WITHOUT A DOG'S CHANCE

James Cousins holds a PhD in history from Simon Fraser University, Canada, and master's degrees in political science and Indigenous public policy. James is originally from the Annapolis Valley of Nova Scotia, and he currently works as a Senior Policy Advisor for the Ontario Ministry of Indigenous Affairs, specialising in matters related to Indigenous governance and self-determination.

WITHOUT A DOG'S CHANCE

THE NATIONALISTS OF NORTHERN IRELAND AND THE IRISH BOUNDARY COMMISSION, 1920–1925

JAMES A. COUSINS

IRISH ACADEMIC PRESS

First published in 2020 by
Irish Academic Press
10 George's Street
Newbridge
Co. Kildare
Ireland
www.iap.ie

9781788551021 (Paper)
9781788551038 (Kindle)
9781788551045 (Epub)
9781788551052 (PDF)

British Library Cataloguing in Publication Data
An entry can be found on request

Library of Congress Cataloging in Publication Data
An entry can be found on request

Typeset in ITC New Baskerville 11/14.5 pt

Cover front: Searching civilians in Belfast, 13 March 1922. Photograph courtesy of *Belfast Telegraph*.

Cover back: Incendries set fire on Talbot Street, picture shows back of Messrs J.P. Corry, 22 May 1922. Photograph courtesy of *Belfast Telegraph*.

For my wife, Dr K. Nicole Power, and
my parents, Roy and Helen Cousins

Contents

Acknowledgements

I am profoundly grateful to the many people who have helped with the research and writing of this book. First and foremost, I would like to thank John Stubbs, Willeen Keough and Leith Davis who read multiple drafts of my research and offered advice and encouragement throughout the long process of writing the chapters that follow. My work also benefitted from thoughtful comments and criticisms provided by Alec Dawson, John Craig and the late Peter Hart. Thank you all, for the time you have invested in me and the kindness you have shown.

I wish to acknowledge Irish Academic Press and express my gratitude to Publisher and Managing Director Conor Graham, Managing Editor Fiona Dunne and Marketing Manager Maeve Convery for the faith they have shown in this project and the incredible support they have given me. I am grateful to Latte Goldstein of River Design for designing the book's cover art and while any errors that remain are exclusively my responsibility, I would like to thank copy editor Heidi Houlihan and the reviewers, proofreaders, indexers, typesetters and others who have left their mark on the pages that follow through the publishing process and made this work better as a result.

Compiling the source material for this research required me to visit a number of record repositories in Ireland where I was given the privilege to view and quote from various manuscript collections. I would like to thank the Deputy Keeper of the Records, Public Record Office of Northern Ireland, and the donors of the Cahir Healy Papers and the J.H. Collins Papers for granting me permission to quote from these valuable sources. I am grateful to the Board of Trinity College Dublin for allowing me to cite materials from the E.M. Stephens Papers. The University College Dublin Archives has kindly permitted me to quote from the Eoin MacNeill Papers and the Ernest Blythe Papers. I was able to view the Papers of the Irish Boundary Commission at the National Library of Ireland. These documents contain public sector information licensed under the Open Government Licence v3.0 and I am thankful to the National Archives of the United Kingdom for helping me to navigate the UK Government Licensing Framework.

This book contains a number of maps and photographs and I would like to thank the people and institutions that have allowed me to reproduce these materials in my book. The cover photograph was made available courtesy of the *Belfast Telegraph* and I am grateful to the National Library of Ireland and the National Portrait Gallery for permitting me to reproduce photographs appearing in the plates. I owe a huge debt of gratitude to Kevin O'Sullivan for drawing the maps, and I would like to acknowledge that these maps were based on work previously produced by Sarah Gearty and Kieran Rankin and are used here with their kind permission.

I deeply appreciate the assistance that was given to me by the staff members of all of the institutions that I visited and I would like to offer a special word of thanks to the Interlibrary Loans division of the Bennett Library, Simon Fraser University, for tracking so many of the rare printed materials that I requested. I am also grateful to the numerous individuals who were kind enough to answer my emails and were willing to share information. These include: the late A.C. Hepburn, University of Sunderland; Richard Kirkland, King's College London; Charles K. Matthews, George Mason University; Mark O'Brien, Dublin City University; Marianne Elliott, University of Liverpool; Kieran Rankin and Jane Maxwell, Trinity College Dublin; Rebecca Geddes and Heather Stanley, Public Records Office of Northern Ireland; Glenn Dunne, Justin Furlong, James Harte and Berni Metcalfe, National Library of Ireland; Lisa Olriche, National Portrait Gallery; Aideen Ireland and Patricia Fallon, National Archives of Ireland; Judy Nokes, National Archives UK; Mrs Ebrahim, of the British Library; newspaper historian Hugh Oram; *Irish News* Librarian Kathleen Bell; Darren Farnan of the *Derry Journal*; Kris Brown of the Linen Hall Library; Mary Gallagher, Company Secretary of Independent News & Media PLC, and Martin Hill, Associate Editor of the *Belfast Telegraph.*

I am thankful for the many friends, colleagues, classmates and co-workers across the spectrum of my personal, academic and public service life who have contributed in some way to the completion of this book. They include: Theresa Mulligan and Arilea Sill, who were there from the beginning of this project, and Adam Kamp, Dana Hollick-

Kenyon and Rob Lutener who encouraged me to see it through. I also wish to thank Alejandra Espinosa, Kaitie Hoffman, Amanda Horn-Hudecki, Sarah Toole, David Tortell, Beatrice D'Angelo, Melanie Gennings, Arie Molema, Devon Martin and Donna LaPointe for the advice and technical assistance they provided, and fellow travellers Alison Norman and Daniel Laxer for establishing a Manuscript Writers Group at the Ontario Ministry of Indigenous Affairs

I am blessed to have had many mentors who have contributed to my professional development, and whose example I have endeavoured to emulate. I wish to offer an especially warm note of gratitude to Professors Barry Moody, Bruce Matthews, Greg Pyrcz and Doug MacArthur, as well as my OPS role models Kate Stewart, Stephanie Prosen, Trish Malone and Alan Kary. I recently heard Kate say that 'We are all the sum of our relationships.' I think this is true and I know that I am a better person, scholar and public servant because of that arithmetic.

Finally, I would like to acknowledge the unconditional love of a chocolate lab named Russell R. Stewart (2007–18), who always had much more than a dog's chance of never being forgotten by the people he touched, as well as my bipedal family. In particular, I would like to thank those for whom this book is dedicated: my parents, Roy and Helen Cousins, who have always supported my academic pursuits, and my wife Dr K. Nicole Power, a chemist who has absorbed much Irish history over our time together and encouraged me in every stage of my work to revise, edit and publish this book. This dedication does not begin to describe the debt that I owe to each of you, but I offer it with love and appreciation.

Jolly good and that is all.

Religious Affiliations in Ulster Based on the 1911 Census

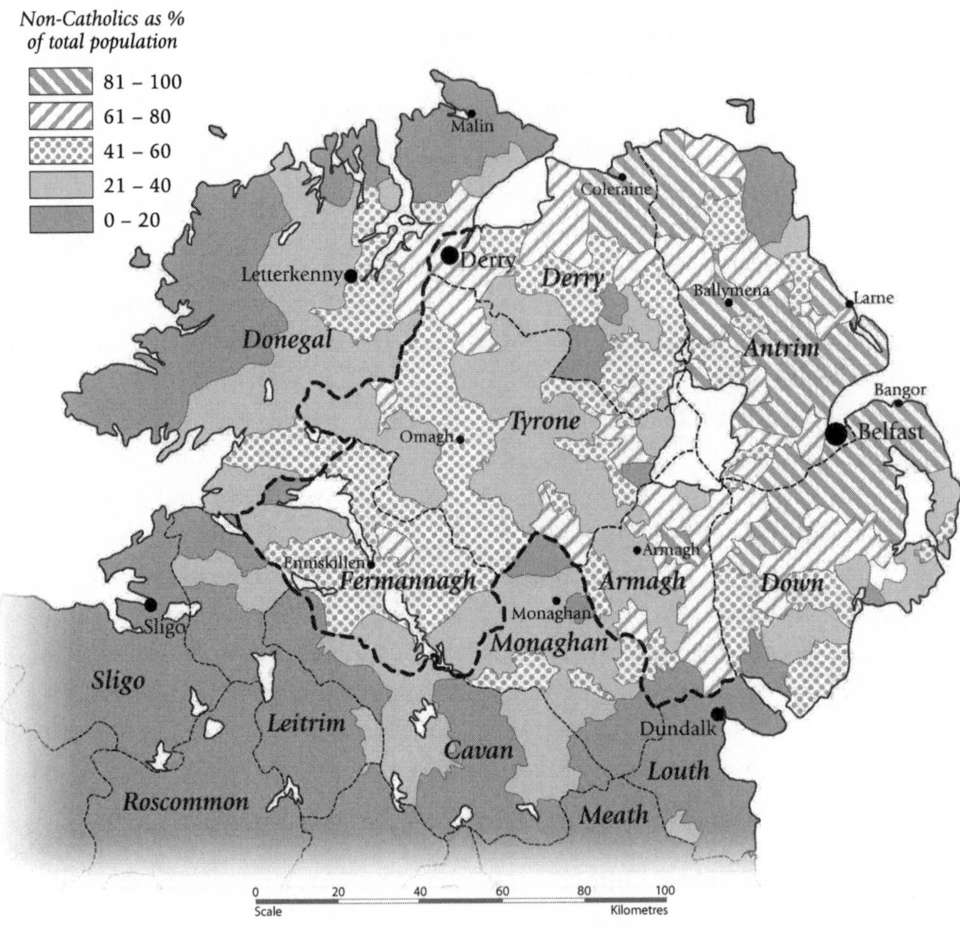

Source: Drawn by Kevin O'Sullivan based on a map drawn by Sarah Gearty, which has previously appeared in M. Laffan, 'The Emergence of the Two Irelands, 1912–25', *History Ireland* (Winter, 2004), p. 40.

The North Eastern Boundary Bureau's Proposed Territorial Demand at the Boundary Commission

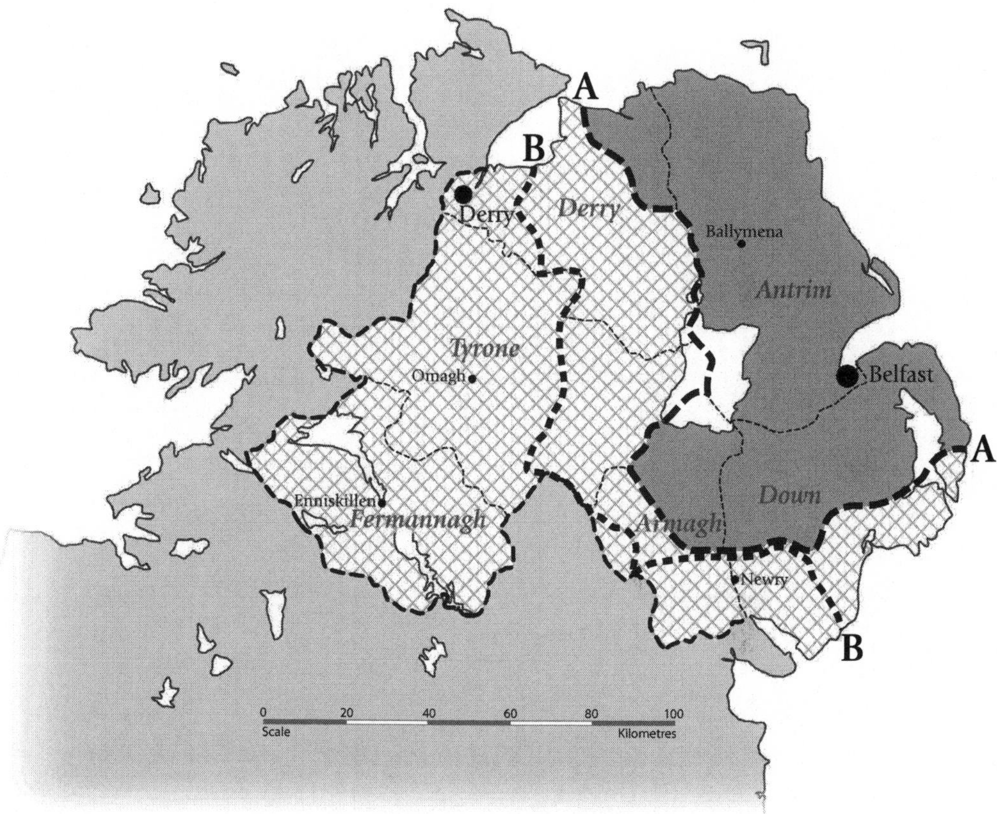

Areas of Northern Ireland territory under claim by the Irish Free State

(A) The 'Maximum Line' representing the best territorial award considered possible based entirely on 'the wishes of the inhabitants'

(B) The 'Minimum Line' representing the best territorial award considered possible taking into account the 'the wishes of the inhabiatants' in conjunction with 'economic and geographic conditions' as per Article 12 of the Treaty

Source: Drawn by Kevin O'Sullivan based on K. Rankin, 'The Role of the Irish Boundary Commission in the Entrenchments of the Irish Border: From Tactical Panacea to Political Liability, *Journal of Historical Geography* 34, 3 (2008), p. 435.

INTRODUCTION

The 'Tips of Dangerous Icebergs': Partition, the Nationalists of Northern Ireland and the Trapped Minority Framework

> The Almighty made of this green island set in these western seas a self-contained unit. In history, in traditions, in racial characteristics, in resistance to wrong, in sacrifices for the right, in all the manifest heritage of mingled failure and success that makes up our chequered story, there is but one Ireland.
>
> – Joseph Devlin[1]

After decades of wrangling between the primarily Protestant Irish unionists, who wanted to preserve the United Kingdom without alteration, and the largely Catholic Irish nationalists, who had spent more than a century seeking to dismantle it, Ireland was partitioned in 1920. Northern Ireland was born out of this intended compromise and, as a consequence of the controversial Anglo-Irish Treaty, by the end of 1921, a second polity was emerging in Ireland known as the Irish Free State. Because unionist and nationalist minorities found themselves scattered along either side of the new border in the wake of these developments, provisions were also made for the establishment of a Boundary Commission to redraw the border. Northern Ireland's reluctance to participate in its proceedings and the outbreak of the Irish Civil War in the Free State postponed the sitting of the Boundary Commission until the autumn of 1924, and it collapsed amidst controversy the following November.

For Northern Ireland's nationalist minority, partition was an intensely traumatic event. It was traumatic not only because it consigned an estimated half a million Northern nationalists to a government that was not of their choosing but also because members of that nationalist minority regarded partition as the mutilation of their nation and mourned what they saw as the loss of their Irish citizenship and patrimony. As one nationalist newssheet argued at the time when the British parliament was preparing to bisect the island, partition robbed Ireland of the most cherished of all its rights as a nation – 'the right to preserve intact its Oneness and Indivisibility'.[2]

As exemplified by Geoffrey Hand's work,[3] efforts to have the Boundary Commission assembled before 1924 are often seen as a mammoth struggle between an eager Free State and a reluctant Northern Ireland with London acting as either a mediator or an enabler. This approach largely ignores the nationalist and unionist minorities that made the Boundary Commission necessary. Starting from the perspective that no section of Northern Ireland's nationalist minority was content to wait passively to be repatriated via the Commission, I wanted to understand Northern nationalists' reactions to the turbulent Southern events that delayed the sitting of the Boundary Commission; the role Ulster nationalists had been afforded in Ireland's post-partition political landscape; and the extent to which these Northern nationalists remained connected to the all-Ireland nationalist movement that they had helped to create.

Until the mid 1990s, Michael Farrell's *Arming the Protestants*[4] was the only study that gave any significant attention to the nationalists of Northern Ireland during the formative 1920s and, with the exception of an important essay penned by Geoffrey Hand, the Irish Boundary Commission has appeared as little more than a footnote in most histories of the period.[5] Serious scholarly interest in the field began with the publication of Eamon Phoenix's authoritative *Northern Nationalism,* which detailed the evolution of minority nationalism within Northern Ireland via a broad political survey.[6] The historiography has since grown to include additional surveys,[7] the first biographies of Belfast MP Joseph Devlin[8] and Kevin O'Shiel, Director of the North Eastern Boundary Bureau,[9] as well as a myriad of titles dealing with such varied topics as the Catholic Church in Ulster,[10] the Northern Divisions of the Irish Republican Army (IRA),[11] political violence in the North,[12] republican internment[13] and the high politics of the Irish Boundary Commission.[14] Each of these works contributes valuable insights on the experiences of Northern nationalists within unionist Northern Ireland; however, this burgeoning historiography has yet to thoroughly explore the complex relationship that bound partition-era Northern and Southern nationalism, and the extent to which Northern anti-partitionists saw a role for themselves in Free State nation-building efforts.

Without a Dog's Chance is a study of Northern Ireland's nationalist minority and their relationship with Southern nationalists during the period between the onset of partition and the collapse of the Boundary Commission. At this time, Northern nationalists were deeply divided amongst themselves between the constitutionally minded supporters of the Irish Parliamentary Party (IPP) MP Joseph 'Wee Joe' Devlin and their rivals within the Sinn Féin movement. Given Sinn Féin's eclipse of the IPP in the 1918 election, the Northern supporters of Sinn Féin feature prominently in this work; however, Devlin and the Devlinite faction of Northern nationalism are my primary focus.

The decision to concentrate on the Devlinites was driven, in part, by Joe Devlin's linkages to the Belfast-based *Irish News* – the North of Ireland's only nationalist daily at the time. Because Devlin controlled the *Irish News*, a unique and stable window into the Devlinite world is available for analysis and that alone makes Devlin and his followers an attractive subject of investigation. Aside from being able to tap into the rich and varied information contained in this important Devlinite mouthpiece, the pivotal, albeit sometimes problematic, role that Joe Devlin personally held within the Irish nationalist movement for more than thirty years also justified making Devlin, his supporters and the Devlinite *Irish News* the focus of this study.

Dubbed the 'duodecimo Demosthenes' by nationalist rival T.M. Healy due to his skill as an orator,[15] by all accounts Devlin was a formidable and spirited debater at Westminster who, the *Times* wrote, could 'fill the House and hold it'.[16] The influence he achieved as IPP leader John Redmond's chief Northern lieutenant during the pre-War Ulster crisis led Winston Churchill to describe Devlin as 'the one figure of distinction in the Irish Party',[17] while his ability as a political organiser and his impressive string of victories in the Catholic and working-class constituency of West Belfast/Belfast Falls made Joe

Devlin an influential figure within Irish nationalism prior to partition. Yet, there were other factors contributing to his influence as well. Once he and his allies gained control of the *Irish News*' board of directors in 1905,[18] the newspaper provided Devlin with a reliable platform for promoting his views and testing his political arguments, while his sway over two key components of his party's political machine – the United Irish League (UIL) and the Ancient Order of Hibernians (AOH)[19] – added immeasurably to his influence within the IPP and nationalist politics. Devlin was able to use his role as General Secretary of the UIL and National President of the AOH, along with his influence over the *Irish News*, to build a virtual fiefdom for himself in Ulster. And, according to Fermanagh Sinn Féiner Cahir Healy, had he chosen to do so, Devlin could have become 'a virtual Dictator in Irish affairs' prior to the rise of Sinn Féin in the later 1910s.[20]

Devlin drew followers from a number of disparate sources. He was a devout Catholic and championed causes that were considered important to his co-religionists – like the protection of Catholic education – and this gave Devlin a significant following among the senior clergy. However, his opposition to the establishment of a Catholic party under clerical control had made him enemies within the Church hierarchy as well.[21] Having come from very humble means himself, as a parliamentarian Devlin was an ardent champion of welfarism and progressive legislation in support of pensioners, the unemployed, widows and children.[22] These efforts, and his determination to improve working conditions in the linen mills and shipyards, endeared Devlin to the Catholic working classes of industrial Belfast and also gave him a smattering of support from the city's Protestant working classes in times when sectarian politics were less pronounced. Although deeply sincere in his effort to address the concerns of those involved in the sweating trades, he was by no means a labour radical and his aversion to the militant syndicalism that Jim Larkin and James Connolly espoused also gained him support from the small community of Catholic businessmen in the North of Ireland.[23] In addition, the election records also show that the majority of those who actually contested Northern Ireland elections as members of Devlin's IPP were from the Catholic middle class – barristers and solicitors, journalists and editors, publicans and hoteliers.[24] With respect to the so-called National Question, Devlin and his followers were every bit as committed to Irish self-government as were the more radical Sinn Féiners, but Devlinism represented a fairly conservative brand of nationalism in which Irish unity, rather than complete separation from Britain, was the most important issue. And, unlike their Sinn Féin rivals, the Devlinites remained committed constitutionalists throughout Ireland's revolutionary period.

Without question, Joe Devlin was the most recognisable and powerful Northern nationalist politician of the Home Rule era but, in later life, he was to be something of a problematic protagonist. Pressed by some 'moderate MPs' to seek the chairmanship of the IPP upon John Redmond's death in 1918, Devlin refused in an effort to avoid a party split by challenging John Dillon for the position, although some of Devlin's more critical contemporaries attributed his acquiescence to a combination of self-doubt and excessive drink.[25] After losing his Westminster seat to redistricting four years later, Devlin was frequently absent from the public eye and considered himself 'out of politics' at this time.[26] When he did speak publicly during these relatively quiet stretches, Devlin often explained his absence by suggesting that, since the torch had passed out of IPP hands in 1918, he did not want to make things more complicated than they already were for Sinn Féin and its successor, Cumann na nGaedhael. Other evidence suggests that Devlin's periods of inactivity coincided with episodes of failing health and depression.[27] Whatever the reason for his reduced presence, and despite the fact that there was frequent chatter in the contemporary sources about Devlin as the IPP puppet-master even during these periods of inactivity, the clearest sense of what might be termed 'the Devlinite perspective' during these lulls comes from examining the editorial line taken by the *Irish News* and the activities of Devlin's surrogates within the AOH and the UIL.

As I worked to piece together Devlinite views on national events and issues, it became abundantly clear that Devlinite perspectives needed to be contextualised within a broader Northern nationalist movement that included a vocal Sinn Féin element. As such, this study also demonstrates how geography and divisions over policy and methods made it difficult for the Devlinites and the Northern Sinn Féiners to work in concert against their common foes – the unionist majority in Northern Ireland and partition. Yet, as important as these lingering divisions were in understanding the various threads of

Northern nationalism, the fact remains that the Devlinites and the Northern Sinn Féiners shared a number of important commonalities as well. Both groups refused to recognise, and did not assimilate into, Northern Ireland, which they each saw as Britain's effort to reconstitute the Protestant Ascendency, or worse, the English Pale. But while their mutual refusal to participate in partition politics and the repressive and disenfranchising measures adopted by Northern Ireland both served to marginalise the Devlinites and Sinn Féiners within the Unionist regime, the Northern nationalists found themselves marginalised within the broader Irish nationalist movement as well. Even when it came to the vital boundary question in which they had an undeniable stake, the Devlinites and the Northern Sinn Féiners each came to believe that their views mattered little to Dublin since, in the words of one Free State advisor, the Southern government was determined to set its own agenda and deal with the boundary 'in its own way and its own time'.[28] These observations about the persistent divisiveness of minority nationalism and the Northern nationalists' marginalisation within Irish politics – North and South – ultimately led me to conclude that the nationalists of Northern Ireland represented an example of what Israeli anthropologist Dan Rabinowitz has called a 'trapped minority'.[29]

Rabinowitz developed the notion of a trapped minority as a way of conceptualising the position held by the Palestinian minority that resides within the borders of Israel.[30] He also speculated that his trapped minority framework had relevance for Ireland, Northern Ireland and a host of other global hot spots. According to Rabinowitz, using the label 'trapped minority' assumes that the people in question belong to 'a mother nation which stretches across two states or more'. He continued: 'Segments of this mother nation may find themselves entrapped as minorities within recently formed states dominated by other groups. Each segment is thus marginal twice over: once within the (alien) state, and once within the (largely absent) mother nation.'[31]

As was the case with the British government's partition of Ireland, Rabinowitz argues that the entrapment of a minority begins with a 'dramatic development' characterised by 'sudden external interference leading to confinement [in which] a door is closed, a fence erected, [or] a wall cemented'.[32] In such instances, public life within the host nation is often 'formally accessible' to a trapped minority, yet in practice they are 'consistently excluded from most political processes'.[33] The existence of a trapped minority in a newly formed state like Northern Ireland also provides its majority population with an ideological Other, and if the trapped ones have 'a real or imagined affiliation abroad', as the nationalists of Northern Ireland did, they are seen by the host state as the 'tips of dangerous icebergs' or 'ominous protrusions of external threats'. This, according to Rabinowitz, is why host states sometimes develop a siege mentality that is 'replete with weakness and vulnerability'.[34]

In elucidating the concept, Rabinowitz identified a number of characteristic elements which denote trapped minorities that can be summarised as follow:

1. Entrapment begins 'at the very historical juncture which the dominant majority associates with victory, redemption and the joyful dawning of a new age'.
2. Trapped minorities exhibit a sense of being 'marginal twice over, within two political entities'. In this instance, the dominant members of the host state treat the minority as 'less than equal citizens' and trapped minorities find that their 'credentials within their mother nations are devalued'.
3. Trapped minorities remain 'non-assimilating'. Whether by choice or otherwise, they neither want nor are genuinely invited to assimilate into the culture or governing apparatus of the host state.
4. Trapped minorities find themselves in the crossfire between at least two nations and their relationship with their host state is 'inevitably influenced, sometimes determined, by the liaison between [those] two nations'. If the latter is 'tense and hostile', the host will see the minority's desire to keep its separate identity as 'dangerously out of line'.
5. Trapped minorities are likely to 'display chronic ideological and political internal divisions, and to experience difficulties in forging a united front both inside and outside the state'. These divisions make it difficult to articulate 'a historic or at least strategic vision, stemming from their dichotomous entrapment, that works against their chances of political unity'.[35]

Prior to this study, Kevin Howard may have been the only scholar to have applied Rabinowitz's trapped minority framework to the anti-partitionists of Northern Ireland. As a jumping-off point for a 2006 working paper, Howard introduced the model, only to reject it because Northern Ireland was 'not a state in the classic Weberian sense'.[36] While it is true that the Northern Ireland parliament was constitutionally subordinate to London's authority, on this point Howard clearly underplays the extent to which the small state was able to control its own destiny, irrespective of its legislative subordination.

Howard's reluctance to adopt the trapped minority designation also rested on his view that Dublin treated the Northern nationalists *not* as an irredenta population but as a part of the 'global Irish diaspora'.[37] This claim only has credibility if one is willing to discount the time, resources and effort that the Free State government actually put into its preparations for the Boundary Commission, and even then it says far more about the limits of Southern nationalism than it does about the disposition of those who were trapped on the Northern side of the Irish border. It is also clear that, because he found indications that the Catholics and nationalists appeared to be developing a separate Northern identity prior to the abolition of the Belfast parliament in 1973, Howard was content to ignore the obvious irredentism of the 1920s and 1930s. As this project attests, while the Irish Free State was not always receptive to the pleas for help that were emanating from the Northern nationalists as they sought an end to partition, the fact that those pleas surfaced with great urgency in the 1921–5 period (and again in the later 1930s) is itself indicative of the fact that Northern anti-partitionists viewed themselves as an irredenta population, even at times when it may have appeared to them that the Irish Free State did not.

Thus, notwithstanding Howard's reservations, this book argues that the nationalists of Northern Ireland of the 1920s are demonstrative of the trapped minority model and that the framework is useful for conceptualising Northern nationalism as an enduring part of the wider nationalist movement whence it emerged. Yet, while the trapped minority concept is a leitmotif throughout this study, my work has revealed that it must be refurbished in one important way to more accurately reflect the cultural vitality of Northern nationalism. In contrast to how Rabinowitz characterises the cultural life of trapped minorities,[38] entrapment did not lead Northern nationalists to 'suppress [their] history' and culture.[39] Rather, my research reveals that a rich sense of Irish history and identity continued to find expression in the columns of the anti-partitionist press, the speeches of Northern nationalist leaders and perhaps most effectively, in the poetry that Northern nationalists wrote and the songs they sung in the post-partition era.

The discrepancy between the archetypal trapped minority, which Rabinowitz claimed was without history and culture within its host-state, and the Northern nationalists clearly owes something to the central place that literary and cultural nationalism held within the wider Irish nationalist movement prior to partition. Political songs and poems have been part of the furniture of Irish nationalism for centuries, harking back to the outlaw poetry of the eighteenth century, the carefully crafted *aislingi*[40] and Jacobite poetry of the seventeenth century and earlier bardic and folk renderings. The Society of United Irishmen was particularly gifted at using this type of material to solicit popular support for its insurrection of 1798. [41] The United Irishmen understood both the emotional appeal of stirring balladry and the affect of its orality. While complex ideas related to nationhood, liberty and ecumenicalism were not easy to convey to a not yet literate public, when these ideas were interspersed within the rhyming couplets of a street singer's songs, the language of reform entered the vernacular becoming more palatable to consume and easy to pass on. Thus, as the literary legacy of the United Irishmen attests, shared poetry and songs of this variety served not only to inform but also to foster a sense of community among those who heard the words or sang them to others.

While the political and cultural influence that the United Irishmen and their predecessors had on later Irish nationalists cannot be ignored, for the nationalists of twentieth-century Northern Ireland, it was Thomas Davis and other members of the Young Irelanders who held the most revered place. As Mary Helen Thuente has shown, even as the Young Irelanders were acting as an adjunct to Daniel O'Connell's Repeal campaign, their newspaper, the *Nation*, contained as much reverence for the United Irishmen – whom O'Connell abhorred – as it did for Repeal.[42] John Kells Ingram's requiem for the participants of the rebellion of 1798, 'The Memory of the Dead', appeared in print during the early 1840s, as did Davis' 'A Nation Once Again'.[43] Because of their popularity, these works became entwined in a shared text that was bequeathed to the Irish nationalists of the nineteenth and twentieth centuries. The names Thomas Davis and John Kells Ingram joined a growing lexicon of nationalist heroes and, indicative of the way in which an evocative message, originally appearing in print, could (and did) become part of the oral culture as it was passed from one individual to another, the words to 'A Nation Once Again' and 'The Memory of the Dead' were still well known and still being sung at various nationalist venues in the 1920s.

The poetry and balladry of Young Ireland, the United Irishmen and earlier Irish bards left a very powerful legacy; however, the later nineteenth century also witnessed a period of cultural revival that was itself both vibrant and influential. Beginning in the last third of the nineteenth century, a number of loosely related cultural, literary and linguistic movements emerged in Ireland. These movements included D.P. Moran's 'Irish-Ireland', which advocated an ethnically defined Gaelic and Catholic Ireland, and the Gaelic Athletic Association (GAA), which promoted Irish sport.[44] The Gaelic League, begun by Douglas Hyde and Eoin MacNeill in 1893, was among the most far reaching of these new cultural movements. Founded to keep the Irish language from dying out, the Gaelic League instituted classes, published Gaelic literature and planned Irish-speaking social events as Gaelic Leaguers petitioned to have Irish Gaelic incorporated into the national school system. This immensely popular movement was not intended to be political but, like so many of the seemingly non-political cultural and literary movements of the late nineteenth century, the League ultimately became intertwined with nationalist politics.[45]

The growth of the Gaelic League coincided with the Anglo-Irish Literary Revival, led by William Butler Yeats, J.M. Synge and Lady Gregory, that sought to recover and re-introduce the myths and folklore of Ireland's past. For instance, in his effort to re-interpret the centuries-old Gaelic motif of presenting a beleaguered Ireland in the guise of woman, Yeats' play *Cathleen Ni Houlihan* (1902) told the story of a poor old woman, weakened by the theft of her 'four beautiful green fields' – the four provinces of Ireland – who was dramatically transformed into a vivacious young queen by those willing to spill blood in her name.[46] As an indication of the way that theatre, like poetry and music, could affect its audience, the constitutional nationalist and literary figure Stephen Gwynn left one of the first performances of *Cathleen Ni Houlihan* with the old woman's mantra – 'They shall be remembered forever/They shall be alive forever/They will be speaking forever/The people shall hear them forever' – still pounding in his head. He would later observe: 'I went home asking myself if such plays should be produced unless one is prepared to go out and shoot and be shot.'[47]

While the Anglo-Irish Literary Revival and the other cultural and literary movements that emerged during the later nineteenth century were influential in their own right, they also provided a channel through which earlier movements, such as the United Irishmen and Young Ireland, could be kept alive and repackaged for later generations. Thus, the fact that Young Irelander poetry and song continued to be referenced in the speeches of Northern nationalist political and religious leaders during the 1920s and that every UIL meeting ended with the singing of Davis' 'A Nation Once Again' is as much a testament to the cultural and literary nationalists who helped to re-introduce Davis to successive generations of Irish nationalists as it is to the attachment that Ulster nationalists had to his body of work.

Northern nationalists also wrote their own songs and poetry. Some of the original material collected for this study represents a clear attempt by anti-partitionist poets and balladeers to emulate art forms and borrow images that were made famous by earlier purveyors of nationalist thought and culture. In this material, the evocation of a nostalgic vision of Ireland's past is used as a way to both reinforce and contribute to the construction of a shared Irish identity that knew no boundary. At other times these poets sought only humour with simple, if not always lighthearted, doggerel. As an example of the latter objective, during the Irish Free State general election of 1932, the ballot boxes in Co. Leitrim were found to contain numerous poetic renderings explaining why voters made the selections they had. As one irreverent voter explained:

I hate the Cumann na nGaedheal crowd,
I hate them; yes I do;
Only for that I'd never
A single vote for you.[48]

Another Leitrim voter had composed a poem explaining in eight rhyming quatrains why he ordered his ballot in the way that he had.

While the examples above have come from the *Fermanagh Herald*, material of this sort could be found in any number of nationalist newspapers published in nineteenth- or early-twentieth-century Ireland. Michael Wheatley's study of the Redmondite IPP in Leitrim, Longford, Roscommon, Sligo and Westmeath indicates that nationalist newssheets in what he calls 'middle Ireland' were teaming with political rhetoric – including poetry – during the 1910–16 period. Highlighting the pervasiveness of the language of 'The Cause', Wheatley's work has illustrated that materials drawn from nationalist Ireland's oral culture emphasising self-sacrifice and the never-ending fight for freedom 'formed the staple content of speeches, editorials, and poems' in the newspapers he studied.[49]

Much like the newspapers of Wheatley's 'middle Ireland', the Devlinite *Irish News* published poetry, ballads and simple rhymes containing the same type of political rhetoric. As my work attests, when *Irish News* editor Tim McCarthy was seeking to evoke memories of days gone by, to inspire his readers or to contextualise the events he was witnessing, he would often intersperse familiar lines of political poetry and patriotic songs within his editorials. Many letters to the editor – signed by people using pseudonyms such as 'National' or 'Northern Celt' – contained original poetry of this variety, while at other times the authors of these 'people's editorials'[50] cited Davis or Mangan in much the same way. Original verse, written in response to contemporary events, also appeared in a separate column of the *Irish News* along with notes indicating the tune to which they were meant to be sung. Not only do these poetic renderings make accessible a dimension of the feelings of jubilation, angst and betrayal that were embedded in the politics of post-partition Northern nationalism, they also represent part of the process of constructing a shared sense of Irishness by continuing to tap into the language of The Cause as they perpetuated idealised images of Irish heroes, English villains and 750 years of ceaseless struggle. Yet, despite the value that Michael Wheatley has put on this type of material with regard to 'middle Ireland', the songs and poetry from Northern Ireland's anti-partitionist press have been largely neglected by the historians who study partition-era Northern nationalism. Taking advantage of this hitherto unused resource, I have made the poetry and song that appeared in Northern Ireland's anti-partitionist press an important part of this study. This, and the value newspapers more generally offer in understanding identity, helps to explain why they are central to and the most thoroughly examined sources used for this book.

As 'cultural product[s]'[51] that shed light on the societies in which they were published, newspapers have generated considerable scholarly interest of late and some of the credit for this must be given to Benedict Anderson. Anderson's 'modernist' account of *when* nationalism emerged has had its critics and is problematic when it comes to Ireland[52] but his explanation of *how* newspapers helped to spread and reinforce nationalism is still worth consideration.

In *Imagined Communities*, Anderson argues that conceptions of nationhood develop and are spread through an 'extraordinary mass ceremony' in which the readers of newspapers and novels engage in the 'almost precisely simultaneous consumption' of their content. He observed that this mass consumption may be done in 'silent privacy' but, at the same time, each reader is 'well aware that the ceremony he performs is being replicated simultaneously by thousands (or millions) of others of whose existence he is confident, yet of whose identity he has not the slightest notion'. Distilled to its essence by Tom Clyde, this aspect of Anderson's thesis posits that if a nation is an 'imagined community', as he claims, 'then these publications are not just an accidental by-product of that imagining, but a key mechanism by which it takes place, at the same time a forum *for* and an embodiment *of* it'. For Clyde, who applied Anderson's theory to Irish literary periodicals, conceiving newspapers and literary magazines in this way means that reading them or contributing to them represent forms of participating in the process of building or reinforcing a shared identity that allowed readers and contributors 'to label themselves, as "Tories," or "women"' or, in the case of this book, Irish nationalists.[53]

The problem with Anderson's argument when it comes to Ireland is not his suggestion that newspapers were instrumental in spreading nationalist ideas; rather, it is Anderson's conviction that they were unprecedented in doing what, according to Tom Garvin, 'Churches, schools, *seanachaíthe*, *marabouts*, ballad-singers, army officers, and grandfathers can do, and have done ... for far longer than have newspapers.'[54] While I accept Garvin's view that nationalism had roots in pre-modern oral culture, it seems equally clear that the simultaneity that Anderson associates with the reading of newspapers had a significant influence on the spread and consolidation of national affiliation once newspapers did emerge as a communicative medium.

Seen from a different perspective, David Vincent's work has shown that eighteenth-century newspapers actually interacted with, and reinforced, oral culture in important ways. According to Vincent: 'precious dog-eared pages were read and re-read, borrowed and reborrowed until imperceptibly they merged back into the common oral culture whence most had originally come'.[55] Of course, the interaction between newspapers and oral culture did not always follow the exact pattern that Vincent has identified. As my work attests, ballads like Davis' 'A Nation Once Again' often became a part of nationalist Ireland's oral culture after they were printed, only to reappear within *Irish News* editorials throughout the 1920s on occasions when its editor, Tim McCarthy, wanted to tap into the sense of community, patriotism and shared history that was bound up in the singing of those songs. While this neither contradicts Vincent's findings, nor refutes Mark Hampton's view that 'the press was becoming the dominant partner in its relationship with oral culture' by the middle of the nineteenth century,[56] it does offer clear evidence that *Irish News* was still interacting with, and helping to reinforce, aspects of Irish oral culture during the 1920s.

To this end, newspapers need not have had an unprecedented effect in order to have been influential and, as Hampton argues with respect to Britain, the printed press must be seen as 'a central political and cultural artefact'.[57] According to Marie-Louise Legg, by the middle of the nineteenth century, Irish nationalists were actively attempting to turn the penny press into a vehicle for 'recount[ing] the lives of heroes, and project[ing] the nation as looming out of an immemorial past'.[58] Her account, which draws on Anderson, maintains that newspapers played 'a vital role in both spreading and fixing the idea of the nation' and that they were successful in doing so because of their increased popularity among all classes of society that resulted from the elimination of the newspaper tax and Ireland's improving literacy rate.[59] Observing this more educated and news-hungry public first-hand in the 1880s, Professor David King noted that 'more than one-half of the people' that he encountered while traveling in a third-class rail carriage 'read the morning papers, [and] even those who looked the least intelligent, show[ed] a great interest in the news'. In utter amazement, he continued, 'I discovered the man who sat opposite me, and who was a rather ragged looking individual, read the other side of my paper with evident interest.'[60] As surprised as he may have been, King was certainly not the only person to recognise the growing appetite of the people of the United Kingdom for newsprint and many of King's contemporaries were beginning to pontificate about the role the press played in their society.

Studies of the British media have indicated that from the middle of the nineteenth century until the 1880s, it was widely accepted that the printed press wielded considerable clout in shaping public opinion. Hampton associates this period with what he has called the 'educational ideal' – an era in which newspapers were regarded as vehicles for improving their readers and preparing them to be responsible and informed political agents.[61] Because of the perceived influence newspapers had during these years, he maintains that politicians cultivated connections with certain newspapers and actually traded compensation or access to information for positive coverage. Well-connected politicians would also use the press to test and promote political positions they were not yet ready to endorse publicly.[62] As Stephen Koss has argued, it became 'mandatory for any political movement to have its own organ, or preferably several that might boom its slogans in unison. It was equally a matter of self-respect, for, without adequate journalistic backing, a party neither seemed to take itself seriously nor could it expect to be taken seriously by its rivals.'[63] Thus, according to Michael de Nie, nineteenth-century politicians and advocates both 'courted and feared' newspapers 'for the authority at their disposal'.[64]

The 'educational ideal' was eclipsed by what Hampton calls the 'representative ideal' during the 1880s – the period during which the *Irish News* was founded. This change was occasioned by the growth of the newspaper industry as a profitable commercial enterprise and the circulation wars that followed. Advertising became the chief source of revenue for newspapers when the 'representative ideal' held sway and since advertisers courted the newspapers that would reach the largest number of people, educating the reading public became far less important for the press than was reflecting public tastes.[65] Indicative of this important shift in focus, the *Irish News*' 1922 descriptive entry in *The Newspaper and Press Directory* boasted that it was 'a good example of [an] up-to-date provincial daily newspaper which bids for general popularity by making its contents readable and its appearance attractive', while its advertisement in the same publication added that it was the 'Best Advertising Medium for Belfast and the Northern Counties'.[66]

Recognising the value newspapers had 'as documentary sources for the study of ideology', Pamela Clayton[67] and Denis Kennedy[68] have both used newspapers to study unionism in 1920s Northern Ireland. However, newspapers have not yet been extensively used to understand the politics of Ulster nationalism and the Northern nationalist identity during the formative first decade after partition. Thus, in addition to conceptualising the nationalists of Northern Ireland as a trapped minority and telling their story, the concentration that I give to the Devlinite *Irish News* and the Sinn Féin-oriented *Derry Journal* and *Fermanagh Herald* is also an important contribution to the historiography. As the *Irish News* is central to this book, this opening chapter will proceed by detailing the often bumpy early history of the Devlinite newspaper before concluding with a brief examination of the *Derry Journal* and the *Fermanagh Herald.*

From its inception in 1891, the *Irish News* identified religiously with Irish Catholicism and, in political terms, with Irish Home Rule. Its first edition appeared on 15 August 1891 and the newspaper's emergence was directly related to the Parnellite/anti-Parnellite split that was then dividing Irish nationalist politics. Occasioned by the fall from grace of IPP leader Charles Stewart Parnell, this messy split outlasted Parnell himself and led to the formation of Parnellite and anti-Parnellite factions across the island. The *Belfast Morning News,* which was the North of Ireland's only nationalist daily, ultimately came out in support of the Parnellite faction but this editorial stance did not reflect the views of most Ulster nationalists and, with the strong backing of the Catholic Church, the *Irish News* soon emerged as the mouthpiece of Northern anti-Parnellism.[69]

The Irish News Ltd was registered in April 1891, its directors held their first meeting a month later and it went on sale later that summer at a cost of one penny. Cardinal Logue and his Ulster Bishops were among the *Irish News*' largest shareholders but a total of 11,000 shares were sold at a cost of £1 each all over the nine Ulster counties and beyond. In addition to clerical elements, the newspapers' directors included leading Belfast professionals and a host of wealthy Catholic distillers, linen manufacturers and businessmen. The *Irish News* soon outsold the *Belfast Morning News* and, indicative of the type of circulation wars that characterised this period,[70] in July 1892 the anti-Parnellite *Morning News* was absorbed by its competitor, officially becoming the *Irish News and Belfast Morning News.*[71] It now had a monopoly position as *the* Catholic/nationalist daily in Belfast and its environs.

Because the *Irish News* was inextricably linked with Joe Devlin for a period of nearly thirty years, it is difficult to envision it as being anything other than a vehicle for the brand of constitutional nationalism that he espoused but before 1905, the newspaper was by no means a Devlinite organ. At that time, the IPP remained divided between Parnellite and anti-Parnellite factions but the latter group was itself divided between the followers of John Dillon and T.M. Healy. Joe Devlin supported the Dillonite wing of the party but the *Irish News* was controlled by staunch Healyites. It was not until the Parnellite John Redmond was able to reunite the IPP in 1900 and took on Joe Devlin as his chief Northern lieutenant that Devlin was strong enough to engineer a takeover of the newspaper's board of directors. He joined its board of directors in 1905 and became Chairman of the Irish News Ltd in 1922.[72]

The fact that the *Irish News* had sixty-nine clerical shareholders in 1921 speaks to the continued support that the Catholic Church was still giving the newspaper[73] but, after his election to its board of directors, the *Irish News* was effectively Joe Devlin's newspaper and the 'Official Organ' of the AOH.[74] Among other things, this meant a change of editors. In 1906, Tim McCarthy replaced T.J. Campbell as editor and the witty and well-read Cork native remained at the helm of the *Irish News* until his death in 1928.[75] Prior to taking the post as *Irish News* editor, McCarthy had worked for the *Cork Herald,* the *Freeman's Journal,* T.P. O'Connor's *The Evening Sun,* as well as Devlin's own short-lived *Northern Star.* As a testament to McCarthy's ability as a newsman, O'Connor once dubbed him 'the greatest political and most versatile journalist in the country'.[76] Under the stewardship of Devlin and McCarthy, the *Irish News* championed John Redmond's Home Rule scheme and the IPP. It had a solid base of support among the working-class Catholics of Devlin's West Belfast constituency and also among Catholic businessmen, publicans, senior clergy and those who remained IPP supporters during the turbulent years that followed.[77] Neither the *Irish News*, nor Devlin, lost the support of these disparate groups when Northern nationalism split and the geographic scope of Devlinism and the IPP contracted after the 1918 general election. Although the Devlinite movement had begun to recuperate by 1922, given how closely the *Irish News* was associated with Devlinism, one might conjecture that the newspaper's readership also suffered during the early 1920s but no circulation figures can be found to confirm this hypothesis.[78] Still, the fact that a department of the Irish Free State, the North Eastern Boundary Bureau, was habitually worried that 'Devlin and Coy. and the "Irish News"' were turning Northern nationalists against Dublin[79] says a great deal about the continued influence that Devlin and his newspaper commanded between 1921 and 1925. This alone attests to the value of using the *Irish News* as a key source for studying post-partition Northern nationalism in general and Devlinism in particular.

Because this book seeks to contextualise Devlinism within the broader Northern nationalist movement, two newspapers that were part of the Sinn Féin oriented border nationalist press have also been examined. These were the *Derry Journal* and the *Fermanagh Herald*. The tri-weekly *Derry Journal* is Ireland's second oldest newspaper still in print today and it began its life in 1772 as the *London-Derry Journal and General Advertiser* – a 'staunchly Protestant and Conservative' newspaper.[80] The *Journal* changed ownership in 1829, becoming a liberal newssheet devoted to Catholic Emancipation, before evolving into a broadly nationalist and then a Sinn Féin oriented newspaper. In the early 1920s, it was edited by Patrick Lawrence Malone, of whom little is known, but after 1924, J.J. McCarroll took the helm of the newspaper. McCarroll had worked for the *Derry Journal* for more than a decade before he became its editor in 1924 and the McCarroll family owned the newspaper from 1925 until 1998.[81] With respect to the third newspaper used in this project, the North West of Ireland Printing and Publishing Company began printing the weekly *Fermanagh Herald* in 1903 – two years after the Lynch family had established the company. Michael Lynch, who was the managing director of the Omagh-based company, had initially been a supporter of the IPP but as Sinn Féin successfully positioned itself as a viable alternative to the IPP during the First World War, Lynch switched his allegiance and brought the five newspapers that his chain owned into the Sinn Féin orbit in 1917.[82]

The newspapers, published by the Derry Journal Ltd and the North West of Ireland Printing and Publishing Company, were the chief competitors of the *Irish News* and it is for this reason that the *Journal* and the *Herald* were selected to explore Sinn Féin perspectives on the events of the day. The editorial pages, letters to the editor, public announcements, poetry and 'the news' that each of these newspapers printed provide important insight into the nature of Northern nationalism during the 1920s and this diverse material forms the nucleus of my study.

Taken together, the chapters that make up this book work to include Northern anti-partitionists within nationalist Ireland's grand narrative and to weave their unique experiences as a trapped minority into the broader history of the period. At times, this approach requires greater attention be given to analysing the role of Northern nationalists in seemingly Southern issues and events, while on other occasions the narrative is driven by the examination of Free State efforts to repatriate these nationalists (via the Boundary Commission) and the conditions under which they lived. Using this approach, I ultimately conclude that, irrespective of their differences on policy and methods, Northern nationalists shared the same uncertain existence as they waited to learn where the Boundary Commission would leave them. Moreover, as they waited, individuals belonging to both political traditions witnessed the diminishment of their credentials within the broader Irish nationalist movement which they had helped to create.

Feeling undervalued, abandoned and exploited by their peers in the South, the nationalists of Northern Ireland were also marginalised within a host state that regarded them with fear and suspicion. As a result, they endured hardships and faced challenges that were materially different from those encountered by the nationalists of the Free State, yet they never ceased to identify with the Irish mother nation, even as they watched the prospect of Irish unity flounder under Dublin's trusteeship. The poetry they wrote and recited, the language of The Cause and the frequent references that the press and Northern nationalist leaders made to what Joe Devlin called the 'mingled failure and success' that made up Ireland's 'chequered story'[83] must be seen as an attempt to remain connected with what was once regarded as an indivisible nation. In the end it was this, the desire to remain part of Ireland's story, which made the ultimate failure of the Boundary Commission all the more tragic.

Notes

1 *Irish News*, 15 August 1924.
2 *Derry Journal*, 27 February 1920.
3 G. Hand, 'MacNeill and the Boundary Commission', in F.X. Martin and F.J. Byrne (eds), *The Scholar Revolutionary: Eoin MacNeill, 1867–1945, and the Making of the New Ireland* (Shannon: Irish University Press, 1973), pp. 201–75.
4 M. Farrell, *Arming the Protestants: The Formation of the Ulster Special Constabulary and the Royal Ulster Constabulary, 1920–27* (Pluto Press, 1983).
5 Hand, 'MacNeill and the Boundary Commission', pp. 201–75. Also see M. O'Callaghan, 'Old Parchment and Water: The Boundary Commission of 1925 and the Copperfastening of the Irish Border', *Bullan: An Irish Studies Review* 4 (2000), pp. 27–55.
6 E. Phoenix, *Northern Nationalism: Nationalist Politics, Partition and the Catholic Minority in Northern Ireland, 1890–1940* (Belfast: Ulster Historical Foundation, 1994).
7 E. Staunton, *The Nationalists of Northern Ireland, 1918–1973* (Dublin: The Columba Press, 2001); J. Bardon, *A History of Ulster* (Belfast: Blackstaff Press, 2001).
8 A.C. Hepburn, *Catholic Belfast and Nationalist Ireland in the Era of Joe Devlin, 1871–1934* (Oxford: Oxford University Press, 2008).
9 E. Sagarra, *Kevin O'Shiel: Tyrone Nationalist and Irish State-Builder* (Dublin: Irish Academic Press, 2013).
10 M. Harris, *The Catholic Church and the Foundation of the Northern Irish State* (Cork: Cork University Press, 1993); A.C. Hepburn, *A Past Apart: Studies in the History of Catholic Belfast, 1850–1950* (Belfast: Ulster Historical Foundation, 1996). O. Rafferty, *Catholicism in Ulster, 1603–1983: An Interpretative History* (London: Hurst & Company, 1994).
11 R. Lynch, *The Northern IRA and the Early Years of Partition, 1920–1922* (Dublin: Irish Academic Press, 2006).
12 A. Parkinson, *Belfast's Unholy War: The Troubles of the 1920s* (Dublin: Four Courts Press, 2004); A. Parkinson and E. Phoenix, *Conflicts in the North of Ireland, 1900–2000: Flashpoints and Fracture Zones* (Dublin: Four Courts Press, 2010).
13 D. Kleinrichert, *Republican Internment and the Prison Ship Argenta, 1922* (Dublin: Irish Academic Press, 2001).
14 P. Murray, *The Irish Boundary Commission and its Origins: 1886–1925* (Dublin: University College Dublin Press, 2011); K.J. Rankin, 'The Role of the Irish Boundary Commission in the Entrenchment of the Irish Border: From Tactical Panacea to Political Liability', *Journal of Historical Geography*, 34 (2008), pp. 422–47.

15 *The Times*, 19 January 1934.

16 Hepburn, *Catholic Belfast and Nationalist Ireland in the Era of Joe Devlin*, p. 275.

17 Winston Churchill to King George V, 8 February 1911, in Randolph Churchill (ed.), *Winston S. Churchill: Companion Volume II Part 2, 1907–1911* (Boston: Houghton Mifflin Company, 1969), p. 1035.

18 E. Phoenix, 'History of a Newspaper, the *Irish News*, 1855–1995', in E. Phoenix (ed.), *A Century of Northern Life: The Irish News and 100 Years of Ulster History, 1890s–1990s* (Belfast: Ulster Historical Foundation, 1995), p. 20.

19 The UIL had been formed in 1898 by nationalist rival William O'Brien but by the time Devlin became the General Secretary of the organisation in 1905, it had been converted into a constituency and fund-raising association for the IPP. The AOH was an Irish-American and Catholic friendly society. The origins of the AOH can be traced back to the seventeenth century but Devlin had modernised it and reintroduced it into Ireland from America around the turn of the century. The Devlinised AOH is often seen as a counter to the Orange Order and Devlin served as its National President from 1905 until his death in 1934. Hepburn, *A Past Apart*, p. 159.

20 Cahir Healy, 'Late Joseph Devlin, MP: An Intimate Sketch by a Colleague', n. d., Cahir Healy Papers, D2991/B/140/19, Public Record Office of Northern Ireland, Belfast.

21 Phoenix, *Northern Nationalism*, pp. 5–6.

22 T.J. Campbell, *Fifty Years of Ulster, 1890–1940* (Belfast: The Irish News Ltd., 1941), p. 229.

23 Hepburn, *A Past Apart*, p. 168.

24 J. Knight and N. Baxter-Moore, *Northern Ireland: The Elections of the Twenties: The General Elections for the House of Commons of the Parliament of Northern Ireland* (London: The Arthur McDougall Fund, 1972), pp. 46–56. Also see E. Rumpf and A.C. Hepburn, *Nationalism and Socialism in Twentieth-Century Ireland* (New York: Barnes & Noble Books, 1977), p. 189.

25 Hepburn, *Catholic Belfast and Nationalist Ireland in the Era of Joe Devlin*, pp. 190–2.

26 F. Whitford 'Joseph Devlin: Ulsterman and Irishman' (MA thesis, London University, 1959), pp.160–6.

27 According to A.C. Hepburn, 'ill-health and depression seemed to go together with him and 1923 was one of his bad years'. A.C. Hepburn, electronic letter to the author, 22 February 2008. In his biography of Devlin, Hepburn indicates that minor ailments affected Devlin 'from a least 1908 onwards, and more frequently from his mid-forties' and that between 1912 and 1923, 'no year passed without a least one reference in the Dillon–O'Connor correspondence to Devlin's winter ailments'. Hepburn, *Catholic Belfast and Nationalist Ireland in the Era of Joe Devlin*, pp. 277–3.

28 Memorandum from Kevin O'Shiel, 'Alleged Delay in Holding the Boundary Commission. Should the Boundary Commission Be Held Now?' 7 February 1923, Department of the Taoiseach, NAI/TSCH/S 2027, North East Boundary Secret Documents 1922–4, National Archives of Ireland, Dublin.

29 D. Rabinowitz, 'The Palestinian Citizens of Israel, the Concept of Trapped Minority and the Discourse of Transnationalism in Anthropology', *Ethnic and Racial Studies* 24, 1 (2001), p. 64.

30 Rabinowitz speculated that his model had relevance for Ireland and a host of other global hot spots but his elaboration of the trapped minority model did not involve evidence related to Ireland. Rabinowitz, 'Trapped Minority', p. 78.

31 Ibid., p. 65.

32 Ibid., p. 73.

33 Ibid., pp. 66–7.

34 Ibid., pp. 78–9.

35 Ibid., pp. 72–7.

36 K. Howard, 'Diasporas and Ambiguous Homelands: A Perspective on the Irish Border', Institute for British–Irish Studies, Working Paper no. 62, 2006, pp. 1–2.

37 Howard, 'Diasporas and Ambiguous Homelands', p. 4.

38 Rabinowitz, 'Trapped Minority', p. 76.

39 Ibid., pp. 74–5.

40 Appearing as romantic verses, these vision-poems involved the poet/narrator being confronted by a beautiful woman who tells him of her distress as she laments the loss of her true love: a noble king exiled by a foreign aggressor. Known as Cathleen ní Houlihan, Cáit ní Dhuibhir or some similar moniker, the woman is the personification of Ireland itself and her lost lover represents the Old Pretender, the Young Pretender or some other redeemer-hero. B. Ó Cuív, 'Irish Language and Literature, 1691–1845', in T.W. Moody and W.E. Vaughan (eds), *A New History of Ireland: IV Eighteenth-Century Ireland, 1691–1800* (Oxford: Clarendon Press, 1986), pp. 398, 406–7; D. Kiberd, 'Irish Literature and Irish History', in R.F. Foster (ed.), *The Oxford Illustrated History of Ireland* (Oxford: Oxford University Press, 1989), p. 286.

41 M.H. Thuente, 'The Folklore of Irish Nationalism', in T.E. Hachey and L.J. McCaffrey (eds), *Perspectives on Irish Nationalism* (Lexington: The University Press of Kentucky, 1989), p. 44; Elliott, *The Catholics of Ulster*, pp. 231–2.

42 M.H. Thuente, *The Harp Re-Strung: The United Irishmen and the Rise of Irish Literary Nationalism* (New York: Syracuse University Press, 1994), p. 193.

43 Davis' 'A Nation Once Again', begins: 'When boyhood's fire was in my blood, /I read of ancient freemen, /For Greece and Rome who bravely stood, /Three Hundred men and Three men. /And then I prayed I yet might see/Our fetters rent in twain, /And Ireland, long a province, be /A Nation once again.' As quoted by T. Kinsella (ed.), *The New Oxford Book of Irish Verse* (Oxford: Oxford University Press, 1986), p. 305.

44 Kiberd, 'Irish Literature and Irish History', pp. 277–8; D. McCartney, 'From Parnell to Pearse 1891–1921', in T.W. Moody and F.X. Martin (eds), *The Course of Irish History* (Cork: Mercier Press, 2001), pp. 246–7; D.J. O'Neill, 'D.P. Moran and Gaelic Cultural Revitalization', *Eire–Ireland* 12, 4 (1977), pp. 109–13.

45 McCartney, 'From Parnell to Pearse 1891–1921', pp. 246–8; *BBC*, 'Cultural Nationalism' BBC – History – Easter Rising – Prelude, http://www.bbc.co.uk/history/british/easterrising/prelude/pr02.shtml (accessed 23 July 2019).

46 W.B. Yeats, *Cathleen Ni Houlihan* (Stratford-Upon-Avon: Shakespeare Head Press, 1911), p. 9.

47 M. Phelan, 'The Critical "Gap of the North": Nationalism, National Theatre, and the North', *Modern Drama*, 47, 4 (Winter, 2004), p. 598.

48 *Fermanagh Herald*, 19 March 1932.

49 M. Wheatley, *Nationalism and the Irish Party: Provincial Ireland, 1910–1916* (Oxford: Oxford University Press, 2005), p. 80.

50 P. Clayton, *Enemies and Passing Friends: Settler Ideologies in Twentieth Century Ulster* (London: Pluto Press, 1996), p. xvi.

51 M. de Nie, *The Eternal Paddy: Irish Identity and the British Press, 1798–1882* (Madison: University of Wisconsin Press, 2004), p. 28.

52 Rejecting the modernist view in a way that seems to support Anthony D. Smith's modernist–perennialist synthesis, D.G. Boyce argues that 'the Gaels possessed a strong sense of cultural identity, which, under the impact of colonization, was transformed into a sense of national identity, and by the end of the Tudor period into an embryonic ethnic nationalism'. The 'strong sense of cultural identity' that Boyce identified as the building blocks of Irish nationalism included such things as the ethnic distinctions that the bardic poets recognised in their work as early as the Viking invasions – the distinction between the Gael (Irish) and the Gall (foreigner). On this point Marianne Elliott maintains that this distinction should not be seen as nationalism *per se*, yet she concludes that 'no one has yet come up with a satisfactory concept to encapsulate the pride in culture and place' which was present in Ireland prior to the eighteenth century. D.G. Boyce, *Nationalism in Ireland* (London: Routledge, 1995), p. 19; Elliott, *The Catholics of Ulster*, p. 46.

53 T. Clyde, *Irish Literary Magazines: An Outline History and Descriptive Bibliography* (Dublin: Irish Academic Press, 2003), p. xii.

54 T. Garvin, *Mythical Thinking in Political Life: Reflections on Nationalism and Social Science* (Dublin: Maunsel & Company, 2001), p. 55.

55 D. Vincent, *Literacy and Popular Culture: England, 1750–1914* (Cambridge: Cambridge University Press, 1989), p. 198, quoted in M. Hampton, *Visions of the Press in Britain, 1850–1950* (Chicago: University of Illinois Press, 2004), p. 29.

56 Hampton, *Visions of the Press in Britain*, p. 29.

57 Ibid., p. 19.

58 M. Legg, *Newspapers and Nationalism: The Irish Provincial Press, 1850–1892* (Dublin: Four Courts Press, 1999), p. 73.

59 Legg, *Newspapers and Nationalism*, pp. 11, 30, 73.

60 Ibid., p. 149.

61 Hampton, *Visions of the Press in Britain*, p. 9.

62 Ibid., p. 25.

63 S. Koss, *The Rise and Fall of the Political Press in Britain, Volume 1* (Chapel Hill: University of North Carolina Press, 1981), p. 9, quoted in Hampton, *Visions of the Press in Britain*, p. 26.

64 de Nie, *The Eternal Paddy*, p. 32.

65 Hampton, *Visions of the Press in Britain*, p. 9; de Nie, *The Eternal Paddy*, p. 32.

66 *The Newspaper Press Directory* (London: C. Mitchel and Co., 1922), pp. 208, 581.

67 Clayton, *Enemies and Passing Friends*, p. xv.

68 D. Kennedy, *The Widening Gulf: Northern Attitudes to the Independent Irish State, 1919–49* (Belfast: Blackstaff Press, 1988).

69 H. Oram, *The Newspaper Book: A History of Newspapers in Ireland, 1649–1983* (Dublin: MO Books, 1983), p. 87; Phoenix, 'The *Irish News*, 1855–1995', pp. 12–13.

70 Hampton, *Visions of the Press in Britain*, p. 9.

71 Phoenix, 'The *Irish News*, 1855–1995', pp. 14–16; Oram, *The Newspaper Book*, p. 87.

72 Hepburn, *Catholic Belfast and Nationalist Ireland in the Era of Joe Devlin*, p. 272.

73 P. Buckley, *Faith and Fatherland: The Irish News, the Catholic Hierarchy, and the Management of Dissidents* (Belfast: Belfast Historical and Educational Society, 1991), pp. 90–1.

74 V. Glandon, 'Index of Irish Newspapers, 1900–1922 (Part I)', *Eire–Ireland* 11, 4, (1976), p. 91.

75 Campbell and Joe Devlin had started school together at St Mary's Christian Brothers School, and they worked together as reporters for the *Irish News* in the 1890s. Campbell had been editor of the newspaper since 1895 and, while he chose to leave the post in 1905 so that Devlin could make the newspaper his own, he and Devlin were on very good terms. Campbell's respect and admiration for Devlin is clearly evident from his autobiographical memoir. Campbell, *Fifty Years of Ulster*, pp. 4–8, 227–38.

76 Phoenix, 'The *Irish News*, 1855–1995', p. 21.

77 Ibid., p. 25.

78 The *Irish News* does not keep circulation figures from the 1920s. Neither the newspaper's entries in *Willings' Press Guide* nor its advertisements during the 1920s cite readership statistics and the documents held by the Companies' Registry do not offer any insight.

79 Memorandum from Kevin O'Shiel, 'The Glenavy Affair', n.d., Department of the Taoiseach, NAI/TSCH/S 2027, North East Boundary Secret Documents 1922–4, National Archives, Dublin.

80 Oram, *The Newspaper Book*, p. 50.

81 Ibid., pp. 35, 50; *Derry Journal: 225th Anniversary Supplement*, 6 June 1997.

82 'About', *Fermanagh Herald*, https://fermanaghherald.com/about/ (accessed 23 July 2019); Staunton, *The Nationalists of Northern Ireland*, p. 15; Phoenix, *Northern Nationalism*, p. 40.

83 *Irish News*, 15 August 1924.

CHAPTER 1

The Making of a Trapped Minority

> Henry II, Henry VIII, Elizabeth, James I, Cromwell, William III, and Castlereagh (with whom was associated William Pitt) were enemies of Ireland. But not one of them contemplated partition. Up to Cromwell's time the favorite plan for Conquest was Colonization plus Extermination of the 'natives.' Elizabeth, James and Oliver put this plan into operation with great zeal. But they did not think of splitting Ireland into warring factions.
>
> – Fear Na Traigh[1]

It is tempting to begin any study of Irish nationalism with an examination of the bumpy path by which Ireland came to be controlled by the Protestant planters of Ulster and the Pale, or the eighteenth-century Penal Laws that their descendants used to build the Protestant Ascendancy. It would be, perhaps, more tempting still to probe the deeper recesses of Anglo-Irish relations in search of antecedents of, and unionist responses to, the cultural, political and insurrectionary nationalism that flourished under the United Irishmen and their Young Ireland followers or the constitutionalist brand of nationalism that Daniel O'Connell developed to fight for Catholic Emancipation. Yet, as fruitful as such an investigation could be in understanding nationalism and unionism in Ireland, the immediate origins of Northern Ireland's nationalist *minority problem* are to be found in the Ulster Crisis of the late nineteenth century and the Home Rule movement whence it grew. Thus, demonstrating the process by which the nationalists of Northern Ireland came to be a trapped minority should also begin there, in the era of William Gladstone and Charles Stewart Parnell. With that in mind, this chapter examines the well-trodden history of Ireland during the second half of the nineteenth century, while focusing on the competing visions of the island's proper place in the world that was then emerging.

In 1868, William E. Gladstone became leader of the Liberal Party and Prime Minister of Great Britain and Ireland, and he immediately began searching for a way to reconcile Ireland to its place within the United Kingdom. The United Kingdom was born in 1800 in the aftermath of the United Irishmen's failed rebellion in 1798 and had endured both insurrectionary and constitutionalist threats to its integrity thereafter. Having taken a menacing Fenian form by the time Gladstone took the reins of power in 1868, physical force Irish nationalism was on the rise. Fenianism had emerged in America and Ireland during the late 1850s and represented a confluence of numerous oathbound and republican secret societies including Jeremiah O'Donovan Rossa's Phoenix Society, the Irish Republican Brotherhood (IRB) launched by James Stephens and the American Clan na Gael within which John Devoy was to become a consummate fixture. Unlike the followers of constitutionalist Daniel O'Connell, Fenians saw engaging in parliamentary politics as recognition of Britain's right to make rules for Ireland as well as a corrupting force that subordinated Irish issues to the vagaries of British politics. Moreover, as undignified as they believed it was to grovel for concessions at Westminster, it was equally clear to the Fenians that no such display could bring about the independent Irish republic they envisioned. O'Donovan Rossa made this point clear when he observed: 'I don't believe the Saxon will ever relax his grip except by the persuasion of lead and cold steel.'[2]

It was with O'Donovan Rossa's form of lead and cold steel persuasion in mind that the IRB embarked on a series of ill-fated insurrectionary acts in Britain, Ireland and British North America between 1866 and 1871. From a military perspective, Fenianism was inconsequential but a Fenian mythology, and indeed a martyrology, emerged nonetheless. It was this rising tide of Fenian sentiment that Gladstone was determined to halt and then harness when he became Prime Minister of the United Kingdom.

In his own words, Gladstone sought to 'draw a line between the Fenians and the people of Ireland and to make the people of Ireland indisposed to cross it'.[3] To achieve these ends and with the intention of making Ireland a contented part of the United Kingdom, Gladstone embarked on a conciliatory Irish policy that included the disestablishment of the Church of Ireland, land reform and, ultimately, Irish Home Rule.[4] Loosely defined as local self-government for Ireland within the United Kingdom, Home Rule was at the centre of Irish nationalist politics from 1870, when Isaac Butt founded the Home Government Association, until the rise of Sinn Féin at the end of the First World War. Home Rule reached the zenith of its influence under the leadership of Protestant landowner Charles Stewart Parnell, who made parliamentary obstructionism the hallmark of his Irish Parliamentary Party (IPP).[5] Not only did this approach threaten to clog the wheels of government but Parnell's aggressive style and language also put an edge on parliamentarianism that made him and Home Rule more appealing to the radical elements on the periphery of Irish politics.[6] In 1879, Parnell forged an alliance with Mayo land agitator and Fenian Michael Davitt, which put him in a position to exploit and harness a serious wave of violent land agitation that was then gripping rural Ireland. Davitt and Parnell were able to convert this Land War (1879–82) into a national movement in which Home Rule came to be seen as a panacea for all of Ireland's ills.[7]

When the Land War had subsided, Home Rule became the primary preoccupation of Parnell and the IPP.[8] Irish Protestants had been active within the agrarian movement but were soon alienated by Parnell's renewed focus on the national question and his increasingly deferential attitude towards the Catholic Church that accompanied this shift. This was a decisive turn, especially since it coincided with the Reform Acts of 1884–5, which enfranchised Ireland's tenant farmers for the first time. The full impact of electoral reform became clear enough after the 1885 election in which the Liberal Party was wiped out in Ireland and the IPP, having won eighty-six seats, was left holding the balance of power at Westminster.[9] The ability to make or break governing administrations became the chief weapon of the IPP during this period of flux as both the Liberals and Conservatives vied for its support.

Initially, Parnell allied with the Marquess of Salisbury on the basis that the Tories pursue a conciliatory Irish policy. Salisbury's own foray into land reform – the Ashbourne Act – should be seen in this light; however, at that time, there was also an indication that Randolph

Churchill and other English Tories were amenable to some form of devolved local government for Ireland.[10] Significantly, Gladstone was also moving in the direction of supporting Irish self-government and when this was leaked to the press in December 1885, the Conservatives responded by clothing themselves as the defenders of the Union against Home Rule. This hastened the collapse of Salisbury's minority government and returned Gladstone to power in 1886.[11]

Gladstone's conversion to Home Rule has been seen as both a genuine moral conviction that devolution was needed to keep the people of Ireland 'indisposed to cross' the line that he first spoke about in 1868,[12] as well as a cynical ploy to outmanoeuvre rivals. Both of these factors came into play when, in April 1886, Gladstone introduced the first of his two Home Rule Bills.[13] The legislation of 1886 called for the establishment of a devolved Irish assembly with its own executive. The measure required Irish MPs to withdraw from Westminster and it included a long list of fields that were to remain the preserve of Westminster, including the crown, foreign policy, trade, customs and the ability to make peace and war.

The legislation was complex and, perhaps, even 'unworkable'[14] but it was something that Parnell was more than prepared to pursue; yet he had to do so without the support of the Whig and Radical factions of the Liberal Party, which both abandoned Gladstone over the Irish Question. Home Rule also met with frenetic opposition by both Irish Protestants and British Conservatives, who cast the measure as an attack on the Empire as well as the Union. The opposition of Irish Protestants came principally from the Anglican landed elite in the South of Ireland and the Presbyterians of Ulster – a region that had benefited from the industrialisation that they associated with the Act of Union.[15] Under the circumstances, Tory unionists were quick to exploit Ulster hostility as Randolph Churchill became the flag-bearer of the Union, marshalling the forces of the North with the suggestive watchwords: 'Ulster will fight, Ulster will be right!'[16]

Home Rule was ultimately defeated in the Commons by this alliance of Liberal and Tory unionists, causing a re-orientation of the party structure in 1886 that kept Union-oriented parties in power for all but three of the twenty years that followed. Moreover, as Home Rule came to be construed as 'Rome Rule' by Irish Protestants, the murky sectarianism that had long been a part of Irish life evolved into the rigidly confessional politics that still haunt modern Ulster.[17] Gladstone submitted a subsequent Home Rule Bill, much the same as the first, during his short-lived fourth administration in 1893 but it was defeated by a unionist majority in the House of Lords.[18] While this legislation met a similar fate as the first Home Rule Bill, Gladstone's 1893 measure was lost under very different circumstances. The IPP had by then become deeply divided after the news surfaced in 1890 that Parnell had been carrying on an affair with Katherine (Kitty) O'Shea – the wife of a former IPP colleague. The scandal brought the condemnation of the Catholic Church and destroyed the constitutional nationalist movement as supporters broke up into Parnellite and anti-Parnellite factions. Factionalism within the IPP was widespread and Ulster was among the most anti-Parnellite regions on the island. The emergence of the anti-Parnellite *Irish News* in 1891 was itself a testament to the anti-Parnellite leanings of Ulster nationalists.[19] Parnell's struggle to hold onto the leadership of the IPP contributed to his sudden and unexpected death in 1891 but the fissures created by this tumultuous period remained open until the party was reunited by John Redmond and Joe Devlin at the turn of the century.[20]

The intervening years between the spectacular fall of Parnell and Redmond's rejuvenation of the party witnessed a flowering of cultural and literary nationalism. This was, in part, a by-product of Standish James O'Grady's immensely influential *History of Ireland* (1878–80) which helped Irish men and women rediscover their mythological past but it also grew out of Michael Cusack's Gaelic Athletic Association (GAA), founded in 1884 to promote ancient Irish sports. The activities of the Gaelic League, which Douglas Hyde and historian Eoin MacNeill established in 1893, 'to keep the Irish language spoken in Ireland', were also influential.[21] Appealing to the same base, both the GAA and Gaelic League were infiltrated by the IRB and became veritable incubators for Anglophobia and ultra-nationalist thought.[22] As Peter Hart has shown, while the GAA was 'highly regionalized' and its role can be 'overestimated', the fact that so many GAA members joined the Irish Volunteers says much about the organisation's political impact on these young athletes.[23] Like the GAA, the Gaelic League, described by Cahir Healy as 'that training school from which so many of the revolutionaries of 1916 emerged', had a similar affect on many of its members.[24] This was clearly apparent to the editors of the Belfast-based literary periodical the *Shan Van Vocht*, who noted in 1899: 'The Irish boy who takes up his Gaelic grammar and reading-book will learn [to say] one thing even should he not become a scholar, namely, this – I am not an Englishman.'[25]

The political realm was far from dormant during this era of cultural and literary awakening. Home Rule still held the allegiance of most politically minded nationalists, and would continue to do so until at least 1916,[26] but the recovery of the reunified IPP also facilitated the emergence of a new and rival political organisation – Arthur Griffith's Sinn Féin movement, founded in 1905. Griffith was a Dublin journalist, publisher, Gaelic Leaguer and, for a time, IRB member. A follower of Parnell but frustrated by the factionalism that incapacitated the IPP after the split, in 1899 Griffith cynically observed: 'Grattan is dead and O'Connell is dead and Parnell is dead, but Emmet and Davis, Mitchel and the Fenian Men are living in the twentieth century.'[27]

The name Sinn Féin, which translates as 'Ourselves Alone', was itself something of a tribute to Young Irelanders Thomas Davis and John Mitchel with whom Griffith identified. One of the earliest references to the ideals embodied by the words Ourselves Alone can be found in a poem by that name that first appeared in the Young Ireland periodical the *Nation* during the 1840s:

Too long our Irish hearts we schooled,
In patient hope to bide;
By dreams of English justice fooled,
And English tongues that lied.
That hour of weak delusion's past,
The empty dream has flown:
Our hope and strength, we find at last,
Is in OURSELVES ALONE.[28]

The self-reliance embodied by the words Ourselves Alone and Sinn Féin resonated with Griffith and helped to shape the ideas that were emerging in his publications.[29]

In the pages of the *United Irishmen* and later *Sinn Féin*, Griffith explored the possibility of establishing an Anglo-Irish dual monarchy (modeled on his reading of Austro-Hungarian history), while advocating economic self-sufficiency and passive resistance to Britain.

The notion that Irish MPs should withdraw from Westminster and form their own counter-state was the capstone of the Sinn Féin programme.[30] Cahir Healy, who came to symbolise Fermanagh nationalism during the 1920s, was an early convert to Sinn Féin and was in attendance at a 1908 rally in Leitrim for Charles Dolan, the party's parliamentary candidate. According to Healy, Griffith did not exactly woo this crowd with the statistic-filled speech he delivered, leading one spectator to observe: '[i]f yez keep the boys at it ye'll win the election, but for God's sake send home the wee bloke with his goggles and his figures'.[31] Still in its infancy and lacking a charismatic leader to complement Griffith's intellect, the movement did not attract many followers at this stage but Griffith's ideas resonated with elements of the IRB and a small body of advanced nationalists that was then beginning to stir.[32]

Such stirrings were temporarily stalled, however, when the House of Lords defeated a Liberal budget presented by David Lloyd George in 1909, which triggered a constitutional crisis in Britain over the powers of that Unionist dominated body. In these circumstances, Home Rule was put back on the table after two elections failed to solve the political impasse and Liberal Prime Minister Herbert Asquith became reliant on the support of John Redmond's IPP to continue the fight. The Parliament Act of 1911, passed with IPP support, left the House of Lords with the power to delay (by two years) but not block legislation and, with this measure in place, Asquith's Liberal Party repaid its debt to the IPP by introducing a third Home Rule Bill in April 1912.[33]

Asquith's legislation closely mirrored the two previous Home Rule Bills and, like Gladstone, he underestimated unionist – and specifically Ulster unionist – hostility to Irish self-government, which was now more deeply entrenched and extreme. Ulster unionists had found an effective spokesman in Edward Carson, a Dublin MP and leading barrister, and were supported by the Southern unionists of the Irish Unionist Alliance (IUA) and many English Tories.[34] Indicative of the cooperation between English and Irish unionists, at the Blenheim Palace rally of 1912, Conservative leader Andrew Bonar Law told supporters in a widely reported speech that 'they would be justified in resisting [Home Rule] by all means in their power, including force'.[35]

Bellicose statements such as these were welcomed in Ulster, where unionists had been contemplating the need to resort to extra-parliamentary measures to ward off Home Rule. As early as 1905, a cadre of young Ulster unionists, which included future Northern Ireland Prime Minister James Craig, had established the Ulster Unionist Council (UUC) as a counter to the parliamentary forum[36] and to differentiate the Ulster movement from Southern unionists of the IUA.[37] The most overt sign of unionist intransigence was the celebrated signing of the Solemn League and Covenant and the women's Declaration in September 1912. The 218,206 male signatories of the Ulster Covenant and 234,046 female signatories of the Declaration pledged to resist Home Rule even to the point of using armed resistance.[38]

The signing of the Covenant coincided with plans to set up a provisional government for Ulster as a means to resist Home Rule and the establishment, in early 1913, of a paramilitary organisation known as the Ulster Volunteer Force (UVF).[39] The UVF became a credible threat to political stability in March 1914 when, believing that they might be compelled to use force against Ulster, a number of British cavalry officers at the Curragh encampment chose to resign their commissions. The Curragh Mutiny cast serious doubts about the government's ability to use any type of coercion to enforce Home Rule and this became all the more significant the following month after the UVF succeeded in landing arms in the North.[40]

Irish nationalists of various stripes responded in kind to the martial zeal of the UVF by establishing their own paramilitaries. Numbering some 180,000 members, the Irish Volunteers was the largest nationalist paramilitary force and gun-running had given this precursor of the Irish Republican Army access to a limited number of arms by the summer of 1914. The Irish Volunteers were the brainchild of Professor Eoin MacNeill and the force was eventually controlled by John Redmond; but even before the emergence of this nationalist paramilitary, James Larkin's radical Irish Transport and General Workers Union (ITGWU) had formed the Irish Citizen Army to protect workers during a severe period of labour unrest in Dublin. The ITGWU and the Citizen Army fell under the control of socialist republican James Connolly after Larkin left Ireland for the United States in October 1914.

The most immediate result of the proliferation of rival Irish paramilitaries was Herbert Asquith's realisation that Home Rule would not be possible unless Ulster was excluded and this effectively meant the partition of Ireland. According to Patrick Buckland, Edward Carson had come to endorse exclusion in 1913 strictly as a tactic to be used to destroy the Home Rule Bill and 'maintain the Union in its entirety'. In contrast, the Ulster-born UUC leaders 'had no such compunction about throwing over the Southern Unionists' believing that '[i]f they could not save the whole country for the Empire, they could at least save themselves'.[41] Lloyd George, Winston Churchill and Irish Chief Secretary Augustine Birrell had each been urging Prime Minister Asquith to consider some form of exclusion but, until 1914, he had steadfastly ignored their warnings.[42] For his part, Joe Devlin, the IPP leader who had the most to lose if Ulster were not included in the Home Rule Bill, emphatically rejected any form of exclusion in October 1913, suggesting that he 'would sooner have his head cut off than consent to such a settlement'.[43] Irrespective of Devlin's opposition to the idea, once Asquith was finally forced to accept exclusion, parliamentary efforts to resolve the Ulster Question via an amending bill spiralled into a bitter debate over the number of counties to be excluded by that bill and whether exclusion would be permanent or temporary. This is where things stood when the United Kingdom was pulled into the First World War in August 1914.

The outbreak of war offered Asquith a temporary reprieve from the Irish quagmire as the Prime Minister managed to place his Home Rule Bill on the statute book, without the proposed amending bill that would have made special provisions for Ulster. But, while a Suspension Act rendered Home Rule inoperable until the cessation of hostilities, Asquith pledged to draft a new amending bill to deal with Ulster exclusion before Home Rule became operable.[44] For their part, John Redmond, John Dillon and Joe Devlin threw their full weight behind the war effort and encouraged members of the Irish Volunteers to enlist in the British army. Because Unionist leaders offered the UVF for military service as well, members of both paramilitaries served together in Europe, albeit under different terms.[45] Redmond, Dillon and Devlin, like their unionist counterparts, clearly hoped that encouraging their supporters to enlist in the military would bolster their standing with the British government but there were unfavourable consequences of this tactic for the IPP leaders. For his effort to encourage Irish Volunteer enlistment, Redmond was ridiculed in the pages of James Connolly's the *Workers' Republic*:

> Full steam ahead, John Redmond said,
> and everything is chum.
> Home Rule will come when we are dead
> and buried out in Belgium.[46]

While it did not seem so at the time, Redmond's support for the War was a serious tactical blunder from which the IPP would never fully recover. Not only did it leave Redmond and Devlin open to attack by Connolly and other extremists, it also led to a split in the ranks of the Irish Volunteers.[47] With Professor Eoin MacNeill as Chief-of-Staff, 12,000 of the Irish Volunteers broke with Redmond, forcing the IPP leader to recast his army as the National Volunteers.[48] Although he was unaware of it at the time, the IRB had infiltrated MacNeill's Irish Volunteers and these radical elements likely formed the majority on its HQ staff by the time the poet revolutionaries Patrick Pearse, Thomas MacDonagh and Joseph Mary Plunkett were elevated to positions of influence.[49]

Pearse, MacDonagh and Plunkett had been involved with Ireland's cultural and literary awakening and they were all deeply affected by the heroic martyrdom and blood sacrifice that those movements so prized. The notion that '[l]ife springs from death' was clearly evident in Pearse's graveside tribute to the memory of the Fenian O'Donovan Rossa in 1915[50] and it is also telling that Pearse used Cúchulainn's adage, 'I care not if I live but a day and a night, so long as my deeds live after me', as the motto of St Enda's College, the bilingual school he founded.[51] Yet they were also IRB men and MacDonagh's notion that the Irish Volunteers were the heirs to 750 years of 'Irish Nationality handed down from revolt to revolt' also had traction – especially since these extreme elements of MacNeill's Volunteers were planning their own insurrection.[52]

This conspiracy took shape within a Military Council that the IRB set up in 1915. Members of this Military Council would eventually include: the Fenians Eamon Ceannt, Sean MacDermott and Thomas Clark; Citizen Army leader James Connolly; as well as MacDonagh, Pearse and Plunkett. These Irish insiders were aided in their preparations by John Devoy of Clan na Gael and former British diplomat Sir Roger Casement, who sought to secure German arms for the rising that was slated to begin on Easter Sunday 1916.[53]

MacNeill had intended the Irish Volunteers to be used for defensive purposes and only discovered the plans for the Easter Rising at the last moment. He proved unable to stop the rebellion even after Casement's collusion with Germany was discovered, yet MacNeill's counter-orders did transform the rebellion into an exercise in self-sacrifice. Beginning on Easter Monday 1916, 1,500 insurgents drawn from the Irish Volunteers, the women's auxiliary Cumann na mBan and the Citizen Army seized a number of strategic positions in Dublin. At the General Post Office, a republican tricolour flag was raised in place of the Union Jack. It was from this location that Pearse read out the words of a document, posted throughout the city, which proclaimed the birth of an Irish Republic and named himself as the President of its provisional government.[54] The rebels were able to hold portions of the city for several days but in the end, they were no match for a well-equipped modern British army and on 29 April, Pearse ordered the rebels' unconditional surrender.[55]

'Isn't it all like a comic opera founded on the Wolf [*sic*] Tone fiasco a hundred years ago,' commented Belfast unionist A. Duffin in a letter to his daughter, adding, 'it is good business its having come to a head, & I hope we shall deal thoroughly with these pests'.[56] Betraying their conservatism, mainstream Irish nationalists initially also wanted the 'pests' dealt with and voiced hostility to the insurgents but nationalist opinion soon swung in the rebels' favour.[57] This was largely the result of the coercive measures and executions that followed the Rising. Pearse, Connolly and the Rising's other principal planners were brought before firing squads during the first two weeks in May. The American-born Éamon de Valera had been the last commandant to surrender and he, too, was sentenced to death but the ambiguity of his citizenship status ultimately helped to spare his life. Nearly 2,000 supposed subversives were interned without trial in the aftermath of the rebellion and in England, Roger Casement was convicted of treason and hanged. For many members of the increasingly indignant public, the 'dirty traitors' of Easter Week were transformed by the government's reaction into 'gallant martyrs and national heroes' within weeks of the initial bloodletting.[58] Moreover, for these people, the constitutional Home Rule movement was beginning to look a lot less palatable than the republic for which the rebels had died.

As public opinion underwent its metamorphosis outside the halls of power, the Easter Rising made Ireland a priority once again at Westminster. Believing that he no longer had the luxury of waiting until the end of the War to make Home Rule operable, Asquith put Lloyd George in charge of finding a solution to the intractable crisis and it soon seemed that one had been found. In May, Lloyd George was able to convince Carson, Redmond and Devlin to accept a plan which allowed for the immediate activation of Dublin's Home Rule parliament while simultaneously excluding six of Ulster's nine counties from its jurisdiction. Religion being regarded as the primary indicator of political preference, the counties in question were Derry, Antrim, Down and Armagh, which each had Protestant majorities, in addition to Tyrone and Fermanagh, which had significant Protestant minorities.

For Devlin, who had once 'threatened to do tragic things to his own head if Ulster [was] left out',[59] accepting the principle of partition proved to be a fatal mistake despite the questionable tactics that Lloyd George had used to gain his confidence. While he and Redmond had been induced to accept exclusion as a strictly temporary solution to the political impasse, Carson had been led to believe that the excluded counties would be permanently represented at Westminster and this ultimately made the scheme unworkable as soon as the inconsistencies were apparent. His role in the debacle earned Joe Devlin the unflattering sobriquet 'the Lloyd George of Ireland', reported T.P. O'Connor,[60] and it left Devlin 'tarred by the brush of partition'.[61] Naturally enough, permanent partition was anathema to Ulster nationalists collectively but not all of them were convinced that temporarily excluding Northern counties, as a political tactic, was without merit (especially since the establishment of a separate Northern parliament was not yet a part of the scheme).[62] In this regard, on 23 June 1916, a representative conference of 770 Ulster nationalists met at St Mary's Hall, Belfast, to discuss this question.[63]

Notwithstanding the blow that his reputation had taken over Lloyd George's exclusion plan, Joe Devlin remained the most powerful Northern nationalist of his day and his position on partition was still highly influential. Having come to the conclusion that some form of partition was now inevitable, Devlin actively encouraged delegates at the conference to accept *temporary exclusion* from Home Rule, believing that it was 'the best means of carrying on the fight for a united self-governing Ireland'.[64] If Home Rule were put into operation outside the excluded area of Ulster, Devlin argued, it would take only good Irish government and a bit of arm twisting to convince the excluded counties to throw in their lot with the rest of Ireland. Given the rancour that had characterised the pre-War fight over exclusion, Eamon Phoenix is correct in suggesting that this line of thinking had 'an air of unreality' but it is important to bear in mind that, at this stage, exclusion still meant rule from Westminster. Since there would be few Westminster MPs from Ulster, this eventuality was bound to give Ulster unionists less influence than they had wielded while Ireland remained a hot topic in the British parliament or they would likely have in Dublin's much smaller Home Rule parliament and, as such, Devlin's argument was not without its merits. As veteran Derry Home Ruler Joseph Davison observed: 'Temporary exclusion opens the door to complete inclusion and we should have no hesitation in accepting it.'[65]

According to Lloyd George's observer at the meeting, Joe Devlin's forty-five-minute speech before the voting was 'wonderfully eloquent and delivered with great force'.[66] This clearly contributed to the result, as roughly 65 per cent of the delegates agreed to accept temporary exclusion if it meant Home Rule for the rest of Ireland. This amounted to a healthy majority in favour of exclusion but voting patterns demonstrate that fissures were beginning to emerge within Ulster nationalism as most of the 265 dissenting delegates were from the counties that were to form the expected border zone of the excluded area – Derry, Fermanagh and Tyrone. The day of the St Mary's Hall conference would be remembered as 'Black Friday' as a consequence of the divisions it had exposed between the centre and periphery of Ulster nationalism.[67]

Despite ambivalence from some Northern quarters, by the end of 1916, it was clear to the British government that partition would prevail and the politics of Ireland at Westminster became engrossed in the debate over the nature that exclusion would take. It was at this juncture that Lloyd George replaced Asquith as Prime Minister of Britain's coalition government, after which Irish policy became the preserve of the English Conservative Walter Long who would chair the Irish committees tasked with drafting Home Rule legislation.[68]

As Long and his cabinet colleagues worked on their legislative scheme, Lloyd George attempted to halt the growth of extremism in the South of the island by releasing republican prisoners. Significantly, Éamon de Valera, the most senior leader to survive the Easter Rising, was one of those released in 1917. Arthur Griffith had not participated in the rebellion but it was around his republican Sinn Féin organisation that de Valera and other released rebels coalesced, transforming it into an ardently republican movement. Sinn Féin candidates contested seven by-elections before the end of the war but refused to take their seats.[69] Moreover, despite the IPP's rejection of conscription, a growing conviction that it would have to be imposed on Ireland fed into Sinn Féin hands as it enabled Sinn Féin to remind voters that both Redmond and Devlin had enthusiastically endorsed the War. The bulk of Sinn Féin's propaganda focused on Joe Devlin after Redmond died unexpectedly in 1918.[70]

The declining stock of the IPP was made all the more apparent after the United Kingdom's first post-War general election in December 1918. Lloyd George's Tory-dominated coalition was returned to power. Unionist-oriented candidates won twenty-five seats in Ireland (mostly in Ulster) and in the Falls Division of Belfast, Joe Devlin soundly defeated Sinn Féin leader Éamon de Valera but the IPP returned only five other MPs in Ireland and all but one of these was in the North.[71] Having secured seventy-three seats in the contest – including former IPP constituencies in Ulster – Sinn Féin was the election's biggest winner.

As Arthur Griffith had advocated, the triumphant Sinn Féiners abstained from Westminster and promptly established their own republican parliament in Dublin, which they called Dáil Éireann. Éamon de Valera became the face of Irish republicanism as President of the Dáil in April 1919 and, with the intention of securing official recognition of Sinn Féin's revolutionary achievement, he set sail for America in June, leaving Griffith to act in his stead.[72]

The establishment of Dáil Éireann coincided with the beginning of open war between Sinn Féin and Britain. It was during this bitter struggle that Michael Collins emerged as a powerful and charismatic politician, military leader and intelligence officer, rivalling the influence enjoyed by either Griffith or de Valera. Limited by lack of resources, the Volunteers-*cum*-IRA fought what amounted to a guerrilla war, using ambush and assassination as their primary weapons. The months that followed were characterised by sanctioned reprisals and counter-reprisals committed by both the IRA and the agents of the British Government – specifically, the Royal Irish Constabulary (RIC) and the notorious Black and Tans and the Auxiliaries that supplemented the regular police force.[73]

Dismissed as 'humbug and tomfoolery' by Devlin,[74] Sinn Féin's policy of abstention from Westminster effectively meant that British parliamentarians were not encumbered by what could have been strong nationalist opposition as they devised Britain's legislative solution to the Ulster Question. Equally important for Northern nationalism, while Joe Devlin still commanded an incredible advantage over Sinn Féin in Belfast, the national eclipse of the IPP robbed him of any influence that he might have otherwise had with respect to the coalition government's Irish policy.[75] Under these circumstances, Ulster nationalists were left to the mercies of Long's Irish committee that, despite the changes occasioned by the rise of Sinn Féin, was still naïve enough to believe that Southern Ireland would be satisfied with Home Rule.

The Better Government of Ireland Act, which received royal assent in December 1920, was the ultimate result of the Irish committee's deliberations and represented the 'sudden external interference' that led to the confinement of a trapped Northern nationalist minority.[76] Although the committee accepted partition as the basis of any legislation, its Bill departed from all previous proposals as it envisioned establishing not one but two Home Rule parliaments in Ireland. Long's fascination with federalism and his desire to reduce congestion at Westminster and remove Ireland as much as possible from British party politics were responsible for the committee's decision to create a separate parliament for 'Northern Ireland'.[77]

Walter Long's Irish committee had made the decision to establish a separate parliament for Northern Ireland early in their deliberations but vacillated over how many counties to exclude from the jurisdiction it intended to give Dublin. Ultimately, the legislation provided for the exclusion of the four Ulster counties that had Protestant majorities – Antrim, Armagh, Derry and Down – in addition to Fermanagh and Tyrone, which each had large Protestant minorities. This was the only option that the UUC was prepared to accept and, while James

Craig raised the idea of using a European-style boundary commission to finetune the border,[78] it did not seem to matter that dividing Ireland in this way effectively trapped some half a million nationalists in Northern Ireland and a smaller number of unionists in Southern Ireland. Article 5 of the statute prohibited either government from enacting discriminatory laws but provisions for the use of proportional representation to elect MPs to each Home Rule legislature was the only real safeguard that the Bill offered to these minorities.

Another important provision of the Better Government of Ireland Bill provided for the establishment of a Council of Ireland to be comprised of representatives from both parliaments. The Council was intended to facilitate co-operation between the two Irish governments on common concerns but it was also meant to encourage eventual Irish unity. Under the terms of the Bill, the two legislatures were left with the option of dispensing with partition and the Council in favour of establishing a single Home Rule parliament for all of Ireland if they so chose. Indicative of London's desire to draw the two Irish legislatures into a single parliament, the Bill left the control of customs and excise in British hands unless the two states agreed to merge. Barring reunion, the financial provisions of the Better Government of Ireland Bill were severely restricted, as Great Britain retained control of taxation on excess profits, corporation profits and personal incomes in addition to customs and excise.

Preferring to be represented by Westminster alone, Ulster Unionists had never asked for their own parliament and only grudgingly accepted the offer, knowing that the alternative, Asquith's still suspended 1914 Act, would leave them in a worse position. 'We would much prefer to remain part and parcel of the United Kingdom,' observed Captain Charles Craig in the House of Commons, '[b]ut we have enemies in this country, and we feel that an Ulster without a parliament of its own would not be in nearly as strong a position as one in which a parliament had been set up.'[79] While Southern Protestants remained hopeful that the UUC would use its influence to prevent Home Rule from functioning in any part of Ireland,[80] unionists in Donegal, Cavan and Monaghan felt betrayed by the fact that they would not be included in Northern Ireland and because the UUC did not seek to block the legislation.[81] Over time and in keeping with the trapped minority model, surviving the onslaught of Irish nationalism would ultimately be considered a major 'victory' and partition the 'joyful dawning of a new age' for Northern Ireland's dominant majority.[82]

Given the fact that Sinn Féin and the IRA were still in the midst of a war in defence of the Irish republic, it was naïve for the British government to think that they would do anything but ignore what was, in essence, a nineteenth-century solution to twentieth-century circumstances.[83] Meanwhile, partition and the imposition of a Home Rule parliament in Belfast was clearly the last thing that any section of Northern nationalist opinion had wanted and the legislation was universally despised by both the Devlinite rump of the IPP and Northern Sinn Féiners.

While the Sinn Féiners took no part in the debate on the legislation and the IPP did not have the numbers to influence the government's Irish policy, both Devlin and Thomas Harbison spoke passionately in opposition to the Bill at Westminster. Arguing that he had devoted thirty-five years 'to fight legitimately, and according to constitutional means, for the right [of] the majority of the people to rule in their native land', Harbison declared the Bill to be 'an insult to the Irish nation', 'a sentence of death' for the nationalists of Ulster and 'the case of the Act of Union over again'.[84] For his part, Devlin purported to loath every aspect of the legislation, arguing that creating a Belfast parliament imposed a 'permanent barrier' against Irish unity. 'The right hon. Gentlemen may not agree with me,' he noted, 'but they do not know Ireland as well as I do, and they do not know Ulster as well as I know it, and they do not know the spirit of hon. Members opposite as well as I know [them].'[85]

Devlin's harshest criticisms of the Bill concerned an amendment made by the House of Lords that added an upper chamber to each of the Home Rule parliaments, albeit with different methods for selecting senators. In a stark contrast to the nominated Southern Senate, which was designed to over-represent the Southern Unionists, senators in Northern Ireland were elected by its House of Commons on the basis of proportional representation. This ensured that membership in the Northern Ireland Senate would mirror the composition of the Northern lower house[86] and denied the Six-County minority of the added influence that was to be enjoyed by Southern Unionists. It was this incongruency that so troubled Joe Devlin, who described the Senate arrangement as 'one of the most disgraceful things [he had] ever known'.[87]

Given the extent of their disdain for the Bill, it is doubtful that more peaceful conditions would have in any way softened the anti-partitionism of the Northern nationalist minority but it certainly did not help matters that both Belfast and Derry City erupted into intense sectarian violence as the Better Government of Ireland Bill was making its way through the British parliament. The fighting had begun in Derry in April of 1920 and intensified after the July killing of an RIC officer in Cork. In Belfast, the rioting occurred in conjunction with the expulsion of Catholic workers from the city's shipyards and from their homes and businesses. As many as 5,000 Catholic workers were expelled from the shipyards within the first week of the disturbance and it is estimated that between 8,700 and 11,000 Catholics were eventually driven from their workplaces. Thousands more were forced from their homes; as many as 500 Catholic businesses were destroyed and between 416 and 498 people were killed as a consequence of sectarian fighting in Belfast. These events, in which Catholics were disproportionately affected, lasted well into 1922 and are remembered by Northern nationalists as 'the pogrom'.[88]

In defence of the Catholic victims of the disturbances and as an attempt to prove that dividing north-eastern Ulster from the rest of Ireland would cripple the economic position of the North, in August 1920, Dáil Éireann imposed a boycott on Belfast goods.[89] The British government responded to the deteriorating conditions in the North by strengthening policing. Established in November of 1920, the bulk of the recruits for the Ulster Special Constabulary (USC) came from the UVF – Edward Carson's Protestant paramilitary force.[90] The sectarianism and ill-discipline of the UVF rendered the Specials every bit as high-handed as were the Black and Tans and Auxiliaries operating in the South of Ireland.

And so it was while the southern and western parts of Ireland were being ruled by an illegal and republican counter-state that was at war with Britain and the north-eastern part of the island was experiencing serious sectarian disturbances, British parliamentarians were preparing to solve all of Ireland's ills by imposing a piece of legislation that no Irish faction really wanted. 'I confess I cannot understand the logic of your English statesmanship,' exclaimed Joe Devlin during a debate on the Bill, as he described the 'chief recommendation' of the partition

Bill as being 'that nobody believes in it, that nobody supports it, nobody has asked for it, and nobody will stand by it except the Government!'[91] Powerless to kill the Bill and unable to bear the humiliation of seeing it pass, Devlin and his tiny cohort of nationalists at Westminster chose to abstain in the final vote on the legislation.

The Better Government of Ireland Act received royal assent on 23 December 1920 and, as later nationalists were fond of pointing out, not a single Irish vote was cast in its favour. Now cut off from the majority nationalism of the South, the divided nationalists of Ulster's six excluded counties had effectively become a trapped minority. Analysing the responses of the Northern nationalists to the forces that had ensnared them while examining the nature of the relationship that this trapped minority would be able to maintain with nationalists in the South of Ireland will be the subject of the chapters that follow.

Endnotes

1 *Irish News*, 23 December 1920.

2 C. Townshend, *Ireland: The Twentieth Century* (London: Arnold, 2001), pp. 23–5; D.G. Boyce, *Nationalism in Ireland* (Gill and Macmillan, 1982), p. 177.

3 D.G. Boyce, *Nineteenth-Century Ireland: The Search for Stability* (Dublin: Gill and Macmillan Ltd, 1990), p. 149.

4 Ibid., p. 151; J. Smith, *Britain and Ireland: From Home Rule to Independence* (Essex: Pearson Education Limited, 2000), pp. 26–7.

5 The Home Government Association became the Home Rule League in 1873 and parliamentarians espousing Home Rule were known interchangeably throughout the 1870–1918 period as the Home Rule Party, the Nationalist Party or the Irish Parliamentary Party. As conditions in Ireland changed, it also became known as the Old Party.

6 Parnell was led into obstructionist tactics by fellow Home Ruler and Fenian Joseph Bigger. In July 1877, Parnell led a forty-five-hour filibuster in the House but such a display was usually scorned by Isaac Butt. Townshend, *Ireland*, pp. 29–32.

7 The Land War (1878–82) involved coordinated demonstrations, rent strikes, boycotting, cattle-maiming, burnings, physical attacks and various forms of ostracism intended to prevent tenant farmers from breaking the unity of the movement as they pressed for redress. M. Hughes, *Ireland Divided: The Roots of the Modern Irish Problem* (Cardiff: University of Wales Press, 1994), pp. 16–18; Boyce, *Nineteenth-Century Ireland*, p. 163.

8 T.W. Moody, 'Fenianism, Home Rule and the Land War, 1850–91', in T.W. Moody and F.X. Martin (eds), *The Course of Irish History* (Cork: Mercier Press, 2001), p. 241.

9 The IPP won eighty-five seats in Ireland including seventeen in Ulster and one in Liverpool. Salisbury's Tories won sixteen Ulster seats and the two Dublin

University seats giving them a total of 250 MPs across the UK as compared with 333 Liberal MPs. Smith, *Britain and Ireland*, p. 36.

10 L. McCaffrey, *The Irish Question: Two Centuries of Conflict* (Lexington: The University Press of Kentucky, 1995), p. 97.

11 Hughes, *Ireland Divided*, p. 19; Smith, *Britain and Ireland*, p. 37.

12 Boyce, *Nineteenth-Century Ireland*, p. 149.

13 J. Bardon, *A History of Ulster* (Belfast: The Blackstaff Press, 2001), p. 376; Hughes, *Ireland Divided*, p. 16; Smith, *Britain and Ireland*, pp. 36–7.

14 Boyce, *Nineteenth-Century Ireland*, p. 177.

15 Ibid., pp. 186, 192, 202–3, 205.

16 G. Martin, 'The Origins of Partition', in M. Anderson and E. Bort (eds), *The Irish Border: History, Politics, Culture* (Liverpool: Liverpool University Press, 1999), p. 59.

17 M. Elliott, *The Catholics of Ulster: A History* (London: Penguin Books, 2000), p. 294.

18 The most significant difference between Gladstone's two Home Rule Bills was that the first required Irish MPs to withdraw from Westminster, while the second provided for representation in that assembly.

19 E. Phoenix, 'The History of a Newspaper: The *Irish News*, 1855–1995', in E. Phoenix (ed.), *A Century of Northern Life: The Irish News and 100 Years of Ulster History, 1890s–1990s* (Belfast: Ulster Historical Foundation, 1995), pp. 13–16; Elliott, *The Catholics of Ulster*, p. 295.

20 Smith, *Britain and Ireland*, p. 44.

21 P. Johnson, *Ireland: A Concise History from the Twelfth Century to the Present Day* (Chicago: Academy Chicago Publishers, 1996), p. 156; D. Kiberd, 'Irish Literature and Irish History', in R.F. Foster (ed.), *The Oxford Illustrated History of Ireland* (Oxford: Oxford University Press, 1989), pp. 277–8; D. McCartney, 'From Parnell to Pearse, 1891–1921', in T.W. Moody and F.X. Martin (eds), *The Course of Irish History* (Cork: Mercier Press, 2001), pp. 246–7.

22 L.J. McCaffrey, 'Components of Irish Nationalism', in T.E. Hachey and L.J. McCaffrey, *Perspectives on Irish Nationalism* (Lexington: The University Press of Kentucky, 1989), pp.14–15.

23 According to Hart, 'a frenzy of collective joining' led many individuals to become members of the GAA, the Gaelic League, the Irish Volunteers and Sinn Féin at the same time and, revealingly, some GAA teams not affiliated with the Volunteers joined the paramilitary '*en bloc* in 1917 and 1918'. P. Hart, *The IRA & its Enemies: Violence and Community in Cork, 1916–1923* (Oxford: Oxford University Press, 1998), pp. 206, 210–11. For the impact that these organisations had on Michael Collins, see P. Hart, *Mick: The Real Michael Collins* (London: Penguin Books Ltd, 2006), pp. 37–74.

24 C. Healy, 'Late Joseph Devlin, M.P.: An Intimate Sketch by a Colleague', n.d., Cahir Healy Papers, D2991/B/140/19, Public Record Office of Northern Ireland, Belfast.

25 Shan Van Vocht translates as 'poor old woman' and was the title of a folksong-*cum*-political ballad made popular by the United Irishmen. Richard Harp, 'The "Shan Van Vocht" (Belfast, 1896–1899) And Irish Nationalism', *Eire–Ireland* 24, 3 (1989), p. 50.

26 According to McCaffrey, the continued domination of this moderate strain of nationalism is often overlooked. McCaffrey, 'Components of Irish Nationalism', pp.15–16.

27 Johnson, *Ireland*, p. 156.

28 As quoted in E. Macdonnell, 'The Crisis Unmasked', *The Quarterly Review* 72, 144 (1843), pp. 586–7. For Macdonnell, this poem was emblematic of the 'deadliest rancour, the most audacious falsehood, and the incendiary provocations to war' that English audiences could expect from the *Spirit of the Nation* – a collection of Young Ireland poetry and prose drawn from editions of their periodical, *The Nation*.

29 Harp, 'The "Shan Van Vocht" (Belfast, 1896–1899) And Irish Nationalism', p. 48.

30 McCartney, 'From Parnell to Pearse, 1891–1921', pp. 248–9.

31 Cahir Healy, 'Memories of Political Figures', n.d., Cahir Healy Papers, D2991/C/28/44, Public Record Office of Northern Ireland, Belfast. 'Memories of Political Figures' is the designation that I have given to this untitled manuscript.

32 McCartney, 'From Parnell to Pearse, 1891–1921', pp. 248–9.

33 E. Phoenix, 'The Political Background: From Parnell to Partition, 1890–1921', in E. Phoenix (ed.), *A Century of Northern Life: The Irish News and 100 years of Ulster History, 1890s–1990s* (Belfast: Ulster Historical Foundation, 1995), p. 48.

34 P. Buckland, *Irish Unionism 1: The Anglo-Irish and the New Ireland, 1885–1922* (Dublin: Gill and Macmillan, 1972), pp. xxiii, 17.

35 *The Times*, 29 July 1912. For an examination of how historians have interpreted Bonar Law's controversial Blenheim speech, see R.J.Q. Adams, *Bonar Law* (Stanford: Stanford University Press, 1999), pp. 108–9.

36 A. Jackson, *The Ulster Party* (New York: Oxford University Press, 1989), pp. 235–6.

37 Buckland, *Irish Unionism 1*, p. 17.

38 D. Urquhart, *Women in Ulster Politics, 1890–1940: A History Not Yet Told* (Dublin: Irish Academic Press, 2000), p. 62; Smith, *Britain and Ireland*, p. 63. With respect to female participation in Ulster politics, Urquhart's research has shown that unionist women were much more active than nationalist women in the province throughout this period. She attributed this disparity to the role of the Catholic Church within Ulster's nationalist movement and the fact that John Redmond and other IPP leaders were 'slower to recognize the potential of women's political work than their unionist counterparts'. Urquhart, *Women in Ulster Politics*, p. 98.

39 Jackson, *The Ulster Party*, p. 314.

40 Phoenix, 'The Political Background: From Parnell to Partition, 1890–1921', p. 49; P. Jalland, *The Liberals and Ireland: The Ulster Question in British Politics to 1914* (Sussex: The Harvester Press, 1980), pp. 133–4, 239–47; Townshend, *Ireland*, p. 67.

41 P. Buckland, *James Craig: Lord Craigavon* (Dublin: Gill and Macmillan Ltd, 1980), p. 34.

42 This quotation has been attributed to Churchill. McCaffrey, *The Irish Question*, p. 128.

43 *The Times*, 21 October 1913.

44 As Asquith told the House of Commons: 'in view of the altered circumstances, the assurance which I gave will in these circumstances be in spirit and substance completely fulfilled. The Home Rule Bill will not and cannot come into operation until Parliament has had the fullest opportunity by an Amending Bill of altering, modifying, or qualifying its provisions in such a way as to secure at any rate the general consent both of Ireland and of the United Kingdom.' *The Times*, 16 September 1914.

45 The UVF were permitted to enlist as a separate unit with their own officers and insignia – honours denied to the Irish Volunteers. McCaffrey, *The Irish Question*, p. 135.

46 Phoenix, 'The Political Background: From Parnell to Partition', p. 50.

47 A.C. Hepburn, *Catholic Belfast and Nationalist Ireland in the Era of Joe Devlin, 1871–1934* (Oxford: Oxford University Press, 2008), pp. 168–70.

48 McCaffrey, *The Irish Question*, p. 133.

49 MacDonagh was Director of Training; Plunkett was Director of Military Operations; and Pearse was Director of Military Organisation. Boyce, *Nationalism in Ireland*, p. 307.

50 D.G. Boyce, *Nationalism in Ireland* (London: Routledge, 1995), p. 309.

51 Kiberd, 'Irish Literature and Irish History', p. 288.

52 As quoted by Boyce, *Nationalism in Ireland*, p. 308.

53 McCaffrey, *The Irish Question*, pp. 134–6.

54 Ibid. p. 137.

55 Boyce, *Nationalism in Ireland*, p. 309.

56 A. Duffin to Dorothy Duffin, 25 April 1916, in P. Buckland (ed.), *Irish Unionism, 1885–1923: A Documentary History* (Belfast: Her Majesty's Stationary Office, 1973), p. 404.

57 While Bishop MacRory could initially dismiss the rebels as 'desperate socialists' and 'sincere but silly patriots', following the executions, a report from the Inspector-General of the RIC warned that 'popular sympathy is turning in favour of the rebels'. Cited by Hepburn, in *Catholic Belfast and Nationalist Ireland in the Era of Joe Devlin*, pp. 174–5.

58 The injuries which Connolly had sustained during the fighting necessitated that he be strapped into a chair in order to receive his punishment. McCaffrey, *The Irish Question*, p. 139.

59 *The Times*, 17 November 1913.

60 Upon being informed of Devlin's new nickname, Lloyd George, the Welsh Wizard, quipped that of course he and Devlin 'were alike in their perfect simplicity and freedom from guile'. Cited by Hepburn in *Catholic Belfast and Nationalist Ireland in the Era of Joe Devlin*, p. 177.

61 Phoenix, 'The Political Background: From Parnell to Partition', p. 51.

62 Martin, 'The Origins of Partition', p. 65.

63 E. Staunton, *The Nationalists of Northern Ireland, 1918–1973* (Dublin: The Columba Press, 2001), p. 14.

64 Ibid.

65 E. Phoenix, *Northern Nationalism: Nationalist Politics, Partition and the Catholic Minority in Northern Ireland, 1890–1940* (Belfast: Ulster Historical Foundation, 1994), pp. 28, 30.

66 Hepburn, *Catholic Belfast and Nationalist Ireland in the Era of Joe Devlin*, p. 178.

67 Staunton, *The Nationalists of Northern Ireland*, p. 14.

68 The first of these committees sat in 1918 and the second between 1919 and 1920. Lloyd George selected Long to Chair the 1918 Irish committee because he wanted to link Irish Home Rule with conscription for Ireland. Long was known to oppose this connection but, because the Prime Minister surmised that he could not resist the opportunity to draft the government's new Home Rule Bill, the chairmanship was intended to muffle Long's objections to the Home Rule-conscription linkage. By the time that the committee appointed in 1918 had wound up its deliberations, a number of possible legislative alternatives had been submitted for consideration. The Irish committee that sat between 1919 and 1920 was instructed to 'examine and report on the probable effect on Ireland, on Great Britain, and on opinion abroad of each of the possible alternative Irish policies' and to 'advise the Cabinet as to the policy they recommend for adoption'. J. Kendle, *Walter Long, Ireland, and the Union, 1905–1920* (Montreal & Kingston: McGill-Queen's University Press, 1992), pp. 132, 146–8, 180.

69 McCaffrey, *The Irish Question*, pp. 139–40.

70 One piece of Sinn Féin anti-conscription propaganda charged: 'An Irish Nationalist is one who works for the Independence of Ireland. CARSON and DEVLIN alike by strengthening the Forces which hold Ireland in subjugation make Ireland more than ever Dependent on England.' *Where is the Difference?* (Dublin: Sinn Féin, 1918).

71 In the Falls Division of Belfast (formerly West Belfast) Devlin received 8,488 votes as compared with de Valera's 3,245 votes. There were no other candidates. B.M. Walker (ed.), *Parliamentary Election Results in Ireland, 1801–1922* (Dublin: Royal Irish Academy, 1978), p. 384.

72 McCartney, 'From Parnell to Pearse, 1891–1921', pp. 256–8.

73 Beginning in January 1920, ex-soldiers were recruited to supplement the regular RIC and, because of the colour of the makeshift and mismatched uniforms they wore, these soldier-policemen became known as the 'Black and Tans'. Demobilised military officers recruited for service in Ireland were rolled into an Auxiliary Division of the RIC beginning in July of 1920. In the most disturbed parts of Ireland, the Auxiliaries were largely unfettered by RIC control. Both the Auxiliaries and the Black and Tans were poorly trained and notoriously undisciplined.

74 Hepburn, *Catholic Belfast and Nationalist Ireland in the Era of Joe Devlin*, p. 203.

75 According to Patterson's tabulations, in 1920, the United Irish League (the IPP constituency organisation) boasted 6,533 Belfast members as compared with Sinn Féin, which registered only 980 members. Likewise, the National

Volunteers, which had remained loyal to Redmond in 1914, had 1,300 Belfast members in 1920, while the republican Irish Volunteers had only 500 members. P. Bew, P. Gibbon and H. Patterson, *Northern Ireland, 1921–1994: Political Forces and Social Classes* (London: Serif, 1995), pp. 22–3.

76 D. Rabinowitz, 'The Palestinian Citizens of Israel, the Concept of Trapped Minority and the Discourse of Transnationalism in Anthropology', *Ethnic and Racial Studies* 24, 1 (2001), p. 73.

77 Long thought that establishing two Home Rule parliaments for Ireland was compatible with his larger plan for the eventual creation of a 'Federal system for the United Kingdom', while immediately reducing congestion at Westminster since local Irish affairs would be handled by the two regional legislatures. In contrast, Ulster Unionists would have preferred to be ruled directly by Westminster. Kendle, *Walter Long, Ireland, and the Union*, pp. 181–2.

78 Buckland, *James Craig: Lord Craigavon*, p. 44.

79 *Parliamentary Debates*, Commons, 5th ser., vol. 127 (29 March 1920), cols 985–93.

80 Even at this late stage, many Southern Unionists still believed that Irish unity could be maintained and Home Rule defeated if the UUC simply refused simply to accept the Bill. As Southern Unionist John Walsh argued in a letter to a colleague, 'we feel a little puzzled about Ulster's attitude. We gather that Ulster would only establish her parliament in the event of the southern parliament being established, but the speeches of some northern members lead one to believe that Ulster is inclined to jump at the idea of a parliament. If Ulster merely accepts her parliament in the event of the southern parliament being established, or demands to be omitted from the bill altogether, the road to the union would remain open.' Clearly sharing the view that Joe Devlin had expressed in his 13 February letter to Bishop O'Donnell, Walsh concluded: 'Once, however, the Ulster parliament is established, the road back to the union would be closed.' As quoted in Buckland, *Irish Unionism* 1, p. 199.

81 Lobbying hard to get the UUC to retract its approval of the Home Rule Bill, unionists from Donegal, Cavan and Monaghan published a pamphlet entitled *Ulster and Home Rule. No Partition of Ulster* (April 1920), which argued that there would still be a viable Protestant majority in a Northern state that included these three counties. The pamphlet angrily objected to what these Unionists regarded as the UUC's violation of the Solemn League and Covenant. 'The facts about the three Counties were clear when the Covenant was signed as they are to-day, and they have not altered,' insisted the pamphlet, '[t]he position as a whole remains the same. Why were we asked to come in and sign if, when the emergency comes, we are to be thrown over?' Extracts from *Ulster and Home Rule. No Partition of Ulster*, April 1920, as quoted in Buckland, *Irish Unionism, 1885–1923: A Documentary History*, pp. 412–13.

82 Rabinowitz, 'Trapped Minority', p. 73.

83 Martin, 'The Origins of Partition', p. 67.

84 *Parliamentary Debates*, Commons, 5th ser., vol. 134 (11 November 1920), cols 1460–2.

85 Ibid. cols 1450–1.

86 Buckland, *James Craig: Lord Craigavon*, p. 42; A. Ward, *The Irish Constitutional Tradition: Responsible Government and Modern Ireland, 1782–1992* (Washington: The Catholic University of America Press, 1994), pp. 108–9; Elections: Northern Ireland ELECTIONS, 'The Northern Ireland Senate, 1921–72', http://www.ark.ac.uk/elections/hnisen.htm (accessed 23 July 2019).

87 *Parliamentary Debates*, Commons, 5th ser., vol. 136 (16 December 1920), cols 783–5.

88 While in no way trivialising the loss of innocent Protestant lives, Elliott points out that Catholics accounted for well over 50% of the casualties but only represented 25% of Belfast's population. Elliott, *The Catholics of Ulster*, p. 374; A. Parkinson, *Belfast's Unholy War: The Troubles of the 1920s* (Dublin: Four Courts Press, 2004), pp. 12–13; Townshend, *Ireland*, p. 180.

89 Parkinson, *Belfast's Unholy War*, pp. 73–82; D.S. Johnson, 'The Belfast Boycott, 1920–1922', in J.M. Goldstrom and L.A. Clarkson (eds), *Irish Population, Economy, and Society: Essays in Honour of the late K.H. Connell* (Oxford: Clarendon Press, 1981), pp. 287–307.

90 M. Farrell, *Arming the Protestants: The Formation of the Ulster Special Constabulary and the Royal Ulster Constabulary, 1920–27* (London: Pluto Press, 1983), pp. 30–6.

91 *Parliamentary Debates*, Commons, 5th ser., vol. 134 (11 November 1920), col. 1445.

CHAPTER 2

'A Triumph of Gilbertian Humour': Partition and the Anglo-Irish Treaty

I just plod on in quiet peaceful paths
For your dear sake – believing that the sword
Is not at all times Freedom's truest friend
Nor surest weapon in a nation's fight:
And yet – through scarcely heard – I never cease
To plead for you. Say, Ireland, am I right?
What does it matter if no wild applause,
Now greets the humble efforts that I make?
Unpopular – the paths I choose – and yet
Conscience bids me go forward for thy sake.

– National, 'Unpopular, But –'[1]

Although it has become a cliché of sorts, there is still something alluring about Michael Laffan's contention that in 1911, 'Irishmen of all political opinions would have been amazed if they could have foreseen the division of Ireland into two separate states.'[2] Laffan's observation exposes the extent to which both British and Irish opinion had changed between the introduction of Herbert Asquith's all-Ireland Home Rule Bill in 1912 and the ratification of David Lloyd George's Better Government of Ireland Act eight event-filled years later. As it was, when preparations were being made for the implementation of Lloyd George's Act in early 1921, Sinn Féin and the IRA were at war with Great Britain. And, while parts of Ulster were still experiencing a serious wave of sectarian violence, there remained a glimmer of hope that the May elections slated to establish the two Home Rule parliaments would proceed as scheduled. Trapped as they were within a would-be host state poised to begin governing the Six Counties and uncertain how being cut off from their Southern brethren would affect their anti-partitionist struggle, the nationalists of Northern Ireland were truly in an unenviable position. This chapter examines the Northern minority's reactions to the chaotic events that befell Ireland as the Anglo-Irish war drew to a close and a series of new, equally daunting challenges emerged as a consequence of a controversial peace treaty. The chapter begins with a brief overview of the conditions prevailing in Ireland as the elections approached, before shifting its focus to examine Northern nationalists' hopeful responses to the news that an Anglo-Irish Treaty had been reached.

As 1920 faded into 1921, a pall of violence hung thick over Ireland – so thick that in early January, the British cabinet chose to extend martial law over all of Munster and part of Leinster.[3] Although Bloody Sunday, the Kilmichael ambush[4] and the burning of Cork were, perhaps, the most notorious incidents in what was a grisly end to 1920, these were but a few examples of the style of warfare in which both the crown forces and the IRA were now engaged. Moreover, it was about to become even more difficult to distinguish between the barbarous acts committed in the name of the crown and equally barbarous acts committed in defence of the Irish republic, as January also witnessed the first sanctioned reprisals carried out by agents of the British government. Whatever else might be said of this stage in the conflict, the situation on the ground did not bode well for the successful establishment of a Home Rule parliament for Southern Ireland.

Despite sectarian disturbances in the North, plans for the installation of the Northern parliament continued apace; yet a notable change was occurring within Unionist ranks. On 4 February, Sir Edward Carson resigned as leader of the UUC and Sir James Craig, who had been instrumental in the establishment of that body, was selected to take his place. Few nationalist tears were shed upon learning of Carson's departure. 'He is a wily lawyer, and having created a mess here he is leaving Sir James Craig to clean up,' remarked Joe Devlin at a Belfast rally as he inserted Carson's name into a piece of subversive French Revolutionary doggerel:

King Carson a gallant captain was –
In battle much delighting;
He fled full soon in the month of June,
And bade the rest keep fighting.[5]

According to the *Irish News,* since Craig had been handed the 'crown, sceptre, and other insignia of domination' as the new leader of the Ulster Unionists, it was now going to be up to him to head the devolved government soon to be installed in Belfast.[6]

Be they supporters of Devlin and the rump IPP or Sinn Féiners, the discourse emanating from Northern nationalist quarters at the beginning of 1921 was filled with as much anger and apprehension about partition as it was with a lingering disbelief that their nation had really been dismembered by an act of the British parliament. In late January, Fermanagh Sinn Féiner Cahir Healy used the forum of the Enniskillen Board of Guardians to proclaim his intention never to 'take part in the tragedy of [Ireland's] dissection' and expressed a determination never to recognise or set foot inside the Belfast parliament.[7] 'We are Irishmen first and Belfastmen second,' boasted Devlin to roaring crowds in Belfast as he vowed to 'fight on until every green sod in the fields of Tyrone and Fermanagh, and every humble cabin and workmen's cottage in Belfast [were] incorporated in a United Ireland'. And, striking a similar tone, Thomas Harbison, the IPP MP for Tyrone and long-time member of the AOH, advised the same audience that all was not yet lost and encouraged his supporters to find comfort in the 'unity and solidarity of the Nationalists of Belfast and North-East Ulster'.[8]

Harbison's own unique position as both an IPP MP and a border nationalist who had opposed temporary exclusion in 1916[9] may have allowed him to overlook the very real division that had since come to separate Devlinite Belfast from the Sinn Féin dominated periphery. Owing to his association with the Black Friday meeting and the pre-partition electoral infighting between the IPP and Sinn Féin, Devlin and his AOH had both become objects of hate by distrusting Sinn Féiners, North and South. John Dillon, who had lost his own East Mayo seat to Sinn Féin leader Éamon de Valera in the 1918 election, publicly avowed that there was little possibility of uniting 'those who still believe[d] in the program and policy of Parnell and the Old

Party with the forces of Sinn Fein';[10] however, the urgency of the situation ultimately forced the two wings of minority nationalism to come together temporarily in advance of the May elections. By the middle of March, the Southern Sinn Féin leadership and Joe Devlin were able to formulate a strategy of limited cooperation. They agreed to contest the impending election, which was to be conducted using proportional representation,[11] as an 'Anti-Partition ticket'.

Under the terms of the election agreement, anti-partitionist voters were instructed to give their first preference votes to the candidates of 'their own party', be they Devlinites or Sinn Féiners, and their 'next immediate preference' to their nationalist rivals – i.e. Devlinite supporters would assign all other preferences on their ordered ballot to Sinn Féin candidates and *vice versa.* The election agreement permitted each party to field as many as twenty-one candidates in Northern Ireland's ten multi-member constituencies and all candidates on the Anti-Partition ticket pledged not to recognise the Government of Northern Ireland or take their seats in the Northern parliament.[12]

The Devlinites were ultimately only able to find twelve candidates to stand and Devlin was forced to offer himself in two constituencies[13] but Sinn Féin was able to field a slate of twenty candidates. These included Southern political heavyweights such as Éamon de Valera, who had returned from America in late December, along with Michael Collins, Arthur Griffith and Eoin MacNeill, the Antrim-born Professor and founder of the Irish Volunteers. Nine of the Sinn Féin candidates were incarcerated at the time of the election.[14]

While they were working with Sinn Féin in preparation for the Northern election, the Devlinites continued to chip away at Lloyd George's partition plan. A public statement issued on behalf of these candidates in early May declared partition to be a 'trick of English politicians' that aimed to prevent reconciliation amongst the Irish. 'No legislative outrage, more needlessly irritating or wantonly insane, has ever been perpetrated by any British Government,' declared the statement, adding:

> The scheme of Partition was rashly conceived, insufficiently considered, and hastily rushed through Parliament as a trumpery expedient to suit the political exigencies of the moment. Even in its puerile purpose it has magnificently failed. Northern Unionists

> regard the forthcoming Parliament as a white elephant. They would be delighted if some one would take it off their hands, and conveniently dispose of it. Were it not for the grim tragedy it so painfully adumbrates, the Partition scheme might justly be regarded as a triumph of Gilbertian humour – purporting to accomplish a great work of national appeasement by giving every section of the community what it most abhors.[15]

Seeking to connect in some way with their Unionist opponents in a last desperate effort to undermine the Act, the Devlinites spent the run up to the election urging all Irish men and women to come together in a 'genuine Constituent Assembly' in an effort to pursue their own Irish settlement.[16] Indicative of both the extent to which Sinn Féin demands had moved beyond what the Devlinites now seemed willing to accept and the strained nature of the Sinn Féin–IPP election agreement, at a joint Derry City rally in May, Sinn Féin supporter John McLaughlin gloated that his party had done more in their 'two and a half years representing the Irish Nation' than had the Irish Party over the previous forty.[17] This was more than just a passing jab from a boastful rival; McLaughlin's statement was a clear reminder of the underlying schism that separated the Sinn Féin and IPP branches of Irish nationalism. In keeping with how Rabinowitz characterises trapped minorities' endemic lack of cohesion and strategic vision, and defined in the Irish context by differences over policy and methods, the inability of Northern nationalists to marshal a genuine united front against partition exposed the fragility and limited nature of the election pact.

As the uneasy anti-partitionist ticket in the North prepared for election day, any hope Britain had that the Southern Ireland parliament would actually function was quickly evaporating. In mid-February, General Nevil Macready, GOC of the British forces in Ireland, privately admitted to the government that there was no 'ground for optimism in regard to anything like a permanent settlement of the country outside Ulster'.[18] The lack of progress on the military front led Lord Midleton and other Southern Unionists to advise Lloyd George in March of the 'gravest consequences' that would result if the Sinn Féiners were allowed to use the elections in order to re-confirm their right to speak for Southern Ireland.[19] By April, Irish Chief Secretary

Harmar Greenwood was predicting that Sinn Féin would easily sweep the Southern election and would thereafter refuse to take the oath of office, forcing the British government to rule 'Southern Ireland' as a crown colony. This prospect did not appeal to Lloyd George; however, the alternative, as Arthur Balfour pointed out during a 27 April cabinet meeting, was to postpone the election and thereby prove to the dominions and America that the British government did not believe in its own plan for Ireland.[20]

The Prime Minister eventually decided to proceed with the Southern election but in the end, none was needed as 124 Sinn Féiners and four Independent Unionists were ultimately returned unopposed. As expected, the Sinn Féiners did not recognise the Better Government of Ireland Act or the parliament of Southern Ireland it sought to create; thus, they effectively became Deputies (TDs) of the Second Dáil. The Home Rule parliament of Southern Ireland was essentially stillborn on nomination day.

The election for the parliament of Northern Ireland took place on 24 May and an impressive 88.1 per cent of the electorate turned out to vote.[21] In comparison with Unionists, Labour and Independents, the Sinn Féin–IPP election alliance combined for 32.3 per cent of the vote across Northern Ireland and 54.7 per cent in the critical border constituency of Fermanagh–Tyrone,[22] with each of the anti-partitionist parties winning six seats. The IPP returned Devlin in both Antrim and West Belfast, ardent Hibernian John Nugent in Armagh, Patrick O'Neill in Down, Tom Harbison in Fermanagh and Tyrone, and George Leeke in Derry. Under the Sinn Féin banner, de Valera won a seat in Down, as did Collins in Armagh and MacNeill in Derry, while Griffith, Seán Milroy and Seán O'Mahony won seats in Fermanagh and Tyrone, but the combined anti-partitionist total of twelve seats paled in comparison to the forty MPs elected by the Unionist Party. The Devlinites and Sinn Féiners both stood by their agreement to abstain from the Belfast parliament, effectively boycotting the 1921 Senatorial elections in which twenty-four Unionists were returned.[23]

The election of key Southern Sinn Féin leaders to the Belfast parliament in concert with the IRA's attack on the Customs House in Dublin on the day after the Northern election only increased the pressure Lloyd George was already feeling regarding the unsettled South. Moreover, the British cabinet was, by then, voicing grave concerns about the resources that were being tied up in an Irish conflict that had no end in sight. These issues, along with the realisation that military victory would require an escalation of the war that would likely hurt Britain's relationship with America[24] and the dominions, was pushing the government into seeking some form of settlement with Sinn Féin.

Sinn Féin and the IRA were also under increased pressure at this juncture. Britain had made progress against the IRA after the police were rearmed and motorised in 1920, and these improvements were expected to have their greatest impact during the upcoming campaigning season. Both arms and ammunition were getting harder for the IRA to acquire and, as Richard Mulcahy would later recall, the insurgents were not yet 'able to drive the enemy from anything [larger than] a fairly good-sized police barracks'.[25] By May and June, both he and Collins were starting to worry that the insurgency would dissipate before the autumn. For these reasons, the Sinn Féin leadership was largely receptive to the idea of negotiation when it came.

As General Macready tried to warn the Irish Committee that Britain would need to go 'all out or [adopt] another policy',[26] a diplomatic démarche emerged as a consequence of an intervention spearheaded by South African Premier Jan Smuts. King George V was planning personally to open the Northern parliament on 22 June and General Smuts, with the King's approval, wrote to Lloyd George on 14 June urging the Prime Minister to use the occasion of the King's speech to 'foreshadow the grant of Dominion status to Ireland' as a way of indicating a willingness to negotiate. Smuts' letter included a draft of a statement that he hoped would be inserted into the address.[27] Although the end product was a composite of drafts written by many hands, the speech that the King eventually delivered was in keeping with the purpose Smuts had in mind. In it, the King appealed to all Irishmen 'to join in making for the land they love a new era of peace, contentment, and goodwill', adding his hope that the opening of the Northern parliament might be 'the prelude of a day in which the Irish people, north and south, under one Parliament or two, as those Parliaments may themselves decide, shall work together in common love for Ireland upon the sure foundation of mutual justice and respect'.[28]

The King's speech raised few eyebrows and even fewer hopes among Northern anti-partitionists. Casting aspersions on George V's hopeful wish that the Craig administration would govern with the moderation and goodwill that he intended, the *Derry Journal* declared that the King 'might as well have been furnished with a passage for reading from Hans Anderson's Fairy Tales'.[29] The *Irish News* asserted indignantly that: 'Mr Lloyd George's hand [was] visible in every sentence' of the speech, which 'utterly falsify[ed] – the hopes of those who believed that he [the King] was to figure as a bearer of glad tidings to any part of the country'.[30] Whereas the anti-partitionist press in the North did not see past the lofty words of the King's speech, Sinn Féin leaders recognised the gesture as a tentative appeal for peace. Having been bombarded by misgivings over coercion from political moderates in London and buoyed by the reception of the King's speech from the dominions, Lloyd George agreed to float the idea of a peace conference before Sinn Féin.[31] As prelude to the negotiations, a truce was reached in early July that prevented either side from reinforcing or upgrading its forces.[32]

The negotiations did not get off to a good start when the British Prime Minister and the Irish President took part in a series of meetings between 14 and 21 July. At this preliminary stage of negotiation, neither party was ready to budge on thorny issues related to constitutional status and unity. During this series of talks, de Valera insisted that allegiance should be sworn to Dáil Éireann, rather than the crown, and he sought to gloss over Britain's requirement that Ireland remain a committed member of the Empire by pressing the idea of 'external association' between the British Empire and an independent, republican Ireland. External association, which figured prominently over the course of the negotiations, implied a very loose connection between Ireland and the Empire that included recognition of the British crown as the symbol of that association but still left Irish sovereignty intact and unencumbered by the bond.[33] By contrast, the offer that Lloyd George ultimately made on 20 July did not move beyond a qualified form of dominion status that gave the would-be Southern polity only limited control of its finances while also allowing Britain to maintain military rights within Ireland.[34] Moreover, since the Prime Minister considered the Ulster problem to have been solved by the Better Government of Ireland Act, no compromise could be made on the unity front. The British proposal was submitted to the Dáil but, at de Valera's urging, it was formally rejected on 11 August.

Following the breakdown of negotiations, Lloyd George chose to disclose the terms of the rejected proposal and related correspondence.[35] The disclosure not only served to ratchet up the rhetoric emanating from London and Dublin but it also gave the trapped Northern minority the opportunity to comment on the negotiations in which neither they nor the Ulster Unionists had been afforded a formal role. In this regard, the *Irish News* came out strongly against Lloyd George's proposal, questioned the Prime Minister's tactics and searched among the spoils of the rejected deal for reasons to hope. 'It is hard to believe that the Government who passed the partition act are genuinely anxious for a settlement,' commented the Devlinite organ as it attributed what it regarded as a disingenuous British proposal to the Prime Minister's desire to pass all of the blame for the breakdown of talks on Ireland.[36]

With respect to the proposal itself, the *Irish News* was convinced that the rejected settlement would have amounted to a 'death-dealing stranglehold' on account of the limited fiscal powers it provided. However, the proposal's failure to make any provision for the essential unity of the island was seen as its greatest weakness. For the time being, the fault for this was placed squarely on Lloyd George – the man who had 'forged a deadly weapon and used it to butcher Ireland'.[37] '[T]he Nationalists of the Six Counties [will] be supported by all of the People of the twenty-six counties,' declared the *Irish News*: 'let not the fault and blame rest on Irish shoulders' if the talks could not be salvaged.[38]

Despite the *Irish News*' show of confidence in the Dáil, the failed negotiations fuelled the uneasiness of many Northern nationalists. It was apprehensiveness of this sort that led the nationalist representatives of Co. Down's public bodies to meet in Castlewellan on 1 September to discuss their position on partition and any Irish settlement that might arise. As a clear indication of anti-partitionists' fears that an Anglo-Irish settlement could be reached that did not remove the blight of partition and in an effort to make sure that their county's voice was heard by the Dáil, the nationalists of Co. Down issued a 'Memorial to President de Valera and the Cabinet of Dail Eireann' on 6 September 1921.

The petition – signed by representatives from Downpatrick, Kilkeel, Newry, Warrenpoint and Banbridge – expressed their 'unalterable opposition' to partition and British coercion of the Northern nationalist minority. The representatives also sought to highlight the unintelligibility of the existing Six-County boundary as a means to guide de Valera's hand in any future negotiations that Dublin might have with Great Britain. The anti-partitionists of Co. Down were evidently eager to show Dublin that east and south Down represented a significant area in terms of population, geographical area and valuation. This was an area contiguous to Southern territory and was every bit as committed to anti-partitionism as were Tyrone and Fermanagh – counties that, by virtue of their Catholic majorities, had received greater press than had Co. Down. 'It is interesting to point out,' insisted the memorial, 'that in this area [east and south Down] there is a still greater proportion of the population opposed to Partition than in either of the more extensive Counties of Tyrone or Fermanagh.' Moreover, the petitioners continued: 'The portion of the County [Down] referred to is not incomparable in area with some of the smaller Counties in Ireland; in rateable valuation it exceeds nineteen, while its population exceeds fourteen of the Irish Counties.' In addition, the petitioners asserted, the machinery of local government in the area was under nationalist control and, from an emotional, historical and religious perspective, 'no District in Ireland fill[ed] a larger page', since it was said that St Patrick began his mission in Down and was buried in Downpatrick. Continuing this sentimental appeal, the memorial concluded: 'We know it is the determination of Down, and we trust of the people of Ireland, that the spot where our National Apostle rests shall remain Irish Earth.'[39]

That Northern nationalists wanted no part of partition and the regional parliament in Belfast was well known, but the timing of this démarche was significant. Coming shortly after the publication of the particulars of a failed Anglo-Irish settlement, which did not preserve the essential unity of the island, this petition and the deputation that followed it offer a clear indication of the level of anxiety felt by Northern nationalists over the place partition would have in any future Irish settlement, as well as the negative affects of their entrapment in Northern Ireland. From a different perspective, however, the decision of the Co. Down representatives to press their justification for inclusion in the Southern Irish polity *vis-à-vis* the well recognised claim of Tyrone and Fermanagh offered an indication of how geographic location affected Northern nationalists' political fortunes and contributed to their disunity. Dublin would receive additional advice from other nationalist groups in the weeks that followed. History and myth buttressed these appeals for support as the nationalists of Northern Ireland wasted no chance to remind their Southern peers the national significance Ulster had had in the centuries-long fight for Irish independence and the sacrifices that Ulstermen, like the O'Neills and O'Donnells, had made in the name of the Irish nation.[40]

It was well into September before the British and Irish governments were able to agree on how to rekindle their talks. The most striking difference between the July talks and those that followed was the absence of de Valera from the Irish delegation. There is no simple explanation as to why the Dáil President did not attend this crucial conference. When, in September, de Valera's decision not to lead the delegation was challenged by Local Government Minister William Cosgrave and others, the Dáil President argued that, as 'the symbol of the Irish Republic', he could not be party to any compromises that would need to be made. Others have attributed de Valera's absence to his desire to remain in Dublin and provide a restraining influence on hardline republican cabinet members Austin Stack and Cathal Brugha, and the tactical advantage that having to confer with Dublin would give the Irish plenipotentiaries.[41]

President de Valera's reasons for not leading the Irish negotiating team remain the subject of speculation but in his absence Arthur Griffith, Michael Collins, Robert Barton, George Gavan Duffy and Eamon Duggan were granted plenipotentiary powers to negotiate for Dáil Éireann when the conference began in October. A known moderate, Griffith, was to lead the delegation and Collins was expected by his government to play the role of diehard republican. They, in conjunction with delegation secretary, Erskine Childers, were to be the main players on the Irish side. As T.P. O'Connor observed disapprovingly, the Sinn Féin delegation 'refuse[d] to make any approach whatsoever to Joe [Devlin]' for advice on Ulster and relied instead on a 'gentlemen named Milson', whom O'Connor did not know.[42] The 'Milson' that O'Connor had referenced was none other than Cavan TD Seán Milroy. While perhaps less known in IPP circles, Milroy, with Eoin MacNeill, had established a Committee of

Information on the Case of Ulster in September 1921 to support the Irish delegation.[43]

Hoping to keep Irish unity foremost in the minds of the plenipotentiaries, Fermanagh Sinn Féiner Cahir Healy requested that something akin to a liaison committee be assembled to keep the Northern anti-partitionists informed of any changes in their status. Tellingly, Healy's suggestion was rebuffed coldly by Milroy, bearing out a key distinction that Anthony Hepburn has made between Devlin, who despite his lack of influence in Sinn Féin or IRA circles, 'remained in political terms the leading Northern representative' of the period, and those other figures born in the North like Milroy, Eoin MacNeill, Ernest Blythe, Sean MacEntee and Kevin O'Shiel, who may have taken 'an interest in the North' but whose 'commitment was to Southern politics' and 'were in effect advisors *on* the North, rather than spokesmen *for* the North'.[44] As it was, the exchange above between Healy and Milroy would be the first of many instances to follow in which those Northern nationalists who were entrapped within Northern Ireland would find their interests marginalised by national leaders who put Southern policy objectives ahead of all other concerns.

This round of talks was ostensibly brought about in order to ascertain 'how the association of Ireland with the community of nations known as the British Empire [could] best be reconciled with Irish national aspirations'[45] and the starting positions of the two negotiating teams had not changed since the summer. The Irish delegation, conscious of the need to safeguard their republican ambitions, sought to procure a unitary state severed from the British Empire, while Britain insisted that any settlement of Irish grievances would require acceptance of the King as Head of State and membership in the Empire/Commonwealth.[46]

As difficult as the question of status would be, both negotiating teams recognised that the unity issue could scuttle the talks, a fact that seemed to favour the Irish representatives. Believing that the supporters of Irish self-government in Ireland and in the dominions accepted the primacy of the unity issue, the Irish negotiators had entered into the negotiations with the intention of letting Ulster destroy the conference if the talks soured.[47] Lloyd George had been expecting this line of attack and was prepared for the challenge when it came.[48] As it was, ending partition turned on the willingness of Britain and Ireland to use force as a means of coercing James Craig's Unionist government into accepting Dublin's rule – a prospect that was flatly rejected by both sides – or their ability to convince the Northern Prime Minister to willingly consent to Irish unity. Craig, however, proved to be unyielding and he resisted intense pressure from Lloyd George to submit to any form of Irish unity.

Unionist intransigence might have prevented the negotiations from going any further but at this juncture, Lloyd George and Assistant Cabinet Secretary Thomas Jones were able to convince the Irish negotiators to shelve the unity issue temporarily. In this instance, the plenipotentiaries agreed that, if the Northern government ultimately refused to accept the terms of any settlement they had reached, 'at some undefined time after a treaty was signed a boundary commission should meet to adjust the border in accordance with the wishes of the inhabitants, so far as may be compatible with economic and geographic conditions'.[49] Jones had raised the idea of appointing a boundary commission in conjunction with his (and Lloyd George's) assurances that Northern Ireland would share the tax burden of the Empire, be subject to the same limited financial powers it had accepted under the Better Government of Ireland Act and would not be given dominion status.

Collins may have had private 'misgivings' about how a boundary commission could advance the cause of Irish unity;[50] however, it is certain that he and Griffith interpreted the idea as Lloyd George's willingness to allow financial pressures to nudge Belfast into the Irish Free State and an assurance that the proposed commission would render Northern Ireland economically unworkable through contraction.[51] Thus, it was this assumption that the Irish border would ultimately be drawn around Belfast and its hinterland – a polity too small to be viable in the long term – that led the Irish negotiators to set aside the unity issue in favour of a boundary commission.[52]

Although neither would have appreciated the comparison, the principal Irish negotiators had essentially agreed to the same sort of temporary solution to the Northern problem as had John Redmond years earlier; but in this instance, the Irish delegation had inadvertently relinquished its strategic advantage.[53] The advent of a boundary commission meant that the Irish team could no longer use national unity as a means to extricate itself from a situation if they thought that it was not going Ireland's way. The trapped Northern minority was left unaware of this tactical error.

As one might have expected, during this prolonged period of closed-door negotiations, the Irish and British press had become saturated with conjecture and rumours about the talks, possible breaking points and the prospects of success.[54] Apparently lacking the connections that made this sort of supposition possible, the *Irish News*' reporting during this tense period focused on the advisability of maintaining the truce, the centrality of Irish unity if there was to be a permanent Anglo-Irish settlement and rumours claiming that Ulster was the cause of a supposed diplomatic deadlock. But the newspaper used nearly as much ink at this time urging the press and those not directly involved in the deliberations to 'leave the members of the Conference alone' and let them do their work.[55] 'The delegates on both sides had been repeatedly referred to as plenipotentiaries – persons invested with full powers to negotiate and to decide,' wrote the Devlinite organ on 24 October, adding: 'Therefore we said – "Leave the members of the Conference alone." But no one left the members of the Conference alone.' The *Irish News* continued: 'If the delegates were plenipotentiaries, they had a legal and moral right to act as plenipotentiaries, and their discretion should not have been impinged, directly or indirectly. If they were not plenipotentiaries, their status and functions should have been defined from the outset.'[56] The powers given to the plenipotentiaries would become a controversial issue in the weeks and months that lay ahead but in the meantime, the talks continued and so too did the speculation of the broader press.

Once the Irish and British negotiators had agreed to set aside the unity issue, concerns relating to fiscal arrangements and the defence of the island proved relatively easy to tackle, which left status as the sole remaining vexatious issue. As Tom Garvin has argued, the problem of reconciling Irish autonomy with British monarchical and imperial connections had become such an emotional issue that compromise and concession, even when they emerged, could scarcely be recognised.[57] As autumn wore on, however, it became clear that a republic would not be in the offering and concessions were made. In what amounted to Britain's final offer, the Irish representatives were presented with a more palatable oath of allegiance and a modified form of dominion status – stylised as a *Saorstat Éireann*[58] or Irish Free State – which would be required to recognise the crown, have a Governor General in place of the Lord Lieutenant and remain a part of the Empire/Commonwealth. Britain would also retain defensive military rights in Ireland under the agreement. As expected, any hope of achieving essential unity was lost since the proposal also gave the Northern parliament the right to opt out of the new polity. But, if it chose to do so, Article 12 of the agreement provided for a 'Boundary Commission' to be convened in order to adjust the border.[59]

The Irish plenipotentiaries may have been far from enthused with the compromise they had before them, but Lloyd George's strong-arm tactics on the night of 5 December had left little room for manoeuvre. The Irish team was presented with two letters addressed to Sir James Craig: one indicating that a deal had been struck and the other announcing the breakdown of negotiations, and the plenipotentiaries had two hours to decide which letter would be sent. Reluctantly, and without referring the proposed settlement to the Dáil cabinet as de Valera had expected,[60] the Irish negotiators signed the Articles of Agreement for a Treaty on the early morning of 6 December.

As news of the settlement began to filter out to the wider world, jubilant messages from Europe, the dominions and the United States poured into London and Dublin.[61] The Ulster Unionist Party met on 8 December to discuss the Treaty, yet it was some time before any official public pronouncements came from the Northern Prime Minister. In the absence of any official comment from Craig, the Belfast correspondent of *The Times* offered a general sense of the mood amongst leading Ulster Unionists. 'I have heard the phrase "England has deserted us" dozens of times in the last two days,' noted the correspondent.

> Last night I was dining with a number of prominent businessmen, and their bitterness against England was remarkable. 'I hate England,' said one, and there were murmurs of assent. To-day another prominent man said quite seriously, 'If the Sinn Feiners had not murdered so many people it would serve England right if we joined the South in a demand for a Republic.' The popular jest in the North now is that its title should be 'the Orange Free State.'[62]

Without providing any details, St John Ervine, Prime Minister Craig's biographer, makes the claim that 'many of the most helpful suggestions during the Conference' that produced the Treaty had come from Craig.[63] Despite this, the Prime Minister was decidedly less obliging when he finally addressed the Northern parliament on 12 December. 'We were not included in that Treaty,' declared Craig, adding that he was 'not invited to sign the Treaty' but that his government had 'reserved to [itself] the right to go into conference with British Ministers when Ulster's rights and privileges became affected'. According to Craig, those British Ministers made a pledge to the Northern government that they would neither sacrifice nor prejudice its rights[64] but, the Prime Minister asserted, 'the Treaty has not carried out that solemn pledge to this House and to the Ulster people'. It was no secret that the Boundary Commission, proposed in Article 12 of the Treaty, was the chief cause of Craig's despair.[65]

Given the tenor of Irish politics throughout the revolutionary period and the potential of the Boundary Commission to affect the territorial integrity of Northern Ireland, Sir James Craig's reaction was anticipated. In contrast to the Ulster Unionist prospective on the Treaty, Northern nationalists, collectively, saw things in a much different light. The poem 'Free', which appeared in the *Irish News* on 7 December, offers an indication of how one Belfast nationalist greeted the initial news that an agreement had been reached. Given that the terms of the Treaty had not even been published in the *Irish News* until the day that the poem appeared, the anonymous author could not have known much about the agreement but still, in words that were intended to evoke memories of Young Irelander Thomas Davis, the poet rejoiced:

> At the foot of thy throne I stand and
>   hail thee, Ireland,
> Crowned as thou art in all the splendor
>   of thy liberty – A Nation once again.
>
> Thy hands are no longer bound nor are
>   thy feet in shackles now;
> The open paths of an open world are
>   thine to tread,

And the freedom of the winds that sweep
the sea but tells thee how free are thou;
And not in vain were all the sacrifices of
thy dead.

Seven hundred years and fifty spent in
ceaseless struggle to be free
Have only made the fruits of triumph
taste more sweet

Than might have been had freedom come
without a drop of blood being shed for thee,
Or had the paths been rose-strewn for
thy feet.

Not in stranger's hand rest now the
glory or the darkness of thy destiny,
But in thy own – to beautify or break
thy rising power:

To-day thy scattered children – the living
and the dead – acclaim thee free –
IRELAND A NATION: This is thy
longed-for hour.[66]

The poet, identified as 'F.H.' was clearly seeking to draw an emotional tie between contemporary politics and Davis' most celebrated ballad, 'A Nation Once Again'. Although his/her references to the human costs of victory would prove to be eerily ironic in view of subsequent events, the poet's ecstatic enthusiasm was as impossible to deny as was his/her desire to cast the historic moment as the fulfilment of Davis' hopeful prophecy that 'Ireland, long a province, be/ A Nation once again.'[67]

In contrast to the words of the anonymous bard cited above, the *Irish News*' initial reactions were guarded. Having received news from the Press Association in the early morning hours of 6 December that a deal had been struck, the newspaper cautiously observed: 'We know nothing of the terms at this hour. It is too much to look for a wholly satisfactory settlement; it is enough to know that an Agreement has been arrived at and that International Peace will be secure if nothing untoward happens hereafter.'[68]

Curiously, the overall sense of achievement served to distract the *Irish News* from the clauses of the document that affected Ulster when the full text of the Treaty appeared in the press on 7 December. But, consumed as it was by the memories of the Treaty of Limerick – 'disgracefully "broken ere the ink wherewith 'twas writ could dry"' – the newspaper remained suspicious of Lloyd George, while also predicting that Sir James Craig would present the most serious stumbling block. With a greater sense of hope after taking time to digest the document, the newspaper added:

> Really, there is not a sane man or women in any part of Ireland who doubts for a moment that a vast majority of the Irish people are not merely willing but intensely anxious to 'work' this Agreement rationally and thoroughly, in the completest possible association and harmony with Great Britain and their own countrymen, and with all the nation's powers and opportunities to the best advantage for the common weal.

Eager to work the deal, the enthusiasm of the *Irish News* remained, in its own words, 'tempered' but it, as with most informed observers of Irish affairs, naturally felt 'entitled to assume the acceptance by Dublin'.[69]

The border press keenly welcomed the Treaty. The *Derry Journal* praised the Irish plenipotentiaries for their prudent, skilful and earnest work and declared the agreement free of any contradiction with Ireland's 'National struggle'.[70] 'Excellent as it appeared at the first view,' exclaimed the *Journal*, 'the Treaty further improves on closer acquaintance.' Clearly buoyed by the document, the *Journal* declared the work of the Irish delegation to be the 'most stimulating and inspiring experience in living memory', which opened up an 'entirely new vista'.[71] Cognisant of the renewed hope that the Treaty would provide nationalist border regions like Derry City and Counties Tyrone and Fermanagh, even if Belfast exercised its right to contract out, the *Derry Journal* was thus convinced that the Treaty had 'obliterated partition' and given Ulster Unionists every reason not to exercise their option in this regard.[72]

With supportive comments coming from Cardinal Logue, Archbishop of Armagh and Bishop Fogarty of Killaloe,[73] it appeared that the Irish Catholic hierarchy was also behind the agreement but the actual impact that it would have on the practical politics of the Northern minority was not immediately clear. Thus, in order to de-mystify the Treaty, a deputation of Northern Sinn Féiners and constitutionalists met with Dáil representatives in Dublin on the evening of 7 December.[74]

Eoin MacNeill, who chaired this Mansion House Convention, began the proceeding by acknowledging the fact that the Northern nationalists would be forced, through their continued entrapment, to 'bear the brunt in the fight for national unity' but he asserted that they would not face the danger alone. Acknowledging that partition had put the Northern nationalist minority in a perilous position, he claimed that theirs was an 'artificial' danger, lacking both strength and permanency. Therefore, to combat the threat which the Northern regime posed, MacNeill proposed a 'concrete program of non-recognition' against the authority of the Belfast parliament. In addition to parliamentary abstention, this meant non-recognition of the courts, of summonses and any commands or instructions issued from Belfast, as well as non-payment of taxes and non-recognition of the 'Education Authority'. MacNeill advocated this call to arms, claiming to be speaking as a Northerner – 'as one of yourselves' – not as an agent of the Dáil or as a spokesman for the position of Dáil Éireann and he strongly urged the representatives to adopt a programme based on 'National Grounds and not on Ecclesiastical grounds'.[75]

In spite of MacNeill's demonstrative appeal for support, not to mention the universal approval given to the Treaty by the Northern nationalist press, the proceedings of this convention reveal that not all of the Northerners were satisfied with the Treaty or the programme set out by MacNeill. Mayor O'Doherty of Derry City was particularly critical. 'Our representatives have given away what we have fought [to achieve] for the last 750 years,' observed an angry O'Doherty:

> It is camouflaged. Once the Northern Parliament [was] put into operation there [was] a breach in the unity. We are no longer a united nation. You have nothing to give us for the sacrifices you call

> upon the people to make. If in the first instance Belfast contracts out, you are handing over manacled the lives and liberties of the Catholics who live in that area ... If they contract in, the position you hand over to the Northern Parliament is that they have full legislative powers in the Act of Parliament that will enable them to jerrymander [*sic*] us out of existence as they have done from time immemorial.

Sharing the concerns of the Mayor, Father MacFeely asked what help Dublin could offer them on questions related to education since, as he noted, '[t]his thing is now signed'. George Leeke, the Devlinite MP for Derry, echoing the concerns of the others regarding Catholic education and fear of the Ulster Special Constabulary (USC) in the North, lamented the possibility of starting the fight from scratch after 750 years of struggle but expressed the hope that these matters could be addressed before the Treaty was ratified by Dáil Éireann. While MacNeill attempted to assure the increasingly agitated assembly that the Treaty actually safeguarded their rights, he also reminded his audience that treaties were compromises and that the alternative to this Treaty was war. The meeting retired at this frosty juncture with the proviso that a smaller contingent of Northern representatives would meet with President de Valera the following morning.[76]

Spokesmen for the nationalist deputation met with de Valera, Seán Milroy and MacNeill on the morning of 8 December. At that time, the President's responses to Northern concerns seemed cold, distant and disinterested. Upon being advised of the reason for the meeting by MacNeill, de Valera told the deputation that 'he could not give them any advice' but would convey their views to cabinet.[77] After being questioned by Father MacFeely about how the new situation would affect Northern education, de Valera responded that 'the position of the Irish Government was to-day the same as it was five days ago' and '[w]hatever was decided in the past holds good'.[78] President de Valera left the Northern representatives to attend a cabinet meeting and, with MacNeill in the chair, the representatives attempted to coordinate the non-recognition tactics that they intended to employ in the Six Counties.

Significantly, Sinn Féiners A.E. Donnelly of Omagh and J.H. Collins of Newry were noticeably more enthusiastic about the proceedings and MacNeill's proposed programme than most of their colleagues had been. Clearly, this nuanced position owed much to the fact that the Treaty and Article 12, in particular, gave a great deal of hope to nationalists in border regions.[79] It was at this juncture, with the appearance of Article 12 and the Boundary Commission as reasons for border nationalists to think that their repatriation was at hand, that any chance of Northern nationalist unity all but disappeared. The overwhelming majority of Northern nationalists would ultimately support the Treaty but, being presented with an agreement that seemed poised to perpetuate the entrapment of some while freeing others to re-join their mother nation, division over how, when or if the boundary clauses should be put into operation would prove to be very difficult to avoid.

Endnotes

1 *Irish News*, 5 March 1921.

2 M. Laffan, *The Partition of Ireland, 1911–1925* (Dundalk: Dublin Historical Association, 1983), p. 1.

3 J. Curran, *The Birth of the Irish Free State, 1921–1923* (n.p.: The University of Alabama Press, 1980), pp. 43–4.

4 P. Hart, *The IRA & its Enemies: Violence and Community in Cork, 1916–1923* (Oxford: Oxford University Press, 1999), pp. 21–38.

5 *Irish News*, 14 February 1921.

6 Ibid., 5 February 1921.

7 Ibid., 1 January 1921.

8 Ibid., 14 February 1921.

9 E. Staunton, *The Nationalists of Northern Ireland, 1918–1973* (Dublin: The Columba Press, 2001), p. 79; E. Phoenix, *Northern Nationalism: Nationalist Politics, Partition and the Catholic Minority in Northern Ireland, 1890–1940* (Belfast: Ulster Historical Foundation, 1994), p. 47.

10 *Irish News*, 1 February 1921.

11 As opposed to the single-member plurality or 'first past the post' system used in Westminster elections.

12 For instance, eight candidates – three Unionists, two IPP candidates, two Sinn Féiners, and one Independent Labourite – contested the four seats which were available in Devlin's West Belfast constituency. S. Elliott, *Northern Ireland Parliamentary Election Results, 1921–1972* (Chichester: Political Reference Publications, 1973), p. 8.

13 Devlin contested both West Belfast and Antrim. *Irish News*, 23 April 1921.

14 Ibid., 15 April 1921.

15 Ibid., 7 May 1921.

16 Ibid.

17 *Derry Journal*, 23 May 1921.

18 M. Hopkinson, *The Irish War of Independence* (Montreal & Kingston: McGill-Queen's University Press, 2002), p. 95.

19 K. Middlemas (ed.), *Thomas Jones Whitehall Diary, Volume III, Ireland, 1918–1925* (London: Oxford University Press, 1971), p. 54.

20 *Thomas Jones Whitehall Diary, Volume III*, p. 56.

21 The total electorate was 582,464 and there were 5,212 spoilt ballots. Elliott, *Northern Ireland Parliamentary Election Results*, p. 105.

22 Elliott, *Northern Ireland Parliamentary Election Results*, pp. 16, 89.

23 Phoenix, *Northern Nationalism*, p. 132. No anti-partitionist would be elected to the Northern Ireland Senate until 1929 when T.S. McAllister, T.J. Campbell and John McHugh were returned. Elections: Northern Ireland ELECTIONS, 'The Northern Ireland Senate, 1921–72', http://www.ark.ac.uk/elections/hnisen.htm (accessed 23 July 2019).

24 G. Martin, 'The Origins of Partition', in M. Anderson and E. Bort (eds), *The Irish Border: History, Politics, Culture* (Liverpool: Liverpool University Press, 1999), p. 62.

25 *Dáil Debates*, vol. 3 (22 December 1921), col. 143, https://www.oireachtas.ie/en/debates/find/ (accessed 23 July 2019).

26 *Thomas Jones Whitehall Diary, Volume III*, p. 76.

27 Ibid., p. 75.

28 Ibid., pp. 78–9.

29 *Derry Journal*, 24 June 1921.

30 *Irish News*, 23 June 1921.

31 Curran, *The Birth of the Irish Free State*, p. 58.

32 Ibid., p. 61.

33 Hopkinson defined external association as 'an association with Britain and the British dominions from the outside; recognition of the crown as the bond of association, but with the right to remain neutral in wartime'. M. Hopkinson, 'From Treaty to Civil War, 1921–2', in J.R. Hill (ed.), *A New History of Ireland: Ireland 1921–84* (Oxford: Oxford University Press, 2003), p. 3.

34 J. Knirck, *Imagining Ireland's Independence: The Debates Over the Anglo-Irish Treaty of 1921* (Lanham: Rowman & Littlefield Publishers, Inc., 2006), pp. 78–9.

35 Curran, *The Birth of the Irish Free State*, pp. 64–8.

36 *Irish News*, 15 August 1921.

37 Specifically, the *Irish News* was incensed by Lloyd George's use of the words 'Ireland', 'the Irish people' and 'the people of Ireland' to describe matters pertaining exclusively to the portion of the island not under James Craig's control in his correspondence with de Valera. The implication here was that the Prime Minister was, by omission, depriving the people of Antrim, Down, Armagh, Derry, Fermanagh and Tyrone of their Irish citizenship. *Irish News*, 15 August 1921.

38 *Irish News*, 15 August 1921.

39 'Memorial to President de Valera and the Cabinet of Dáil Éireann', 6 September 1921, Department of the Taoiseach, NAI/TSCH/S 1801/Q, National Archives of Ireland, Dublin.

40 A deputation from Tyrone and Fermanagh arrived in Dublin on 30 August, a week before the Co. Down group noted above. In presenting the case for Tyrone, Alex Donnelly argued that the Battle of the Yellow Ford (1598) and Hugh O'Neill's campaigns against Queen Elizabeth, the Battle of Benburb (1646) and the Dungannon Convention (1782) made Tyrone an inseparable part of the Irish nation. *Fermanagh Herald*, 3 September 1921. On 16 September a deputation representing Co. Armagh arrived in Dublin and later issued a statement unequivocally rejecting partition, while noting: 'Armagh holds the most glorious landmarks of Ireland's history. Armagh is the ecclesiastical Capital of Ireland. It is the See of St. Patrick. Its National Cathedral appeals to Irishmen everywhere, and it is hardly to be even considered that any nation would tolerate the severance of its ecclesiastical Capital from the Motherland.' *Irish News*, 16 and 17 September, 1921. On 20 September, a south Derry deputation comprised of both IPP and Sinn Féin advocates met with the Irish President. *Irish News*, 21 September 1921. And on 28 September, a group of nationalists representing Belfast met with Éamon de Valera and Eoin MacNeill. This deputation claimed to represent 100,000 citizens of the city and presented a petition which appealed 'to An Dail to refuse to recognize or consider any scheme of government which would partition Belfast and the six counties of the North-East from the government self-determined by the will of the big majority of the Irish people'. *Irish News*, 29 September 1921.

41 Knirck, *Imagining Ireland's Independence*, p. 85; P. Hart, *Mick: The Real Michael Collins* (London: Penguin Books Ltd, 2006), pp. 284–5.

42 In his correspondence with John Dillon, O'Connor found the circumstances to be 'one of the most comic passages of the whole business' but was glad to report that 'Joe accepts the situation quite philosophically.' As quoted by A.C. Hepburn, *Catholic Belfast and Nationalist Ireland in the Era of Joe Devlin, 1871–1934* (Oxford: Oxford University Press, 2008), p. 228.

43 Bishops MacRory, Mulhern, McHugh, McKenna and O'Donnell and eight priests were consulted by Milroy. M. Harris, *The Catholic Church and the Foundation of the Northern Irish State* (Cork: Cork University Press, 1993), p. 103.

44 Hepburn, *Catholic Belfast and Nationalist Ireland in the Era of Joe Devlin*, p. 270.

45 *Irish News*, 11 October 1921.

46 A. Jackson, *Ireland, 1798–1998: Politics and War* (Oxford: Blackwell Publishers, 1999), p. 261.

47 Knirck, *Imagining Ireland's Independence*, pp. 89–90.

48 At a 7 September Cabinet meeting, Lloyd George argued: 'De Valera will talk Tyrone and Fermanagh and the break will come on forcing these two counties against their will. Men will die for the Throne and Empire. I do not know who will die for Tyrone and Fermanagh.' *Thomas Jones Whitehall Diary, Volume III*, p. 110.

49 Hopkinson, 'From Treaty to Civil War, 1921–2', pp. 3–4. Jones' notes on the conference reveal that the idea of using a boundary commission to deal with the Ulster issue did not emerge until 8 November but the Jones diary also indicates that Lloyd George, Collins, Griffith and Gavan Duffy had discussed boundary commissions as early as 14 October. At that time, Collins noted: 'There is no analogy in the Dominions in this particular case but there are some in the Treaty of Versailles.' His understanding of the Versailles commissions – whatever it was – may have induced Collins to accept this form of boundary rectification. *Thomas Jones Whitehall Diary, Volume III,* p. 131.

50 P. Murray, *The Irish Boundary Commission and its Origins, 1886–1925* (Dublin: University College Dublin Press, 2011), p. 109.

51 While there is little doubt that Griffith and Collins were convinced that the proposed boundary commission would have the power to make extensive changes and completely reconfigure the Northern state, historians are divided on whether the Irish delegates misconstrued what they were hearing, placed their own inaccurate interpretation on what the boundary commission was intended to do or were purposely misled by Lloyd George and Jones. In the first comprehensive history of the Irish Boundary Commission, Paul Murray has assembled a significant amount of evidence to support his view that Griffith and Collins would not have agreed to the boundary clause without assurances that the Commission would deliver a generous reward to the Free State, along with further documentary evidence to show the extent to which British interpretations of the clause evolved between 1921 and the convening of the tribunal in 1924. Murray, *The Irish Boundary Commission and its Origins,* pp. 97–151. Also see Knirck, *Imagining Ireland's Independence,* p. 152; Curran, *The Birth of the Irish Free State,* pp. 103–4; G. Hand, 'MacNeill and the Boundary Commission', in F.X. Martin and F.J. Byrne (eds), *The Scholar Revolutionary: Eoin MacNeill, 1867–1945, and the Making of the New Ireland* (Shannon: Irish University Press, 1973), p. 204; Martin, 'The Origins of Partition', p. 70.

52 Lloyd George had given Collins written assurances on 5 December 1921 that, if Northern Ireland rejected Irish unity, the Boundary Commission 'could be directed to' adjust the border to 'conform as closely as possible to the wishes of the population'. As quoted by Murray, *The Irish Boundary Commission and its Origins,* p. 99.

53 Jackson, *Ireland, 1798–1998,* p. 259.

54 For instance, one of the newspapers in Lord Beaverbrook's chain was reporting that the government was pushing 'a new proposal for establishing an All-Ireland Dominion'. Another London newspaper was reporting that rumours fixing 'the crux of the problem' on Fermanagh and Tyrone were 'not only unfounded, but are not even well-informed guesses', while an additional London press organ was suggesting that all rested on Ulster agreeing to allow those contentious counties to hold a plebiscite. As quoted by the *Irish News,* 2, 4 November 1921.

55 *Irish News,* 13 October 1921.

56 Ibid., 24 October 1921.

57 T. Garvin, *1922: The Birth of Irish Democracy* (New York: St Martin's Press, 1996), pp. 51–2.

58 In theory, the plenipotentiaries were negotiating for the entire island of Ireland; thus, the term *Southern Ireland* – as the twenty-six southern counties had been called in the Government of Ireland Act (1920) – would not suffice. A new term had to be found that could be applied to the island which would not be affected by any decision that might be made by Northern Ireland regarding the Anglo-Irish talks. In this regard, two terms coined by Irish nationalists in the nineteenth century were considered for this purpose. *Poblacht* (republic) – a word derived from the Irish *pobal* and the Latin populus and used during the Easter Rising of 1916 – was ultimately rejected by Lloyd George for obvious reasons. *Saorstat Éireann* was derived from the genitive case of *Érin,* the Irish Gaelic word for Ireland – and the Irish Gaelic words *saor* (free) and *stat* (state). Basically, the term is Irish Gaelic for *the Free State of Ireland.* M.W. Heslinga, *The Irish Border as a Cultural Divide: A Contribution to the Study of Regionalism in the British Isles* (The Netherlands: Assen, 1971), pp. 30–1.

59 Hopkinson, 'From Treaty to Civil War', pp. 2–4.

60 Knirck, *Imagining Ireland's Independence,* p. 96.

61 A synopsis of the messages sent to Lloyd George from the French Prime Minister, the American Ambassador, representatives in South Africa and India, and a host of Canadian newspapers appeared in the *Irish News,* 10 December 1921.

62 *The Times,* 9 December 1921.

63 St J. Ervine, *Craigavon: Ulsterman* (London: George Allen & Unwin Ltd, 1949), p. 475.

64 For a discussion of the 'pledge' that British leaders purportedly provided Carson and Craig, see Murray, *The Irish Boundary Commission and its Origins,* p. 133.

65 *The Times,* 13 December 1921.

66 *Irish News,* 8 December 1921. The poet, identified as 'F.H.' was clearly making reference to Thomas Davis' most famous ballad 'A Nation Once Again'.

67 As quoted by T. Kinsella (ed.), *The New Oxford Book of Irish Verse* (Oxford: Oxford University Press, 1986), p. 305.

68 *Irish News,* 6 December 1921.

69 Ibid., 7 December 1921.

70 *Derry Journal,* 7 January 1922.

71 Ibid., 9 January 1922.

72 Ibid.

73 Logue told an interviewer on 8 December that 'I think it [the Treaty] is very satisfactory but I would like to see Irish unity. I would like to do away with all those divisions, and let us all pull together.' *Irish News,* 10 December 1921. Likewise, Fogarty released a statement suggesting that '[t]his treaty is well worth the price paid for it'. He continued: 'Ireland is now free to live her own life without interference from outsiders. The moral effect of the treaty throughout the world will be worth half a navy to England. The men who made it will be immortal. I have confidence that the Irish Free State will soon have the cordial allegiance of every Irishman.' *Irish News,* 10 December 1921.

74 A transcript of this meeting was sent to Cahir Healy – who was in attendance – by J. Bonner in 1938 after he had come across it in his files. It has been given the designation 'Remembrances of the Mansion House Convention'.

75 'Remembrances of the Mansion House Convention', 7 December 1921, Cahir Healy Papers, D/2991/B/2/4, Public Record of Northern Ireland, Belfast.

76 Ibid.

77 Ibid.

78 Ibid.

79 Ibid.

CHAPTER 3

Sisyphus Redux: Northern Nationalists and the Treaty Debates

Oh! Ireland, land of sorrow,
When shall thy tears be dried?
In thy heart there rankles an arrow,
The memory of sons who have died.
For liberty sweet thou sighest;
Pray that thou sigh not in vain;
For oft' when thy hopes were highest
They were dashed to the ground again.

– Anonymous, 'Liberty Sweet'[1]

Many Northern nationalists had greeted news that a Treaty had been reached between Britain and Ireland with guarded optimism. Some measure of scepticism was not without warrant as the proposed settlement was about to expose deep, heretofore ignored, fissures between pragmatists and republican purists within Sinn Féin and the IRA. Unbeknownst to the outside world, emotions were running so high in Dublin when news of the Treaty's terms surfaced that some staunch republicans actually wanted the Irish plenipotentiaries arrested as they made their way home.[2] It was the Treaty's oath of allegiance, which maintained Ireland's connection to the British crown, that was chiefly responsible for transforming an historic achievement into a bitter political split between the pro-Treaty Sinn Féin and an emergent anti-Treaty/Republican Party. Picking up the story at the first public signs of division in Dublin, this chapter demonstrates how closely the anti-partitionist press followed every stage of the Treaty debate in the Dáil. It also reveals the increasingly frustrated attitude Northern nationalists felt towards the political fissures that were emerging in the South of Ireland – fissures that appeared to jeopardise a proposed settlement that was 750 years in the making and which seemed destined to prolong the nationalist minority's entrapment within Northern Ireland.

The first public signs of division came on 8 December after the Dáil cabinet voted on the agreement. Arthur Griffith, Michael Collins, W.T. Cosgrave and Robert Barton endorsed the Treaty while de Valera, Cathal Brugha and Austin Stack were in opposition. What alarmed befuddled Northern nationalists the most, however, was de Valera's decision to issue a press release, stating in part: 'The terms of this agreement are in violent conflict with the wishes of the majority of this nation as expressed freely in successive elections during the past three years. I feel it my duty to inform you immediately that I cannot recommend the acceptance of this Treaty either to Dail Eireann or the country.'[3] For the *Irish News*, de Valera's rejection of the Treaty presented a 'regrettable circumstance' that only served to reinforce the fact that 'perilous pitfalls' still stood in the way of national liberty.[4]

As was the case with Belfast, the prevailing mood in Derry regarding the news from Dublin was bewilderment. According to the *Irish News*' Derry correspondent, while anti-partitionists of the region may have expected some objections from Dáil Éireann over the terms of any settlement, they 'never dreamt' that events would take such an unexpected, bizarre and 'dangerous' turn. Since the Irish President had refused to lead the delegation, which had been given full plenary powers, these Northern nationalists were reportedly 'astounded' by the actions taken by de Valera and his republican cohort. Given the division of the cabinet, it was widely believed in the North that those who were opposed to the Treaty should have remained silent until the views of the Dáil at large could have been ascertained and only then, if the situation warranted, the issue should have been taken to the public for a definitive verdict on the merits of the document. Thus, from the perspective of Derry nationalists whom this reporter interviewed, de Valera's actions were regarded as 'improper and unwarranted'.[5]

As the Northern anti-partitionists nervously awaited the Dáil debate on the Treaty, the clarion call of unity sounded across the island. A particularly poignant plea came from an anonymous letter (and accompanying verse) to the editor of the *Irish News* written on 10 December:

> Sir – We must not allow any man to stand in the way of the Irish Nation. We have signed this treaty, and must stand by it. To do otherwise, would be to forfeit the good will of all the people of the earth. We had them with us in our struggle for freedom: we will have them against us if we persist in breaking faith.
>
> Shall we stain our well-won laurels,
> And our sacred cause disgrace,
> With more petty feuds and quarrels –
> So unworthy to our race?
>
> Have we given our allegiance
> To a cause, or to a man?
> Did we promise our obedience?
> To a country or a clan?
>
> In the sacred cause of freedom
> Sink all jealousy and spite,
> Fools may quarrel: who's to lead them?
> But the true men will unite.[6]

Taken as an example of how those Northern bystanders to the treaty-making process sought to have their voices heard, this material demonstrates a deep appreciation of the dangers caused by factionalism in Dublin; however, the format that this appeal took is itself significant. Letters to the editor represent what Leon Svirsky has called 'the people's editorials' – that is, a key mechanism by which newspaper readers converse with, and attempt to win over, each other and the press.[7] Convincing fellow readers of the *Irish News* that the choice facing the nation was between war and peace – not between a republic or a Free State – was so important to the author of this piece that the plea for unity was made both intellectually using a reasoned argument and emotionally by using verse. Evidently, this particular correspondent had no qualms about choosing the 'cause' over the 'man'.

Believing that Sinn Féin was heading towards a split 'more fatal' and 'far less defensible than the Parnell "Split"', the editor of the *Irish News* took his own opportunity to offer a keen assessment of events for the benefit of any would-be Southern trouble-makers:

> The treaty is just – so far as it goes: and it goes further and means more for the Irish nation than any practicable proposal for a Settlement on National principles ever yet discussed by Irishmen and Englishmen on level terms. When Nationalists in the N.E. of Ireland admit so much – although, for the time, they are compelled to stand outside and know they must wait in peril and anxiety the efflux of events presently unforeseen – it should not be hard for their countrymen to form a definite judgement on the issue.[8]

The implication of these observations was clear: nationalist Ireland, including the self-sacrificing excluded counties, wanted the Treaty, so Dublin should let reason overpower passion and take the opportunity that it had been given. Notwithstanding their differences, this was something upon which Devlinites and the vast majority of Northern Sinn Féiners were able to agree.

With deep fissures beginning to open up in the Dáil, it was not surprising that the eyes of the Northern minority were firmly fixed on Dublin. It was at this juncture that Joe Devlin chose to withdraw from the impending discussions of the Treaty in the British House of Commons, stating that the 'business there was for British members only' whereas 'Ireland's decision' would be taken in Dublin.[9]

The Treaty debates began in both the British parliament and Dáil Éireann on 14 December. In Britain, the most acrimonious events occurred in the House of Lords. Although Lords Morley and Dunraven reportedly 'bestowed blessings on the Treaty' and Curzon argued that it 'brought peace with honour', Edward Carson was not so kind. In 1920, Lloyd George's cabinet had assured Lord Carson and Sir James Craig that the six Ulster counties 'should be theirs for good and all and there should be no interference with the boundaries',[10] yet now, in the context of a signed Treaty, Carson defiantly observed: '[t]he people of Ulster are expected to be the compliant puppets of the Government and without demur to take off their hats to the Foreign Secretary and the rest who have done everything which they have previously said would ruin the United Kingdom'. According to Carson, the Coalition had 'betrayed Ulster' and asking Ulster Unionists to submit to Sinn Féin in this way was 'like shooting a man in the back and then going up to him and patting him on the shoulder saying, "Good man, die as quietly as you can."'[11]

Britain ultimately approved the Treaty with relative ease but this was not to be the case in Dublin, where the tone and temperament of Dáil Éireann's first short session on 14 December turned out to be just the beginning of a long and acrimonious battle. As the debate opened, Michael Collins and the principal supporters of the Treaty brandished largely practical, tactical and defensive arguments, focusing on the fear of the return to war if the Treaty were rejected. In contrast, de Valera and the anti-Treatyite republican cohort charged that the plenipotentiaries had overstepped their authority by signing the agreement[12] and rested their position on the assumption that a republic could have been won. After tumultuous exchanges of words during this public session, the decision was made to continue the debates in private session.[13]

In response to this first day of debates in the Dáil, the *Irish News* seized upon what it considered to be the absurdity of jeopardising the Treaty over 'matters of technique and etiquette proper to the making of Treaties'.[14] While defending the actions of the accredited plenipotentiaries, the newspaper also took the opportunity to once again point out the fact that Northern nationalists – who were, for the first time, excluded from a proposed Irish settlement – would be affected to a greater extent and in more intrusive ways than anyone south of the border but, regardless, they were still its most vocal champions. 'This fact should be borne in mind,' wrote the editor, 'by all who are now discussing and, perhaps, dissecting the Treaty between Great Britain and Ireland.'[15]

Undaunted by the unruly course of events in the Dáil and uninfluenced by the scornful sentiments expressed by the *Irish News*, Catherine McCay of Larne, in her poem 'The Golden Moment', wrote of the gleeful anticipation she felt while waiting for news from Dublin. The verse read in part:

We are watching for the signal
    That will flash along the valleys

To unfurl the Flag of Freedom
    And light the Fire of Joy:
And the banners waving proudly
    Will proclaim our country's glory,
With a record down the ages
    That no malice can destroy.[16]

Encouraged by the same sentiments which seemed to have touched McCay, the Fermanagh County Council decided to put Eoin MacNeill's non-recognition strategy[17] to work on 15 December by passing a resolution which repudiated the authority of the Belfast parliament, pledged allegiance to Dáil Éireann and directed the Council Secretary not to communicate with the Local Government Department of either the British or Belfast government. In so doing, the Fermanagh County Council had joined a growing list of public bodies across the North which had sworn allegiance to the Dáil under the threat of dissolution.[18] This anti-partitionist victory proved to be costly however, since, as the Council Chairmen had expected, only minutes after the meeting had finished, police took charge of the Council Chamber.[19]

In private session, the Dáil continued to debate the merits of the Anglo-Irish settlement and it was at this juncture that the spectre of de Valera's alternative to the Treaty first appeared. That alternative – known as Document No. 2 – was based on the President's long-cherished notion of external association with Great Britain.[20] De Valera presented his proposal as a compromise position and it was summarily rebuffed by both Griffith and Collins, who argued that it was a dead issue because Britain had already rejected the idea, and by republican diehards, who saw it as a half-way measure. President de Valera ultimately withdrew this proposal from consideration and asked that details of the proposal not be divulged.[21]

Secrecy surrounding this mysterious Treaty substitute only amplified its allure in the press when the Dáil decided to return to public sessions on 19 December. While not knowing the exact content of the proposal, the mere thought that an alternative to the Treaty could even exist bemused the *Irish News*. The newspaper asked rhetorically:

> If an Irish Army had defeated a British Army in a dozen great battles on Irish soil, involving the loss of 20,000 men each battle

> to each force ... would Plenipotentiaries of the Irish Nation be in a position to extract, or exact, from a British Government terms much more favourable to this country than those contained in the Treaty while the British Navy still held unchallenged control in the Atlantic Ocean outside our coasts?[22]

Confident that the answer to this hypothetical question was an assertive 'no', the editor continued by addressing the sparse details of de Valera's proxy document. He wrote:

> If the Treaty is rejected, what is the alternative Irish National policy? Mr de Valera formulated an alternative policy: it was produced and discussed at the secret sittings; it was not brought forward yesterday: its author stipulated that it should not be debated or published: is it so rare and fragile a plant that exposure to the light of public opinion may shrivel it up and wither the sap in its veins? We have said that the people of Ireland want to know where they are bound should the Treaty be rejected. Mr Griffith and Mr Collins stand for the Treaty. It is a tangible fact – a definite proposal. Mr de Valera and Mr Erskine Childers would reject the Treaty. What then?

The fact that de Valera and Childers wanted Ireland to follow them into the unknown seemed to be nonsensical to the *Irish News* – especially since, according to Griffith, the difference between the Treaty and de Valera's document was 'merely a quibble of words'.[23]

The anti-partitionist press also seized upon the allegations that the plenipotentiaries only signed the Treaty out of fear of the return of war. Although they were real enough, these claims of duress, which ostensibly came from Robert Barton and Gavan Duffy,[24] appeared ridiculous to the *Irish News* editor. Peace had not been declared in July 1921 when the Dáil and the British government began their negotiations. The *Irish News* asked rhetorically: 'Was there not a man in Ireland or Great Britain who realised from the outset that "war would follow immediately" if the Conference of Plenipotentiaries failed to frame a Treaty?'[25]

While certain information was being kept from the public on either side of the Irish border, the advocates' ability to form persuasive arguments for and against the Treaty also had an impact on the print media and the public at large. In this regard, de Valera's impassioned pleading was often interpreted as a fierce and rambling tirade, 'long-drawn-out and unconvincing', while Collins and Griffith looked calm and confident, their arguments considered to be 'concise and to the point'.[26] Notwithstanding these differences in tactics and style, however, most Irish nationalists north and south of the Six-County border had lost all patience with the debate by 22 December when Dáil Éireann adjourned its proceeding until the New Year.[27]

Indicative of the prevailing mood in the North, it was at this juncture that the *Irish News* issued a scathing rebuke of Dublin for quibbling over the terms of a sound deal that should have freed a large portion of the Irish nation from alien rule before Christmas. The editor wrote:

> The people of five-sixths of Ireland are the masters of their own destinies – for the moment. They can choose; in fact, they have chosen mentally but have yet to see that their decision is registered and made effective. Well nigh half a million Nationalists in the severed one-sixth of Ireland are far differently placed. They were Irish citizens twelve months ago. They have not surrendered their Irish citizenship: but they cannot exercise it: and the Christmas of 1921 is for them a time of anxiety beyond all previous experience.[28]

Clearly dismayed by Dublin's apparent disinterest in the sacrifices that Northerners were prepared to make in the interests of the Irish mother nation, the *Irish News* editor had identified another significant facet of the debate over the Treaty: the will of the people, as shown in the actions of groups, boards and public bodies, seemed to have no impact on the debates.

During the interval between the Dáil's adjournment and its return after the holidays, support for the Treaty across Ireland tilted dramatically in favour of ratification. According to Curran, by 7 January – the day that the vote was finally taken – 369 county councils, borough corporations, urban and rural district councils, Sinn Féin clubs, farmer's associations and labour organisations had thrown their support behind the Treaty, while only fourteen bodies had gone on record as opposing the agreement.[29] According to Hopkinson, the

Connachtman was the only Southern newspaper to reject the Treaty.[30] Éamon de Valera's constituents on the Clare County Council had endorsed the Treaty and diehard republican Liam Mellows could not deny the fact that his Galway constituency was firmly behind it as well.[31]

In the North, the Christmas recess witnessed the consolidation of anti-partitionist forces behind the agreement. Emphasising the political influence of the Ulster Bishops, Mary Harris has given considerable credit to the Catholic Church for bringing the Northern minority in line with the pro-Treaty Party in the South, arguing that 'Christmas sermons became pro-Treaty speeches.'[32] In this respect, the sermons of Bishop Fogarty of Killaloe and Bishop MacRory of Down and Connor are worth noting. From his cathedral in Ennis, Bishop Fogarty used the pulpit to mock the motives of the anti-Treaty opposition and brought a heavy dose of fear to bear by telling his congregation:

> Let the people have no mistake about it, the rejection of this treaty must lead inevitably to war [with Britain], and war of such a destructive character as will lay Ireland out dead in a very short time, if, indeed, the country wants war, and war, be it observed, not for any advance in the Treaty powers, but for the pleasure of writing 'external association' over the door.

Convinced that the country wanted the Treaty ratified, the Bishop continued scornfully: 'The discussions in the Dail have, however, revealed a disquieting fact. I mean the callous disregard openly avowed by some deputies for the national will and the wishes of their constituents on this question.'[33]

Sparing much, but not all, of the fire and brimstone, Bishop MacRory, a Sinn Féiner, admitted that there were aspects of the Treaty – such as partition – that he did not like and, had the circumstances been different, he would have 'objected strenuously to them'. However, MacRory had become convinced by the divisiveness exhibited in Dublin that there would be 'nothing but chaos before the country unless the Nation approv[ed] the Treaty'. The Bishop suggested that the Treaty would put the Irish nation in a better position than it had been in for some 750 years and that there would be no dishonour in 'accepting the better when the best is unattainable'. MacRory left his congregation with the disquieting assertion that the only alternative to accepting the Treaty would be division, demoralisation, emigration and 'the millstone of foreign Government still round their necks'.[34]

Since the Six-County nationalists' initial responses to the Treaty in the press and elsewhere were overwhelmingly in support of the agreement, Harris may have overestimated the impact of the Bishops' Christmas sermons on the already convinced Northern nationalists. As it was, the *Irish News*' Enniskillen correspondent, after interviewing a cross-section of Fermanagh nationalists during the Christmas hiatus, felt confident enough to suggest that the people of the area were firmly behind the Treaty. While he had encountered half a dozen anti-Treatyites who were disappointed over both partition and the denial of a republic, the correspondent was assured that a plebiscite on the Treaty would receive at least 95 per cent approval. As one unidentified Sinn Féiner told the reporter, 'I see no way out of the morass that rejection would create.'[35] Similarly, a Sinn Féin advocate from Lisnaskea, disappointed by the continuation of partition, warned that their 'purgatorial existence' would be prolonged if the Treaty was rejected.[36]

The opinions of the Enniskillen correspondent and those with whom he spoke were reinforced on 30 December, when a special meeting of the Sinn Féin executive for north and south Fermanagh assembled. The twenty-three *cumann* (Sinn Féin clubs) represented there voted thirty-four to eight in favour of Cahir Healy's resolution: 'That we, the Comhairle Ceanntair of North and South Fermanagh, while not approving of the Treaty in all respects, consider that in the present circumstances it should be ratified, and we call upon our T.D. in An Dail, Mr Sean O'Mahony, to carry out the wishes of his constituents.' According to a press representative in the region, Co. Armagh's clergy, 'influential' anti-partitionists, and nationalists on the City Council were also in favour of ratification.[37]

An anti-partitionist meeting in Omagh, Co. Tyrone, illustrated similar support for the Treaty. The large gathering passed a resolution demanding its ratification and requested that the Dáil permit TDs holding two constituencies to vote twice so that the voice of the people could be heard. Chairman Father Philip O'Doherty enthusiastically told the assembled Tyrone nationalists that '[t]he Treaty provided what the country aspired to for many years, and rejection would mean disaster'. He continued: 'The men who made victory possible – the Collinses and Mulcahys and others – were all in favour of the treaty, and what was good enough for Michael Collins was good enough for them all. (Applause.) What was good enough for their great statesman Arthur Griffith was also good enough for them. (Applause.)'[38] With an eye to the reasons for the division in Dublin, Tyrone solicitor and Sinn Féiner George Murnaghan took this opportunity to pledge his willingness to stand by the plenipotentiaries, while Alex Donnelly – also a Tyrone Sinn Féin advocate – suggested that the Dáil's choice of representatives was a tacit recognition of the fact that the republic had been abandoned by Dáil Éireann in October and not by the plenipotentiaries sent to London.[39]

The Dáil debates resumed in public session on 3 January 1922.[40] From the Northern nationalist perspective, the long-winded protestations by both sides in the debate during the December sessions in no way helped the cause of national freedom. Rather, these discussions were seen as a 'spectacle' by the *Irish News*, which claimed that the unnecessarily prolonged Dáil debates were only serving to provide fodder for the Unionist assertion that Irishmen lacked the ability to govern themselves. The 'world was watching', claimed the press, and this was Ireland's only opportunity – in the words of Tennyson – to prove that they had the wherewithal to 'take occasion by the hand, and make the bounds of freedom wider yet'.[41]

Although the nature and duration of debates had clearly tried the patience of many Northern anti-partitionists, by now, Treaty advocates found little difficulty attributing blame for the lack of movement in Dublin. According to the *Irish News*: 'Those Deputies of Dail Eireann who have deliberately resolved to defy it are withholding from the Irish people the right that British Governments and British military power had forcibly denied to all generations of Irish men … since Henry II left Dublin in 1172.' The newspaper continued:

> A group of men and women in Dublin say to these anxious and expectant people: 'you shall not be free, because the freedom offered to you is not branded as we desire!' The sum and substance of all the speeches against the treaty is embodied in the 17 short words thus emphasised, although the speakers must have used up words by the hundred thousand.[42]

The *Derry Journal* found ample satisfaction in the case put forward by Kerry TD Piaras Béaslaí during the opening session of the New Year. Béaslaí argued that Ireland's enduring struggle with England was not a 'fight for a republic but for Ireland for the Irish. They [a century of Irish nationalists] fought for liberty. It is ready to their hands. Will they be denied the right to hold and use it?'[43]

Reflecting border nationalist opinion, the *Derry Journal* echoed the sentiment expressed in Belfast, declaring that the freedom achieved by the Treaty was immensely greater than that sought by 'the repealers of Butt's day' and proceeded to advocate the peaceful evolutionary position that was associated with Collins, Griffith and the pro-Treaty Sinn Féin. 'Why,' the *Journal* asked, 'should there not now be a period of peace and a stretch of earnest, united work to test practically the beneficial potentiality claimed for the Treaty?'[44]

As revealing as these observations may have been, Northern criticism of the anti-Treatyite position intensified as a consequence of the decision, in the first week of January, to make public the details of de Valera's alternative to the Treaty – Document No. 2. The anti-partitionist press in the North found Document No. 2 entirely unpalatable. In the interval between its first mention in the Dáil record and its publication, de Valera amended the document's Ulster clauses, leading the *Journal* to mockingly refer to it as Document No. 3 while claiming that there was 'sinister significance' in that fact that it had been endorsed by some Northern Unionists.[45] The *Irish News* declared the republican proposal to be an 'amateur political essay' not worth serious attention.[46] In this regard, the document's similarity to the Treaty – which the newspaper claimed had the support of the public as well as the plenipotentiaries and British Government – was not lost on the *Irish News*: '[N]o sane Irishmen would deem the difference [between the Treaty and Document No. 2] worth half a drop of blood.'[47] The Treaty and de Valera's alternative were alike in all but a few 'semi-essentials' and 'trivial' details, according to the newspaper.[48] De Valera's proposal recognised the 'British connection' and therefore, 'however it might be construed, it did not, in any sense, or by any flight of the most vivid imagination', secure a republic.[49] Thus, since Document No. 2 seemed to merely split hairs with 'unproven assertions' and 'vague generalities', it was regarded as 'nothing but wreckage' and futile because 'it [could] go no further' and would merely confuse the debate over the real issue – the signed Treaty that lay before them.[50]

Momentous as the schism in Dublin appeared to be and notwithstanding the view taken in the North, the real difference between the pro-Treaty and anti-Treaty positions was between 'a *de facto* and *de jure* republic'.[51] Partition and the essential unity of Ireland, in contrast, were purely secondary concerns for the TDs in Dublin. This fact is evident, as Lyons has argued, by a simple page count of the Dáil debates – only nine pages out of 338 dealt with partition.[52] Moreover, de Valera's Document No. 2 offered no solution to the Northern minority problem. This omission was particularly irksome for the border nationalists. 'It must be confessed,' wrote the *Derry Journal* '[t]hat the production at An Dail of the much-talked-of Document No. 2 promoted numerically to No. 3, is not calculated to ease a critical situation. It is advanced as an alternative to the Treaty, but it has not even the redeeming feature of effacing the worst flaw in that instrument, namely Partition.'[53] Since Document No. 2/3 recognised and accepted partition, wrote the *Irish News,* de Valera had shown himself ready to give Ulster what he 'impeached, denounced, and would reject inconstantly' in the Treaty.[54] The fact that there were no substantive differences between the pro-Treaty and anti-Treaty positions on Ulster helps to explain why partition did not figure more prominently in the debates, but there were other reasons as well. According to Clare O'Halloran, the indifference on the part of Southern nationalists to the plight of the Northern minority went as far back as the first Home Rule crisis – a time when the Southerners had no clearly defined perceptions of their Northern co-religionists and were prone to stereotype them as troublesome Northerners not unlike Ulster Unionists.[55]

The vast majority of the Irish Bishops came out in favour of the Treaty but they, like the anti-partitionist press, were dismayed by the fact that it left Ireland divided and that no one in the Dáil seemed to care about essential unity. Indicative of this sense of pessimistic resentment, Bishop McKenna of Clogher – a supporter of the Treaty – wrote to Rome in late January: 'The big blot on the Treaty to which no one in the Dáil seemed to give a thought is the uncertainty surrounding the position of the Catholics in the North-East. Everything may come right yet, but meantime we cannot enthuse.'[56]

Apart from the hair-splitting over republican aspirations and the 'big blot' which McKenna later identified, most Northern nationalists were clearly and anxiously fixated on what they considered to be the real alternative to the Treaty – the resumption of war with England. If the Treaty was rejected, warned Cardinal Logue, 'the country will be thrown back into a state even more drastically oppressive than that through which we have passed'.[57] The Northern press was overflowing with dire predictions at the thought of an anti-Treaty victory in the Dáil but, on closer inspection, this pessimism represented more than just fear of the unknown. Rather it was underscored by the desire to prevent the loss of ground that had been won valiantly by the sacrifices that generations of Irish nationalists gave to The Cause. Cardinal Logue's assessment of the situation complemented a view held by many Northern nationalists who considered the rejection of the hard-fought-for freedoms secured by the Treaty to be tantamount to national suicide.

For the Belfast anti-partitionist press the choice was simple: the gains secured by the Treaty represented a lifeboat for the nation but if it was rejected by those desperate to 'wreck the Irish ship', they would all be left without even 'a leaking punt' beneath their feet. Thus, from this perspective, there was an urgent need for Dublin to act quickly and decisively while there still existed in London a government pledged to the Treaty.[58] With the very real fear that an anti-Treaty victory would nullify nationalist progress, the *Derry Journal* drew a tantalising comparison between Irish nationalism and Sisyphus – the tragic figure of Greek mythology condemned to roll a large boulder to the top of a high peak only to have it fall back to the ground again, forcing him to begin anew each day.[59]

After much cajoling and consternation, when the vote was finally taken in the Dáil, the results made plain the fact that Sinn Féin unity would not easily be restored, for the Dáil accepted the Treaty by a slim margin of 64 to 57 on 7 January 1922. The *Irish News* greeted this news with relief, claiming in no uncertain terms and with little embellishment that 'the Nationalists of the Six Counties approve the verdict'.[60] In fact, the entire nationalist press in the North endorsed the Treaty.[61] While one Donegal reader of the *Derry Journal* claimed to have been handed a 'death-blow' by the result of the Dáil vote,[62] opposition to the Treaty within the excluded portion of Ulster was all but nonexistent.[63]

The nearly unanimous conviction of the entrapped Northern minority could not be parleyed into a coherent and cohesive policy for dealing with the new situation created by the Anglo-Irish Treaty and this would be their greatest pathology. A number of public boards and councils that were under the control of anti-partitionists heeded the call from pro-Treaty TD Eoin MacNeill for a policy of passive non-recognition by pledging allegiance to the Dáil. This was a costly strategy since any government body that recognised the Dáil (or refused to give allegiance to the Northern parliament) risked being dissolved by the parliament of Northern Ireland. Public bodies in Fermanagh, South Down and South Armagh had followed this course of action. In contrast, Tyrone nationalists, believing that it would be a greater advantage to have a functioning council under the control of an anti-partitionist majority when the Boundary Commission was convened, chose to save itself from dissolution by recognising the Northern parliament on a temporary basis.[64] Likewise, on 11 January, after a rancorous debate between the Mayor of Derry and a small group of diehard Sinn Féiners on the Derry Corporation, Mayor O'Doherty successfully prevented the city from pledging its allegiance to the Dáil. However, the Corporation chose not to recognise the Northern parliament as Tyrone had.[65]

Aside from the divisions on policy which divided some anti-partitionists on the border, the Northern nationalists' unanimous support for the ratification of the Treaty masked what was perhaps the most damaging and persistent division preventing them from agreeing on a 'strategic vision' for dealing with their entrapment.[66] This division was between the border regions, which had a vested interest in the functioning of the boundary clause of the Treaty, and the non-contiguous pockets of anti-partitionists in areas such as Belfast and the Glens of Antrim, which, as Kevin O'Higgins would later declare, did not have 'a dog's chance of getting out of the Boundary area'.[67] Support for the Treaty in the border regions was contingent upon the timely functioning of the boundary clause, while as early as 16 December, the *Irish News* was telling its readers: 'It is to be hoped that the "Boundaries Commission" will never sit.'[68] Clearly clinging to the hope that essential unity could be achieved by negotiation and without resorting to Article 12, the *Irish News* experienced no noticeable ill-will for saying as much at this juncture but, in the future, the Devlinite newspaper would discover that the mere suggestion of abandoning the Boundary Commission would bring on vehement protests and charges of perfidy from those who were counting on repatriation via the tribunal.

Divisions between the border regions and the interior on the rationale for supporting the Treaty, and amongst border nationalists themselves on questions of policy, existed alongside divisions which naturally sprang up between the Northern minority as a whole and their allies on the other side of the border, and this too corresponds with the general parameters of the trapped minority model.[69] Whether any nationalist chose to recognise it or not, the fact remained that partition existed and Dublin's predilection for philosophical debate over the form of freedom that the people in the South of Ireland could accept without humiliation only served to illuminate the fact that the Northern minority had no real choices before them. As such, more than a hint of resentment could be detected in the *Irish News*' observation that:

> For those people of the six excluded counties whose devotion to Irish nationality stood a thousand tests never applied elsewhere, and who look across the border of the Irish Free State at the squabbles and the quibbles and the charges and allegations that have tortured the country for a month, can do nothing more than face the terrible realities of their own position.[70]

In addition to the disillusionment illustrated above, the nationalist Belfast press was deeply concerned that the anti-Treaty opposition would refuse to admit defeat and would seek to use the sacrifice of the excluded area as a rallying point. Seizing on this emerging sore spot, the paper continued: 'The Nationalists of "Northern Ireland" had been "sacrificed" ever since the day when it was made possible for the British Parliament to pass the Partition Act of 1920. That was done in 1918 – not in 1921.'[71] The sullenness and cynicism that accompanied this not so subtle dig at Sinn Féin abstentionism in 1918 was clearly rooted in the realisation that, whether or not the Treaty represented a settlement in the lasting sense, the South controlled its own destiny while the fate of the Northern nationalists was, as it had been since 1918, in the hands of others.

In addition to the discord apparent in the passages cited above, it is also evident from the reportage of both the *Irish News* and border newssheets, such as the *Derry Journal*, that most Northern nationalists wanted nothing more than for their Southern compatriots to mend fences, lay the groundwork for the repatriation of the North and get on with the work of governing the, albeit incomplete, Irish nation. The *Derry Journal* was eager to point out that, while the vote in the Dáil was 'not as deep as a well or wide as a church door' it was 'amply sufficient'. According to the *Journal*, the mere seven votes which separated the pro-Treaty Sinn Féin from the Republicans in the Dáil was misleading as a consequence of the way in which the votes were tallied. Each of the TDs in the Dáil was given a single vote but five of the TDs held dual constituencies. Four out of these five dual constituency holders were in favour of the Treaty; thus, had the vote been taken by constituency rather than by TD, the margin of victory would have been greater. Moreover, Eoin MacNeill, who also represented two constituencies, was denied a vote on the Treaty since he was the Speaker of Dáil Éireann. And finally, there was the case of Alderman Kelly – an acknowledged supporter of the Treaty – who was unable to record his vote due to illness. Had these circumstances been taken into consideration, wrote the *Derry Journal*, an additional six votes would have been recorded in favour of the Treaty, widening the margin of victory.[72]

Regardless of the fact that the vote was close, the indisputable fact remained that more TDs had voted to accept the Treaty than opposed it and this was applauded by the Northern press as a triumph for democratic principles and the popular will over the autocratic 'Prussianism' with which they associated the anti-Treaty opposition. According to the *Derry Journal*:

> Irrefutable logic supports the statement that it is no more within the rights or competency of a minority in this country to thrust a Republic upon the majority of the people against their will than it is within the competence of the British Government to thrust alien rule upon Ireland against the wishes of the Irish people.[73]

As harsh as the criticisms of the anti-Treaty opposition often were, however, at this juncture the Northern press was still able to draw a line of demarcation between the poor judgment of the misguided anti-Treatyites and their patriotic intent and honourable character. The intended purpose for making such a distinction was explicit: now was the time for mending fences. John Clinton O'Boyce's poem, which appeared in the border press on 13 January in response to the Dáil vote, is clearly indicative of the Northern view that the time for debate and dissension had passed. The poem, entitled 'Close up the Ranks Again', reads as follows:

Close up the ranks again, stand shoulder to shoulder,
The voice of the country demands that you do;
With pale face uplifted, appealing, behold her–
To old Mother Eire be faithful and true.

Close up the ranks again, no longer divided,
But bury dissension deep down in the dust;
The fate of our country to you is confided,
As brothers united be true to your trust.

Close up the ranks again, stand firmly together;
On both sides we know there are good men and true,
Who strove for the homeland thro' all sorts of weather
To further the cause of our loved Roisin Dhu.

Close up the ranks again, your forces uniting;
The eyes of the world are on you to-day;
To finish the compact, sans further back-biting,
And millions shall bless you we fervently pray.

Close up the ranks again, and pull all together;
United we stand, but divided we fall;
A long pull and strong at same end of the tether,
For old Erin's Freedom, with God over all.[74]

Alluding to the seventeenth- and eighteenth-century *aislingi* that cast Ireland as a woman – old Mother Eire and Roisin Dhu – this poetic appeal called on the 'good men and true' to put aside their differences and come together in *her* defence.[75] The central message of the poem was unequivocal: there was much more work to be done and Ireland would need all of its heroes – Treatyite and Republican – to face the next challenge. That next challenge, stated the *Derry Journal*, would be testing the value of the Treaty through practical politics, since 'it is actual wear that will prove the worth of the fabric or the reverse'.[76]

The practical work of testing the Treaty would not begin immediately as tensions between the Treatyites and anti-Treatyites in the aftermath of the Dáil vote left both factions jockeying for position. Éamon de Valera's presidency was the first obvious political casualty of the pro-Treaty Party's victory in the Dáil debates. He sought and narrowly lost a vote of confidence and was replaced by Arthur Griffith as President of Dáil Éireann.[77] Then, as specified by the Treaty, on 14 January, Sinn Féin's pro-Treaty TDs and the Dublin University representatives assembled for the first and last time as the Better Government of Ireland Act's Southern Parliament, ratified the Treaty and selected a Provisional Government, led by Michael Collins as Chairman.[78] Two days after this historic meeting, which the anti-Treatyite TDs boycotted, the outgoing British viceroy handed over Dublin Castle to Collins – thus, in the words of the *Irish News*, bringing about a political transformation that 'twenty generations of Irishmen lived in the hope that they would see'.[79]

Notwithstanding the tension in the air created by continued division in Dublin, the *Irish News* claimed that the Provisional Government had begun 'splendidly'. However, the newspaper was eager to point out that it did not constitute *the* government of Ireland, since its jurisdiction did not extend over all Irishmen and women; but it was, in contrast to centuries of alien rule, at least *an* Irish government. Describing its place in connection with the accomplishments of Grattan and Flood in the eighteenth century, Emmet's short-lived rebellion of 1803 and the rebels who declared Ireland a republic in 1916, the newspaper proudly pointed out that the Provisional Government was the first recognised and representative Irish government since the reign of Rory O'Connor – the last High King of Ireland.[80]

As long and daunting as the process of achieving it had been, one could argue that, for Great Britain, the Anglo-Irish settlement was a triumph. It is true that Dublin had won a significant measure of freedom heretofore considered unthinkable; but the agreement fell short of granting a republic, kept Ireland in the Empire and seemed to allow Britain to extricate itself from the quagmire that had engulfed the politics and politicians of the United Kingdom for the better part of a century. And, while it did not seem so to the anti-Treatyites, the Articles of Agreement may have represented the best that Dublin could have hoped for under the circumstances; however, if the Treaty was a victory for the South it was clearly a pyrrhic one and renewed violence seemed all but certain once the IRA split into pro- and anti-Treaty factions later that spring. The gravity of that development became all the more clear in early April when recalcitrant anti-Treatyites – led by a self-styled Army Executive – occupied Dublin's Four Courts, established a base of operations and hunkered down waiting to be confronted by the Provisional Government.

For their part, the Treaty (and Dublin's responses to it) could only mean continued uncertainty to the peoples of the North. Ulster Unionists could take comfort in the fact that they had weathered the threat posed by a century of Irish nationalism and maintained their dominant position in Northern Ireland but the victory was far from complete since the prospect of a Boundary Commission provided a glaring reminder that their ultimate future was not yet certain. Clearly, the Northern nationalists suffered from a degree of uncertainty as great as that afflicting Ulster Unionists but unlike their Ulster adversaries, Northern Ireland's trapped nationalist minority could not meet the threats they faced as a united force. Northern nationalists of virtually every hue and region applauded the acceptance of the Treaty by the Dáil and feared the possibility that continued acrimony in the South would forestall irredentism; but divisions persisted regarding the nature of the policy that was needed. The Treaty debates also served to highlight the different circumstances that would now be faced by the Northern minority, who were – at least for the moment – ensnared on the wrong side of the border, and their Southern brethren, who controlled their own destiny but seemed poised to waste the opportunity for which they had all suffered.

Notes

1 *Irish News*, 15 March 1922.

2 Hopkinson, 'From Treaty to Civil War, 1921–2', in J.R. Hill (ed.), *A New History of Ireland VII: Ireland, 1921–84* (Oxford: Oxford University Press, 2003), p. 7.

3 *Irish News*, 9 December 1921.

4 Ibid.

5 These observations of the general mood in Derry were based on the opinions of the *Irish News*' Derry correspondent. *Irish News*, 10 December 1921.

6 *Irish News*, 13 December 1921.

7 As quoted by P. Clayton, *Enemies and Passing Friends: Settler Ideologies in Twentieth Century Ulster* (London: Pluto Press, 1996), p. xvi.

8 Emphasis added. *Irish News*, 12 December 1921.

9 *Irish News*, 13 December 1921.

10 P. Murray, *The Irish Boundary Commission and its Origins, 1886–1925* (Dublin: University College Dublin Press, 2011), p. 133.

11 *The Times*, 15 December 1921.

12 That the debate on the Treaty would become, in part, an argument over the powers of the plenipotentiaries was interesting, given the *Irish News*' support for them in October. As the debate progressed, both the *Derry Journal* (on 7 January) and the *Irish News* (on 10, 15, 20, 28 December) continued to defend the Irish plenipotentiaries. The *Irish News*' most blatant attempt to weigh in on the issue came on 29 December, however, when the newspaper used all upper-case letters to publish extracts from de Valera's instructions to the plenipotentiaries on 11 October 1921. The portion cited read: 'OUR DELEGATES ARE KEENLY CONSCIOUS OF THEIR RESPONSIBILITIES. THEY MUST BE MADE TO FEEL A UNITED NATION HAS CONFIDENCE IN THEM UNFLINCHINGLY ... THE UNITY THAT IS ESSENTIAL WILL BEST BE MAINTAINED BY AN UNWAVERING FAITH IN THOSE WHO HAVE BEEN DEPUTIED TO ACT IN THE NATION'S BEHALF, AND A CONFIDENCE MAINTAINING ITSELF AS HITHERTO IN ELOQUENT DISCIPLINE.' *Irish News*, 29 December 1921.

13 *Dáil Debates*, vol. 3 (14 December 1921), cols 7–16, https://www.oireachtas.ie/en/debates/find/ (accessed 23 July 2019).

14 *Irish News*, 15 December 1921.

15 Ibid.

16 Ibid., 16 December 1921.

17 'Remembrances of the Mansion House Convention', 7 December 1921, Cahir Healy Papers, D/2991/B/2/4, Public Record of Northern Ireland, Belfast.

18 For instance, every Rural District Council and every Board of Guardians in south and east Down had taken similar measures by 14 December. *Irish News*, 16 December 1921.

19 *Irish News*, 16 December 1921.

20 Curran has traced the idea of external association back to February 1920, when the President waxed philosophical about the analogy that could be drawn between what Ireland was prepared to accept from Britain and the 1903 treaty between the United States and Cuba. That treaty had prohibited Cuba from entering into agreements with nations that were hostile to the United States. De Valera first broached the idea of external association with his Cabinet colleagues

in June 1921. The Dáil Cabinet supported external association as a worthy objective but it appears that some ministers did not realise just how committed de Valera was to the idea. J. Curran, *The Birth of the Irish Free State, 1921–1923* (n.p.: University of Alabama Press, 1980), pp. 45, 76.

21 Curran, *The Birth of the Irish Free State*, p. 148.

22 *Irish News*, 20 December 1921.

23 Ibid.

24 Barton explained his reluctant decision to sign the Treaty during the Dáil debate on 19 December. He insisted that, faced with the prospect of immediate war if they did not sign, he 'preferred war' but in the final analysis he could not bring himself to commit the country to war under these circumstances. 'The alternative,' said Barton, 'which I sought to avoid seemed to me a lesser outrage than the violation of what is my faith. So that I myself, and of my own choice, must commit my nation to immediate war, without you, Mr. President, or the Members of the Dáil, or the nation having an opportunity to examine the terms upon which war could be avoided. I signed, and now I have fulfilled my undertaking I recommend to you the Treaty I signed in London.' *Dáil Debates*, vol. 3 (19 December 1921), col. 49, https://www.oireachtas.ie/en/debates/find/ (accessed 23 July 2019). Duffy spoke on 21 December. His recollection of the events that immediately preceded the signing of the Treaty mirrored those of Barton, as did his rationale for 'reluctantly, but very sincerely' recommending the Treaty. Duffy referred to his signature on the Treaty as a 'pledge' that was 'extorted' from him as a consequence of Lloyd George's ultimatum but said he saw no real alternative. *Dáil Debates*, vol. 3 (21 December 1921), col. 85, https://www.oireachtas.ie/en/debates/find/ (accessed 23 July 2019).

25 For the *Irish News*' account of the duress issue, see its 21 December 1921 issue. As Duffy's testimony during the Dáil debate suggested, however, the matter was not as clear-cut as the *Irish News* would have had the reader believe. According to Duffy, 'The complaint is not that the alternative to signing a Treaty was war; the complaint is that the alternative to our signing that particular Treaty was immediate war.' *Dáil Debates*, vol. 3 (21 December 1921), col. 85, https://www.oireachtas.ie/en/debates/find/ (accessed 23 July 2019).

26 *Irish News*, 22 December 1921.

27 Given the level of factionalism in the Dáil over the Treaty, it is not surprising that even the issue of whether or not to take a short adjournment brought division. An amendment to Collins' motion calling on the Dáil to remain in session until after midnight daily was defeated by a vote of 44–77. *Dáil Debates*, vol. 3 (22 December 1921), cols 167–71, https://www.oireachtas.ie/en/debates/find/ (accessed 23 July 2019).

28 *Irish News*, 24 December 1921.

29 Curran, *The Birth of the Irish Free State*, p. 150.

30 Hopkinson, 'From Treaty to Civil War, 1921–2', p. 5.

31 Curran, *The Birth of the Irish Free State*, p. 151. The *Irish News* took great pleasure in the fact that de Valera's constituency clearly backed the pro-Treaty position.

The newspaper carried a full story on the Clare Council vote. *Irish News*, 23 December 1921.

32 M. Harris, *The Catholic Church and the Foundation of the Northern Irish State* (Cork: Cork University Press, 1989), p. 104.

33 *Irish News*, 29 December 1921.

34 Ibid., 27 December 1921.

35 Ibid., 28 December 1921.

36 Ibid.

37 Ibid., 31 December 1921.

38 Ibid., 29 December 1921.

39 Ibid.

40 *Dáil Debates*, vol. 3 (3 January 1922), col. 173, https://www.oireachtas.ie/en/debates/find/ (accessed 23 July 2019).

41 *Irish News*, 4 January 1922.

42 Ibid.

43 *Derry Journal*, 6 January 1922.

44 Ibid.

45 Ibid.

46 *Irish News*, 5 January 1922.

47 Ibid., 7 January 1922.

48 Ibid., 5 January 1922.

49 Ibid., 7 January 1922.

50 Ibid., 5 January 1922.

51 A. Jackson, *Ireland, 1798–1998: Politics and War* (Oxford: Blackwell Publishers, 1999), p. 263.

52 F.S.L. Lyons, *Ireland Since the Famine* (London: Weidenfeld and Nicolson, 1971), p. 443. Lyons stated further that two thirds of those nine pages of discussion on partition were contributed by three County Monaghan TDs. Sean McEntee was, perhaps, the best advocate for the North in the Dáil debates.

53 *Derry Journal*, 6 December 1922.

54 *Irish News*, 7 January 1921.

55 O'Halloran maintains that these Southern perceptions of Northern nationalists persisted into the 1920s. As evidence, she cites a 1923 Irish Free State memorandum in which E.M. Stephens suggests: 'Ulsterman of both religions have in their subconscious minds a feeling that they have something in common which they do not share with their fellow countrymen of the south. This feeling lies below the threshold of consciousness where the Ulsterman is moving in an Ulster environment. Probably this feeling has its roots deep in Irish history. It may go back to the cycle of Cuchulain.' C. O'Halloran, *Partition and the Limits of Irish Nationalism: An Ideology Under Stress* (Dublin: Gill and Macmillan, 1987), pp. 57–8.

56 Harris, *The Catholic Church and the Foundation of the Northern Irish State*, p. 106.

57 *Derry Journal*, 6 January 1922.

58 *Irish News*, 5 January 1922.

59 *Derry Journal*, 6 January 1922.

60 *Irish News*, 9 January 1922.

61 E. Phoenix, *Northern Nationalism: Nationalist Politics, Partition and the Catholic Minority in Northern Ireland, 1890–1940* (Belfast: Ulster Historical Foundation, 1994), p. 161.

62 *Derry Journal*, 13 January 1922.

63 The large number of organisations and bodies that came out in favour of the Treaty has already been noted. In addition to this, there is some indication – for instance on the Dundalk Urban Council – that those voting against resolutions supporting the Treaty were voting against interference in Dublin, not voting to reject the Treaty. *Irish News*, 4 January 1922. While Downpatrick solicitor John H. King, in a letter to Seán Milroy in mid-January, made note of the fact that the south Down Comhairle Ceanntair went against the Treaty, he was convinced that this was the result of propaganda and fear of the unknown and did not represent the 'majority view of the electorate'. King to Milroy, 24 January 1922, Department of the Taoiseach, NAI/TSCH/S 1801/Q, National Archives of Ireland, Dublin.

64 Phoenix, *Northern Nationalism*, p. 155.

65 *Derry Journal*, 11 January 1922.

66 D. Rabinowitz, 'The Palestinian Citizens of Israel, the Concept of Trapped Minority and the Discourse of Transnationalism in Anthropology', *Ethnic and Racial Studies* 24, 1 (2001), p. 77.

67 'Deputation to the Provisional Government', 11 October 1922, Department of the Taoiseach, NAI/TSCH/S 11209, National Archives of Ireland, Dublin, 18.

68 *Irish News*, 16 December 1921.

69 According to Rabinowitz, the 'chronic ideological and political internal divisions' that plague trapped minorities make it difficult to forge 'a united front both inside and outside the [host] state'. Rabinowitz, 'Trapped Minority', p. 73.

70 *Irish News*, 9 January 1922.

71 Ibid.

72 *Derry Journal*, 9 January 1922. As Knirck notes, the unique situation created by the existence of TDs holding dual constituencies was raised by Seán Milroy but his charge that the voters of second constituencies were being disenfranchised did not change the procedure that gave each TD one vote. Griffith and Milroy continued to protest but Collins was of the view that the Treaty should not pass by a 'sharp practice'. J. Knirck, *Imagining Ireland's Independence: The Debates Over the Anglo-Irish Treaty of 1921* (New York: Rowman & Littlefield Publishers, Inc., 2006), p. 117.

73 *Derry Journal*, 9 January 1922.

74 Ibid., 13 January 1922.

75 See the introduction for the definition of an *aisling* (plural *aislingi*).

76 *Derry Journal*, 11 January 1922.

77 Curran, *The Birth of the Irish Free State*, pp. 157–8.

78 The Provisional Government, which existed in conjunction with the Griffith-led Dáil administration, was to operate until the Irish Free State could be formally constituted.

79 *Irish News*, 17 January 1922.

80 Ibid., 16 January 1922. While Grattan's Parliament had been looked upon with reverence by some nineteenth-century Irish nationalists, the *Irish News* was critical of it because it did not include Catholic representation and did not control Dublin Castle. Robert Emmet, in 1803, and those who rebelled in 1916 had proclaimed independent republics which became emotional milestones but neither could be maintained.

CHAPTER 4

'The Matter is Too Serious': The Craig–Collins Pacts and Northern Conditions

> I will not reply to a single interruption. I could squash that gentleman with a breath. I could blow him out as the last of the Die-hards, but I do not notice him; the matter is too serious.
>
> —Joe Devlin, on the sectarian violence in Belfast[1]

The occupation of the Four Courts did not immediately lead to war between the Provisional Government and the anti-Treaty Republicans. Rather, as Chairman of the Provisional Government, Michael Collins still hoped to avoid an open clash with his former allies and for this purpose, the Northern minority provided a convenient diplomatic device. Both Collins and his Republican counterparts became markedly more interested in the plight of those Catholics and nationalists who were trapped on wrong side of the Six-County border as relations between the Southern factions deteriorated and the escalating cycle of sectarian violence that was then gripping Belfast became the focal point of Southern criticism. What shape this increased Southern interest would take and how the government of Northern Ireland would respond to the changing circumstances remained to be seen, as did the extent to which the liaison between Belfast, Dublin and London would have an impact on Northern nationalism. With that in mind, this chapter examines the series of metropolitan outrages and border crises that Northern Ireland experienced during the spring of 1922. It will show that, while Northern nationalists were seldom furnished with accurate information about the activities of the Provisional Government, much less the anti-Treatyites, they nonetheless recognised a relationship between the volatile politics of Southern Ireland and the further deterioration of Northern conditions.

There is an old Belfast street rhyme which offers a droll, yet no less candid, observation of the nature of inter-communal relations within the city. It reads:

> Belfast's a famous northern town,
> Ships and linen its occupation;
> And the workers have a riot on
> The slightest provocation.[2]

Anxious and dissatisfied Catholics and Protestants within Northern Ireland found plenty of provocation to riot as events were playing out in Dublin during the spring of 1922 and the results of these confrontations were very often deadly. Political uncertainty and a post-War economic slump in the Northern economy contributed to the frequency and intensity of bloody disturbances,[3] and the rise of rival and militant armed forces in the North undoubtedly aggravated these tensions. Under the terms of the truce which halted the Anglo-Irish War, the IRA was officially recognised by Britain and was even permitted to open a liaison office at St Mary's Hall in Belfast.[4] Under these circumstances, troop strength increased and, much to the dismay of the Unionist government, the IRA set up training camps in various locations across the North and began to drill recruits.[5] Unbeknownst to Belfast or London, it was also at this juncture that the General Headquarters (GHQ) of the IRA set up its Ulster Council to organise Northern activities.[6]

In March 1922, the Northern government estimated that there were some 8,500 members of the IRA living within its borders.[7] If the growth of the Northern IRA was a cause of anxiety for Sir James Craig, estimates that the total strength of the organisation in Ireland was in the neighbourhood of 112,650 must have been profoundly alarming and this helps to explain Craig's own efforts to secure his territory.[8] As of January 1922, a contingent of approximately sixteen battalions of the British army remained in the North and, although plans were underway for its replacement, the RIC continued to function as the regular police force.[9] However, the bulk of the Northern government's security forces were drawn from the ranks of the notorious Ulster Special Constabulary (USC).[10] The USC was established in 1920 and was divided into three sections: the full-time 'A' Specials; the part-time 'B' Specials; and the 'C' Specials, which represented a reserve unit.[11] The Specials, in general, inspired the same sort of fear and contempt in the minds of Northern nationalists as had the Black and Tans in the South but the 'B' Specials were particularly hated. They were drawn largely from the sectarian Ulster Volunteer Force and were undisciplined, poorly trained[12] and, in many cases, linked to the very outrages they were expected to prevent. Moreover, because of Lloyd George's unwillingness to allow the British army to interfere with the IRA on the border, the government of Northern Ireland became dependant on the 'B' Specials for security and their numbers swelled.[13]

Regardless of the ways in which Northern nationalists and unionists chose to justify their accumulation of armed forces – or that some outrages and reprisals were committed by ordinary hooligans – the mere existence of an ever-increasingly sectarian police force and an active IRA straddling the border made political and sectarian violence within Northern Ireland difficult to avoid. As a consequence, the sporadic outrages, reprisals and border incidents that had punctuated Northern life since the shipyard expulsions had escalated amidst the tensions of the Treaty negotiations.[14]

One particularly serious incident occurred in Tyrone one week after Dáil Éireann voted to accept the Treaty. On 14 January 1922, Dan Hogan, OC of the IRA's 5th Northern Division, which was based in Co. Monaghan, and a number of his officers were arrested by the USC. Known to history as the 'Monaghan footballers', these men had been on their way to Derry City to attend the Ulster GAA finals when they were arrested. The Monaghan men were armed and they were also in possession of incriminating documents, including plans for the rescue of three men held in Derry jail awaiting execution.[15] The uproar caused by this daring attempt was enough to grab the attention of Winston Churchill, Colonial Secretary of Lloyd George's governing coalition. Owing to the increased level of violence in the North and as a means to deal with some unanswered questions stemming from the shaky Treaty settlement, the Colonial Secretary invited Sir James Craig and Michael Collins to meet with him. As the British government now considered Collins as the 'custodian' of Northern nationalism[16] and the Chairman of the Provisional Government knew that he would be 'bitterly attacked by some of his own friends' if he were to seek advice from the likes of Joe Devlin,[17] Collins represented both the interests of the Northern minority and those of his administration when he met Craig and Churchill on 21 January in London.

Expectations regarding the outcome of the meeting were decidedly low in all quarters; however, the conference produced a broad, if somewhat vague, agreement now known as the first Craig–Collins pact. In it, the signatories pledged to seek a bilateral solution to the boundary question, thus repudiating the provision for both the Boundary Commission called for in Article 12 of the Treaty. Collins declared an end to the Belfast boycott and promised to cease IRA activity in the North, and Craig vowed to facilitate the return of Catholic workers to the Belfast shipyards and sought relief aid from Great Britain to help improve their lot. They also agreed to seek a better way of dealing with problems affecting both regimes than the Better Government of Ireland Act's proposed Council of Ireland, which had never functioned. Craig and Collins made plans to meet again in the near future to hammer out an agreement on the release of political prisoners.[18]

In certain circles, the pact signalled a note of hope for Ireland. The agreement was praised in London and Dublin; however, Craig encountered harsh criticism from Unionist hardliners.[19] The pact's reception among Northern nationalists was more complex owing to the pre-existing 'internal divisions' and inability to forge a 'united front' that marked them as a trapped minority.[20] For instance, the *Irish News* greeted the signing of the agreement with optimism, suggesting that by casting aside the 'grotesque', 'feeble', 'futile' and 'unworkable' Council of Ireland, the signatories of the pact were 'laying the foundation of re-union'.[21] Expressing its own particular brand of irredentism, the newspaper asked: 'How could one even determine which problems were all-Ireland problems' worthy of the Council since it was 'impossible to imagine any question of capital importance … that does not affect Derry and Donegal in some degree if it affects Waterford and Tipperary [?]'

The cessation of the 'ugly business' caused by the boycott was also applauded by the *Irish News,* which claimed that the measure had hurt nationalists as much as it had unionists. The newspaper's optimism over the pact was mitigated, however, by concern about the boundary. While endorsing the desire of Collins and Craig to take Britain's external influence away from the boundary question, the Devlinite organ speculated that the new procedure agreed to at the conference would make the border question no easier to settle. 'Assuming that "politics" are still to be conducted on "religious" lines,' it asked rhetorically, 'how do the Catholics of Belfast, Antrim, Derry, half of Armagh, two-thirds of Down, and indeterminable fractions of Tyrone, and Fermanagh [the areas that would likely remain under Belfast's control] like the prospect?' According to the newspaper, the only foreseeable solution to the boundary question would be to hold off on border rectification of any sort and expend the necessary energy to devise and work the pact's proposed replacement for the Council of Ireland. This response reflected Joe Devlin's view that improving the liaison between the North and South of Ireland, rather than the enforcement of Article 12, was the surest way to achieve Irish unity, especially since the nationalists of Belfast and the interior were trapped too deeply within the heart of Northern territory to benefit from any border changes. Insinuating that Collins had, in effect, recognised Northern Ireland as a consequence of the pact, the *Irish News* concluded that mounting tensions in Dublin would soon force Northern nationalists to formulate their own anti-partitionist strategy. 'This fact should clarify the situation for all Nationalists in the Six Counties,' observed the newspaper. 'They are living under a government fully recognised by the responsible Nationalist Government of the Twenty-Six Counties. It is their duty to take the fact into account at once, and to "devise a more suitable method" of preserving and advancing their vital interests than the simple but curiously ineffective method of doing nothing.'[22]

In contrast to the *Irish News*' cautious optimism about the Craig–Collins pact, border nationalists were less than enthused. Betraying their differing context from the Devlinites, even the hint of recognising the government of Northern Ireland was anathema to those nationalists who expected to benefit from the Boundary Commission.[23] Moreover, the primary reason that the vast majority of border nationalists had endorsed the Treaty had been because of the Boundary Commission with its British Chairman whom, it was hoped, would act with impartiality. Dislike of the pact was so intense among Sinn Féin supporters at the grass-roots level that many local branches of the party purposely sought out 'anti-pact delegates', at the expense of prominent party stalwarts, to represent them at the organisation's February *Ard Fheis* in Dublin.[24]

The new circumstances brought about by the pact called much into question and intensified fears that Northern Ireland would be granted a veto on border changes. In the days immediately following the announcement of the agreement, Collins received petitions and entertained nationalist deputations, each seeking to impress their own views on the Provisional Government and to determine what effect the pact would have on them.[25] The proceedings of a conference held at the Newry Town Hall attended by nationalists from Newry, South Down and South Armagh were indicative of the broader concerns of border nationalists. Speaking for many in attendance, R. O'Hagan noted that the Northern nationalists' 'great difficulty was in understanding the nature of the terms Mr Collins had made with Sir James Craig'. O'Hagan continued, 'If Mr Collins had given away the greatest weapon they ever had – the Boycott – without anything in return but sentiments, it would be their duty to fight against the ruin of their interests.'[26] Echoing O'Hagan's concerns, John Quinn called for a deputation to be sent to meet Collins in order to 'ascertain from him whether he had given anything away and to what extent'.[27] Likewise, Daniel Dowdall informed the assembly that he too was 'very much annoyed to see that any such agreement should be arrived at ... without the people in districts such as theirs being consulted'.[28]

As the above excerpts suggest, the overriding concerns of these border nationalists pertained to the ending of the boycott, which they considered to have been an effective weapon, and the lack of information they had been given by Collins. Consistent with what Dan Rabinowitz describes as the double marginality of trapped minorities, there was a certain expectation, feared as it might have been, that Catholics and nationalists would be marginalised within Northern Ireland but these border nationalists were also finding that their views could and would be marginalised by Southern nationalists if it was in Dublin's interest to do so. As time passed there would be little doubt that Northern nationalists' 'credentials' within their mother nation had been 'devalued' by their entrapment.[29] As transplanted Northerner Kevin O'Shiel later commented disapprovingly, 'North-East Nationalists have always been very jealous of their particular status' and they expect to be kept informed of any 'departures of policy'.[30]

Hated as it was in some quarters, it was not long before the January pact began to unravel. Northern Ireland's struggling economy prevented Craig from fulfilling his obligation to return the expelled shipyard workers to their jobs and Collins proved unable to end the boycott.[31] The inability to fulfil these key elements of the agreement may have been sufficient on their own to scuttle it but the immediate cause of the pact's failure came on 2 February when the signatories sat down ostensibly to discuss the release of political prisoners. The intransigence of each man over questions of the boundary proved to be the pact's undoing. While Craig would consider only minor changes to the border, Collins took this opportunity to reveal maps which, according to the Prime Minister, 'indicated to me clearly that he has already promised to bring into the Free State almost half the area of Northern Ireland, including the counties of Fermanagh and Tyrone, large portions of counties Armagh and Down, Derry City, Enniskillen, and Newry'.[32] Since their views on the border were clearly contradictory and because neither man was willing to bend on this crucial question, the conference, and for all practical purposes, the agreement, ended in failure.[33]

The Mayor of Derry reportedly celebrated the news that the pact had failed;[34] however, the *Irish News* offered a more sobering assessment of the new situation as it took a jab at what it regarded as the more short-sighted border nationalists. 'Mr Collins has been praised and blamed in connection with the "Pact" of January 21st,' claimed the newspaper, but

> most of the blame has come from people who think more of political tactics than a genuine National Settlement. We are convinced that the head of the Free State gave a thought yesterday to the position of 300,000 Ulster Nationalists, as faithful as any in Ireland, who do not live on the borders of Down, Armagh, Tyrone and Fermanagh, or in Derry City. Most of Mid and North Armagh, two-thirds of the county of Down, all the counties of Derry, Antrim,

> and the City of Belfast are well within any 'boundaries'... [and those areas] contain an overwhelming majority of the Nationalists of the Six Counties.[35]

Given the suspected impact that devising a boundary settlement would have had on the nationalists who would in no way benefit from it, the *Irish News* returned to what was becoming its familiar refrain. The newspaper urged Ireland's leaders, North and South, to devise a scheme that would enable them to work together in the hopes that civility, time and common interests would eventually lead to political and economic unity.[36] In spite of this hope, however, the more subdued atmosphere caused by the pact proved to be a mere respite from cold war between the two Irish governments and disorder in Northern Ireland.

The deterioration of relations between the North and South of Ireland coincided with Sir James Craig's anxious efforts to get his own house in order. The Northern Ireland executive had existed for the better part of a year but the transfer of authority from Westminster to Belfast was not yet complete. Not sure how far Lloyd George could be trusted to defend what Craig would later call his 'Protestant Government for a Protestant people', according to Buckland, the Northern Prime Minister was inclined to believe that '[t]he more entrenched it was, the harder it would be to dismantle'.[37] Of the transferred powers which Northern Ireland had received by early February of 1922, for the Northern minority, few were more worrisome than education.

Beginning on 1 February, Northern Ireland's Ministry of Education – headed by Lord Londonderry – was to start paying the salaries of Northern teachers.[38] Since the bulk of Six-County anti-partitionists had committed themselves not to recognising the functioning of the Unionist government, it was now imperative that they decide how to deal with the vexing question of funding. Dublin ultimately agreed to foot the bill and, in mid-February, began the costly experiment of paying the salaries of those Northern teachers who refused to recognise the Northern Ireland's Ministry of Education.[39] According to Harris, 270 of Northern Ireland's schools chose to seek funding from Dublin and avoided being forced to recognise the Northern government. In addition, all of the Northern Catholic intermediate schools, as well as technical schools in Armagh and Newry and St Mary's Teacher Training College, sought help from the Provisional Government.[40]

A small victory of sorts for the minority, the Provisional Government's effort to protect Catholic education from the perceived dangers of Londonderry's Ministry did not assuage persistent nationalist anxieties over dangers to their personal security and economic well-being. As an illustration of the long-term economic affects that sectarian violence had on Belfast Catholics, a report generated by Hugh McCartan on behalf of the Provisional Government in November 1923 indicated that 149 of the 430 spirit grocers in business at the time of the shipyard expulsions were no longer open three years later. Defined as 'small grocer shops with a six day license for consumption off the premises', spirit grocers had been 'almost entirely Catholic in every part of the city' when the troubles began but by 1923, the trade was evenly divided between Catholic and Protestant proprietors. According to McCartan's contact with the Ulster Licensed Vintner's Association, there was also a 20 per cent reduction in the number of Catholic publicans as a direct or indirect result of the pogrom. D. Bradley, one of the spirit grocers with whom McCartan spoke, claimed that the weekly turnover in one of his shops had dropped from £150 to £15 since 1920 – a result Bradley attributed to '30% bad trade and 70% bigotry'.[41]

For the people of Belfast and the border regions in February and March of 1922, a major cause of the political and economic instability they were experiencing was the continued detention of Derry's three death-row inmates – who were to be executed mid-month – and their would-be rescuers, the Monaghan footballers.[42] Lord Lieutenant FitzAlan[43] ultimately reprieved the men but not before the IRA had taken matters into its own hands. Beginning late on the evening of 7 February, IRA raiding parties – with Collins' clandestine approval[44] – crossed the borders of Tyrone and Fermanagh and succeeded in capturing forty-two unionist sympathisers, including the former High Sheriff of Fermanagh.[45]

In response to these provocative actions, on 8 February at Westminster, Unionist MP Captain Charles Craig[46] attempted to ask Lloyd George for an update on the situation and 'whether every assistance [would] be given to the local authorities to hunt down the perpetrators'. Significantly, and before the Prime Minister could answer, the enquiry was ruled out of order by the Speaker of the

House. '[A]s we have transferred the responsibility for these matters to the Northern Parliament,' ruled the Speaker, 'this is a question which should be asked there rather than here.'[47] Although this exchange did not cause much of a stir in the nationalist press at the time,[48] the Speaker's ruling, innocuous as it might seem, actually set an important constitutional precedent by putting limits on what issues could or could not be raised in the British House of Commons regarding Northern Ireland. Ultimately, this was to have a significant effect on the efforts of nationalist representatives to use Westminster as a check on the actions of the government of Northern Ireland (and granting it the practical status of a Weberian state despite its legislative subordination) but for the moment, it left the Unionist MP without the answers he sought.[49]

As Captain Craig and other Unionists looked for reassurance in the wake of the Fermanagh kidnappings, the situation was made worse less than a week later because of a serious incident that occurred at the Clones train station, which was just across the Fermanagh–Monaghan border. Unlike the border kidnappings, the facts surrounding this incident are disputed and responsibility is more difficult to assign.[50] What is clear, however, is that a small group of armed 'A' Specials were travelling from a training centre in Newtownards to Enniskillen on 11 February and the route they took brought them into the Irish Free State.[51] Upon being informed of the presence of armed Specials in Free State territory, a local IRA detachment confronted the security officers at the station and the skirmish that followed left four Specials and the IRA Commander dead. The remainder of the Specials were either wounded or taken captive.

The Northern government's reaction to the Clones incident was immediate. Sir James Craig implored Churchill to authorise the deployment of a rescue force to seek the return of the captured men and also urged the Colonial Secretary to reoccupy border territory belonging to the Free State.[52] It is likely that the event also reinforced the Prime Minister's decision to seek security advice from Field-Marshal Sir Henry Wilson, the former Chief of the Imperial General Staff and the recently selected Unionist candidate for North Down's seat in the Westminster parliament.[53] Belfast's anti-partitionist press responded to these border crises with unbridled, albeit misinformed, outrage. Seeking to link the incidents with the worsening split in Dublin over the Treaty and unaware of Collins' involvement,[54] the *Irish News* lashed out at de Valera for selfishly giving 'licence' for violence to those individuals with a predilection towards such action. The newspaper asked rhetorically: 'How are their [Northern Catholics'] present interests to be served or their future fate affected by the continuance of this interchange of shots, and deaths and "raids," and "reprisals" along the border line from Carlingford to Derry?'[55] Calling for Collins to restore order, using language and tone clearly intended to implicate anti-Treatyite Southern agitators, the editor continued:

> All this concerns the Twenty-Six Counties directly, as they are the arbiters of their own destinies. They can choose for themselves and no 'outside influences' can determine their choice. Before the issue is knit, however, 450,000 Nationalists inside the Six Counties are entitled to know whether they are to be victimized wholesale and without scruple in connection with the struggle between the Treaty-makers and the Treaty-breakers in the Twenty Six Counties. If the Provisional Government are unable to deal, promptly and effectively, with the situation created in the Six Counties by the events of the past week, they will fail in Ireland, and lose Ireland, and leave the whole country in a state as hopeless as on the morrow of the Act of Union.[56]

The Specials and other hostages were eventually released but the *Irish News* had good reason to disavow these 'meaningless and destructive struggles'[57] committed on the border in mid-February, since the dire consequences of the skirmishes were felt most deeply in Belfast. Reaction to the Clones incident in particular unleashed days of intense sectarian backlash in the city. In only three days of rioting, beginning on 13 February, thirty-one people – Catholics and Protestants – were killed as a consequence of the mayhem. The religious tenor of the fighting was undeniable, as was the partiality of the security forces, since the city's 'lawless but "loyal" men'[58] were allegedly protected by police when they targeted Catholic homes and assaulted Catholic inhabitants.[59] With the pall of religious violence hanging over his city, a Belfast man, R. Bryson Calwell, made this poetic plea for calm in 'The Devil's In Between':

Ireland, these tears are thine;
    Ireland, the pain thine own;
Ireland, the sound you hear
    Is thine own groan;
Ireland, thy sons who fall
    Were born within thy border;
'Tis thine own cities, Ireland
    Which rot with foul disorder.
Ireland, some remedy
    Is surely badly needed;
A house divided within itself
    Must fall if left unheeded.
Open yon Book of Holy Writ
    Which Patrick brought to you:
Read there a lesson which is old –
    It tells the thing to do.
If brother won't love brother,
    Whom he has often seen,
He may say the Christ is leading him,
    But the Devil's in between.[60]

While Calwell sought guidance from Patrick, Ireland's Patron Saint, and the 'Book of Holy Writ' in order to cope with the sectarian carnage, Eoin O'Duffy, the Provisional Government's Chief-of-Staff, was urging Collins and Richard Mulcahy to take direct action in order to protect Belfast Catholics. These concerns led to the establishment of the Belfast City Guard – a protection force drawn from the ranks of the IRA.[61] The upsurge in sectarian unrest, in conjunction with the introduction of the Irish Free State (Agreement) Bill, was also enough to bring about Joe Devlin's return to the British parliament after months of boycotting the institution. During his speech in support of the Irish Bill,[62] Devlin was given considerable latitude by the Speaker to discuss security in Northern Ireland[63] and he proceeded to explain his reasons for not publicly addressing the deteriorating condition in the North sooner and why he was so eager to do so now. 'The function of a Member of Parliament is to defend his own people,' observed Devlin, adding: 'I have remained absolutely silent for 12 months although I felt my blood boiling with indignation at the way my people were being treated. I remained silent because I did not want to make any speeches which would endanger the chance of peace between Northern and Southern Ireland.'

Devlin had, by his own admission, said little publicly about the worsening conditions in Belfast in recent months but he had not been idle. While indicating that he did not want to do anything that could cause a breakdown of the truce, on 24 November 1921, Devlin had written to Prime Minister James Craig voicing concerns about his constituents. In that letter, Devlin cited numerous instances of attacks on the lives and property of Belfast Catholics both at the hands of their neighbours and the Special police. With more than a hint of derision, his letter asked the Northern Prime Minister: 'Are the Catholics of Belfast to be handed over to the tender mercies of an armed mob; are they to be left to their own resources to defend their lives and Liberties?' According to what Devlin told his Westminster colleagues on 16 February 1922, this letter was never acknowledged by the Northern Prime Minister. Believing as Devlin did that, 'unless he is devoid of human instinct', no MP could 'stand idly by' and watch his constituents be 'treated as outlaws', 'hunted', 'persecuted' and attacked by 'liveried servants' of the British government, the Belfast MP sought to put clear focus on what he saw as a double-standard condoned by many parliamentarians. 'One of the things that amazes me,' said Devlin, 'is when I hear Ministers on that bench, and Unionist private Members in this House, talking about this outrage here and that outrage there in Southern Ireland, they do not seem to think there is a Northern Ireland at all.'[64]

In fairness, Britain was neither oblivious to the Northern outrages nor indifferent to them. The torrent of sectarian violence in Northern Ireland only intensified fears among Lloyd George's inner circle that the plight of Northern Catholics could lead to a *rapprochement* between the Provisional Government and the Republicans, endangering the Treaty, or worse, leading to an anti-Treaty *coup d'état*.[65] As Curran noted, coalition politicians had 'staked their political reputations on the Treaty'[66] and understood the public relations nightmare that would befall the government if sectarian violence in Ulster, rather than issues related to constitutional status, caused the collapse of the settlement.[67] But, preoccupied with the post-War recovery and beholden to Tory support in order to maintain his shaky coalition government, Lloyd George was very much caught in the crossfire.[68]

With Britain unwilling (or unable) to do anything to stem the tide of violence in the North and Dublin preoccupied with its own political instability, it was at this time that leading Devlinite propagandist J.P. O'Kane introduced the controversial idea of recognising and entering the Belfast parliament. Referring to the Sinn Féin–IPP election pledge of 1921, which prevented either party from recognising Northern Ireland, O'Kane told a United Irish League audience on 12 March that circumstances had changed since that pledge was made and it was now 'desirable to reconsider the whole question'. Because the Treaty included provisions concerning Northern Ireland, O'Kane claimed, Dáil Éireann's acceptance of the agreement amounted to recognition of the Northern regime; thus, in his view, Six-County nationalists would not be violating their pledges by taking their seats.

> By the acceptance of the Treaty Dail Eireann, which includes elected representatives of the Six Counties, has decided to recognise Partition. This alters the whole political position ... Is it not, then, unreasonable and absolutely impracticable, seeing that Dail Eireann has recognised the northern Parliament, that the supporters of Dail Eireann in Ulster should be expected to suffer fearful persecution in the attempt to deny recognition to that Parliament?

Arguing that committed abstentionists 'should produce the plan of campaign by which they propose to fight the Northern Parliament and to protect the Catholics of Carsonia,' O'Kane observed, '[i]t must be remembered that abstention from the British Parliament by the Irish members enabled the Partition Act to be passed. The policy that produced Partition won't get rid of it'.[69]

While there may have been many reasons for the Devlinites to recognise Northern Ireland, doing so was considered sacrilege by a significant number of Six-County nationalists. In rebuttal to O'Kane's UIL speech, Archie Savage, who had unsuccessfully contested East Belfast as a Sinn Féiner in 1921, penned a letter to the *Irish News* lambasting the recognition argument. Suggesting that asking Northern Catholics and nationalists to recognise the Northern parliament was 'pretty safe' in Belfast owing to Devlinite strength in the city, Savage argued that recognising partition would only 'pay homage' to the forces that had made their lives unbearable since the pogrom began. '[I]t is gratifying,' wrote Savage, 'that no organized body from amongst the minority ... has ever yet advocated Mr O'Kane's views, and I shall be greatly surprised if any ever shall.'[70]

As it turned out, Savage was only partially correct in his assessment. While Northern Sinn Féiners, like himself, could be counted on to oppose recognition and IPP supporters from the border regions, such as Fermanagh–Tyrone MP Thomas Harbison, were not willing to jeopardise their case before the Boundary Commission by entering the legislature, Belfast was not as 'safe' as it may have appeared. A number of Belfast's Catholic businessmen, including staunch Devlinites Raymond Burke and Hugh Dougal, were known to support nationalist recognition of the Northern parliament but working-class Catholics inhabiting portions of the city that were rife with sectarian violence did not see matters in the same light. Speaking to the Smithfield Branch of the UIL, Alderman John Harkin argued that '[i]f partition was "national suicide"' when the IPP and Sinn Fein decided on non-recognition, 'it was the same vile evil yet'. Intimating that there was 'no guarantee' that 'adoption of the recognition policy would bring peace and security', Harkin concluded that '[s]uch an assertion betrayed complete misunderstanding of the mentality of the mob and its masters'.[71] As this West Belfast division of the UIL was in full agreement with Harkin's view, it was clear that there was serious opposition to O'Kane's proposal to recognise the Northern parliament, even within the ranks of those who considered themselves Devlinites.

Since he stayed clear of the issue publicly, it is impossible to know with certainty how Joe Devlin felt about his colleague's proposal. But, as a self-described 'constitutionalist' who had spent his life 'look[ing] to Parliament for the redress of public grievances',[72] it is reasonable to assume that Joe Devlin would have looked kindly on O'Kane's argument for ending abstention.[73] In addition to the personal convictions that surely made recognising Northern Ireland attractive to the long-time parliamentarian, Belfast publicans, traditionally Devlin supporters, were pushing the MP to enter parliament in order to defend their interests,[74] while his clerical supporters were becoming increasingly worried that continued abstention would endanger Catholic education.[75] Yet, regardless of how appealing recognition would have appeared to him, the controversy O'Kane had caused by merely suggesting this policy change undoubtedly shaped Devlin's response: he remained at Westminster and took no steps to put the recognition plan into action. Nonetheless, the divisive public episode had the effect of associating all of the Devlinites with O'Kane's recognition scheme and further exacerbating the divisions separating Northern nationalists at a time when unity amongst the trapped Northern minority was of the utmost importance.

As the recognition issue was playing out in Belfast, events in Dublin were by no means making matters easier for the Northern minority, who were now finding themselves resigned to the role of bystanders to the Southern game. However, de Valera's decision to establish a new organisation – *Cumann na Poblachta* or League of the Republic – in order to crush the 'humiliating' Treaty did succeed in bringing a particularly scornful reaction from the *Irish News*. Lamenting how empty 'resonant words and beautiful sentiments "launched" in Dublin' were to northern nationalists' 'desperate struggle for existence', the newspaper warned: 'Should the people of the Twenty-Six Counties respond in large numbers to Mr de Valera's invitation, they will make their intention of abandoning 450,000 or 500,000 Nationalists in N.E. Ulster plainer than the proverbial pikestaff.'[76] With the resurgence of violence in the South almost a foregone conclusion, the Devlinite organ once again offered this sage advice to its interested Northern readers:

> Until the Nationalists of the Twenty Six counties have definitely settled the great question that has been forced upon them for solution by a section of themselves, the Nationalists of the Six Counties must stand together in defence of their own interests and spare no thought from the principle of Self-Reliance to the possibility of help from outside their borders. Were the Ireland outside the Six Counties united, all the people of the North-East would be in a wholly different situation. It is hopeless to expect from them that practical assistance that can be rendered only by Government acting on a national mandate and assured of national support. The Nationalists of the N.E. Ulster must

> depend on their own efforts for months to come: they will not be helped but victimized, by any section of the community outside the North-East who think of resorting to unorganized, sporadic, futile methods of resistance to organized and well-armed forces ruthlessly commanded.[77]

Notwithstanding the *Irish News*' desire to champion self-reliance in the fight for Irish unity, by early March any existent political machinery which would have enabled Northern nationalists to defend their interests was being dismantled. The King's speech opening the Northern Ireland parliament made it clear that a serious coercion bill would be introduced during the session.[78] And in continuation of the process that had begun in December 1921, within days of the parliament's opening, seven more nationalist-controlled local councils were suspended for refusing to recognise the government.[79]

Amidst this cloud of uncertainty, March witnessed continued violence against Northern Catholics and an escalation of IRA activity and reprisals. In that context, Michael Farrell argues that pressure exerted on the GHQ of the pro-Treaty IRA over the Northern situation had forced Beggar's Bush to give its Northern Divisions a freer hand in attacking crown forces. As a consequence, on 19 March, Northern Divisions launched attacks on the Maghera RIC Barracks in Derry and the Pomeroy Barracks in Tyrone. These attacks left four Specials dead.[80] On 23 March, two more Specials – Thomas Cunningham and William Cairnside – were killed near Great Victoria Street in Belfast.[81] These incidents led directly to what was, perhaps, the most nefarious and grisly attack committed against Northern Catholics at the time – the murder of the McMahon family.

In a likely retaliation for the murder of the Specials, Owen McMahon – the prosperous owner of the Capstan Bar – three of his sons and a male employee of his bar were killed in the McMahon home on 24 March. Two other McMahon sons survived the attack but a fourth son died of wounds in hospital. The perpetrators of the attack, alleged to have been uniformed members of the USC, prefaced their assault with the ominous warning: 'You boys say your prayers.' No one was ever arrested for the crime.[82]

The McMahon murders, which the *Irish News* noted had occurred 'at a time [1:20 AM] when no civilian dares walk abroad without incurring imminent danger of arrest',[83] sparked immediate outrage among nationalists north and south of the border. The massacre was said to have driven Richard Mulcahy nearly to the point of breaching the Treaty,[84] while equally frustrated, Michael Collins availed himself of the situation for propaganda purposes. Treatyite outrage and condolences may have been appreciated; however, de Valera's effort to speak about the tragedy led to the accusation that he was just 'making fruits of the factions in N.E. Ulster an excuse for his insanity'.[85]

Reacting to the outrage, Joe Devlin, who considered Owen McMahon 'a very close and intimate personal friend', told parliamentarians at Westminster that the attacks were 'a deliberate plot to exterminate the Catholics of Belfast and drive them out of the city'.[86] Devlin's solid reputation as a proponent of non-violent constitutional nationalism brought an ever-sharper focus to a situation that now seemed to face Belfast Catholics.[87] He observed incredulously: 'if Catholics have no revolvers to protect themselves they are murdered. If they have revolvers they are flogged or sentenced to death. Was there ever anything like it in any Christian land?'[88]

Although Colonial Secretary Winston Churchill made short shrift of Devlin's claims in the House of Commons,[89] evidence of Whitehall's growing weariness over Northern conditions and Craig's security apparatus in particular, were made manifest in Thomas Jones' 17 March letter to Lloyd George. This letter clearly outlined the uneasiness that he, as Assistant Cabinet Secretary, and Lionel Curtis, as Colonial Office Advisor on Irish Affairs, felt over Ulster. In particular, Jones questioned Westminster's decisions to continue paying for the USC, to make 'other grants' to Ulster, to allow Craig to cloak 'a military force under the guise of a police force' and to permit Sir Henry Wilson to continue with his aggressive plans for Northern security. Jones added: 'Is it not the duty of the British government to undertake the control of the Border and to remove all justification from the Northern government for these swollen police forces?'[90]

For those like Jones and Curtis, the implications of Craig's security measures were clear. The Northern government had 'assumed the military functions specifically reserved to the British government simply by calling their forces police' and – in addition to their ineffectiveness in stemming the tide of violence – this force would pose a very serious problem if that government refused to accept border changes in the future.[91] During his lengthy speech at Westminster on 28 March, Joe Devlin had drawn a similar conclusion and offered his own solution – disband the Specials and put Belfast under martial law; a tactic which, he claimed, the government had no hesitation in doing 'when there was an odd murder here and there' in the rest of Ireland. Suggesting that there would be 'an absolute uprising amongst the indignant' British taxpayers if they knew how much they were spending to 'maintain a force like that [the Special Constabulary]', the Falls MP called on Britain to establish a religiously mixed police force that was independent of the Northern government.[92]

Devlin was not personally involved in the negotiations but Devlinite ideas about policing had a definite impact on the discussions that led to the second Craig–Collins pact. Businessmen Raymond Burke and Hugh Dougal, both strong supporters of Joe Devlin, had acted as the 'link-men' between the two Irish governments as preparations for this important meeting were taking place and they had even submitted a draft agreement of their own that included provision for a mixed police force.[93] Since the delegations from the Provisional Government and the government of Northern Ireland were slated to return to London on 29 March, the day after Devlin's speech, it seems clear that the Belfast MP was, in part, using the unhappy occasion of the McMahon murders to signal his support for the efforts being made by Burke and Dougal.[94]

Clearly, the situation in Belfast warranted some sort of action from the Provisional Government but it is also evident that Collins and his colleagues were eager to seek some sort of accommodation with the Northern Prime Minster before relations between the Provisional Government and Southern Republicans reached their breaking point. Craig was reluctant to attend the conference but he ultimately did appear and the discussion produced a second pact – a formal agreement countersigned by Great Britain, which triumphantly proclaimed: 'Peace is today declared.' This second Craig–Collins pact provided for the end of IRA activity in Northern Ireland and called on the Northern Prime Minister to use whatever influence he had to facilitate the return of Catholics to the Belfast shipyards. Although Craig's ability to fulfil his part in the bargain depended as much on an improvement in the depressed Northern economy as it did on the political will of the Unionist government, Britain also provided a fund of £500,000 in order to subsidise relief schemes and one-third of this total was intended to aid Northern Catholics. With that said, however, the most ambitious clauses of the pact concerned criminal justice. The pact proposed non-jury trials for crimes related to sectarian incidents and an overhaul of policing in Northern Ireland. Mirroring the ideas presented by Devlin, Burke and Dougal, the pact pushed for Catholic inclusion in the USC and the use of religiously mixed police to conduct searches and patrols in areas of Belfast with mixed populations. In order to facilitate these bold plans, three committees were to be set up: one to administer the relief fund, a second to oversee matters related to policing and a third that was to act as a conciliation committee.[95]

Declaring the sum total of the conference to have been the attainment of 'Far Reaching Proposals To Restore Order and Security', the *Derry Journal* published the agreement in full.[96] To a chorus of cheers in London, Joe Devlin called the talks that led to the pact 'the best day's work ever done for Ireland and for the Empire and for the World'.[97] In a similar vein, the *Irish News* advised readers that, because of the pact, 'the seeds of Peace had been planted' and it was their duty to 'cherish and nourish the new plant'.[98] The newspaper also strongly urged the abandonment of the Northern government's proposed coercion legislation and, as a show of support for the idea of Catholic Specials, it published a recruitment advertisement for the Ulster Constabulary that under other circumstances would have been unthinkable.[99]

Sanguine reactions to the agreement would not last long, however, as the first bloody test of the pact materialised only hours after peace was declared. On 1 April, RIC Constable George Turner was murdered while on patrol near Old Lodge Road in Belfast. If this attack was difficult to justify, then the repercussions of the killing were truly appalling. Witnesses would later report that uniformed men travelling in a Lancia cage car raided homes in the Catholic district of the city, leaving two dead on Stanhope Street and Park Street. The perpetrators then moved on to Arnon Street, where they targeted William Spallen, killing the elderly man in the presence of his grandson and stealing the money Spallen had set aside to cover the cost of his wife's funeral (she had been buried the day before). The perpetrators then proceeded to the neighbouring home of Joseph Walsh, an ex-soldier. The raiding party used a sledgehammer to gain access to the home before turning the instrument on Mr Walsh, whom they found asleep with his two young children.[100] This assault spawned the usual spate of outrage from nationalist Ireland's press and politicians and would go down in history as the Arnon Street massacre.

Notes

1 Hansard does not indicate which MP these comments were directed towards. *Parliamentary Debates,* Commons, 5th ser., vol. 152 (28 March 1922), cols 1282–95.

2 S. Baker, 'Orange and Green', in H.J. Dyos and M. Wolff (eds), *The Victorian City: Images and Realities Volume 2* (London: Routledge & Kegan Paul, 1973), p. 797.

3 A global decline in the price of agricultural products, innovations in other linen producing countries and a post-War downturn in Belfast's shipbuilding industry strangled the Northern Ireland economy throughout the 1920s. Northern Ireland had an unemployment rate of 23 per cent in 1922. P. Buckland, *A History of Northern Ireland* (Dublin: Gill and Macmillan, 1981), pp. 27–8, 34; St J. Ervine, *Craigavon: Ulsterman* (London: George Allen & Unwin Ltd, 1949), p. 440; J. Bardon, *A History of Ulster* (Belfast: The Blackstaff Press, 2001), pp. 515, 523–5.

4 E. Phoenix, *Northern Nationalism: Nationalist Politics, Partition and the Catholic Minority in Northern Ireland, 1890–1940* (Belfast: Ulster Historical Foundation, 1994), p. 141.

5 M. Farrell, *Arming the Protestants: The Formation of the Ulster Special Constabulary and the Royal Ulster Constabulary, 1920–27* (London: Pluto Press, 1983), p. 65.

6 Ibid. p. 90.

7 This figure is based on the estimate tabulated by the Northern government in March 1922 and is frequently cited. See, for instance, D. Kleinrichert, *Republican Internment and the Prison Ship Argenta, 1922* (Dublin: Irish Academic Press, 2001), p. 5; B. Barton, 'Northern Ireland, 1920–25', in J.R. Hill (ed.), *A New History of Ireland VII: Ireland, 1921–84* (Oxford: Oxford University Press, 2003), p. 171; F. O'Donoghue, *No Other Law: The Story of Liam Lynch and the Irish Republican Army, 1916–1923* (Dublin: Irish Press Limited, 1954), p. 248.

8 Kleinrichert, *Republican Internment and the Prison Ship Argenta, 1922,* p. 5.

9 The RIC was disbanded at the end of May in favour of the Royal Ulster Constabulary (RUC). The RUC had 'absorbed' approximately 1,000 RIC officers when it began to function on 1 June 1922. G. Ellison and J. Smyth, *The Crowned Harp: Policing Northern Ireland* (London: Pluto Press, 2000), pp. 18–31. Also see C. Ryder, *The RUC: A Force Under Fire* (London: Methuen, 1989); C. Ryder, *The Fateful Split: Catholics and the Royal Irish Constabulary* (London: Methuen Publishing Limited, 2004).

10 P. Canning, *British Policy Towards Ireland, 1921–1941* (Oxford: Clarendon Press, 1985), p. 58.

11 Kleinrichert, *Republican Internment and the Prison Ship Argenta,* p. 4.

12 M. Hopkinson, 'From Treaty to Civil War, 1921–2', in J.R. Hill (ed.), *A New History of Ireland VII: Ireland, 1921–84* (Oxford: Oxford University Press, 2003), p. 24. According to Rafferty, the Northern government refused to disclose how many members of the USC were drawn from the UVF. O. Rafferty, *Catholicism in Ulster, 1603–1983: An Interpretative History* (London: Hurst & Company, 1994), p. 216.

13 In March 1922, the USC had approximately 32,000 members and by June the number had reached as high as 48,000. Rafferty has argued that before the end of 1922 there was one armed agent of the Northern government for every two adult male members of the Catholic minority. Rafferty, *Catholicism in Ulster*, p. 219. Also see Farrell, *Arming the Protestants*, p. 144.

14 Between 6 December 1921 and the end of May 1922, 147 Catholics and seventy-three Protestants were killed in Belfast and thirty others lost their lives outside the city. M. Hopkinson, 'The Craig–Collins Pacts of 1922: Two Attempted Reforms of the Northern Ireland Government', *Irish Historical Studies* 27, 106 (November 1990), p. 145.

15 Farrell, *Arming the Protestants*, pp. 92, 322.

16 Barton, 'Northern Ireland, 1920–25', p. 177; M. Harris, *The Catholic Church and the Foundation of the Northern Irish State* (Cork: Cork University Press, 1993), p. 109.

17 Collins had relayed this to a friend of Dillon's at the end of January, 1922. Cited by Hepburn, *Catholic Belfast and Nationalist Ireland in the Era of Joe Devlin*, p. 233.

18 Hopkinson, 'The Craig–Collins Pacts of 1922', p. 147.

19 M. Farrell, *Arming the Protestants*, p. 91.

20 D. Rabinowitz, 'The Palestinian Citizens of Israel, the Concept of Trapped Minority and the Discourse of Transnationalism in Anthropology', *Ethnic and Racial Studies* 24, 2 (2001), p. 77.

21 *Irish News*, 23 January 1922.

22 Ibid.

23 Hopkinson, 'The Craig–Collins Pacts of 1922', p. 148.

24 Phoenix, *Northern Nationalism*, p. 176.

25 Hopkinson, 'The Craig–Collins Pacts of 1922', p. 148; Phoenix, *Northern Nationalism*, p. 179; J. Dooher, 'Tyrone Nationalism and the Question of Partition, 1910–25' (M. Phil. thesis, University of Ulster, 1986), p. 409.

26 'Vigorous Protest from Newry, South Down, and South Armagh', n.d., J.H. Collins Papers, D 921/4/1/7, Public Record Office of Northern Ireland, Belfast.

27 Ibid.

28 Ibid.

29 Rabinowitz, 'Trapped Minority', p. 74.

30 O'Shiel was born in Tyrone but made his career in the South. At this juncture he was a legal advisor to the Provisional Government. As cited by Phoenix, *Northern Nationalism*, p. 171.

31 Hopkinson, 'From Treaty to Civil War, 1921–2', p. 27; Phoenix, *Northern Nationalism*, p. 177.

32 *Irish News*, 4 February 1922.

33 How Collins and Craig could have held such different views on this key matter and, nevertheless, come to an agreement in January, is somewhat baffling. The 4 February edition of the *Irish Times* noted: 'The astonishing thing is that the two Irish leaders could have met for five minutes in London without discovering that someone had blundered.' A letter from Mrs Churchill to her husband seems to offer a suggestion as to who that *someone* may have been. She wrote: 'Surely the P.M. must have misled Collins over the Ulster boundary? I do hope Craig will not think he has been treated in a slippery way.' Hopkinson, 'The Craig–Collins Pacts of 1922', p. 149.

34 Phoenix, *Northern Nationalism*, p. 180.

35 *Irish News*, 3 February 1922.

36 Ibid.

37 *Parliamentary Debates*, Northern Ireland House of Commons, vol. 17 (21 November 1934), col. 73, http://stormontpapers.ahds.ac.uk/search.html (accessed 23 July 2019); Buckland, *A History of Northern Ireland*, p. 34.

38 For an examination of this issue, see M. Harris, *The Catholic Church and the Foundation of the Northern Irish State*, pp. 110–24.

39 According to Dooher, the fact that 'responsible educated people were prepared to risk their jobs and future prospects in such a protest seemed to augment the extent of Catholic alienation'. The non-recognition experiment cost the Provisional Government as much as £18,000 each month. Dooher, 'Tyrone Nationalism and the Question of partition, 1910–25', pp. 427–9.

40 Harris, *The Catholic Church and the Foundation of the Northern Irish State*, p. 119.

41 H. McCartan, 'North Eastern Boundary Bureau. Report on Visit to Belfast and Derry', n.d., Department of the Taoiseach, NAI/TSCH/S 2027, North East Boundary Secret Documents 1922–4, National Archives of Ireland, Dublin.

42 According to Eoin O'Duffy, IRA Chief-of-Staff, the 'erection of scaffold and the bringing of the hangman into the prison was the culminating point'. *Derry Journal*, 10 February 1922.

43 FitzAlan remained Lord Lieutenant of Ireland until the Irish Free State was formally constituted in December 1922. The Lord Lieutenancy was replaced in Northern Ireland by a Governorship and the King's representative in the Irish Free State became known as the Governor General.

44 Collins hid his involvement in these border disturbances from both Britain and his own moderate allies. C. Day, 'Political violence in the Newry/Armagh area 1912–1925' (PhD diss., Queen's University, Belfast, 1999), p. 245.

45 Ironically, these raids began after FitzAlan intervened on behalf of the Derry men. *Derry Journal*, 10 February 1922.

46 Captain Charles Craig was the brother of Northern Ireland Prime Minister James Craig.

47 *Parliamentary Debates*, Commons, 5th ser., vol. 150 (8 February 1922), cols 1282–95.

48 The *Irish News* printed a transcript of the debate but did not discuss it editorially. *Irish News*, 9 February 1922.

49 Although space does not allow the issue to be fully explored here, this was a very significant constitutional convention which gave the government of Northern Ireland far greater latitude than was specified in the Better Government of Ireland Act. This ruling was one of the reasons why, as Paul Arthur has suggested, the British government was able to 'quarantine the Irish issue from British politics' in later years and how Northern Ireland went from being a devolved government with limited powers to being 'a self-governing province with some of the trappings of sovereignty'. P. Arthur, *Special Relationships: Britain, Ireland and the Northern Ireland Problem* (Belfast: Blackstaff Press, 2000), pp. 18–30.

50 The contentious point here regards the question of who shot first. The nationalist press tended to run with the statement issued by the IRA Liaison Office, which claimed that Fitzpatrick was shot from behind after demanding that the Specials surrender, while contemporary Unionist sources – citing the report given by USC Headquarters – described the incident as an IRA ambush. For the text of the contemporary statements, see the *Fermanagh Herald*, 18 February 1922.

51 They had actually been in the Free State for approximately thirty miles and passed through the town of Monaghan (the county's principal commercial centre) before the confrontation at Clones Junction. See the *Derry Journal*, 13 February 1922.

52 Farrell, *Arming the Protestants*, p. 93.

53 Wilson's selection notice appeared in the *Derry Journal*, 13 February 1922.

54 Although Collins denounced the kidnapping of Ulster loyalists, he had in fact postponed the mission in order to meet with Craig on 2 February.

55 *Irish News*, 13 February 1922.

56 Ibid.

57 Farrell, *Arming the Protestants*, p. 3; *Irish News*, 13 February 1922.

58 This phrase appeared in a 5 January article of the *Irish News*, which blamed 'the "authorities"' for inciting violence and protecting Protestant rioters.

59 M. Elliott, *The Catholics of Ulster: A History* (London: Penguin Books, 2000), p. 375; Rafferty, *Catholicism in Ulster*, p. 217.

60 The poem was dated 12 March 1922. Emphasis in the original. *Irish News*, 14 March 1922.

61 According to Peter Hart, 'the desire to protect "our people"... drove GHQ efforts thereafter'. P. Hart, *Mick: The Real Michael Collins* (London: Penguin Books Ltd, 2006), p. 382.

62 The Irish Free State (Agreement) Bill gave legal force to the Anglo-Irish Treaty. Despite some angry words, it easily passed by a margin of 302 to 60 on 8 March. Canning, *British Policy Towards Ireland*, p. 32; K. Matthews, *Fatal Influence: The Impact of Ireland on British Politics, 1920–1925* (Dublin: University College of Dublin Press, 2004), pp. 70–1.

63 Quick to seize on the constitutional convention limiting discussion of Northern Ireland at Westminster, on three occasions during this speech, Devlin's political opponents asked the Speaker to rule him out of order but the Speaker ruled that Devlin was 'speaking in reply to taunts of other Members from Northern Ireland who [had] directed attention entirely to certain happenings in Southern

Ireland'. *Parliamentary Debates*, Commons, 5th ser., vol. 152 (16 February 1922), cols 1365–6.

64 *Parliamentary Debates*, Commons, 5th ser., vol. 152 (16 February 1922), cols 1360–72.

65 If the Republicans did gain control of the government, General Macready was prepared to side-step the Provisional Government and declare martial law in the South. Canning, *British Policy Towards Ireland*, p. 32.

66 J. Curran, *The Birth of the Irish Free State, 1921–1923* (n. p.: University of Alabama Press, 1980), p. 179.

67 Ibid.

68 Farrell, *Arming the Protestants*, p. 94.

69 *Irish News*, 13 March 1922.

70 Ibid., 18 March 1922. In response to Savage's letter, O'Kane published his own rebuttal in the *Irish News* on 20 March and Savage reciprocated on 21 March. *Irish News*, 20, 21 March 1922.

71 Phoenix, *Northern Nationalism*, pp. 193–4.

72 These references are drawn from a speech Devlin gave after the murder of Owen McMahon, a close friend, and his family two weeks later. The events surrounding that incident and Devlin's speech are examined elsewhere in this chapter. *Parliamentary Debates*, Commons, 5th ser., vol. 152 (28 March 1922), cols 1282–8.

73 Phoenix, *Northern Nationalism*, p. 193. O'Kane was very active in the UIL and he later served as the joint leader, with Gerald Kennedy, of a Devlinite deputation that met with Eoin MacNeill in the spring of 1923. These activities indicate that he was a trusted confidant of Devlin and suggest that he would not have initiated this controversial debate without discussing it with Devlin beforehand. *Irish News*, 12, 20 March, 28 August 1922; Phoenix, *Northern Nationalism*, p. 283; Joseph P. O'Kane and J. Gerald Kennedy to President Cosgrave, 11 April 1923, Department of the Taoiseach, NAI/TSCH/S 2027, North East Boundary Secret Documents 1922–4, National Archives of Ireland, Dublin.

74 The fear that the Craig government would impose prohibition, or 'local veto', on Northern Ireland had been very strong in 1921 and the *Irish News* frequently published news regarding prohibition efforts around the world. For instance, see the *Irish News*, 3 March, 7 April, 17 September 1921.

75 Phoenix, *Northern Nationalism*, p. 172.

76 *Irish News*, 16 March 1922.

77 Ibid.

78 On the occasion of the speech, Craig heightened nationalist fears by suggesting that the impending legislation would be, as paraphrased by the *Irish News*, 'one of the most drastic [pieces of legislation] ever proposed in any Parliament; it will mean Martial Law, with the fatal distinction that the powers vested in passably impartial military authority after Martial Law has been proclaimed are to be exercised by civil officials in whom a large and increasing minority of the people have not a particle of confidence'. *Irish News*, 15 March 1922.

79 Farrell, *Arming the Protestants*, p. 97.

80 Ibid., p. 100.

81 A. Parkinson, *Belfast's Unholy War: The Troubles of the 1920s* (Dublin: Four Courts Press Ltd., 2004), p. 229.

82 Parkinson, *Belfast's Unholy War*, pp. 230–1.

83 *Irish News*, 27 March 1922. A night-time curfew had been in effect since August 1920. For the details related to the implementation of the curfew see Ryder, *The Fateful Split*, p. 18.

84 Farrell, *Arming the Protestants*, p. 100.

85 *Irish News*, 30 March 1922.

86 *Parliamentary Debates*, Commons, 5th ser., vol. 152 (28 March 1922), cols 1282–8.

87 Parkinson, *Belfast's Unholy War*, p. 236.

88 *Parliamentary Debates*, Commons, 5th ser., vol. 152 (28 March 1922), cols 1285–6.

89 After expressing disgust at the murder of the McMahon family, the Colonial Secretary noted that he could 'find other instances in other places in Ireland equaling it in horror'. Indicating that government policy in Ireland was to carry out the Treaty and defending Ulster, Churchill noted: 'What Englishmen, Scotsmen, and Welshmen are asking themselves is: Why is it that Irishmen will go on doing these things to one another?' *Parliamentary Debates*, Commons, 5th ser., vol. 152 (28 March 1922), cols 1290–2. Churchill's rebuttal had a much greater impact on Austen Chamberlain than did Devlin's remarks. In a letter to the King on 29 March, Chamberlain noted that the House of Commons 'listened with marked and almost breathless attention' to Churchill's claim that Englishmen and Scotsmen could not understand Irish factionalism. Austen Chamberlain to King George V, 29 March 1922, in M. Gilbert (ed.), *Winston S. Churchill: Volume IV Companion Part 3 Documents April 1921–November 1922* (London: William Heinemann Ltd, 1977), p. 1837.

90 K. Middlemas (ed.), *Thomas Jones Whitehall Diary, Volume III, Ireland, 1918–25* (London: Oxford University Press, 1971), p. 195.

91 Farrell, *Arming the Protestants*, pp. 97–8.

92 *Parliamentary Debates*, Commons, 5th ser., vol. 152 (28 March 1922), cols 1289–90.

93 Staunton, *The Nationalists of Northern Ireland*, p. 74; Farrell, *Arming the Protestants*, pp.105–6.

94 The minutes of the conference do not make any mention of Devlin or his speech. 'Irish Conference Minutes, 30 March 1922', in Gilbert, *Winston S. Churchill: Volume IV Companion Part 3*, pp. 1837–9.

95 Hopkinson, 'The Craig–Collins Pacts of 1922', p. 150.

96 *Derry Journal*, 31 March 1922.

97 Ibid.

98 Ibid.

99 Ibid.

100 Parkinson, *Belfast's Unholy War*, pp. 245–6.

CHAPTER 5

'Hope Deferred': The Northern Advisory Committee and Continued Instability in Ireland

> The course of events in the Twenty-six counties has had a deplorable influence on the fortunes of the minority in the North-East. Now it seems likely that an attempt will be made to exploit the situation here for the advantage of the section who have bent themselves to the creation and promotion of anarchy in the three-and-a-half provinces outside the 'Northern Area.' Half a dozen persons can create trouble on the 'Border'... Then 'raids' will take place; 'reprisals' will be exacted; innocent blood will be shed; deeds of ruthless barbarity will be recorded and the apostles of anarchy from Dublin to Cork and Castlebar will proclaim to the Four Winds of Erin that a dastardly Free State Government have abandoned the nationalists of North-East Ulster to a horrible fate! It is a cruel and conscienceless device: but it is in operation.
>
> – *Irish News,* 4 April, 1922[1]

In the aftermath of the grizzly Arnon Street murders, Michael Collins pushed for an inquiry to test his agreement with the Northern Prime Minister, Sir James Craig. It is likely that the massacre also had a role in the Provisional Government's decision to establish a Northern Advisory Committee, comprised of Ulster nationalist leaders, to advise Dublin on key Northern matters. This short-lived committee had been struck amidst escalating tensions in both parts of Ireland and the minutes from its inaugural 11 April 1922 meeting provide a rare glimpse at the rapport, or lack thereof, which existed between the Provisional Government and its Northern Sinn Féin supporters. Placing its first focus on this sometimes acrimonious meeting among pro-Treaty Sinn Féiners, this chapter demonstrates how the onset of partition had created differing conditions in the North and South of Ireland and how those differing conditions had contributed to divergent priorities. The remainder of the chapter analyses how the anti-partitionist press, its correspondents and the leaders of Northern Ireland's trapped nationalist minority reacted to the security measures introduced in Northern Ireland and the further slide towards civil war between pro- and anti-Treaty factions in the South.

The Northern Advisory Committee had been brought together ostensibly to solicit Northern views on the second Craig–Collins pact and the implications that the Arnon Street murders would have on its implementation but the talks turned to more general points of policy as well. It is telling that committee participants were drawn exclusively from Northern Sinn Féin ranks – a decision that was likely informed by advice received from Frank Aiken, the influential OC of the 4th Northern Division, who warned Collins not to 'recognize Joe Devlin or his clique' in his dealing with Ulster.[2]

Collins opened the discussion by asking the Northern members how forcefully the Provisional Government should push Belfast for an inquiry into the Arnon Street murders.[3] This was a pointed question and the Chairman of the Provisional Government no doubt hoped for a direct answer. However, on this question, as on many others, the Northern members of the committee responded by sharing their detailed accounts of the Northern government's continued raiding of nationalists' homes and the hard-handed approach of the Specials. These digressions were certainly related to the question that Collins had raised but did not go far in providing an answer.

Attempting to steer the discussion back to the question posed, Collins outlined the alternatives as he saw them. They could (1) convene an inquiry without Belfast, forcing Britain to either send a representative or accept the findings or (2) push the matter to breaking point with Craig. If they could convince Belfast to cooperate with the inquiry, cease the raiding and release their political prisoners, Collins argued, then it would be worthwhile to maintain the pact; otherwise it would be prudent to break it.[4] At this point, Bishop Joseph MacRory observed: '[T]hose people in Brown Square Barracks [those implicated in the murders] are very much "in the know" in Belfast'[5] and are therefore unmolested; 'you will get no inquiry from Craig'.[6] Solicitor George Murnaghan, equally sceptical of Belfast's commitment to the agreement, added that the 'raiding and arresting' in his own district – Omagh, County Tyrone – had actually worsened since the March pact.[7] 'I think this is a test case,' said Murnaghan, 'we should press to the breaking point on this matter.'[8] Recognising that the discussion had been by and large a dialogue between Collins, Bishop MacRory and Murnaghan, and preoccupied with a differing set of political priorities, it was at this juncture that Arthur Griffith reprimanded the reticent Northern representatives.

> It seems to me your lordships and gentlemen, you are all here from the area affected. What we want is guidance as to your opinions. In fact, only one or two of you gentlemen have yet spoken. We are sitting here as a cockshot for our political opponents and we are trying to defend the people of the north east, and our political opponents then come along and call us traitors. We are quite prepared for that, but we want to know exactly where do you stand. We called you together to get your opinions. We have not got your opinion. [9]

There is little doubt that Griffith's overriding concern throughout the entire exchange was to make sure that the Northern nationalists took some responsibility for the policy that the Provisional Government would ultimately adopt. When Belfast Doctor Russell McNabb asked how Dublin was prepared to aid the Northern nationalists in the event of the pact's failure, he, too, was chided. Griffith retorted: 'You must take some responsibility, not leaving us here to be attacked by Mr de Valera and his friends, and then some people in the North East saying they were never consulted.'[10]

Griffith's gruff response could not mask the fact that the Northern nationalists – especially those who resided in Belfast – were vulnerable.[11] According to Francis MacArdle, they were becoming ever-more ghettoised[12] – 'huddled in the Falls'[13] to use MacRory's phrase – and, as Father Hassan noted, 'on their last legs'.[14] What could be done about the situation in Belfast remained to be seen; however, some representatives, like Dr McNabb, advocated a return to the 'beautiful fires' which he claimed had made matters uncomfortable for the Unionists. The problem, as McNabb saw it, was that Catholic areas were now disarmed, 'searched daily' and could no longer put up a fight.[15] Collins acknowledged that the Protestants 'think a great deal more about property than human life' but he had evidently not been satisfied with McNabb's suggestion and he returned to the question that he would ask with some regularity: 'What is the proposal?'[16] This was indeed an excellent question. If lack of arms and free movement blocked a return to property destruction – a proposal which Griffith, Mulcahy[17] and others were leery of even if it were possible – and if the military position was 'impossible' in Belfast,[18] as Seamus Woods would report – then what could be done?

Although it would permeate much of the disparate discussions, it is in this context that the committee's consideration of policing and, in particular, the recruitment of Catholic Specials, should be viewed. The March pact had advocated the recruitment of Catholics into the police force but, as these interactions would illustrate, this would not be an easy proposal to sell. A number of Northern representatives seemed supportive of the idea to send Catholic nationalists into the police force but were torn by fears that this would interfere with the non-recognition programme which had been in effect since before the Mansion House Conference of December 1921.[19] This conflict of objectives was immediately recognised by Bishop MacRory:

> The mixed parts of Belfast would benefit immensely by the arrangement made in this pact that there would be as much [*sic*] Catholics in the raiding parties as Protestants and in searching for arms … I am quite convinced that Catholic Specials would be useful if we have them. I see, on the other hand, that we are acknowledging the Northern Government by setting them up.[20]

Largely echoing what J.P. O'Kane had had to say in his UIL speech, Kevin O'Higgins, then Minister of Economics, attempted to quash this concern by shifting attention onto the Treaty settlement that all present claimed to support. 'The Treaty recognises the Northern Parliament and until such time as the boundary commission sits it recognizes the jurisdiction of the Northern Parliament,' insisted O'Higgins adding, 'anyone who stands on the Treaty would be inconsistent in saying that he did not recognize the Northern Parliament'.[21] Realising the way this comment would be received, Richard Mulcahy immediately added that the recognition which O'Higgins alluded to meant only that they 'recognise that Parliament in order to destroy it'.[22] If this was indeed the case, MacRory retorted, then the proposal might actually 'strike a blow'[23] for the Catholics of Belfast. Still not convinced, however, Dr Gillespie maintained that 'nothing will give the Northern Parliament greater recognition than a thing like this'.[24] Gillespie's scepticism, in spite of the reassurance offered, was enough to bring on another attack from an obviously irritated Arthur Griffith who, by virtue of these comments, seemed completely out of touch with what life was like in the North.

> I don't see where the question comes in of recognizing the Northern Parliament by your joining the police force. I don't see how you recognise it more than you do at present as you are living there. This arrangement is provisional until the Northern parliament and the provisional Government meet together and see can a basis be found [*sic*] for unity. If that can't be done the matter reverse [*sic*] to its original position. It's a temporary provision during the present time. I do say that *some of the gentlemen who are giving their opinions now should have gone to London and given their opinions there.* And not be leaving all the responsibility on us.[25]

Notwithstanding that both factions of the Northern nationalist minority were relegated, by the Southern leadership, to the role of bystanders to the events in London, Griffith's outburst sparked no rejoinder from the Northern representatives. Rather, this aspect of the discussion ended with George Murnaghan's observation that sooner or later, at least some of Northern Ireland would have to be recognised as such, once the Boundary Commission had awarded its settlement.[26]

Aside from the obvious defensive reason that made the idea of Catholic Specials palatable for MacRory and others, there were other reasons to support the idea as well. For instance, Francis MacArdle had suggested earlier in the exchange that having Catholics in the police force could give Northern nationalists access to arms,[27] while Murnaghan saw it as a way to gather intelligence. They could 'go in just to keep their eyes open and see what is going on', he advised.[28]

Whatever the reasons were for accepting the plan, some attention would also have to be given to making sure that – to quote Murnaghan – the 'proper men' got into the force.[29] Above all, there was a need to prevent Craig from filling his suggested Catholic quota with what MacRory called the 'chums of the Black-and-Tans' – Southern Catholics who had distinguished themselves in defence of the realm during the Anglo-Irish War.[30] As the Northern representatives at this meeting were all Sinn Féin advocates, there was also some noticeable uneasiness over the prospect that Joe Devlin's supporters would join the force but, despite the persistence of the IPP–Sinn Féin rivalry, Devlin had some defenders. For instance, Archdeacon Tierney argued that they would 'get good enough men from Devlin's rank' as he sought to vouch for the respectability and patriotism of the Devlinites.[31] Concern over who was likely to be drawn to the force also served to highlight the fact that certain political opponents had already repudiated the plan. According to McNabb, supporters of de Valera in Belfast had issued a statement which threatened that Catholics who joined the Specials should be 'shot at sight'.[32] And, despite Eoin O'Duffy's suggestion that the 'cream of the flying column'[33] should be sent into the Specials, there was palpable disbelief that any members of the IRA would consider joining the force, even if they could be slipped by the scrutiny of the Northern government.[34]

The question of Catholic Specials was left up in the air, pending the outcome of Collins' effort to secure an inquiry into the Arnon Street murders. The future of the pact really rested on this question, so the committee ultimately decided that it would not be in their best interest to break the pact and opted instead to back Collins' suggestion that they continue to push hard for an inquiry, demand the end to aggressive police activities and work for the release of the political prisoners. The discussion then turned to the question of local government.

As Minister for Local Government, William Cosgrave took the leading role in the equally animated discussions that followed. At issue here was the future of the local councils which, following the Fermanagh County Council, had been dissolved and replaced by Commissioners for refusing to recognise the Northern parliament – a plan that had come from Sinn Féin's Southern leadership. Here Cosgrave all but admitted the failure of the 'Local Government war', complained that Northern bodies had made unreasonable economic requests of his Ministry and urged the members of these councils to reverse their policy and apply for reinstatement by the Northern government.[35]

Given the rancorous debate over recognition in the context of policing, it was not surprising that Cosgrave's suggestion was not well received. In this context, Cahir Healy, a member of the dissolved Fermanagh Council, squared off against the Minister:

> They [nationalist councils] were put out of existence for recognizing An Dáil and to-day we hear the Dáil recommends a policy of surrender. It may be a good policy, but it is not a palatable one. It is rather a humiliating position to be put into that they should go back now without apparently any new circumstances. If anybody is to put that into force it should be An Dáil.[36]

As was the case with policing, Healy's bitter exchange with Cosgrave over local government says much about the way in which the Northern representatives viewed their contribution to the anti-partition policy of the Provisional Government. They had been asked by the Provisional Government to engage in a non-recognition campaign and, as Archdeacon Tierney had noted, they had made 'great sacrifices' for the fulfilment of Dublin's policy[37] but now they were being accused of making unreasonable requests of the Provisional Government and they were being urged to give in to Belfast because the strategy no longer served Dublin's interests. This was an example of double marginality writ large.

Although Cosgrave may have been correct in suggesting that 'the situation had altered since the Treaty' was signed,[38] the Northern representatives on the Advisory Council were still very much attached to the 'little experiment'[39] and it was decided in the end that the affected bodies should come together and decide their fate as a group. Before the meeting had concluded, however, the discussion would turn once again to the topic of recognition – this time in the context of education. Unlike the previous exchanges on the matter, those who spoke on the issue of education – primarily Archdeacon Tierney and Bishop McKenna – seemed resigned to the fact that Dublin could not continue to fund the Northern teachers and also seemed to see the practicality in recognising the Northern parliament in the limited realm of education without much protest.[40] By all accounts, the protection of Catholic education was a very high priority for Northern nationalism and eventually the Northern schools would reach an accommodation with Belfast.[41] The high priority of this issue might account for the different atmosphere in which the idea of recognising the Northern government's jurisdiction over education was received during the Advisory Committee meeting; however, following the heated exchange over recognition in the context of policing and local government, the Northern delegates may also have seen the writing on the wall.

Even a perfunctory glance at the minutes of this Northern Advisory Committee meeting would bear out Clare O'Halloran's observation that the Southern leadership was 'unsympathetic' to the Northern minority – both the pro-Treaty Sinn Féiners like themselves and the Devlinites.[42] Given the clear drift towards civil war in the South, perhaps Arthur Griffith's overriding desire to have the Northern delegates share the responsibility for his government's Northern policy could be excused, as could the increasingly irritated way in which he and Michael Collins struggled to get clear answers to the questions they raised. Northern dithering might also be understandable when one considers that while Dublin may have been perched on edge of war, the nationalists of Northern Ireland had been on the front lines of a very different war since partition. As Alec MacNeill – a young transplanted Belfast Catholic from Michael McLaverty's semi-autobiographical novel *Call My Brother Back* – lamented after witnessing the sectarian outrages of the early 1920s: 'In the South they have to fight one war and that's a political one. Here we have to fight a religious and a political one.'[43]

Whether the members of the Northern Advisory Committee were willing to admit it or not, it was painfully clear that partition had created very different conditions in the two parts of the island and because of these different conditions, the political priorities of Irish nationalism were diverging. In the North, Joe Devlin and his supporters were perhaps quicker to recognise this divergence than were the Northern Sinn Féiners. The Devlinites' earlier attempt to get Northern nationalists to recognise the Northern government bears this out, as does the *Irish News*' close monitoring of Southern conditions in a way which clearly and consistently linked Northern conditions with Southern instability. On the latter point, it is worth noting that on the very day that the Northern delegation of Sinn Féin supporters were in Dublin discussing the pact, the *Irish News* chose to focus its editorial on the worsening conditions in the South, exhorting patience, courage and clear-headed statesmanship. The paper cited the last lines of M.J. Barry's 'Bide Your Time' in warning: 'Danger makes the brave man steady/Rashness is the coward's crime/ Tranquil be – but ever ready/Calm and patient, Bide Your Time.'[44]

The use of this poetic call for discipline, written by a member of the Young Irelanders, was surely intended by the *Irish News* to evoke memories of the ill-planned and poorly executed Young Ireland revolt of 1848, which resulted in the scattering and incapacitation of a once vibrant national movement because of its lack of restraint. To be more specific, the *Irish News*' reference to the poem was most certainly directed at Rory O'Connor who, as a leading spokesman for the newly established IRA Executive, seemed far too willing to squander the gains of the Treaty and the sympathy of the world with the imposition of what the *Derry Journal* indelicately called 'a touch of Mexican politics'.[45] Regardless, in a bold step, on 13 April, the IRA Executive seized the Four Courts, making it a republican base of operations.[46] O'Connor's apparent unwillingness to 'bide his time' caused political instability in Dublin and, because of the pressure that this exerted on Collins and the uncertainty it caused Craig, the *Irish News* claimed, with some justification, that repercussions were also felt in Northern Ireland.[47]

The Arnon Street Massacre, which the Northern Advisory Committee had spent so much time discussing, was but one example of the continued disturbances which gripped Belfast. Many more incidents had followed Arnon Street, leaving behind both Protestant and Catholic victims. With this in mind, on 7 April, the Belfast Catholic Protection Committee – a propaganda organisation established by Bishop MacRory[48] – sent telegrams to both Winston Churchill and Michael Collins protesting the 'desperate' position of the city's minority population since the signing of the pact and giving a detailed list of deaths and injuries incurred by Catholics.[49] Much to the dismay of Northern Catholics, James Craig's government approached security during the first weeks of the pact's existence in much the same way that they had in the past – through heavy-handed policing that included the destruction of roads, bridges and homes.[50] Perhaps more galling for the Catholic community were such matters as the uneven administration of justice with respect to firearms offences[51] and allegations that claimed ill-treatment of Northern priests and clerics. On this second point, the *Fermanagh Herald* reported several incidents which implicated the Specials in the unreasonable search of priests and parishioners on their way to church, interference with the conduct of church services and the raiding of and theft from homes belonging to prominent priests like Sinn Féin advocate Father Eugene Coyle.[52] The worst of these incidents would occur in June, when the elderly Cardinal Logue and his Coadjutor Bishop O'Donnell were roughly searched at gun-point on two separate occasions.[53]

In this atmosphere in which trust, transparency and fair play were rare commodities, the second Craig–Collins pact had little chance for success. Collins would continue to use the idea of an inquiry into the outrages as a 'diplomatic weapon'[54] but a series of IRA hostage takings and border raids in April served to show that the commitment of some pro-Treatyites to the agreement was suspect. Moreover, Collins was unable to bring an end to the boycott that had been re-imposed by the anti-Treatyites.[55] Likewise, Craig – who was often 'subverted' by Richard Dawson Bates, his sectarian Minister of Home Affairs[56] – released very few prisoners and made no greater effort to earnestly make the pact work than did his Southern adversary.[57] As a consequence, the machinery of the accord failed to function. In fact, only the relief committee performed its duties and it was plagued by issues related to the proper representation of the interested parties. While it continued to occupy discussions until the beginning of the Irish Civil War, the second Craig–Collins agreement was, practically speaking, all but dead by the end of April.[58]

Having failed to get results from either his non-recognition programme or his diplomatic negotiations with Craig, Michael Collins' Northern policy took on a new form in May and June – coercion. Although both Collins and de Valera had each pledged not to coerce Ulster into political unity on numerous occasions, the plans for a Northern offensive had been in the works since early spring and, significantly, this offensive was to include both factions of the divided IRA.[59] Supplies and provisions for the attack were to come from IRA divisions outside Northern territory but action was to take place away from the border and to be carried out by IRA units from within Northern Ireland.

The Northern offensive and the security crackdown that followed made May the bloodiest month yet. During a short fifteen-day period, the IRA set forty-two large fires causing some £500,000 of damage to Unionist-owned property in both Belfast and the rural countryside.[60] Amidst the carnage of the incendiary campaign, the 2nd Northern Division launched attacks on police barracks in Derry and Tyrone, which were followed on 18 May by the raid on the Musgrave Street Barracks (the HQ of the Belfast police).[61] By the end of the month, as many as seventy-five lives had been lost in the North and, significantly, Northern Ireland Unionist MP William Twaddell was among the victims.[62] Despite the extent of the destruction, however, the offensive was a debacle. Many of the arms and munitions from the South did not make it into the theatre of operations in time.[63] Very few Southern volunteers were able to take part in the action and those who took part in the raid on the Musgrave Street barracks – the *coup de théâtre* that was supposed to begin the offensive – barely escaped with their lives.[64]

As had been the case with the kidnapping of prominent Unionists in February, the *Irish News* was unaware of Michael Collins' involvement in the 'catalogue of horrors'[65] that had befallen Belfast and responded to the events by asking: 'Who are playing these hideous pranks with the very existence of 450,000 men, women and children in the Six Counties?'[66] Seriously doubting the prospect that the action was taken 'in the name of Sinn Fein', the *Irish News* strongly urged the Provisional Government to repudiate the actions of the provocateurs, adding, '[i]t is easier to evoke the demon of bloodshed and lawlessness than to exorcise it'.[67] Hugh McCartan, the Provisional Government's representative in County Down, later observed that the hostilities only served to 'embitter feeling and place the Catholic population at the mercy of the Specials'.[68]

The Northern offensive had succeeded in raising the ire of some anti-partitionists in the North and its military advantages were minimal. Michael Collins and Richard Mulcahy had clearly been active participants in the operation and the whole Treaty settlement would have been in jeopardy had their activities been detected.[69] Thus, the motivation for engaging in such a risky endeavour has been a source of some speculation.[70] Whether Collins and Mulcahy were motivated by a desire to offer some protection to the Northern Catholics or by a last-ditch effort to find some form of accommodation with the anti-Treaty Party, the political ramifications of the Northern offensive would prove to be catastrophic for the Northern minority. The Northern government's willingness to wield its recently acquired coercion legislation – the Civil Authorities (Special Powers) Act – would now be the source of nationalist discomfort.

The Special Powers Act was introduced in March and was given royal assent on 7 April. Often called the 'flogging bill' in nationalist lore,[71] the draconian Special Powers Act gave Sir Richard Dawson Bates, the Minister for Home Affairs, the power to conduct searches or seize property without warrants, suspend *habeas corpus*, prevent inquests, proscribe organisations and newspapers, ban meetings, impose or tighten curfews, block transportation routes, destroy buildings and flog individuals convicted of firearms offences.[72] These exceedingly wide powers were augmented after the burning of Shane's Castle[73] and the murder of William Twaddell by the imposition of internment for political crimes. Armed with these two political weapons, the Northern government began to put an effective end to the insurgency. The night-time curfew was extended, nationalist organisations such as the IRA, IRB and Cumann na mBan[74] were outlawed, transportation routes across the border were destroyed and the USC were active on virtually on every street corner.[75] During the early stages of Northern Ireland's counter-insurgency effort, the *Irish News* ominously observed that the Protestants were 'armed to the teeth' and that: 'If a citizen covets a deadly weapon and is able to walk, he need only apply for admission to the ranks of the "C" Specials. Even if he is aged and vulnerable, or a cripple, Sir Dawson Bates has thoughtfully provided for his case.'[76]

If the experience of ex-serviceman Jack McCusker of Belfast in any way represented the methods of the Specials, the *Irish News*' critique of their actions was well warranted. According to McCusker's letter to an unidentified Belfast priest, on the evening of 26 May, an unruly and inebriated group of Specials broke into his home, ransacked his furnishings and terrorised his family, before dragging him and another ex-soldier (John Turner) to their Lancia cage car. While they were being held – fully expecting to be murdered – the Specials smashed religious items, destroyed his photographs of Joe Devlin and the Pope and harassed an elderly neighbour. McCusker credited the chance arrival of the District Inspector for saving his life. Claiming never to have 'seen the Germans carrying on in such a dirty and brutal manner', McCusker maintained that 'loyal Belfast' had given similar treatment to other Catholic ex-servicemen and like so many other Catholics, the ex-soldier reported that he would be leaving the city for places unknown.[77]

Allegations similar to McCusker's had appeared in the press on numerous occasions but as brutal as the police raids often were, it was the introduction of internment that would cause the greatest havoc. A police raid on the IRA liaison office at St Mary's Hall in mid-March had given the Northern government access to the names of a large number of the active IRA members in the North.[78] This list, supplemented by other intelligence,[79] provided the basis for the large-scale internment raids which followed. Described as 'A Sensational Swoop'[80] by the *Derry Journal*, three days of raids beginning on 22 May led to the internment of some 348 individuals. Within weeks, as many as 500 people had been interned. According to Denise Kleinrichert, all but a handful of the internees were Catholic Sinn Féiners and, in some cases, when security forces were unable to find their target, sons or fathers of the missing individual were taken in their stead.[81] However, as Fermanagh internee Cahir Healy would recall, the individuals who had been picked up by the security forces were not all militant crusaders.[82] Rather, according to Healy, the government of Northern Ireland made 'no distinction between those who favoured physical force and the constitutionalists. The talker was considered nearly as dangerous as the actor – they gave each other support.'[83] In protest at this unfair treatment, Healy later joked that he and his fellow internees sought to punish their captors by the only means available to them; when given writing materials for outgoing letters, they endeavoured to write as much as they could, with the smallest print possible in an attempt to blind the government censors.[84]

Most of the internees were eventually held in the cramped quarters of the prison ship *Argenta*, which was moored outside Larne Lough.[85] As stagnant and stifling a life as it must have been, the *Argenta* internees have left behind some of the most evocative cultural artefacts from this turbulent time. Many of the men kept autograph books in which they scribbled down inscriptions, shared recitations of Young Irelander poetry or recalled the great political speeches of nationalist patriarchs from Parnell to Pearse.[86] They even produced a leaflet called the *Argenta Bulletin* on a cyclostyle machine. Healy, who was detained after the Twaddell murder, recalled that the internees had a fondness for citing John Mitchel's fiery rhetoric and were all 'excited nationally'.[87]

The satirical 'History of the Argenta' of unknown authorship is, perhaps, one of the most frequently cited and caustic expressions of nationalist anger, angst and humour. Highlighting both Northern efforts to quash the IRA and nationalists' disgust at Britain's willingness to prop up Belfast's devolved parliament, verses ten to seventeen of this long poem read as follows:

X
Says Jimmie Craig to Dawson Bates
'Our Government's in a dreadful state
In spite of all our war array
We've failed to strengthen Britain's sway

XI
A year or more has now been spent
To start this bogus Parliament
We're just as if we'd started,
Dear Bates, I'm almost broken-hearted.

XII
We've tried the bayonet, bomb and gun
With Crossleys thrown in for fun.
But use our terrors as we may,
We cannot crush the IRA.'

XIII
'Oh don't despair so Jimmy dear,
For there's no grounds for fear.
Don't think of something doing rash
We're well backed up by Britain's cash.

XIV
We can counter IRA wiles
Sure you and I will make our piles,
And if in failure all this ends
We have the [illegible] to make amends.'

XV
A moment's silence then ensued
Both men looked in a thoughtful mood
Dawson Bates then jumped upright
And says, 'Dear Jimmy, I have struck light.

XVI
The plan I've got which you will find
Will set at ease your troubled mind –
You know the hulk at Belfast Quay?
It's useless both on land and sea.

XVII
We'll fit her out from bow to stern
And in her the IRA intern
And when we have her fitted up
Tis then we'll plan a good round-up.'[88]

As this clever piece of doggerel suggests, those who were interned on the *Argenta* lost neither their wit nor their political acumen and somehow managed to keep subversive material such as this out of sight of their jailers.

The security round-up in Northern Ireland indirectly contributed to what was to be one of the greatest threats to the continuation of peace between Collins' administration and the British government during the months leading up to the Irish Civil War – the Pettigo–Belleek incident. The village of Belleek (Co. Fermanagh) and the neighbouring village of Pettigo (Co. Donegal), together with the northern shoreline of Lower Lough Erne and the River Erne, formed a quirky triangular jut of land which protruded into Co. Donegal. Belleek, which was cut off from the rest of the county by Lough Erne and the river, was predominantly Catholic, as was the triangle but Pettigo and its hinterland were Protestant.

In April the RIC abandoned their barracks near Belleek and shortly thereafter the IRA took up positions in the border salient, using the old fort as a base for raiding operations into Fermanagh. This IRA presence increased in May as men wanted by the Northern government sought refuge in the area. In late May, a USC detachment, commanded by Sir Basil Brooke, crossed Lough Erne and occupied Magerameenagh Castle near Belleek, which was owned by the local parish priest.[89] The Specials were fired on by the IRA and, in the ensuing clash, the USC and their reinforcements were forced to retreat by pleasure craft – the *Lady of the Lake*[90] – across Lough Erne, leaving behind their armoured car. This left the triangle in the hands of fewer than one hundred members of the IRA contingent. The fiasco infuriated Craig, who frantically warned Churchill that a thousand soldiers were preparing to invade Northern Ireland via the border salient, Derry City and Strabane. Lloyd George and General Macready were reluctant to allow the involvement of British troops in a dispute which involved Free State territory but Churchill was persistent. Once Churchill had been suitably convinced by Collins that troops loyal to the Free State were not involved in the engagement,[91] the British Army, without USC involvement, was ordered to clear the combatants from the border salient. During the first week of June, Pettigo and its Free State hinterland were occupied by the British army – leading to an angry demand for an inquiry into the matter by Michael Collins – and soon thereafter Belleek also fell under British control. Pettigo and the Free State territory adjacent to it remained in British hands until January 1923; Belleek remained under military occupation until August 1924.[92]

Although the *Fermanagh Herald* viewed the foray, and the exaggerated press reports describing it, as an effort by 'unionist Die-hards and Ulster Orangemen to smash the Treaty',[93] the skirmish in the Pettigo–Belleek salient was the first incident to involve the British army and the IRA since the truce. The skirmish was clearly overblown but it had occurred during a low point in relations between Dublin and London, and both Collins and Lloyd George breathed a sign of relief when it was over. The nadir in Anglo-Irish relations in this instance stemmed from the forthcoming Dáil election and the related problem of the Irish Free State's draft constitution. While the extent of cooperation between the Provisional Government and the republicans during the Northern offensive was unknown in London,[94] the main thrust of the engagement had actually coincided with the announcement of an election agreement between Michael Collins and Éamon de Valera and news of that agreement had not been well-received in Britain.[95] Had it been strictly adhered to, the agreement would have made the 16 June election a sham, as it proposed that both Sinn Féin factions – the pro-Treatyites and Republicans – assemble a panel of candidates which would contest the election as a slate that reflected the overall Treaty split in the Dáil.[96] Thus, in a further attempt to prevent an irrevocable split, the election would not be fought on the issue of the Treaty, the division in the Dáil over the Treaty would remain unchanged and nothing would have been settled.[97]

Reactions to the announced election pact ranged from hostility to guarded optimism. Colonial Secretary Winston Churchill was particularly dismayed by the Collins–de Valera pact. Privately expressing concerns that the Provisional Government could 'slide into accommodation' with de Valera and the Republicans,[98] Churchill told the House of Commons that the pact appeared to 'raise very serious issues affecting not only the character and validity of the election contemplated in the Irish Free State Agreement Act, but also affecting the Treaty itself'.[99] Since the announcement of the pact came at a point when Northern Ireland was under attack by IRA personnel of unknown affiliation, it was hardly surprising that, as the *Fermanagh Herald* reported, Britain was 'snarling , but as yet afraid to bite';[100] nor was Churchill's eagerness to discuss the issue with Collins and Griffith in London unexpected.[101] For his part, Craig used the announcement of the pact as a pretext for repudiating the Boundary Commission. As Craig defiantly told his parliament: 'What we have we hold.'[102]

Reactions of Churchill and Craig could have been anticipated; however, the lukewarm reception of the agreement by Northern nationalists may not have been. Initially, the *Derry Journal* was buoyed by the news that an agreement had been reached in Dublin but the *Journal* tempered its enthusiasm with the view that the Free State had to 'get on with the heavy arrears of its work'[103] and the assertion that the anti-Treaty Party had secured 'the best of the bargain'.[104] The *Irish News* was even less keen about the pact, calling it a 'lopsided compromise' that would furnish the next Dáil with the same individuals that had 'kept Ireland in a state of something-far-worse-than-suspense during the past five months'.[105] Although the newspaper claimed that 'time and events'[106] would be the best judge of the agreement, its scepticism about the pact was palpable, as was its continued desire to link Southern disunity with the appalling crises wrought in the North. The newspaper urged groups and individuals outside the panel of Sinn Féin candidates to contest the election with vigour.[107]

Regardless of the unpopularity of the Collins–de Valera pact among observers outside the Free State, its durability depended on the ability of the Provisional Government to produce a constitution that would satisfy Republican demands as well as British scrutiny. On 27 May, amidst the chaos of the Northern offensive and just days after the announcement of the election agreement, Dublin submitted its draft constitution to the British government as was required by the Treaty.[108] Notwithstanding Collins' eagerness to use the Irish constitution to placate Republican misgivings over the Treaty, it is hard to imagine how he could have expected this draft to satisfy Great Britain. As the British Law Officers observed, the draft was 'a Republican constitution almost without disguise'.[109] It did not contain an oath of allegiance to the King; the draft gave executive powers to the Executive Council rather than the crown; it allowed Dáil Éireann to assume powers to declare war and sign treaties; and it did not mention British military rights in the Free State, Irish responsibility for a portion of the national debt or the primacy of the Judicial Committee of the Privy Council in Irish judicial matters.[110] Britain rejected the draft unequivocally and the Provisional Government's legal advisor, Hugh Kennedy, and Britain's Lord Chief Justice, Gordon Hewart, set to work re-moulding the document. Suffice it to say here that this new draft was not a republican document.

From the moment that the Anglo-Irish Treaty was presented to the world in December 1921, the spectre of an Irish civil war reared its ugly head. Weeks of wrangling in the Dáil over the document had embittered feelings between Sinn Féin's factions and efforts to re-unify the broken party at the February *Ard Fheis*, through the joint Northern offensive against Northern Ireland and through the production of a republican constitution had all failed. Cognisant of the direction that new constitutional draft would have to take, Collins began to distance himself from his former republican allies and his 14 June speech in Cork is usually seen as a repudiation of his election agreement with de Valera.[111] The Irish constitution, devoid of any republican elements, was published two days later on the morning of the Free State election. However, neither the document nor the apparent collapse of the Collins–de Valera pact had sufficient time to affect the election. In the end the pro-Treaty Sinn Féin won fifty-eight seats, the anti-Treatyites thirty-six and the balance of the Dáil seats were won by an assortment of smaller parties whose total equated to that of the Republicans. Although they did not cast themselves in such terms, the Independents, the Labourites and the Farmer Party candidates all supported the Treaty, as did approximately 78 per cent of the Irish electorate.[112]

The election had given the pro-Treatyite Provisional Government the legitimacy it needed to confront the anti-Treatyite forces that had been holed up in the Four Courts since April. While Griffith and O'Higgins had for some time urged action against the Army Executive, Collins was still reluctant and it took a British ultimatum to tip the scale in their favour. On 22 June, Sir Henry Wilson, Unionist MP and military advisor to the government of Northern Ireland, was assassinated in London by men alleged to have had connections with the IRA. Controversy still surrounds the shocking development. The slipshod methods of the perpetrators have raised questions about the responsibility for the assassination but allegations that either Michael Collins or Rory O'Connor was behind the murder persist.[113] Britain's response to the murder was unequivocal. As Churchill made clear to Michael Collins via Westminster, if the Provisional Government was not now prepared to deal with the Republicans occupying the Four Courts, Britain would take matters into its own hands.[114] As a consequence of Churchill's ultimatum and in conjunction with the pressure being exerted by the anti-Treaty IRA, on 28 June 1922, the Provisional Government finally laid siege to the Four Courts, beginning the long expected Irish Civil War – a war which nobody in Ireland, least of all the nationalists of Northern Ireland, had ever wanted to materialise.[115]

This was not Northern nationalism's war. The war had not arisen over Irish unity; it could not end partition; and, as the *Irish News* had so consistently warned during the first six months of 1922, the war could not help but divert Southern attention away from the needs of Northern nationalism for months to come. Catholics and nationalists in Northern Ireland had endured much since the signing of the Anglo-Irish Treaty. They had witnessed Northern Ireland's rapid descent into an even deeper form of sectarianism; they had suffered through the false piquancy of the Craig–Collins pacts and the disruption of border raids and disturbances. Yet, despite their own dire conditions, they never lost sight of the fact that the Northern minority was but a sideshow in the wider game of Anglo-Irish politics and grew accustomed to having their dreams dashed time and time again by events beyond their control. An anonymous poem, submitted to the *Irish News* on 6 June, provides insight into the way in which at least one Northern nationalist saw himself/herself six months after Dáil Éireann accepted the Treaty.

Sometimes fair ships loom into sight
Far o'er the distant main,
Then cloud and pall of falling night
Hide them from view again.

And so we are left with hope deferred
As on an island shore;
They pass us by our cries unheard
To come again no more.

Au! Could we not see gleaming stars
Above this shrouded vale,
Our feet would wander reckless far,
And hope itself would fail.

But shining fair a deathless gleam
Hope lifts up waning eyes:
Inspired again our spirits dream
Of fairest sunlit skies.

Then oh my soul hope on and on,
Unto that better day
When life's unfading goal is won,
And fear has fled away.[116]

Redolent with images of misplaced optimism and dashed dreams, the message of the poem resonates even deeper when one considers the fact that it was published in early June, just three weeks before the storming of the Four Courts and the beginning of the Irish Civil War. Conditions in the North would stabilise during the summer of 1922, yet it seems clear that the new circumstances triggered by the war had effectively deferred the broader anti-partitionist hopes of Northern nationalists for the foreseeable future.

Notes

1 *Irish News*, 4 April 1922.

2 Accordingly, Aiken warned: 'in your future dealings with Ulster you should not recognize Joe Devlin or his clique ... There can be no vigorous or harmonious policy on our part inside Ulster if his people occupy any position in your circle'. Cited in A.C. Hepburn, *Catholic Belfast and Nationalist Ireland in the Era of Joe Devlin, 1871–1934* (Oxford: Oxford University Press, 2008), p. 235.

3 'Minutes of the Northern Advisory Committee Meeting', 11 April 1922, Department of the Taoiseach, NAI/TSCH/S 1011, National Archives of Ireland, Dublin, pp. 3–4.

4 'Minutes of the Northern Advisory Committee Meeting', 11 April 1922, pp. 7–8. During the spring and early summer, Collins repeatedly requested inquiries into the disturbances in the North as well as the imposition of martial law. Britain was reluctant to concede to these demands – and Craig was openly hostile to them – for reasons largely associated with the public relations nightmare it would bring to the British and Northern governments. Ultimately, a compromise was reached and, instead of a public inquiry, a British civil servant (S.G. Tallents, private secretary to Lord Lieutenant FitzAlan, 1921–22, and Imperial Secretary, Northern Ireland, 1922–26) was employed ostensibly to investigate the failures of the Craig–Collins pacts. The report was issued just before the beginning of the Irish Civil War – too late to make an appreciable difference in North–South relations and Northern conditions. M. Farrell, *Arming the Protestants: The Formation of the Ulster Special Constabulary and the Royal Ulster Constabulary, 1920–27* (London: Pluto Press, 1983), p.141.

5 'Minutes of the Northern Advisory Committee Meeting', 11 April 1922, p. 8.

6 Ibid.

7 Gillespie made similar observations about Cookstown, ibid. p. 13.

8 Ibid., p. 9.

9 Ibid.

10 Griffith responded in a similar way to the wording of a proposed resolution that would have called on Collins to 'use every endeavor' to force Craig to implement the pact. Griffith complained: 'You are placing the whole responsibility on the shoulders of Mr. Collins. You are making him the judge and leaving it open

to yourselves afterwards to complain that he didn't use every endeavor.' Ibid., pp. 9–10.

11 Griffith freely admitted that the Provisional Government was unable to protect Northern Catholics by suggesting, 'I see no effectual means of protecting them except by this pact. Ibid., pp. 16–17.

12 Ibid., p.12.

13 Ibid., p. 22.

14 Ibid., p. 19.

15 Ibid., p. 11.

16 Ibid.,

17 Ibid., p. 16.

18 Ibid., p. 21.

19 'Remembrances of the Mansion House Convention', Cahir Healy Papers, D/2991/2/4, Public Record Office of Northern Ireland, Belfast.

20 'Minutes of the Northern Advisory Committee Meeting', 11 April 1922, p. 27.

21 Ibid., p. 30.

22 Ibid.

23 Ibid., p. 31.

24 Ibid., p. 35.

25 Emphasis added. Ibid., p. 36.

26 Ibid., p. 37.

27 Ibid., p. 12.

28 Ibid., p. 31.

29 Ibid., p. 30.

30 Ibid., p. 27.

31 Ibid., p. 31.

32 Ibid., p. 22.

33 Ibid., p. 32.

34 Ibid., p. 38.

35 Ibid., pp. 39–41.

36 Ibid., p. 44.

37 Ibid., p. 43.

38 Ibid., p. 45.

39 Ibid.

40 Ibid., pp. 51–2.

41 For instance, see M. Harris, *The Catholic Church and the Foundation of the Northern Irish State* (Cork: Cork University Press, 1993), pp. 122–3.

42 C. O'Halloran, *Partition and the Limits of Irish Nationalism: An Ideology Under Stress* (Dublin: Gill and Macmillan Ltd, 1987), p. 133.

43 M. McLaverty, *Call My Brother Back* (London: Longmans, 1939; reprint Dublin: Poolbeg Press, 1979), p. 144.

44 *Irish News*, 11 April, 1922. The full text of the poem has been taken from *Workers Republic*, 25 December 1915, reprinted in A. O'Cathasaigh, *James Connolly: Lost Writings* (Pluto Press, 1997), p. 187.

45 *Derry Journal*, 14 April 1922.

46 J. Curran, *The Birth of the Irish Free State, 1921–1923* (n.p.: University of Alabama Press, 1980) p. 181.

47 *Irish News*, 19 April 1922.

48 A. Parkinson, *Belfast's Unholy War: The Troubles of the 1920s* (Dublin: Four Courts Press Ltd, 2004), p. 63.

49 *Derry Journal*, 10 April 1922.

50 The Northern government was particularly active in the destruction of bridges and the barricading of cross-border transportation routes along the Monaghan border. C. Day, 'Political violence in the Newry/Armagh area, 1912–1925' (PhD diss., Queen's University, Belfast, 1999), p. 247.

51 A report in the *Derry Journal* concerning a band of Protestants who had received a slap on the wrist for firearms offences left the newspaper stunned by the 'Amazing Verdict'. *Derry Journal*, 29 April 1922.

52 *Fermanagh Herald*, 22 April 1922.

53 *Irish News*, 8 June 1922. Craig's response to the bad press that these searches received in England and the United States did not help his cause. He told a correspondent of the *Chicago Tribune*: 'All cars are stopped. If he [Logue] had been anxious for peace in the north he would have been pleased to find the net so fine. You would think the old man had been injured. Our account of it is that he did not give his name until it was all over.' Harris, *The Catholic Church and the Foundation of the Northern Irish State*, p. 133.

54 M. Hopkinson, 'From Treaty to Civil War, 1921–2', in J.R. Hill (ed.), *A New History of Ireland VII: Ireland, 1921–84* (Oxford: Oxford University Press, 2003), p. 30.

55 The border press announced the re-imposition of the boycott on the same day that it reported on the second Craig–Collins Pact, noting that the news about the boycott would be 'welcomed by many'. *Derry Journal*, 31 March 1922.

56 B. Barton, 'Northern Ireland, 1920–25', in J.R. Hill (ed.), *A New History of Ireland VII: Ireland, 1921–84* (Oxford: Oxford University Press, 2003), p. 176.

57 J. Dooher, 'Tyrone nationalism and the question of partition, 1910–25' (M. Phil. thesis, University of Ulster, 1986), p. 414. Craig's 16 May introduction of a bill which aimed to end proportional representation in local elections was but one example of the cavalier attitude of the Northern government towards the pact and political reconciliation. Farrell, *Arming the Protestants*, 124; E. Phoenix, 'Michael Collins: The Northern Question, 1916–22', in G. Doherty and D. Keogh (eds), *Michael Collins and the Making of the Irish State* (Boulder: Mercier Press, 1998), p. 113.

58 Farrell, *Arming the Protestants*, p. 114.

59 Curran, *The Birth of the Irish Free State*, p. 178.

60 Farrell, *Arming the Protestants*, p. 128.

61 Day, 'Political violence in the Newry/Armagh area, 1912–1925', p. 271.

62 Farrell, *Arming the Protestants*, p. 128.

63 E. Staunton, *The Nationalists of Northern Ireland, 1918–1973* (Dublin: The Columba Press, 2001), p. 66.

64 Farrell, *Arming the Protestants*, p. 128.

65 *Irish News*, 20 May 1922.

66 Ibid., 22 May 1922.

67 Ibid.

68 Hopkinson, 'From Treaty to Civil War, 1921–2', p. 29.

69 Curran suggested that the dangers of being caught by Britain offers an explanation as to why 'so much talk produced so little action' once the offensive began. Curran, *The Birth of the Irish Free State*, p. 179.

70 The question here was whether Collins was motivated by Northern or Southern circumstances – i.e., was the offensive meant to alleviate the suffering of Northern nationalists or to sooth tensions between his Provisional Government and the Republicans? For the former view, see Dooher, 'Tyrone nationalism and the question of partition, 1910–25', p. 417. For the latter view, see Barton, 'Northern Ireland, 1920–25', p. 173.

71 D. Kleinrichert, *Republican Internment and the Prison Ship Argenta, 1922* (Dublin: Irish Academic Press, 2001), p. 9.

72 For the details of the Special Powers Act, see Farrell, *Arming the Protestants*, p. 99; Kleinrichert, *Republican Internment and the Prison Ship Argenta*, p. 9. With respect to flogging, according to Cahir Healy, 'The Government found difficulty in securing a man to do the flogging. A Belfast B Special will shoot his supposed enemy at sight, without scruple, but he will not undertake to flog him.' C. Healy, 'Life on a Northern Prisonship', n.d., Cahir Healy Papers, D 2991/B/140/52, Public Record Office of Northern Ireland, Belfast.

73 Shane's Castle, on the shores of Lough Neagh, was the historic seat of the O'Neill family.

74 *Irish News*, 24 May 1922.

75 Ibid., 20 May 1922.

76 Ibid., 19 May 1922.

77 'How Soldiers of the Great War Are Treated in Belfast', May 1922, Department of the Taoisearch, S 1801/A, National Archives of Ireland, Dublin. In particular, this file contains a copy of a letter from McCusker – ex-soldier and former army welterweight champion boxer – to an unnamed Belfast priest. The Belfast Catholic Protection Association claimed to have verified the letter's contents.

78 Hopkinson, 'From Treaty to Civil War, 1921–2', p. 28.

79 *Irish News*, 24 May 1922.

80 *Derry Journal*, 24 May 1922.

81 Kleinrichert, *Republican Internment and the Prison Ship Argenta*, p. 19.

82 Kleinrichert's work supports Healy on this point. In fact, she claims that there was an economic objective behind the internment campaign since many of the men in custody were educated activists who lost their jobs to Unionists while interned. Kleinrichert, *Republican Internment and the Prison Ship Argenta*, p. 278. A number of the Northern representatives on the Advisory Committee hinted at this during their 10 April meeting. This claim is also supported by the Internees Dependents Committee. 'Treatment of the Minority in the Six Counties Under the Government of Northern Ireland' (Belfast: The Internees Dependants Committee, 1924).

83 C. Healy, 'On an Ulster Prison Ship: Some Reflections of 1922–1924', n.d., Cahir Healy Papers, D 2991/B/140/10, Public Record Office of Northern Ireland, Belfast. These reflections appear to have been written after the emergence of the civil rights demonstrations in the 1960s.

84 Ibid.

85 Kleinrichert, *Republican Internment and the Prison Ship Argenta*, p. 84.

86 'Correspondence from the Prison Ship Argenta', Pre-1966 Anti-Unionist Material (1922–) Box 1, Northern Ireland Political Collection, Linen Hall Library, Belfast.

87 Healy, 'Life on a Northern Prisonship', n.d.

88 Kleinrichert, *Republican Internment and the Prison Ship Argenta*, pp. 151–2. As an indication of its popularity, sections of the poem also appear in the Linen Hall Library's collection of internment letters. 'Correspondence from the prison ship Argenta', Pre-1966 Anti-Unionist Material (1922–) Box 1, Northern Ireland Political Collection, Linen Hall Library, Belfast.

89 A. Kinsella, 'The Pettigo–Belleek Triangle Incident', *The Irish Sword* 20, 82 (1997), pp. 147–8; Curran, *The Birth of the Irish Free State*, pp. 198–9.

90 *Irish News*, 3 June 1922.

91 This was a course of action urged by Lloyd George and Thomas Jones. According to Jones, Churchill objected to the interference from the Prime Minister and even offered his resignation. K. Middlemas (ed.), *Thomas Jones Whitehall Diary, Volume III, Ireland, 1918–1925* (London: Oxford University Press, 1971), pp. 210–11.

92 Farrell, *Arming the Protestants*, pp. 132–4. A letter from Belleek resident Martin Keegan to Seán Milroy, dated 11 November 1923 and printed in 'Northern Minorities' complains of harassment at the hand of British troops and the easy movement of Britain in the Free State's section of the salient. The letter ended: 'The Catholic population near the border in the six county area are despairing of any relief seeing that the free state Government is apparently letting the matter slide, and some "loyal" residents in the free State side are contemplating the idea that this part of the Free State now dominated by English troops will in a short time be included in the area on the other side of the border.' 'Northern Minorities', n.d., E.M. Stephens Papers, 4239/1, Manuscript Department, Trinity College, Dublin.

93 *Fermanagh Herald*, 3 June 1922.

94 Curran, *The Birth of the Irish Free* State, p. 179.

95 With regard to the emergence of the pact and Collins' reluctance to deal with the Republicans, Churchill disparagingly described the agreement as a case of 'dog won't eat dog'. P. Canning, *British Policy Towards Ireland, 1921–1941* (Oxford: Clarendon Press, 1985), p. 40.

96 A. Ward, *The Irish Constitutional Tradition: Responsible Government and Modern Ireland, 1782–1992* (Washington: The Catholic University of America Press, 1994), p. 175. For information on the nomination process, see M. Gallagher, 'The Pact General Election of 1922', *Irish Historical Studies* 21, 84 (1979), pp. 406–9.

97 Ibid., p. 405.
98 Ward, *The Irish Constitutional Tradition*, p. 176.
99 *Irish News*, 23 May 1922.
100 *Fermanagh Herald*, 3 June 1922.
101 Upon seeing the draft constitution, Churchill's hostility towards the pact became even more pronounced, and on 31 May, he issued an ultimatum on the floor of Westminster. According to the Colonial Secretary, if members of the anti-Treaty group became part of the Provisional Government after the election, they would be required to sign a declaration vowing to uphold the Treaty and if they refused to sign, 'the Treaty is broken by that very act'. *Irish News*, 1 June 1922.
102 Ibid., 24 May 1922.
103 *Derry Journal*, 22 May 1922.
104 Ibid., 24 May 1922.
105 *Irish News*, 22 May 1922.
106 Ibid.
107 Ibid. Unfortunately, while the pact permitted non-panel candidates to stand for election, those who chose to do so were often subject to intimidation. Gallagher, 'The Pact General Election of 1922', p. 411.
108 Ward, *The Irish Constitutional Tradition*, p. 173.
109 Ibid., p. 174.
110 Ibid.
111 The standard interpretation states that Collins publicly broke with de Valera during a speech he delivered in Cork. Gallagher casts doubt on this interpretation by suggesting that the contemporary press took little notice of his speech. Gallagher, 'The Pact General Election of 1922', pp. 412–13. Also see, Hart, *Mick: The Real Michael Collins*, pp. 389, 392–3; Ward, *The Irish Constitutional Tradition*, p. 177; Curran, *The Birth of the Irish Free State*, p. 220.
112 Ward, *The Irish Constitutional Tradition*, p. 177.
113 In his examination of the historiography of the Wilson assassination, Peter Hart concludes that: '[t]here is no solid evidence to support a conspiracy theory linking Michael Collins or anyone else to the murder. In the absence of such evidence, we must accept the assertions of the murderers that they acted alone, in the (grossly mistaken) belief that Wilson was responsible for Catholic deaths in Belfast.' P. Hart, 'Michael Collins and the Assassination of Sir Henry Wilson', *Irish Historical Studies* 28, 110 (1992), p. 170. This was also the assessment of contemporary *Irish News* reportage. *Irish News*, 27 June 1922.
114 *Parliamentary Debates*, Commons, 5th ser., vol. 155 (26 June 1922), cols 1709–12; *Irish News*, 27 June 1922.
115 Hopkinson, 'From Treaty to Civil War, 1921–2', p. 23.
116 *Irish News*, 6 June 1922.

CHAPTER 6

The Woe that 'Reckless Folly Brings': The Irish Civil War and the Eclipse of the Boundary Commission

God made this land of Beauty
A place for praise and play;
Man's darkened sense of Duty
His dream has swept away.

– Cahir Healy, 'Thoughts'[1]

The Irish Civil War, in all its bitter incarnations, took the Provisional Government/Irish Free State to the brink of bankruptcy, robbed the nation of some its most able leaders and served to ossify the political divisions that emerged during the Treaty debates. This chapter explores Northern nationalists' perspectives on the outbreak of hostilities in Dublin, General Michael Collins' conduct of the war in the months leading up to his death, as well as the Northern minority's role in the bitter armed struggle. It will be seen that, despite the fact that nearly all of the fighting occurred on the Southern side of the border, the consequences of the war were not similarly confined, since any decision regarding the Irish boundary had to be postponed at least until the fighting ended. In the view of the Northern minority, this untimely delay and the loss of key Southern advocates to the internecine struggle would be a lasting legacy of the Irish Civil War.

After months of political instability in Dublin, hostilities finally broke out during the early morning hours of 28 June 1922. The pretext for war came as a result of the kidnapping of J. J. 'Ginger'

O'Connell – Collins' Deputy Chief-of-Staff.[2] As a result of this incident, the administration issued an ultimatum requiring the surrender of the Four Courts and when this demand was refused, the Provisional Government laid siege to the structure using British field artillery.[3]

So long as the fighting remained on the Southern side of the border, Sir James Craig actually welcomed the war as it gave him the freedom to dig in and consolidate his hold on the Six Counties, unmolested by outside interference.[4] Lloyd George's coalition had long favoured a confrontation between the Treatyite regime and the anti-Treaty Republicans and Winston Churchill, in particular, was determined that the attack would not be permitted to fail. Thus, setting aside British misgivings about the fortitude of the small National Army that was emerging from the ranks of the pro-Treaty IRA,[5] the Colonial Secretary made ample resources available to the Irish administration.[6]

British concerns about the fighting ability of the Provisional Government paled in comparison with the palpable anxiety expressed by the anti-partitionist press in the North regrading the outbreak of hostilities. Accordingly, the *Irish News* regretfully informed its readers on June 29 that '[t]he disaster so long anticipated – and dreaded – by Irish Nationalists has befallen the country'. The report continued: 'Civil War has broken out in Dublin; it is raging even now; lives are being sacrificed, great public buildings are being seized by one section and assailed, by another – with destruction as their almost inevitable fate.'[7]

Harbouring no satisfaction in the news, the Devlinite organ could not avoid the temptation of reminding its readers that it had foreseen the carnage and had been counselling against the dangers of faction in the South of Ireland for many months. The newspaper also took a jab at what it considered the giddy attitude of unionist diehards, adding 'these terrible days have filled their black hearts with joy'.[8] Equally discouraged by the disturbances in the Southern capital, the *Fermanagh Herald* reported that Dublin was 'in the throes of a fierce conflict', yet both newspapers were left somewhat buoyed by reports that hostilities were confined to Dublin and had not extended to the provinces. It 'is expected', wrote the *Fermanagh Herald*, 'that the Irregulars [the anti-Treatyite Republican forces] will shortly surrender'.[9]

The initial bombardment of the Four Courts on 28 June caused little damage to the building but, with the employment of high explosive shells, the massive structure soon began to crumble. Having developed no escape plan and in an effort to leave the Republicans outside the garrison in the strongest possible position, on 30 June, Oscar Traynor, OC of the Dublin Brigade and senior Irregular officer outside the building, ordered the surrender of the Four Courts and its inhabitants.[10] Rory O'Connor, Liam Mellows, Joe McKelvey and Dick Barrett were among the prisoners taken captive by the Provisional Government.[11]

Relieved by the fall of the Four Courts, the *Irish News* now substituted a considerable amount of the concern and anxiety it had expressed during its initial reportage of the war with anger and irritation. Stressing in its editorial of 1 July both the perfidy of Republicans' spiteful refusal to surrender before the building was destroyed and the costs of the carnage, the newspaper worried that the reputation of Ireland had been sullied in the eyes of the world. The *Irish News* forcefully called upon the remaining supporters of O'Connor to end their 'campaign of Death and Destruction'.[12]

Given the collapse of one of the most significant bastions of anti-Treaty strength in Dublin and the capture of Rory O'Connor – hitherto the voice of the IRA Executive – it was not coincidental that the *Irish News* also chose to publish, on 1 July, a letter to the editor by a literary critic identifying himself/herself simply as 'J.B.H.'. In an evocative allusion to contemporary conditions, the author cited the opening stanza of a James Clarence Mangan poem, 'Rury and Darvorgilla'.

> List to the tale of a Prince of Oriel –
> Of Rory, last of a line of kings:
> I pen it here as a sad memorial
> Of how much woe reckless folly Brings!

Though his/her message was blatantly obvious to *Irish News* readers, the author of this letter explained: 'Truly, "reckless folly" has brought woe to our dear country – woe and sorrow beyond the mental conception of too many amongst her sons.'[13] Apparently encouraged by the actions of the Provisional Government to restore order and confident that things were already getting better, the author concluded the letter by citing a passage from 'Dark Rosaleen' – a sixteenth-century Gaelic allegory made famous in translation by Mangan.

'Tis you shall reign, and reign alone,
My Own Rosaleen!
'Tis you shall have the golden throne,
'Tis you shall reign, and reign alone,
My Dark Rosaleen!'

The author's reference to 'Dark Rosaleen' in this context was particularly significant. Believed to have been written by a poet in the court of Hugh the Red O'Donnell, the verse was interpreted as a pledge by O'Donnell to restore Ireland – symbolised by Rosaleen – to the glory it knew before Saxon and Norman intervention.[14] In drawing the comparison with contemporary Ireland, J.B.H. sublimely concluded: 'The day of her crowning is nigh. I am not a prophet, or son of a prophet – but I know it.'[15]

The optimism of this letter was not without warrant. Peace efforts sponsored by Irish Labourites and various other civil and religious authorities had surfaced almost as soon as the war began and,[16] and although it was not made public, de Valera was also expressing serious doubts about the value of continued armed resistance.[17] However, politicians such as Éamon de Valera had held little sway within the republican movement since the spring; thus, as subsequent events would attest, the war was far from over.

In the aftermath of the Four Courts surrender, the Provisional Government's attention turned to the east side of O'Connell Street where the Dublin Brigade had established a Republican base of operations in a block of buildings. These buildings became a gathering house for the anti-Treaty elite, as de Valera, Cathal Brugha, Sean T. O'Kelly, Austin Stack and a host of other prominent Republicans had taken refuge there in advance of the Provisional Government's attack.[18]

The National Army which, according to the *Irish News*, was 'fighting to save the country' from those who were 'violently defying the National will', began its assault on the buildings on 2 July.[19] As had been the case with the Four Courts, faced with the destructive might of the Provisional Government's artillery, the resistance soon melted away. Brugha ultimately ordered his small band to surrender on 5 July but, refusing to be taken prisoner, he was fatally wounded in a desperate attempt to escape capture and died two days later. Cathal

Brugha was the first prominent Republican leader to die during the Civil War. His heroism in the fight for Irish independence had been laudable but, as one of the most militant opponents of the Treaty, he, like Erskine Childers, was vilified in certain nationalist quarters as much for his Englishness as for his political views.[20]

The battle for O'Connell Street signalled the end of the first phase of the conflict and thereafter, the war moved out into the provinces. Choosing to hold pockets of fortified buildings in Dublin, the Republicans had employed a defensive strategy reminiscent in many ways of the Easter Rising. Notwithstanding the symbolic value of such a battle plan, the Provisional Government's use of British artillery quickly neutralised the Republican threat in the city.[21] Remarkably, the National Army faced little resistance in the capital and this did not go unnoticed by the supporters of the Provisional Government north of the Irish border. Despite the imposition of military censorship, the anti-partitionist press in Northern Ireland was receptive to the message projected by the Irish government as evidenced by their editorial pages. The *Fermanagh Herald*'s hopeful reports of an early end to the conflict[22] complemented editorials of the *Irish News*, which stressed the bleak prospects for Republican victory in the 'one-sided struggle'[23] while commending the civility and restraint shown by the Provisional Government.[24] Bewildered by the perceived insanity of the Republican cause, the Belfast newspaper asked rhetorically: 'Did Mr de Valera think for a moment that he was advancing the cause of an Irish Republic by seizing thirty or forty valuable houses in the principal street of a hostile city and holding them until millions of pounds' worth of the citizen's property was destroyed?'[25]

The Republicans' makeshift evacuation from the 'hostile city' may have enabled the force to safeguard their arms and carry the fight into the countryside but their resources were essentially finite.[26] In contrast, Britain's determination to see the Provisional Government prevail and its eagerness to provide and replenish Treatyite military resources meant that time was not on the side of the Irregular forces. As Joseph Curran has argued, the Republican battle plan determined the outcome of the war from the opening salvo.[27]

With the fighting for O'Connell Street ongoing, the *Irish News* confidently asserted that the victory of the Provisional Government was assured, though it added that 'it is uncertain how it will be achieved'.[28] As it was, the regime's plan for achieving this most important objective required a reshuffling of the administration. In mid-July, Michael Collins left the Chairmanship of the Provisional Government upon taking up the position of Commander-in-Chief of the National Army.[29] In his place, William T. Cosgrave, formally Minister of Local Government, became the acting head of the Provisional Government and Minister of Finance.[30] Arthur Griffith retained his position as the President of Dáil Éireann – which was still functioning and was due to begin sitting – but Griffith's health had begun to deteriorate and he was therefore spared much of the work of governing.

The Dáil's upcoming session was ultimately postponed until September and, in an attempt to forestall its use by the anti-Treatyites, the Provisional Government also dissolved the Supreme Court of the Republic that had been established during the Anglo-Irish War.[31] In addition, the Provisional Government convened a War Council on 12 July, which consisted of: the Commander-in-Chief, Michael Collins; Richard Mulcahy, who was both the Minister of Defence and Chief-of-Staff; and Eoin O'Duffy, the Assistant Chief-of-Staff and GOC of the National Army's Southwest Division.[32] The government, with its structured political and military organisation, also had the advantage of approaching the war with a clear, uncompromising objective based on neutralising and disarming its enemies and increasing the size of its army. It quickly amassed a force that numbered approximately 30,000 soldiers by November 1922; it had ballooned to 50,000 by the end of the war.[33]

In contrast to the organisational and material advantages of the Provisional Government, the Republicans were a much more nebulous grouping. While Liam Lynch held the position of Chief-of-Staff of the Irregular forces and, therefore, retained the right to veto any peace proposals, he wielded little control over the Divisions outside his own command and often found it difficult to keep abreast of the events in other areas.[34] The Irregulars in the south and west of Ireland were much better armed than they had been at any time during the Anglo-Irish War[35] but, unlike the Provisional Government, they lacked the backing of an outside ally. Moreover, aside from defying the Treaty, the Republicans – dominated since the Treaty debates by the IRA – had no political apparatus to focus their policy aims, lacked an uncensored press organ to espouse their rhetoric and therefore suffered from a lack of popular support.[36] Republican weaknesses were made worse by the defensive military strategy that they were forced to pursue. The bulk of the Irregular forces hunkered down in the so-called 'Republic of Munster', waiting for the Provisional Government to seek them out.[37]

There was frenzied activity among both camps on the Southern side of the border in June and July but the Provisional Government, and Michael Collins in particular, had not forgotten about the problems of the Northern minority. Remarkably, on 28 June, while the siege of the Four Courts was taking place, Collins wrote to Winston Churchill in order to voice his objection to Northern Ireland's impending Local Government Bill.[38] That Bill sought to abolish proportional representation for local elections and this, in conjunction with the gerrymandering that was expected to follow, would surely disadvantage anti-partitionist candidates. Responding to what the *Irish News* called the 'Doom of PR',[39] Collins complained to Churchill that the

> [s]afeguards for the minority under our jurisdiction have been frequently demanded and readily granted by us. Our people in the North are not so slow to notice this, and continually put up to us that their rights under the Craig regime are not protected in the slightest degree. The introduction of this bill has greatly strengthened this standpoint, and in consequence, considerably weakened our influence. The effect of this enactment will be to wipe out completely all effective representation of Catholic and Nationalist interests.[40]

Given the disdain for the Bill among both Devlinites and Sinn Féiners, Collins' intervention would surely have met with their approval.

Ironically, a report, written by British civil servant S.G. Tallents on the reasons for the failure of the Craig–Collins Pacts, was released just as the war in the South was beginning. Although conditions had begun to improve in the North during June and July – a welcome by-product of the Civil War – the political uncertainty, which Tallents blamed for the sectarian violence of the spring, persisted.[41] With that in mind, it is not surprising that the thoughts of the Northern minority were very much fixed on events on the other side of the border. A resolution, issued by Revd B. Laverty on behalf of the Belfast Catholic Protection Committee, was indicative of Belfast nationalists' concern for, and endorsement of, the Provisional Government. It read, be it resolved: 'That this Committee, grateful for the work of the Provisional Government for the Catholics of Belfast, congratulate that Government on the success of its labours for the restoration of peace and good order in Dublin and the country, and wishes them "God speed" in their efforts.'[42] The *Irish News* 4 July editorial represented further evidence of Northern support for Collins and the Treatyite government. Worried that the anti-Treaty Party would exploit 'the sufferings of the Catholics in the North-East for its own partisan ends', the newspaper took the opportunity to express its approval of the general policy being pursued by the Provisional Government.

> All that the Provisional Government of the Free State could have done for the minority in the Six Counties has been done up to the present: in the triumph of Order over Anarchy and of Civil Liberty over irresponsible Militarism within the borders of the Free State lies the final hope of the 450,000 Nationalists who live outside the Twenty-Six Counties.

The newspaper was somewhat put off by Collins' suggestion in an interview that sectarian outrage in the North had brought on the war but in keeping with the Devlinite view that Irish unity could only come via negotiation, the *Irish News* emphatically supported the Southern leaders' vow not to coerce Ulster. The article concluded: 'Mr Collins knows the facts of the situation; the policy of northern nationalists must be based on his plain statement.'[43]

While the Provisional Government had held the overwhelming support of both sections of Northern nationalism since the Treaty debates, the position of the IRA's embattled Northern Divisions were less certain. Since the 1st Northern had not recovered from its role in the Pettigo–Belleek debacle of early June and the 2nd Northern had all but collapsed by the end of the month, the status of the 3rd and 4th Northern Divisions were of the greatest concern to the GHQ.[44] The 3rd Northern Division, which bore the brunt of the fighting during the abortive Northern offensive in the spring, had been led by Joe McKelvey before his defection in April to the Republicans.[45] Thereafter, the solidly Treatyite OC Seamus Woods took over the Division and, according to his own admission in September, he was personally responsible for keeping the 3rd Northern in the government fold.[46] The 4th Northern Division was led by Frank Aiken. His territory straddled the Irish border and it was believed to be the best armed of the Northern Divisions but Aiken had objected to the Treaty's oath of allegiance and, indicative of the independence he and other IRA Commandants wielded, he had not declared loyalty to either side in the Civil War, hoping instead to remain neutral. This was a luxury which Aiken would not long be permitted.[47]

As Frank Aiken and his 4th Northern Division attempted to avoid being drawn into the war, the Provisional Government moved quickly against the Irregular-held areas in the provinces. After a minor skirmish in Blessington, on the outskirts of Dublin, the National Army moved simultaneously into the west and the south of the country, setting the stage for a major engagement of the enemy in Limerick, where forces loyal to the government had reached a tactical truce with the enemy. Once the GHQ sent reinforcements and heavy artillery to the region, the National Army's local commanders ended their truce and quickly drove the Irregular forces out of Limerick.[48] The Republicans, who had also been forced to evacuate Donegal and most of Connacht during mid-July, were likewise dislodged from key positions in Waterford, Kilkenny and Tipperary by the end of the month.[49]

During these early days of the war, the *Irish News* offered high praise to General Collins and his National Army. The newspaper extolled the 'rout'[50] of the Irregular forces near Blessington, gleefully reported resignations from the anti-Treaty ranks of the Tuam Brigade[51] and credited the Provisional Government's 'unity of command' under Collins, Mulcahy and O'Duffy for the government's progress in the field.[52] Treatyite successes and continued murmurings of peace proposals had provided all of Ireland with a measure of hope that the end of the internecine struggle was near. For example, on the occasion of the Feast of the Blessed Oliver Plunkett[53] – which ironically coincided with the first anniversary of the Anglo-Irish truce – the Northern poet 'Benmore' was inspired to urge the 'men of mighty will' to seek an end to the war. Benmore's poem, entitled 'The Angelic Voice', pleaded:

May the Angelic voice in peace resound,
In blood-dyed street and square.
In every town throughout our land
Let the man of peace now dare!
Come forth, ye men of noblest hearts.
Bind every wound and sore
That makes your country sick to death,
From heavy crosses bore![54]

In spite of the *Irish News*' championing and the impassioned urging of individuals like Benmore, all was not well in the North for the supporters of the Provisional Government. In the political sphere, Collins' concerns over the Local Government Bill, which he had voiced in June, finally elicited a response from Churchill in late July but the news was not promising. Rather, the Colonial Secretary flatly denied Collins' allegation that the sole purpose of the Bill was to disenfranchise the Northern minority. Resorting to a tactic that was based on the Speaker's ruling of 8 February, Churchill justified his disinclination to interfere with the legislation by suggesting that local government was a purely domestic matter for Northern Ireland to decide.[55] When it could be utilised, this approach to dealing with controversial Ulster issues would become the hallmark of Britain's policy on Northern Ireland.

As devastating as the effects of the Bill would be for the supporters of the Provisional Government in Northern Ireland, military matters were a more pressing concern for the Commander-in-Chief. The Provisional Government's longstanding dilemma over what to do about Frank Aiken finally reached its climax in mid-July after the GHQ bungled an attempt to gain control of the 4th Northern Division. The 'Dundalk coup'[56] – as the incident was stylised by the press – had the disastrous effect of pushing Aiken and the bulk of his previously uncommitted Division into the Irregular camp.[57] If this news was not bad enough, a series of reports from Seamus Woods made it clear that Northern conditions had rendered the position of his 3rd Northern Division untenable.[58] Woods' assessment of the situation and Aiken's conversion to the Republican cause forced the Provisional Government in early August to re-assess the status of both the military and political components of its Northern policy.

On 2 August, members of the GHQ met with Woods and other Northern officers at Portobello Barracks in order to both reassure them and provide direction to the Provisional Government's Northern allies. Recognising the difficulty which the Northern Divisions found themselves in, General Collins elaborated a new military policy for the pro-Treaty IRA in the North. In conjunction with the Northern Sinn Féiners, with whom the pro-Treaty IRA had connections, and the Devlinites, with whom they did not, Collins advised the Northern officers to continue pursuing a non-recognition policy towards the Craig regime while assuming a defensive role within the Northern borders. The GHQ also decided to permit the members of the untenable Northern Divisions to leave their divisional areas in order to train at the Curragh under their own officers.[59] The direction which Collins gave to the Northern officers, his decision not to roll their Divisions into the growing National Army and his vow to deal with Ulster 'in a very definite way' proved to be enough to placate Woods. By the end of the year, 524 Northern combatants were training at the Curragh.[60]

As members of the GHQ were in conference with the Northern officers, the Treatyite regime was also making plans to overhaul its relationship with Northern nationalism in the political sphere. However, in a radical divergence from the Provisional Government's Northern policy to date, Collins would no longer be pulling the strings. Because the Commander-in-Chief's attention was focused squarely on the war, he was not able to sit on the committee assembled on 1 August to consider the Northern question. Rather, the committee consisted of Ernest Blythe (Minister for Local Government), Patrick Hogan (Minister for Agriculture), J.J. Walsh (Post Master General), Desmond Fitzgerald (Minister for External Affairs) and Michael Hayes (Minister for Education)[61] – with Blythe seemingly taking the leading role in its deliberations. The committee's findings, which did not reach General Collins until 21 August,[62] urged the Provisional Government to cease its longstanding support for the non-complying nationalist-controlled municipal bodies in the Six Counties and recommended terminating the administration's costly funding of the Northern teachers. The committee also counselled against the use of a coercive military policy or aggressive economic tactics to pressure Belfast, while simultaneously advising the Southern regime to use the levers at its disposal to push the Northern nationalists into taking their seats in the devolved parliament.[63]

As indicated by both Collins' meeting with the Northern officers and the Northern committee's recommendations, the Provisional Government was in the process of changing the direction of its Northern policy. It is apparent that the regime was preoccupied – and understandably so – with its own survival but in seeking to tailor its Northern policy exclusively to fit its own exigent circumstances, it was paving the way for the total marginalisation of the trapped Northern nationalist minority. How quickly that marginalisation was to take place and what effect it was to have on anti-partitionism would be determined, to a large degree, by the unforeseen and unwanted events that accompanied the war as it advanced into the remaining Republican strongholds in Kerry and Cork.

The war in the southwest began well for the Provisional Government. In early August, the National Army decided to use a series of coordinated sea landings along the Munster coast in order to liberate the area from the Irregulars' increasingly unpopular control. The Provisional Government's military successes in north Kerry and Cork soon made it clear that Lynch's Republic of Munster was vulnerable and by mid-August, the Provisional Government had succeeded in clearing the Irregulars from every town or population centre of any size in the region.

With the war in the field winding down, General Collins began an inspection tour of the southwest command. The tour was just underway when the Commander-in-Chief was forced to return to the capital upon receiving news that Arthur Griffith had died. Griffith, who had survived a slight stroke earlier in the month, succumbed to the effects of a cerebral haemorrhage on 12 August. Although the health of the Dáil President had prevented him from taking a more active role in the administration of the state for some time,[64] as the architect of the Sinn Féin organisation and a principal signatory of the Treaty, he was widely regarded as the 'brains of the movement'.[65] As Churchill noted in a letter to his wife Clementine, Griffith's death represented a 'serious blow' to the regime.[66] The *Derry Journal* greeted this discomforting news with 'profound shock of surprise and sorrow', noting that Griffith's death represented Ireland's greatest loss since the passing of Young Irelander Thomas Davis.[67] Indicative of his

Irish Parliamentary Party Leaders John Dillon, John Redmond and Joseph Devlin. Reproduced courtesy of the National Library of Ireland, Dublin (NPA RED6).

Joseph Devlin, Belfast MP and Northern Nationalist Leader. Reproduced courtesy of the National Library of Ireland, Dublin (NPA PERS9).

Éamon de Valera, President of Dáil Éireann, photo taken between 1914 and 1923. Reproduced courtesy of the National Library of Ireland, Dublin (KE 31).

Michael Collins, 1921. Reproduced courtesy of the National Library of Ireland, Dublin (NPA MKN40).

Cahir Healy, Fermanagh Sinn Féin politician, seated for a formal portrait on 7 July 1932. © National Portrait Gallery, London (NPG x48253).

Republican group portrait, with Cathal Brugha (centre), and Éamon de Valera peeking out from behind the camera, 10 July 1922. Reproduced courtesy of the National Library of Ireland, Dublin (HOG 235).

National Army troops shelling the occupied Four Courts, summer 1922. Reproduced courtesy of the National Library of Ireland, Dublin (HOG 85).

Michael Collins and Arthur Griffith, the principle signatories of the Anglo-Irish Treaty, shown here in 1922. Reproduced courtesy of the National Library of Ireland, Dublin (NPA POLI9).

The Provisional Government of the Irish Free State, with William T. Cosgrave sitting at the head of the table, flanked by Ernest Blythe and Kevin O'Higgins to his right, 1922. Reproduced courtesy of the National Library of Ireland, Dublin (HOG 97).

William T. Cosgrave at his desk, 1922. Reproduced courtesy of the National Library of Ireland, Dublin (KE 243).

The first sitting of the Irish Boundary Commission in Ireland, 9 December 1924. Left to right: F.B. Bourdillon (Secretary), J. R. Fisher (Northern Ireland), Richard Feetham (Chairman), Eoin MacNeill (Irish Free State), and C. Beerstecher (Feetham's private secretary). Reproduced courtesy of the National Library of Ireland, Dublin (HOG 88).

The Boundary Commissioners while in Armagh, 9 December 1924. Reproduced courtesy of the National Library of Ireland, Dublin (HOG 181).

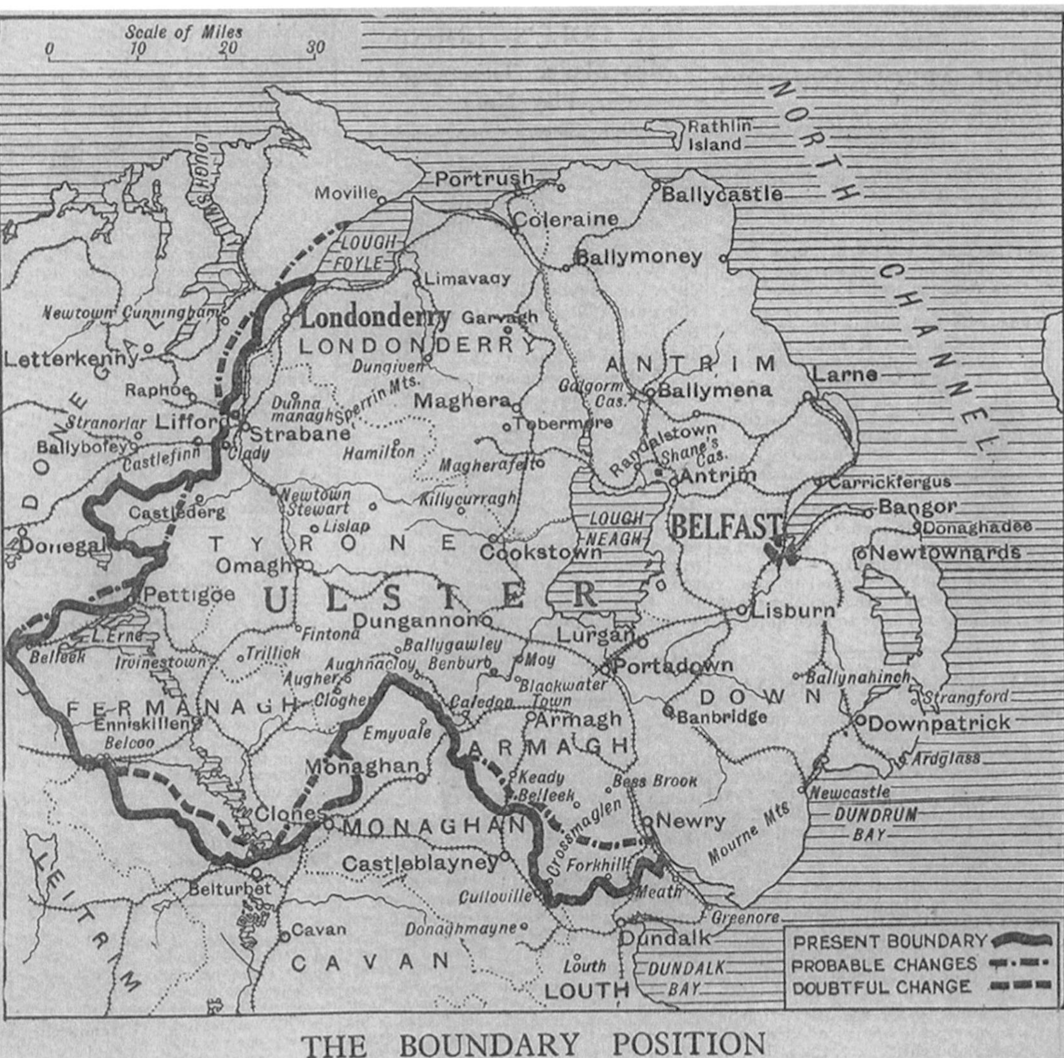

The Morning Post's forecast of the Boundary Commission's findings (*The Morning Post*, 7 November 1925).

integrity, and the moderate strain of the politics he espoused,[68] it is worth noting that it was a Unionist member of the Derry Corporation who – believing that the Dáil President 'was honestly doing his best' – recommended sending a condolence resolution to Griffith's widow.[69]

Already holding the mantle of acting Chairman of the Provisional Government, William T. Cosgrave succeeded Griffith as the President of Dáil Éireann, thus providing a measure of continuity to the business of governing the vulnerable state. Meanwhile, General Collins returned to his military duties on 20 August and resumed his inspection tour of the southwest. Two days later in Co. Cork, Collins' military caravan was ambushed by a small band of Irregulars. During the brief engagement, Collins was mortally wounded. The soldier/statesman died on 22 August 1922, just shy of his thirty-second birthday and only ten days after the death of Arthur Griffith.[70]

The loss of two of the Treatyite regime's most respected and influential members in such a short space of time had an immediate impact on the Provisional Government and its supporters. The public grief of the Dublin population was palpable as thousands of mourners crowded the streets of the city on 28 August, hoping to catch a glimpse of Collins' flag-draped coffin passing by on the way to Glasnevin cemetery.[71] While Dublin may have been shocked and saddened by the loss of the slain leader, the unexpected calamity also caused grave political concerns for Great Britain and, according to Thomas Jones, the news of Collins' death had a 'depressing effect' on Lloyd George.[72] Churchill immediately pledged the 'fullest measure of co-operation and support' to the Provisional Government via Assistant Undersecretary for Ireland Alfred Cope. The Colonial Secretary's uneasiness about the situation was clearly evident in the confidential telegram he sent to Cope, warning of the dangers of a 'sloppy accommodation' emerging between the Provisional Government and de Valera.[73]

The impact of Michael Collins' death was deeply felt among the nationalists of Northern Ireland. Joseph Devlin was reported to be 'deeply shocked and grieved'[74] by the news, while his colleague, J.P. O'Kane, likely expressed the feelings of most Devlinites when he told a UIL audience:

> Michael Collins was done to death by a bullet fired by a fellow-Irishman. We did not agree with Michael Collins politically; this

> does not prevent us expressing our sincere sorrow at his tragic death (hear, hear) He loved Ireland – (applause) – he was prepared to die for her, and, as a matter of fact, did die for her with the noblest Christian sentiments for his slayers and opponents generally on his lips.[75]

In similar fashion, Cardinal Logue issued a statement to the press lamenting the loss of the man whom he claimed 'was the chief hope of a peaceful and prosperous Ireland'.[76]

The *Irish News* had received word of Collins' death in the early morning hours of 23 August – too late to offer its audience anything other than a confirmation of the news.[77] But, rather than adding to the pungent mix of memorials to the slain man,[78] on 24 August, the newspaper chose instead to use the occasion of Collins' death to lash out at the moral depravity of the prevailing conditions in Ireland that had permitted such an act to occur. Its editorial maintained that in the old days when political adversaries disagreed – as was the case in 1918 – they would settle their disputes at the ballot box. Unlike Redmond, Dillon and Devlin who had accepted their defeat with grace, the Republicans had lost both the Treaty debate in the Dáil and the June election but still insisted upon putting Ireland through trials more 'odious' than had Carew or Cromwell. Voicing the sincere hope that Collins' death would awaken the 'dumb and dormant populace ... to their responsibility to Ireland', the *Irish News* also attempted to reassure its readers that anti-partitionism did not die with the Commander-in-Chief. In this instance, the newspaper refrained from speculating on the effect that Collins' death would have on the functioning of the Provisional Government but eagerly asserted that 'political devices' could not sever the six Northern counties from the rest of Ireland.[79]

Symptomatic of their entrapment, the persistence of the Devlinite/ Sinn Féin division was clearly evident in the statements of O'Kane and in the *Irish News* editorial cited above, yet this need not detract from the sincerity of the loss felt. While he may have been a rival for the attentions of the Northern minority and, had they known, the Devlinites would certainly have disapproved of his involvement with the border crises of the spring, Michael Collins was also thought to be critical to the survival of the fledgling state and any hope for a peaceful and united Ireland. Collins had consistently asserted that he would do something to end partition and this, in and of itself, set him apart from the rest of the Southern leadership. But, while there is little doubt that the grief which Devlin and the constitutionalists expressed was genuine, it should be equally clear that the border nationalists were the most deeply affected by the assassination. The *Derry Journal*, citing both the unnatural and un-national character of the ambush, expressed profound shock and anger over the loss of the 'gallant soldier and freedom-loving statesman'.[80] According to Newry's *Frontier Sentinel*, which also circulated in Collins' Northern Ireland constituency (Co. Armagh), the sorrow of the people was 'too great for words'. The newspaper continued:

> Mr Collins had endeared himself to the people by his sterling qualities of heart and mind, and they looked upon him as their chief mainstay in the field as well as in the council chamber against the evil conspiracy to which he has now fallen a victim ... The country mourns the loss of a devoted son and gallant leader, and prays that the calamity may bring the less desperate of those who opposed his policy to a sober realisation of the terrible nature of the course into which they have been seduced.[81]

Although the full impact of the Commander-in-Chief's loss was not yet certain, these statements suggest a realisation among Northern observers that Michael Collins' death would change the face of the Ulster Question.

Whether the Provisional Government would uphold Collins' pledge to deal with Ulster in a definite way now seemed in doubt, as did the status of the Northern Divisions of the pro-Treaty IRA. Had he lived, what General Collins would have (or could have) done to strengthen the Northern Divisions and keep them intact is impossible to know but, as Seamus Woods' 29 September memorandum to his new Commander-in-Chief Richard Mulcahy suggests, at the Curragh, the Northern officers were not getting the level of support that they had expected from the new administration led by William Cosgrave. Woods' lengthy memorandum read in part:

> As I am inclined to believe, the attitude of the present Government towards its followers in the Six Counties, is not that of the late

> General Collins, I am writing this memo. with a view to ascertaining from you what exactly the position of my Division is now, and is likely to be in the future relative to G.H.Q., and I would also like to know through you what policy the Government has for its followers in the Divisional areas.

While Woods was convinced that GHQ 'did their best' to aid the Northern Divisions during the spring of 1922 and had given them direction when the war threatened to set the army in Ulster adrift,[82] it was becoming abundantly clear to the Northern soldiers that Cosgrave and Mulcahy did not share Collins' commitment to their cause.[83] Caution was understandable during this time when allegiances seemed blurred by the Civil War but in keeping with Rabinowitz's trapped minority model, it seems that Northern officers at the Curragh had their nationalist credentials questioned, were treated with suspicion by GHQ and received few resources. Moreover, the administration now seemed intent on folding the Northern Divisions into its National Army, thus severing their ties with Ulster. Because of this, Seamus Woods ultimately left the Curragh, was captured by the Northern authorities and spent the balance of the war in custody. Many of the rank-and-file soldiers in training at the barracks chose to join the National Army, some simply went home, while others found a place in the Irregular forces.[84] Given the extent of these hardships, it was not surprising that, as CO Roger McCorley noted, 'When Collins was killed the northern element [at the Curragh] gave up all hope.'[85]

Notes

1 *Irish News*, 29 September 1922.

2 J. Curran, *The Birth of the Irish Free State, 1921–1923* (n.p.: The University of Alabama Press, 1980), pp. 229–30.

3 M. Hopkinson, 'Civil War and Aftermath, 1922–4', in J.R. Hill (ed.), *A New History of Ireland VII: Ireland, 1921–84* (Oxford: Oxford University Press, 2003), p. 31.

4 R. Lynch, *The Northern IRA and the Early Years of Partition, 1920–1922* (Dublin: Irish Academic Press, 2006), p. 176.

5 The National Army consisted of approximately 10,000 soldiers at the start of the war. Curran, *The Birth of the Irish Free State*, p. 237.

6 Hopkinson, 'Civil War and Aftermath, 1922–4', p. 31.

7 *Irish News*, 29 June 1922.

8 Ibid., 30 June 1922.

9 *Fermanagh Herald,* 1 July 1922; *Irish News,* 29 June 1922.

10 Curran, *The Birth of the Irish Free State,* p. 235; Hopkinson, 'Civil War and Aftermath, 1922–4', p. 32.

11 M. Hopkinson, *Green Against Green: The Irish Civil War* (Dublin: Gill & Macmillan, 2004), p. 191.

12 *Irish News,* 1 July 1922.

13 Ibid.

14 N. Vance, *Irish Literature Since 1800* (London: Pearson Education Limited, 2002), pp. 87–8.

15 *Irish News,* 1 July 1922.

16 Curran, *The Birth of the Irish Free State,* 236; Hopkinson, *Green Against Green,* pp. 183–5.

17 Hopkinson, 'Civil War and Aftermath, 1922–4', p. 32; J. Bowman, *De Valera and the Ulster Question 1917–1973* (Oxford: Clarendon Press, 1982), pp. 76–9.

18 Curran, *The Birth of the Irish Free State,* p. 236.

19 *Irish News,* 3 July 1922.

20 Consider, for instance, the views of a Dungannon man, Cormac MacArt, whose letter entitled 'What's in a Name?' appeared in the *Irish News.* Here MacArt argued that, at the very least, the Republican mutineers were 'curiously un-Irish in their names' and suggested that attempts should be made to 'manufacture' Gallicised names for de Valera, Childers, Barton and Gore–Booth as had been done for Charles Burgess, who cloaked himself in the name Cathal Brugha. The letter continued: 'Well, these names are a pretty cluster. They will shine forth with an odd picturesque effect in the pages of history [while] plain Collins from Cork, and MacKeon from Longford, and O'Duffy from Monaghan, and Mulcahy from Dublin, will appear only commonplace and Irish beside them.' The difficulty of getting up-to-date information during this stage of the war suggests that the timing of the piece may have been coincidental but its racial implications are indicative of the sort of political attacks which the Provisional Government and its supporters would level on Erskine Childers and de Valera throughout the course of the war. *Irish News,* 6 July, 1922.

21 Curran, *The Birth of the Irish Free State,* pp. 136–7; Hopkinson, 'Civil War and Aftermath, 1922–4', p. 37.

22 *Fermanagh Herald,* 1 July 1922.

23 *Irish News,* 4 July 1922.

24 The National Army was commended for its effort to avoid taking the lives of the Irregulars while their enemies 'sought to slay the Free State forces – and their leader mourned over his failure'. *Irish News,* 4 July 1922. In addition, the Provisional Government was also described as being 'loath to demolish' the building inhabited by the Republicans. *Irish News,* 1 July 1922.

25 Ibid., 7 July 1922.

26 Hopkinson, 'Civil War and Aftermath, 1922–4', p. 43.

27 Curran, *The Birth of the Irish Free State,* pp. 236–7.

28 *Irish News,* 4 July 1922.

29 According to Hart, the decision to raise Collins to the position of Commander-in-Chief happened rather nonchalantly and his authority was never defined. P. Hart, *Mick: The Real Michael Collins* (London: Penguin Books Ltd, 2006), pp. 401–2. Yet this seems to have been a seminal event for the survival of the regime which kept 'headstrong' members of the army in line. As Peter Young has argued, Collins' new position also gave the National Army, and the nation, a sense of identity that they otherwise would not have had and likely prevented the emergence of 'local rivalries and animosities' that had hurt the IRA during the Anglo-Irish War. P. Young, 'Michael Collins: A Military Leader', in G. Doherty and D. Keogh (eds), *Michael Collins and the Making of the Irish State* (Boulder: Mercier Press, 1998), pp. 89–90.

30 Hopkinson, 'Civil War and Aftermath, 1922–4', p. 34.

31 Curran, *The Birth of the Irish Free State*, pp. 240, 247.

32 Hopkinson, 'Civil War and Aftermath, 1922–4', p. 34.

33 In their haste to build a National Army, the Provisional Government paid little attention to the health, quality or commitment of their recruits. Curran, *The Birth of the Irish Free State*, p. 238.

34 For instance, in January, James L. O'Donovan complained of 'an almost complete out-of-touchness with affairs' on the part of Liam Lynch. Hopkinson, *Green Against Green*, p. 229.

35 J.M. Regan, *The Irish Counter-Revolution, 1921–1936: Treatyite Politics and Settlement in Independent Ireland* (Dublin: Gill & Macmillan Ltd, 1999), pp. 114–15.

36 For instance, a Capuchin friar complained to Ernie O'Malley that '[w]e are without a government – nothing more in the eyes of the world than murderers and looters'. Hopkinson, 'Civil War and Aftermath, 1922–4', p. 39.

37 Curran, *The Birth of the Irish Free State*, p. 237; Hopkinson, 'Civil War and Aftermath, 1922–4', p 38.

38 The Bill, which according to Phoenix was 'a reflection of the Craig government's limited horizons and lack of generosity', sought to discontinue the use of proportional representation in the state's local elections. E. Phoenix, *Northern Nationalism: Nationalist Politics, Partition and the Catholic Minority in Northern Ireland, 1890–1940* (Belfast: Ulster Historical Foundation, 1994), pp. 243–4.

39 *Irish News*, 27 June 1922.

40 Michael Collins to Winston Churchill, 28 June 1922, in M. Gilbert, *Winston S. Churchill: Volume IV Companion Part 3 Documents April 1921–November 1922* (London: William Heinemann Ltd., 1977), pp. 1923–4.

41 Phoenix, *Northern Nationalism*, pp. 236–40.

42 *Irish News*, 4 July 1922.

43 Ibid.

44 All of the Northern Divisions were in 'terminal decline' by June as a consequence of the Northern offensive. J. McDermott, *Northern Divisions: The Old IRA and the Belfast Pogroms, 1920–22* (Belfast: Beyond the Pale, 2001), pp. 245–6, 257.

45 E. Staunton, *The Nationalists of Northern Ireland, 1918–1973* (Dublin: The Columba Press, 2001), pp. 53, 71; Hopkinson, *Green Against Green*, p. 248.

46 Seamus Woods to the Commander-in-Chief, 29 September, 1922, Department of the Taoiseach, NAI/TSCH/S 1801/A, National Archives of Ireland, Dublin.

47 C. Day, 'Political violence in the Newry/Armagh area 1912–1925' (PhD diss., Queen's University, Belfast, 1999), pp. 258, 297–300. With respect to what Hart called the 'same old IRA independence in action', see his explanation for Collins' 'reimmersion in the army'. Hart, *Mick: The Real Michael Collins*, pp. 401–2.

48 Hopkinson, *Green Against Green*, p. 146–53.

49 Curran, *The Birth of the Irish Free State*, pp. 241–2.

50 *Irish News*, 7 July 1922.

51 Ibid., 20 July 1922.

52 Ibid., 17 July 1922.

53 Oliver Plunkett was the Catholic Archbishop of Armagh and Primate of All Ireland (1669–1681). He was falsely implicated in the Popish Plot – a Catholic conspiracy that began in 1678 and aimed to murder King Charles II. The Archbishop was hanged, drawn and quartered at Tyburn in 1681. He was beatified in 1920 and canonised in 1975. M. Elliott, *The Catholics of Ulster: A History* (London: Penguin Books, 2000), pp. 144–5; J. Bardon, *A History of Ulster* (Belfast: Blackstaff Press, 2001), p. 145.

54 *Irish News*, 11 July 1922.

55 Part of Churchill's reply read: 'In any event I feel bound to observe that the continuing refusal of the Catholic minority in the North to recognize the Northern Government robs of much of their substance and possible validity the arguments urged in your letter against the passage of the Bill ...There is another wider aspect of the case which is of general constitutional importance and has a direct interest for the future Government of the Free State. The matters with which this Bill deals are *prima facie* matters solely of domestic concern to Northern Ireland and, according to constitutional practice, such a Bill, if passed by an existing Dominion Parliament, would not be reserved.' Winston Churchill to Michael Collins, 31 July 1922, in Gilbert, *Winston S. Churchill: Volume IV Companion Part 3*, p. 1943.

56 *Irish News*, 17 July 1922.

57 Hopkinson, *Green Against Green*, pp. 169–71.

58 McDermott, *Northern Divisions*, p. 254; Phoenix, *Northern Nationalism*, p. 245.

59 Staunton, *The Nationalists of Northern Ireland*, p. 71.

60 Seamus Woods to the Commander-in-Chief, 29 September, 1922, Department of the Taoiseach, NAI/TSCH/S 1801/A, National Archives of Ireland, Dublin; Hopkinson, *Green Against Green*, pp. 248–52; Phoenix, *Northern Nationalism*, pp. 246–7.

61 Eoin MacNeill became Minister for Education before the end of the year and Hayes became Speaker of Dáil Éireann in September 1922.

62 McDermott, *Northern Divisions*, p. 265

63 C. Day, 'Political violence in the Newry/Armagh area, 1912–1925', p. 305.

64 Curran, *The Birth of the Irish Free State*, pp. 243–7.

65 *Derry Journal*, 14 August 1922.

66 Winston Churchill to Clementine Churchill, 14 August 1922, in Gilbert, *Winston S. Churchill: Volume IV Companion Part 3*, p. 1957.

67 *Derry Journal*, 14 August 1922.

68 Curran, *The Birth of the Irish Free State*, p. 248.

69 In the end, Mayor O'Doherty decided that it would be inappropriate to send condolences to Mrs Griffith since none had been sent to the family of Sir Henry Wilson. *Irish News*, 22 August 1922.

70 Hopkinson, *Green Against Green*, pp. 176–9.

71 The *Irish News* estimated that as many as 500,000 Dubliners came out onto the streets to witness this historical event. *Irish News*, 29 August 1922.

72 K. Middlemas (ed.), *Thomas Jones Whitehall Diary, Volume III, Ireland, 1918–1925* (London: Oxford University Press, 1971), p. 217.

73 Winston Churchill to Alfred Cope, 24 August 1922, in Gilbert, *Winston S. Churchill: Volume IV Companion Part 3*, p. 1963.

74 *Irish News*, 25 August 1922.

75 Ibid., 28 August 1922.

76 Ibid., 25 August 1922.

77 Ibid., 23 August 1922.

78 With the plight of the Northern minority as its main concern, the *Irish News* saved its memorial to the slain man for the days following his funeral. *Irish News*, 28 August 1922.

79 *Irish News*, 24 August 1922.

80 *Derry Journal*, 25 August 1922.

81 Day, 'Political violence in the Newry/Armagh area', p. 304.

82 Seamus Woods to the Commander-in-Chief, 29 September, 1922, Department of the Taoiseach, S 1801/A, National Archives of Ireland, Dublin.

83 McDermott, *Northern Divisions*, p. 266.

84 Phoenix, *Northern Nationalism*, pp. 252–3, 259; McDermott, *Northern Divisions*, pp. 271, 274.

85 Hopkinson, *Green Against Green*, p. 249.

CHAPTER 7

'No Other Policy': Regime Change, Northern Policy and the 'Hideous Skeletons' of War

> I believe that if the mischief in Ireland can be ended (and I believe the greater part of it can be), it can only be ended if the North of Ireland makes a generous gesture to the South, and if the South holds out its hand generously, as I know it would, to the North (cheers).
>
> – Joe Devlin[1]

That so much emphasis was placed on the effects of Michael Collins' death merely underscores Michael Hopkinson's observation that there was more than one pro-Treaty perspective and many different reasons for supporting the Treaty. Throughout the spring and summer of 1922, the most noticeable division separating the members of the Provisional Government was between the IRA/IRB men like Collins and Mulcahy, who had only grudgingly accepted the need to confront the Republicans, and the politicians who had long urged such a course of action.[2] It is not unimportant, therefore, that William T. Cosgrave – the man tapped to fill the positions left vacant by Collins and Griffith – was a politician rather than a soldier.[3] This chapter explores the Provisional Government's efforts to distance itself from the boundary question as the Civil War entered a particularly dark period. Regime change in both Dublin and the United Kingdom form the backdrop for the chapter, which also discusses Joe Devlin's departure from Westminster politics and Northern nationalists' increasing marginalisation from the politics of the Irish mother nation.

Despite differences that would eventually emerge, in the aftermath of Collins' death, Cosgrave was eager to dispel any doubts about his intention to carry out the general programme set out by his predecessors. The new Irish leader assured a Southern audience at the end of August that:

> The Government so formed has stood, as you know, with unanswering consistency to the program of carrying into full effect in accordance with the declared will of the Irish people and the Treaty which was entered into between the Plenipotentiaries, and recommended by President Griffith and General Collins as offering the fairest hopes to our much tried people. We, their colleagues, have the same faith, stand by the same policy, and though overwhelm[ed] with sorrow take up the same task with the same determination and confidence.[4]

A self-admitted reluctant leader, Cosgrave would prove to be an effective administrator, quickly gaining the respect of the British government,[5] but his responsibilities were far from easy and his decisions not always popular. This was due, in large part, to the fact that he had inherited an administration that was overburdened by the debts of a war that had not yet ended. Cosgrave was also prepared to deal much more firmly with the Irregulars than was his predecessor.

With limited Republican successes in early September, the Irregular campaign had, by and large, deteriorated into a guerrilla war by the end of the month. They set up flying columns, carried out ambushes and sabotaged transportation and communication networks.[6] The Irish press vilified the largely inactive Erskine Childers for this campaign of destruction[7] but in reality, Liam Lynch was directing operations as the Republican Chief-of-Staff and Lynch continued to hope that destructive activities would render the state ungovernable. Sincere as he may have been, however, Lynch's eternal optimism could not mask the fact that his insurgency was in dire trouble and this did not go unnoticed. According to the *Irish News*:

> The 'civil war', as a war, has been easily won by the soldiers of the Free State Government; if these soldiers numbered 300,000, instead of 20,000 or thereabouts, they could not prevent the

> occurrence of incidences like the sudden attack on unarmed men at Cork City on Saturday, the ambushes, in all parts of the Twenty-six Counties, the blowing up of bridges, the uprooting of railway lines, and the robberies planned and carried out by criminals in the cities, towns and rural areas alike.

As this report suggests, the newspaper clearly grasped the protracted nature of guerrilla warfare. In an attempt to hurry the war to its inevitable conclusion, the Devlinite organ boldly called upon the victims of Republican raiding and commandeering to rise up and oust their tormenters.[8]

With the conduct of the war seemingly under control, the Third Dáil began its long-awaited sitting on 9 September 1922. With important work lying ahead, the primary purpose of this opening session was a bit of much needed housekeeping. William Cosgrave was formally elected head of the government and, as expected, he used this occasion to merge the offices he held – the Dáil Presidency and the Chairmanship of the Provisional Government – while also presenting his ministers to the Dáil. The Third Dáil had been selected by the pact election of early June and, for the first time in the history of the legislature, Labour and the Dublin University representatives chose to attend. With the exception of Laurence Ginnell, the Republicans boycotted the proceedings, which left Labour to act as the official opposition.[9]

The Irish Free State constitution was the most pressing business before the Dáil. The Anglo-Irish Treaty mandated that a permanent authority replace the Provisional Government before 6 December; therefore, in late September, the government set to work designing a bill that would secure this provision. It was, however, another piece of legislation that would spark the greatest controversy in the months that followed. On 27 September, the Dáil enacted a Special Powers Act – a device that gave the government and military wide martial discretion, including the power to execute political prisoners.[10] This controversial piece of legislation provided the Provisional Government a new weapon with which to wage war; however, its usage – which did not immediately follow – unwittingly set in motion some of the darkest events of the Irish Civil War.

Although the Six-County supporters of the Provisional Government were fully aware of the importance of the Dáil's autumn sitting, the

Northern nationalists were facing their own challenges at this time. On 11 September, Northern Ireland finally received royal assent for its Local Government Act. Assent had been held back amidst protests from Collins and Cosgrave – as well as Joe Devlin and his associate Raymond Burke – but, as Churchill had implied in June, the British government did not have the authority, much less the stomach, to challenge the Unionist administration over a matter considered to be local in nature. The fact that Craig and his administration had threatened to resign unless the Bill was approved only encouraged Churchill's inclination not to make this a constitutional issue between London and Belfast.[11] The Act not only abolished the use of proportional representation for local elections – a provision which had enabled nationalists to control a number of municipal bodies since 1920 – but also permitted the Home Ministry to alter constituency boundaries, leading to fears of further gerrymandering.[12]

That Derry City's first Catholic Corporation in more than 300 years[13] would inevitably be thrown out of office by the expected consequences of these changes likely explains why the Corporation, in late September, raised the idea of holding an anti-partitionist conference. The proposed conference was to be attended by Sinn Féiners and Devlinites holding seats in the Northern parliament and, as Mayor Hugh O'Doherty explained, it was intended to seek ways of 'bringing about unity in support of a common policy'.[14] Naturally, the Devlinites enthusiastically supported the idea. As the idea for a conference was coming to fruition, the *Irish News* was telling its readers that they 'should work out their own salvation or deliberately consign themselves to political and economic perdition' since, the newspaper continued: 'President Cosgrave and his colleagues have much to learn yet; but they can do nothing for the Nationalists of the Six Counties under the most favourable of southern conditions if these Nationalists sit in pitiful lethargy and refuse to do anything practical for themselves.'[15] For his part, Devlin, in a letter to the editor of the Unionist *Northern Whig*, expressed his support for 'the suggestion of the Mayor of Derry that a conference should be called', adding, 'I am now, as I have always been, most anxious to bring about peace and unity in Ulster and in Ireland, and will always be glad to co-operate with any and every party to secure that most desirable end.'[16]

Devlinite support of the idea of holding a conference bolstered the pleas for anti-partitionist unity that Devlin, his supporters and the *Irish News* had raised with some regularity since the Treaty debates. Perhaps more importantly, because two of the six Sinn Féin members of the Northern parliament – Arthur Griffith and Michael Collins – were now deceased and the anti-Treaty Sinn Féin MPs Éamon de Valera and Sean O'Mahony would both be unwelcome at and unlikely to attend the proposed Derry conference, Devlinite MPs would have a numerical advantage over pro-Treaty Sinn Féin MPs by a margin of five to two. Under these circumstances, the Devlinites would be in a position to shape any policy decisions that came out of the type of parliamentary conference that the Derry Corporation had in mind.[17]

As the *Irish News* was appealing for those of nationalist opinion to give the plan 'Fair Play',[18] the proposed conference was meeting with lukewarm support elsewhere. Leery that the idea might be a precursor to the recognition of the Northern parliament – an idea that all Devlinites were suspected of supporting – the *Derry Journal* likened the conference to a 'web of words' that risked trapping 'unwary flies' in the Ulster 'parlour'.[19] If the reaction of some unreceptive border nationalists was not enough to scuttle plans for the conference, the reluctance of Seán Milroy and Eoin MacNeill to participate in its proceedings was likely to have just that effect. Milroy and MacNeill were both members of the Dáil who held Northern seats[20] and neither was inclined to support the call for a conference along the lines that the Derry Corporation had intended. In particular, Milroy's letter of response to the invitation cited objections to the restricted nature of the conference membership list. He informed the Mayor:

> I am in thorough agreement with the main idea expressed in the resolution which you enclose – viz., 'to try and bring about a rapprochement of parties with a view of establishing unity and the pursuance of a common policy in the area for a united Ireland.' In my opinion, a meeting such as suggested, *consisting only of those who at the moment are the elected Parliamentary representatives,* would not help materially towards that end, and therefore I do not see my way to attend such a meeting. I think, however, that a conference, representative of various phases of opinion in the Six Counties, and not confined to Parliamentary representatives,

> is most desirable and necessary to secure the object indicated in your letter.

The letter continued: 'I am at present consulting with Professor M'Neill, who is the only other representative of the Six County area in the Dail, as to the practicality of summoning such a conference, and I shall acquaint you at the earliest possible moment as to what we propose to do in this connection.'[21] After receiving Milroy's letter, Mayor O'Doherty advised a Dublin interviewer that he had no intention of proceeding with the matter.[22]

Stymied by the poor reception that the Derry conference had received, a group of prominent border nationalists were taking a different tack. Having formed a deputation to wait on the Provisional Government, this delegation had an increasingly rare audience with Cosgrave and members of his administration on 11 October. Alex Donnelly, the Omagh solicitor and Sinn Féiner, spoke first for the deputation and expressed concerns over the Provisional Government's delay in setting up the Boundary Commission. Donnelly scornfully noted that 'the disastrous Civil War which has been raging has strengthened the hands of our enemies in the north. And so long as your energies are engaged in Civil War they will be more truculent.'[23] The Omagh man beseeched President Cosgrave to find a way to force the Northern government to abandon its plan to abolish proportional representation, while ominously warning that the delays were allowing James Craig to consolidate his hold on the border areas, leaving the 'growing feeling in the North that ... the boundary as fixed at present will remain fixed unless something is done as soon as possible'.[24]

Thomas Harbison was, perhaps, more direct in his critique of the Unionist government and what he was expecting from his Southern advocates. '[W]e know our "Ulster",' said the old Hibernian, adding:

> We know our 'Ulster' Orange friends, we know they hate us and we know they will never coalesce with us until they are pressed in, either by financial pressure or by the gun. And if you, Sir, as I may say representing the Irish Nation can't do something to help us I am afraid we are in a perilous condition in the North.[25]

Recognising that Cosgrave had little legal means of influencing Belfast on electoral matters, Newry solicitor J.H. Collins chose instead to raise concerns over Britain's impartiality in the functioning of the Boundary Commission if it were ever convened.[26] This led Frank Bonner and Michael Lynch to press the Irish President to set up an organisation to combat what they considered to be the Craig government's 'mischievous propaganda' – that is, its public protestations that the Boundary Commission would not function and the minority should 'accept the inevitable'.[27] With regard to publicising the anti-partitionist case, Bonner assertively informed Cosgrave, 'the providing of the money will be your end of the stick and not ours'.[28]

That the Provisional Government's Northern policy was in a state of flux during the autumn of 1922 was apparent throughout the course of the meeting. Just days earlier, Kevin O'Shiel, the Assistant Legal Advisor to the Provisional Government, had submitted a telling report to the administration on the North. In addition to fuelling the Provisional Government's distrust of Hibernianism, O'Shiel's report strongly urged the Provisional Government to seek a means of shifting the responsibility for Northern affairs, and any 'unpleasantness' over policy, to the nationalist minority.

> I am strongly of the opinion that the Government should not take on itself the utterly thankless task of elaborating a policy on all these points [the Northern Ireland–Free State relationship and the impact of this relationship on Six-County MPs] without consulting the North-Eastern Nationalists. The onus (and unpleasantness), if any of an ultimate decision in these matters should be placed on the shoulders of those directly concerned, viz: the Nationalists of the North-East. I am convinced that this is the best policy and certainly the safest one for the Government, because: 1) The government cannot be blamed henceforth if anything should go wrong with the taunt that 'It went behind the backs of the Ulster People, and that it let the Ulster people down.' If this suggestion is carried out, the 'letting down' henceforth will be done by themselves.[29]

The callous tone of O'Shiel's report says much about the direction that the Provisional Government's Northern policy appeared to be taking and its increasing marginalisation of Northern concerns. So, too, did the fact that the administration was simultaneously preparing to act on the recommendations of Ernest Blythe's Northern committee with regard to the payment of Northern teachers – a matter that would eventually spark cries of betrayal.[30]

Notwithstanding the Provisional Government's obvious efforts to distance itself from minority politics, anti-partitionism had witnessed at least one positive development in advance of the border deputation's arrival. On 2 October, President Cosgrave established the North Eastern Boundary Bureau (NEBB), thus anticipating the suggestions that would be made by Lynch and Bonner. Placed under the direction of O'Shiel and E.M. Stephens, the NEBB was designed to carry out research, disseminate propaganda and coordinate the collection of evidence.[31] Kevin O'Shiel was given the task of explaining the function of the organisation to the deputation of border nationalists during the 11 October meeting. In a tactic that reinforced the conclusion of his previously tabled report, O'Shiel told the deputation that the NEBB would need at least to appear to be working at a distance from the Irish government. Bonner and Lynch both applauded the measures to be adopted by the NEBB and three of the Northerners in attendance – J.H. Collins, Alex Donnelly and Thomas Harbison – ultimately took up positions as agents for the organisation.[32]

The Provisional Government's overall strategy for defeating partition was one thing that had apparently not changed. With that in mind, unity by contraction continued to be the guiding principle for dealing with Northern Ireland, since, as O'Shiel told the deputation, if they could succeed in removing as little as ten or fifteen square miles from the 'barely self-supporting' Northern government, their case would be won.[33] According to Kevin O'Higgins, the size of the area to be wrestled away from Belfast was crucial because 'area means people and people mean money' and it was on this that Northern Ireland would 'sink or swim'.[34]

Although this line of thinking assumed that Northern Ireland would avail itself of its right to contract out of the Free State and retain its links with Great Britain, which was all but inevitable, the slim possibility remained that Belfast would not take this tack and some border nationalists felt this would present its own risks. According to Harbison, Northern nationalists would be 'hopeless for eternity' if Northern Ireland chose to put itself under Free State jurisdiction in exchange for local autonomy because, in Harbison's view, there would be no way to end Belfast's sectarian policies within the area it controlled.[35] Although these fears were neither understood nor appreciated by the Southern leaders,[36] Harbison's alarm-ridden comments compelled President Cosgrave and Kevin O'Higgins to address issues related to gerrymandering and Northern Ireland's local elections.

The Irish President asserted that he was still attempting to prevent the abolition of proportional representation; however, his comments about Northern Ireland's upcoming local elections were more revealing. It bears remembering that, as the Minister for Local Government, Cosgrave had sparred with Cahir Healy over funding and the Minister's suggested retreat from the non-recognition 'experiment'.[37] Given this history, the continuation of the Civil War and the Cosgrave administration's newfound desire to remain at arms-length from the Northern minority, the President's views on the matter were to be expected. 'You must yourselves make up your minds as to whether you will contest those elections,' said Cosgrave, who continued:

> we take very strong action here against people who don't give allegiance to the Government here. If we were to take the line that would be popular in the North and advise the people there not to give allegiance to that 'Northern' Government it would be used against us down here; and it would also be used against us by the North. So we can't in a matter of that sort interfere. And it must be a question for yourselves.

The Irish President assured the deputation that his government was prepared to push their concerns 'to the bitter end' but it was nonetheless clear that the Michael Collins era was over.[38]

While Cosgrave's comments were indicative of his government's approach to the North, Kevin O'Higgins' closing remarks were undeniably directed at the Northern nationalists themselves and in particular, the need to get their Northern house in order. In his lengthy comments to the deputation, the Home Minister argued that 'the chief difficulty' affecting Northern nationalism was lack of cohesiveness and with this,[39] the absence of what Rabinowitz might have described as a 'strategic vision'.[40] The reason for the disarray, O'Higgins perceptively concluded, was:

> the very human reason of the conflicting interests. There is a conflict of interests between the man who has and the man who has not a dog's chance of getting out of the Boundary area. There is a conflict of interest between the man in Belfast and the man down in the Border. And if we are not careful that conflict of interest will pretty well spoil things.[41]

As O'Higgins observed, while one section of the minority – the Devlinites – were impatiently hoping to make use of the Northern parliament, others had rested all of their hopes on the Boundary Commission. Ultimate unity, he maintained, was going to be a gradual process requiring a uniform policy and, he warned, 'that particular problem can't be solved by the sword or by the gun'. Rather, '[t]he people who know they have not a dog's chance under the Boundary Commission [i.e. the Devlinites], should be prepared to mark time, and give those who have a chance an opportunity of playing their hand'.[42] Attempting to reassure his audience of the Provisional Government's commitment to ending partition, O'Higgins concluded:

> We have no other policy for the North East than the Treaty policy [that is, full use of Article 12 and other economic or diplomatic pressures to secure Irish unity] ... Now any doubts about the intention of this Government with regards to the Treaty and the North eastern question are simply doubts created by the propaganda of Sir James Craig and his immediate followers.[43]

As insightful as the Home Minister's comments were, and aside from the irony provided by the context of the bitterly factional Civil War, it is worth recalling that the Provisional Government had not helped to heal the divisions between Northern nationalists. Seán Milroy and Eoin MacNeill were partially responsible for the failure of Mayor O'Doherty's Derry conference on unity, and Kevin O'Shiel's important report on the North made it clear that the AOH was to be seen as a rival rather than a partner and little effort had thus far been made to seek an accommodation with the Devlinites. It might also be mentioned that O'Higgins' plea for unity was given before an audience that was made up entirely of men from the border regions – those who did have a dog's chance of salvation via the Boundary Commission.

Notwithstanding these contradictions, O'Higgins' comments must have had some effect on J.H. Collins. Following the deputation's meeting with the Provisional Government, the Newry man wrote to Peader Murney – a Northern Republican who was at the time incarcerated in a Free State prison – urging Murney to unite with his political opponents behind the anti-partitionist banner. '[N]o matter what one's individual views are regarding the Republican position[,] the Treaty position or for that matter any other position,' said Collins:

> all hands should join and pull on the one rope, in the effort to reduce Craig's territory ... To my mind at the present time, there is only one fight to hand, and that is on the Boundary question, and all other things should wait till that is decided ... I would suggest to you that without killing 'Mr Principle' you should give him a rest till after the Boundary question is decided, and then wake him up and let him take his old place again, if you think right.[44]

That Collins was unsuccessful in his plea need not invalidate the effort.

As illuminating as J.H. Collins' letter was in the context of divisive Northern politics, it had been penned at a time when an important dimension of Anglo-Irish relations was changing. In a departure from the events of the past, however, this time the *coup de théâtre* was actually taking place in Britain, where David Lloyd George's governing coalition was about to burst at the seams. Fed up by Lloyd George's missteps both at home and abroad,[45] restless Tories were eager for a return to pre-War party politics and the dissidents among them were prepared to depose coalition linchpins within their own party to achieve that aim. It was in this context that Tory leader Austen Chamberlain unwittingly decided to seek a vote of confidence in the party leadership. The meeting was to take place at the Carlton Club on 19 October.[46]

As events in Britain were about to reach their crescendo, the *Derry Journal* could take great joy in the irony that 'office holders having half a lifetime's experience of statecraft' were mired in such a fiasco across the Channel while 'the political sky in Ireland, long gloomy with the menace of successive gales, [was] assuming a distinctly brighter hue'.[47] As such, the relative calm of Dáil Éireann represented a stark contrast to the British House of Commons. The re-emergence of contentious debate in the Dáil surrounding the constitution's draft oath of allegiance did cause some observers to fear a return to 'word-spinning'[48] but political divisions were sufficiently papered over to allow the enactment of the Bill in late October. Moreover, the Provisional Government also gained much needed support from the Catholic hierarchy through the publication, on 10 October, of a fiery Episcopal letter decrying the depravity of the Irregular campaign and mandating stiff punishments for those who engaged in guerilla tactics.[49]

Supporters of the Treaty north and south of the Irish border could also find some solace in the apparent disarray of Irish Republicanism at the time. In mid-October, a series of captured letters written by de Valera, Lynch and other prominent men within the movement were printed in the Irish press. Written a month earlier, the letters revealed how deeply despondent de Valera had become over the conduct of the war and in particular, the submergence of the anti-Treaty Party to the dictates of the army. The letters indicated that the former President of Dáil Éireann had attempted to meet with the Army Executive in the early autumn but was rebuffed by Liam Lynch. As a result, de Valera threatened to 'resign publicly' unless the position of the movements' political organ was 'straightened out' in relation to the army. His opinion would eventually change on this matter but the letters also suggest that de Valera was attempting to block as futile any effort to engineer the establishment of a Republican government to rival the Treatyite regime.[50]

The captured communications represented something of a propaganda godsend for the Provisional Government as it reinforced persistent allegations about Éamon de Valera's powerlessness within the movement. At the time that the letters were written, the *Irish News* was actually reporting that both political and military matters within Republicanism were being 'inspired, controlled, and directed by the

Englishman Childers'[51] and now, in the face of such clear evidence of de Valera's waning influence and the overall weakening of the insurgency, the newspaper could feel justified in asking 'for what tangible or imaginable object is the campaign of national destruction carried on after the disappearance of Mr de Valera from the scene – assuming that he has followed his authority in to oblivion?'[52]

Unbeknownst to the *Irish News*, however, the information gleaned from the captured letters was out of date by the time it was published. Meeting in mid-October for the first time since July, the IRA Executive ultimately paved the way for the establishment of a Republican government and such a body was soon formed from the nucleus of the Third Dáil's anti-Treaty TDs. De Valera, rescinding his earlier objections, accepted the Presidency of this counter-government, appointed ministers and advised the press of the changed circumstances.[53]

That the establishment of a Republican government garnered little attention from the anti-partitionist press betrays the sterility of the movement and its announcement at a time when all eyes seemed fixated on Britain during the heady days of the 'crumbling coalition'.[54] On the day of the fateful Carlton Club meeting, the *Irish News* seemed confident that Lloyd George would be able to fend off the simmering revolt he was facing at the hands of disgruntled Conservatives[55] but this would not be the case. After rousing speeches from Stanley Baldwin and Andrew Bonar Law, the party voted 187 to 87 in favour of breaking the coalition and fighting the next election as an independent party. As a result, Lloyd George resigned and four days later Bonar Law became Prime Minister and leader of the Conservative Party as the United Kingdom prepared for an election.[56]

The *Irish News* boastfully feigned disinterest in the demise of the man who 'wrought the infamy of partition';[57] however, the fall of the coalition clearly had consequences for Ireland and the Treaty. Notwithstanding nationalist fear that it, like the Treaty of Limerick, would be 'disgracefully "broken ere the ink wherewith 'twas writ could dry"',[58] David Lloyd George and his coalition partners had stood by their word, fended off diehard attacks on the Treaty and continued to consider Irish unity as a worthy policy objective.[59] Since a sitting government at Westminster would still need to ratify the Free State constitution before the 6 December deadline, it is little wonder that the emergence of the Bonar Law premiership was a source of anxiety for Dublin. Bonar Law was, after all, a man of impeccable Unionist credentials and there was no way to know how far he would be willing to go in support of the Treaty settlement as Prime Minister or what role he would afford his party's right wing on such matters. It is significant, therefore, that the very timing of the Westminster election was determined by the exigencies of the Irish timetable.[60] The Prime Minister also took great pains to reassure nationalists and unionists alike in advance of the election by pledging to both 'carry out the Treaty' and 'safeguard the freedom of the Government of "Northern" Ireland'.[61] Even a diehard of Lord Salisbury's ilk could apparently see that 'Ireland's clock could not be put back'[62] and, given what might have been, this all boded well for the Treaty settlement.

It was in this context of British instability and urgent electioneering that J.H. Collins had issued his appeal for all anti-partitionists 'to join and pull on the one rope'.[63] While all signs seemed to suggest that Bonar Law was loath to reopen the Irish Question, Collins did have reason to be concerned. The divided Northern nationalists were unprepared to fight an election and although Kevin O'Shiel had advised using the occasion in order to 'register another emphatic protest against Partition',[64] they would have to do so weakened by the disadvantages of redistricting. The greatest hardship in this regard would be endured by Joe Devlin and his supporters since the West Belfast/Falls constituency that Devlin had held since 1906 was no longer a nationalist stronghold. The Better Government of Ireland Act (1920) had reduced the number of Westminster representatives that the six Ulster counties making up Northern Ireland were to have and the 1922 Westminster election was going to be the first election fought in these new and enlarged constituencies.

Known as the Falls Division of Belfast between 1918 and 1922, Devlin's constituency had once had one of the smallest electorates in Ulster; but now, because of the redistricting, West Belfast re-emerged as one of Northern Ireland's largest constituencies and was thought to have a significant Unionist majority.[65] '[T]he Belfast electoral areas have been so shamelessly [g]errymandered as to make the return of a Nationalist Member impossible,' wrote Devlin in a letter to his long-time friend and colleague Alderman Richard Byrne. Despite the good will that the MP had earned from many working-class Protestants in his region of Belfast over the previous sixteen years at Westminster, under the current sectarian conditions there was no chance that Devlin could overcome this electoral change. The MP bowed out of the West Belfast contest and offered himself (unsuccessfully) in the Liverpool exchange seat 'in order to avoid putting [his] friends and supporters [in Belfast] to the trouble and expense of a contest' that he regarded as 'both futile and farcical'.[66]

Similar circumstances also made Derry virtually impossible for nationalists to win; thus, the nationalist-dominated joint constituency of Fermanagh–Tyrone represented the only viable venue to register an anti-partition protest. Thomas Harbison and the Fermanagh Sinn Féiner Cahir Healy were nominated to contest these crucial border seats for the Northern minority.[67] Despite Healy's internment, the lack of any electoral machinery and alleged voter intimidation, the anti-partitionists handily won the constituency. Touting the view that the region had given 'expression through the ballot-boxes', Harbison loudly proclaimed that 'no longer could their enemies blind the world to the verdict'.[68]

In Britain, any hope that Lloyd George would be able to claw his way back to power evaporated on election day. Bonar Law's Conservatives easily won the November election securing 344 seats overall and a 77 seat majority.[69] Though arguably 'less talented' than the previous coalition ministry had been,[70] Bonar Law had clearly avoided, with the exception of Lord Salisbury, assembling an administration dominated by extreme Conservatives of the type James Craig might have preferred.[71] Certainly Bonar Law's Ulster-centred approach represented a change of perspective from his predecessors; however, as Thomas Jones and Lionel Curtis continued to be the conduits through which Irish affairs were channelled, and with no one really wanting to rock the boat, there would be no sudden departures of policy.[72]

As Britain's new Conservative government was finding its legs, the course of the Irish Civil War began to take a very dark turn. In mid-November, the Provisional Government, making use of its emergency powers legislation, executed five prisoners for arms violations. Having been captured in possession of a small pistol on 10 November, there was little doubt that the much-maligned Erskine Childers would soon meet a similar fate and, in a trial that began 17 November, he and eight others were condemned to death by a military court. Robert Erskine Childers was executed on 24 November 1922.[73]

Ironically, upon learning the news of Childers' capture two weeks earlier, the *Irish News* had acerbically quipped, '[I]t is to be hoped he will not figure again as an active factor in the affairs of a nation to which he does not belong.'[74] Regrettably, the newspaper's wish would not come true, since it was in direct response to Erskine Childers' execution that Liam Lynch issued a proclamation authorising the assassination of TDs who had voted for the Special Powers Act and other supporters of the government.[75] This blanket call to arms was not immediately acted upon but it was a harbinger of things to come.

On the political front, the threat of diehard meddling with the Constitution Bill and a press campaign launched by the ultra-Conservative *Morning Post*[76] were having an effect on the shaky confidence of the Northern minority. The *Irish News*, in particular, was worried that the intransigent sections of Toryism were 'determined to retrieve over the Constitution Bill their failure over the Treaty Bill'[77] but if Northern nationalists were to be betrayed, the Constitution Bill would not provide the opportunity. There were, as Jones observed, some 'obstinate' members of the government who refused to see that the constitution – like the Treaty – had to be 'swallowed without change'[78] but the Bill passed the British House of Commons[79] without opposition and received royal assent on 5 December. This paved the way for the formal establishment of the Irish Free State with Joe Devlin's former nemesis T.M. Healy as its first Governor General.

The ease at which the Constitution Bill made its way through parliament likely owes as much to Britain's desire to dispense with Irish affairs, as it does to the political acuity of individuals like Curtis and Jones. The beginning of William Cosgrave's ruthless law-and-order campaign, however, also had an impact on British opinion. In particular, Lionel Curtis at the Colonial Office had shown emphatic support for the Provisional Government's strengthening resolve, as did Lord Derby, the Secretary of State for War, who was urging the withdrawal of British troops.[80] Apparently, the bloodletting had assuaged any remaining fears Britain may have had of a rapprochement between the Provisional Government and the Republicans.

It was under these inauspicious circumstances that the Irish Free State came into being exactly one year after the Anglo-Irish Treaty was signed. Given the dark turn in the protracted and costly Civil

War, Dubliners could be excused for not greeting the long-awaited emergence of the Irish Free State with drum beating, flag waving and celebratory gunfire as some observers seem to have expected.[81] While the emergence of the Free State was surely welcome news for anti-partitionism, given the tragically piecemeal way it had come about and the fact that Northern Ireland quickly and assertively availed itself of the option to 'contract out' of its jurisdiction,[82] it was perhaps not surprising that the occasion was met with mixed emotions among Northern nationalists.

Indicative of the muted mood, Cardinal Logue, when pressed into making a statement, both hailed the Free State constitution for 'open[ing] the way for future progress and prosperity', while simultaneously decrying the 'open sore' of partition, the expense of a 'double government' and the want of peace.[83] A letter to the editor of the *Irish News* was better able to put the occasion into perspective. The letter, which was signed by 'A North of Ireland Nationalist' and dated 4 December, observed:

> The present state of things in the North of Ireland is unstable, unnatural, unwise – and cannot last. The Northern Nationalists do not consider that the Southern Nationalists have treated them at all well. The latter stayed away from the British Parliament and allowed the Act of 1920 to go through without opposition. The Southern Nationalists then made a Treaty with the British Government and obtained full Dominion Self-Government for the South and North-West: but assented to the retention by the Northern Government of the Six County area, with all the injustice to Catholics that follows from its existence. The Southern Nationalists are now in a position to rectify this injustice, and should do so.[84]

As the above letter makes clear, whether the Free State government was or was not *provisional* had changed very little for the lives of Northern nationalists. They still found themselves trapped on the wrong side of a hated border, watching and waiting while others prepared to decide their fate. Thus, harbouring more than a tinge of resentment as the historic day for the Irish Free State approached, an *Irish News* editorial could cynically retort: 'Everything that concerns the days to come –

the days right before us and the days that will not dawn for a hundred years – depends on their action now ... Here we can do no more than merely watch and wait.'[85]

Seemingly forsaken by the vagaries of war and politics, as Northern nationalists resigned themselves to watching and waiting, a series of incidents occurred in the Southern capital that would both intensify the bitterness of the Irish Civil War and hasten its end. On 7 December, two members of the government were set upon outside Leinster House by Republican gunmen. Sean Hales, TD, was killed and Padraic O'Maille, the Deputy Speaker of the Dáil, was wounded in the attack, which apparently had been launched in response to Liam Lynch's call for retribution in the aftermath of Childers' execution. The Free State cabinet reacted swiftly to the development with an act of vengeance that was just as shocking. On the evening of the incident, the administration made the decision to execute four leading Republicans in an official reprisal and on the following morning, Rory O'Connor, Liam Mellows, Dick Barrett and Joe McKelvey were executed at Mountjoy.[86]

Since all four men had been held in captivity since the siege of the Four Courts, had taken no part in the assassination of Sean Hales and had not been afforded any legal recourse, the administration's stern measure came under attack from virtually all quarters. The fact that Dáil Éireann had not been consulted in advance of the cabinet's decision only intensified the ire of the attack that Tom Johnson and other TDs levelled on the administration. Even the *Irish Independent* and *The Times* of London decried the brutal incidents in their pages.[87] Rory O'Connor's personal relationship with the powerful Home Minister made the event all the more tragic; O'Connor had been the best man at Kevin O'Higgins' wedding only one year earlier.[88]

The Hales assassination and summary executions that followed elicited from the *Irish News* a despondent critique, not only of the previous week's activities but also of the general conditions that prevailed in the new state and the growing desperation of its people. Making a not-so-subtle allusion to the near triumph of constitutional nationalism and the 'days when hope filled Irish hearts', the *Irish News* editorial used the gloomy prophecy of James Clarence Mangan's poem 'King Cathal Mór of the Wine Red Hand' in order to contrast 'what might have been with what actually is'. Employing a prophetic vision to describe Gaelic Ireland's dissent after the Anglo-Norman intervention, the poem read in part:

I sought the hall,
    And, behold! A change
From light to darkness, from joy to woe!
    Kings, nobles, all,
Looked aghast and strange;
    The minstrel group sate in dumbest show!
Had some great crime
    Wrought this dread amaze,
This wonder none seemed to understand?
    I again walked forth;
But lo! the sky
    Seemed fleckt with blood, and alien sun
Glared from the North.
    And there shone on high,
'Mid his shorn beams, a skeleton![89]

The connection between the beginning of Anglo-Norman rule in Ireland and the increasingly tragic course of the Civil War would have been obvious to an audience that was so well versed in Irish history and its enduring literary culture. It was during the reign of High King Rory O'Connor and amidst factional strife that Henry II had first ventured into Irish affairs[90] and it was the intransigence of a man bearing the name Rory O'Connor that was partially responsible for bringing on the factional war that was now being fought: the same Rory O'Connor who had been wantonly sacrificed, with his Republican colleagues, in a reprisal by the Irish Free State. 'The hideous skeleton of internecine war is reared between the Irish nation and the sun of Liberty,' explained the disillusioned *Irish News* editorial, which added, '[I]t cannot be repeated too frequently that the people of the newly-constituted Free State can make or mar their own destiny.'[91]

The Free State's destiny certainly did not look encouraging in the foreseeable future. In January and February of the new year, Republicans launched an incendiary campaign against the homes of thirty-seven senators, destroyed communication lines and conducted a costly assault on the Irish rail system.[92] Two senators were kidnapped during these months and Kevin O'Higgins' father was murdered. These dangers forced the seclusion of the Free State cabinet.[93] The fact that no more TDs were killed during this dire period likely owes something to the punitive measures being taken by the administration. During the month of January alone, thirty-four Republicans were executed; seventy-seven would meet their deaths by firing squad before war's end, but Liam Lynch, who retained a veto on any peace proposals, resisted all pressures to concede defeat and the floundering insurgency continued.[94]

Notes

1 *Irish News*, 9 October 1922.

2 M. Hopkinson, 'The Civil War from the pro-Treaty Perspective', *The Irish Sword* 20, 82 (1997), p. 288.

3 Although Cosgrave had participated in the Easter Rising, he had made his career in the field of local government. J. Curran, *The Birth of the Irish Free State, 1921–1923* (n.p.: University of Alabama Press, 1980), p. 251.

4 *Irish News*, 8 September 1922.

5 For instance, on 9 February 1922, Thomas Jones recorded in his diary that '[t]he most diehard among the Secretaries cannot help liking Cosgrave. "I love him," said Curtis'. On 8 June, Jones noted: 'Cosgrave has done better than any of us imagined possible.' Curtis had made a similar comment in October while contrasting Cosgrave's strengths with James Craig's weaknesses as a leader. K. Middlemas (ed.), *Thomas Jones Whitehall Diary, Volume III, Ireland, 1918–1925* (London: Oxford University Press, 1971), p. 225.

6 M. Hopkinson, 'Civil War and Aftermath, 1922–4', in J.R. Hill (ed.), *A New History of Ireland VII: Ireland, 1921–84* (Oxford: Oxford University Press, 2003), p. 46.

7 For instance, when the Irregular forces began cutting telegraph cables, the *Irish News* claimed that Childers – 'the real leader of the revolt' – was 'the originator of the magnificent plan for the establishing a republic in Ireland by destroying the country's internal and external means of communication'. *Irish News*, 8 September 1922. This editorial was, no doubt, a reaction to a similar report that appeared in *The Times* on 7 September and the numerous instances in which Kevin O'Higgins and the late Arthur Griffith had made comments maligning Childers. L. Piper, *Dangerous Waters: The Life and Death of Erskine Childers* (London: Hambledon and London, 2003), pp. 223–7.

8 *Irish News*, 4 September 1922.

9 Curran, *The Birth of the Irish Free State*, p. 252.

10 M. Hopkinson, *Green Against Green: The Irish Civil War* (Dublin: Gill & Macmillan, 2004), pp. 180–1.

11 P. Arthur, *Special Relationships: Britain, Ireland and the Northern Ireland Problem* (Belfast: The Blackstaff Press, 2000), p. 23; E. Phoenix, *Northern Nationalism: Nationalist Politics, Partition, and the Catholic Minority in Northern Ireland, 1890–1940* (Belfast: Ulster Historical Foundation, 1994), p. 244.

12 The widening ramifications of the Local Government Act lurked elsewhere as well. The Act forced an oath of allegiance on all local authorities who drew their salaries from municipal coffers. Thus, it was with both shock and disappointment that Archdeacon John Tierney of Enniskillen discovered that he too would be subject to the oath-taking provision of the Act if he wanted to continue offering his services to the local workhouse. Notwithstanding the Archdeacon's disgust, Guardian Chairman J.M. Geddes declared his position at the workhouse vacant. *Irish News*, 25 October, 1922. For details on the Catholic clergy's reaction to the oath, see M. Harris, *The Catholic Church and the Foundation of the Northern Irish State* (Cork: Cork University Press, 1993), p. 146.

13 R. Gallagher, *Violence and Nationalist Politics in Derry City, 1920–1923* (Dublin: Four Courts Press, 2003), p. 17.

14 *Derry Journal*, 11 October 1922.

15 *Irish News*, 26 September 1922; *Derry Journal*, 2 October 1922.

16 Devlin wrote this letter to the Unionist *Northern Whig* in order to correct errors that the *Whig* had made in reporting on the proposed Derry City conference. Specifically, the *Northern Whig* had reported that Devlin was preparing to 'make a tour among *his constituents* in Co. Down' in order to 'sense the feelings of *his followers*' on the proposed conference. The Unionist newspaper also reported that Devlin and other nationalists had already met in Belfast to discuss the prospect of attending the conference. Although the *Whig* was likely referring to the unofficial leadership role that Devlin had among the remaining followers of the IPP in writing this story, as the elected MP for West Belfast and Co. Antrim in the Northern legislature, Devlin argued: 'I have no constituents in Co. Down.' He also indicated that the Belfast meeting which, according to the *Whig*, involved 'protracted discussions' had never taken place. Emphasis added. As cited in the *Irish News*, 7 October 1922.

17 IPP candidates won six seats (Devlin being returned in both West Belfast and Antrim) and Sinn Féiners won six seats in the first Northern Ireland election. The two surviving pro-Treaty Sinn Féiners were Eoin MacNeill and Seán Milroy. The five IPP members were Joe Devlin, John Nugent, Patrick O'Neill, Thomas Harbison and George Leeke.

18 *Irish News*, 3 October 1922.

19 *Derry Journal*, 2 October 1922.

20 Milroy was one of the two MPs for Fermanagh–Tyrone (as well as TD for Cavan), while MacNeill was the MP for Derry City and a National University representative in Dáil Éireann. Harris, *The Catholic Church and the Foundation of the Northern Irish State*, p. 151.

21 Emphasis added. As cited by the *Irish News*, 9 October 1922. Dated 4 October, the letter was sent directly to Mayor O'Doherty and was subsequently released to the press by the Mayor.

22 Mayor O'Doherty also tried to distance himself from the idea of the conference by making it clear to his interviewer that the plan was not his idea but had come from the 'National members' of his council. *Derry Journal* 11 October 1922. However, this was not the end of the matter. When the Dáil representatives did not immediately arrange for a conference along the lines Milroy had suggested, Frank Harkin, a Belfast Devlinite, wrote a letter to the editor of the *Irish News* criticising Milroy for blocking the conference and 'assuming command of affairs' without doing anything to help bridge the gap between interested parties as they approached both Westminster and local elections. *Irish News*, 25 October 1922. Milroy, once again, became the subject of criticism in the *Irish News* two days later, when the news broke that he had rejected a second plan for a conference that had come from a group of 'northern Nationalists temporarily resident in Dublin'. This plan was rejected on account of the involvement of known anti-Treatyite supporters of Éamon de Valera. Despite the suspicion that de Valera and the Republicans were behind this second overture, the sad irony of the situation – that the destiny of Northern Ireland's permanently resident nationalists was being determined by those who resided either temporarily or permanently in Dublin – was very much a sore spot for the newspaper. *Irish News*, 27 October 1922.

23 'Deputation to the Provisional Government', 11 October 1922, Department of the Taoiseach, NAI/TSCH/S 11209, National Archives of Ireland, Dublin, p. 2.

24 Ibid., p. 3.

25 Ibid., p. 5. Harbison was a politician of the IPP persuasion and remained a prominent member of the AOH throughout his life but, because he voted against temporary partition in 1916 and was eager to have Article 12 of the Treaty put into operation, the Tyrone man was able to co-operate with Sinn Féiners while Devlin and other Hibernians and IPP members could not.

26 Ibid., p. 6.

27 Ibid., p. 7.

28 Ibid., p. 10.

29 C. O'Halloran, *Partition and the Limits of Irish Nationalism: An Ideology Under Stress* (Dublin: Gill & Macmillan, 1987), p. 146.

30 O'Halloran, *Partition and the Limits of Irish Nationalism*, pp. 141–6.

31 E. Sagarra, *Kevin O'Shiel: Tyrone Nationalist and Irish State-Builder* (Dublin: Irish Academic Press, 2013), p. 207.

32 Phoenix, *Northern Nationalism*, pp. 256–60.

33 'Deputation to the Provisional Government', p. 16.

34 Ibid., p. 20.

35 Ibid., p. 16.

36 In a confidential memorandum from Kevin O'Shiel to the Executive Council of the Free State in early 1923, the NEBB Director attributed the predominance of this line of thinking in the border regions to 'the pathology of a political temperament [in the North] which [had] developed very little from the earliest stages through lack of proper education and healthy conditions'. From O'Shiel's perspective, border nationalists holding Harbison's view were putting too much

emphasis on *forcing* territorial changes on the Craig government and did not see the advances that could be made via negotiation. Memorandum from Kevin O'Shiel, 'The Glenavy Affair', n.d., Department of the Taoiseach, NAI/TSCH/S 2027, North East Boundary Secret Documents 1922–4, National Archives of Ireland, Dublin.

37 'Minutes of the Northern Advisory Committee Meeting', 11 April 1922, Department of the Taoiseach, NAI/TSCH/S 1011, National Archives of Ireland, Dublin, p. 44.

38 'Deputation to the Provisional Government', pp. 21–2.

39 Ibid. p. 18.

40 Rabinowitz, 'Trapped Minority', pp. 72–7.

41 'Deputation to the Provisional Government', p. 18.

42 Ibid., p. 19.

43 Ibid., pp. 19–20.

44 J.H. Collins to Peader Murney, 31 October, 1922, J.H. Collins Papers, D 921/2/3/18, Public Record Office of Northern Ireland, Belfast.

45 In addition to Ireland, the sale of honours, Lloyd George's conciliatory policy towards Russia and the Chanak Crisis were the primary areas of concern for the dissident Tories. K.O. Morgan, *Consensus and Disunity: The Lloyd George Coalition Government, 1918–1922* (Oxford: Clarendon Press, 1979), p. 355; P. Clarke, *Hope and Glory: Britain, 1900–1990* (London: Penguin Books, 1996), p. 118.

46 Morgan, *Consensus and Disunity*, p. 347.

47 *Derry Journal*, 13 October 1922.

48 *Irish News*, 29 September 1922.

49 B. Murphy, 'The Irish Civil War, 1922–1923: An anti-Treaty Perspective', *The Irish Sword* 20, 82 (1997), p. 303.

50 *Derry Journal*, 16 October 1922; *Irish News*, 16, 17 October 1922.

51 *Irish News*, 29 September 1922.

52 Ibid., 17 October 1922.

53 Murphy, 'The Irish Civil War, 1922–1923: An anti-Treaty Perspective', pp. 300–3.

54 *Derry Journal*, 16 October 1922.

55 *Irish News*, 19 October 1922.

56 Morgan, *Consensus and Disunity*, pp. 350–1; K. Matthews, *Fatal Influence: The Impact of Ireland on British Politics, 1920–1925* (Dublin: University College of Dublin Press, 2004), p. 88.

57 *Irish News*, 20 October 1922.

58 Ibid., 7 December 1921.

59 Matthews, *Fatal Influence*, pp. 89–90.

60 Ibid., p. 93; *Irish News*, 25 October 1922.

61 At a meeting in Glasgow on 26 October, Bonar Law told his audience that 'whatever our views may be or have been as to the wisdom of the Treaty or as to the events which led up to it this is certain, that in my belief ninety-nine out of every hundred of the people of this country intended to keep that Treaty, as far as we are concerned, and earnestly pray that it may be successful'. *Derry Journal*, 27 October 1922.

62 *Derry Journal*, 20 October 1922.

63 J.H. Collins to Peader Murney, 31 October 1922, J.H. Collins Papers, D 921/2/3/18, Public Record Office of Northern Ireland, Belfast.

64 Kevin O'Shiel to J.H. Collins, 26 October 1922, J.H. Collins Papers, D921/2/3/1, Public Record Office of Northern Ireland, Belfast.

65 The constituency boundaries were the same for Northern Ireland and Westminster elections but because Northern Ireland elections were fought under the proportional representation system in multi-member constituencies, Devlin's West Belfast seat in the Northern parliament was still viable. S. Elliott, *Northern Ireland Parliamentary Election Results, 1921–1972* (Chichester: Political Reference Publications, 1973), pp. 2–9.

66 Richard Byrne had nominated Devlin in West Belfast in 1906 and at every Westminster election that had followed. Devlin's letter to Byrne was published in the *Irish News* along with an editorial lamenting the loss of '[o]ne of the most remarkable of political connections between the people of any Irish constituency and their elected advocates recorded in the history of the country since 1800'. *Irish News*, 28 October 1922. For a reference to his failed attempt to secure the Liverpool Exchange seat, see Harris, *The Catholic Church and the Foundation of the Northern Irish State*, p. 152.

67 Phoenix, *Northern Nationalism*, p. 262; *Irish News*, 28 October 1922.

68 *Irish News*, 18 November 1922.

69 P. Canning, *British Policy Towards Ireland: 1921–1941* (Oxford: Clarendon Press, 1985), p. 74.

70 Curran, *The Birth of the Irish Free State*, p. 262.

71 Given his support in the past, James Craig was expecting great things from the new Tory Prime Minister. The Northern Prime Minister, upon hearing about the defeat of Lloyd George, 'expressed the hope that Mr. Bonar Law would be the leader of the Unionist Party, and would continue to give Ulster his support and loyal assistance'. *Derry Journal*, 20 October 1922.

72 As Canning has argued, the Bonar Law government did not so much differ with its predecessor over whether to uphold its Treaty obligations as it did over what those Treaty obligations were. Canning, *British Policy Towards Ireland*, p. 74

73 Hopkinson, *Green Against Green*, pp. 189–92.

74 *Irish News*, 11 November 1922.

75 Hopkinson, *Green Against Green*, p. 190.

76 Responding to the criticism levelled by the diehard newspaper, the Lord Beaverbrook-owned *Daily Express* (Bonar Law's newspaper of choice) wrote: 'The Irish Constitution will pass through both Houses of Parliament without amendment. Let the dogs bark, and let the caravan pass.' *Irish News*, 25 November 1922.

77 *Irish News*, 21 November 1922.

78 *Thomas Jones Whitehall Diary, Volume III*, p. 218.

79 Ian Macpherson who, as Chief Secretary for Ireland, had introduced Lloyd George's Irish bill three years earlier, took this opportunity to congratulate Bonar Law for 'going down in history as the final author of one of the greatest

Parliamentary achievements of the century'. For Macpherson, there was added significance to the fact that the House had passed 'unanimously a Bill drafted by Ireland's own sons to give the South and West what they regarded as their legitimate rights'. *Irish News,* 30 November 1922.

80 Canning, *British Policy Towards Ireland,* p. 76.

81 A special correspondent of the Press Association described his impressions of the historic day as follows: 'The new state was born, so to speak, on a lovely December day, but without any outward sign of rejoicing. There were no public demonstrations or celebrations in the capital, no beating of drums, no clanging of bells, no flag waving, no firing of guns. Not even the guns of the Irregulars disturbed the peace of the city. A brand new tricolour floating proudly from the temporary Parliament House was the only visible sign of the new state of affairs which makes the Irish people masters in their own country.' *Irish News,* 7 December 1922.

82 At the meeting of the Northern Ireland parliament on 7 December, both Houses unanimously adopted an Address to the King acknowledging the passage of the Free State Constitution Act and stating: 'We, your Majesty's most dutiful and loyal subjects ... do, by this humble Address, pray your Majesty that the powers of the Parliament and Government of the Irish Free State shall no longer extend to Northern Ireland.' As James Craig told the House on that occasion: 'No one in that Assembly, and certainly none of the Loyalists in Ulster have expected any other action on our part for a very long time past, and I am sure hon. Members will acquit me of any ambiguity on this subject since I have had the honour to lead them in this House.' *Parliamentary Debates,* Northern Ireland House of Commons, vol. 2 (7 December 1922), cols 1147–8, http://stormontpapers.ahds.ac.uk/search.html (accessed 27 September 2019); *Irish News,* 8 December 1922.

83 *Irish News,* 7 December 1922.

84 Ibid., 5 December 1922.

85 Ibid., 30 November 1922.

86 Hopkinson, *Green Against Green,* pp. 190–1.

87 In addition to printing GHQ's official statement and excerpts of the bitter Dáil debate, *The Times* described the executions as 'the sternest measures' adding that '[t]he British Government never adopted such drastic measures, even in the darkest days of the fighting before the Truce'. *The Times,* 9 December 1922. For a view on the Irish electorate's response to Free State ruthlessness, see T. Garvin, *1922: The Birth of Irish Democracy* (New York: St Martin's Press, 1996), pp. 102–3.

88 Ibid., pp. 266–7; Hopkinson, *Green Against Green,* p. 191.

89 *Irish News,* 12 December 1922.

90 The poem 'King Cathal Mór of the Wine Red Hand' was written about Cathal Crobderg O'Connor. Cathal was the younger brother of High King Rory O'Connor and he was able to rule the province of Connaught from 1198 until 1224. After Cathal's death, the Anglo-Norman Richard de Burgh conquered the province. G.H. Orpen, *Ireland Under the Normans 1169–1216* (London: Oxford University Press, 1968), pp. 179–98; G.H. Orpen, *Ireland Under the*

Normans, 1216–1333 (London: Oxford University Press, 1968), pp. 158–65; K. Simms, 'Burke (de Burgh)', in S.J. Connolly (ed.), *The Oxford Companion to Irish History* (Oxford: Oxford University Press, 2004), p. 67; K. Simms, 'O'Connor (O'Conchobhair)', in S.J. Connolly (ed.), *The Oxford Companion to Irish History* (Oxford: Oxford University Press, 2004), pp. 419–20.

91 *Irish News,* 12 December 1922.

92 For details on the Irregulars' attack on the rail system, see Hopkinson, *Green Against Green,* pp. 198–200; Hopkinson, 'Civil War and Aftermath, 1922–4', p. 50.

93 Garvin, *1922: The Birth of Irish Democracy,* p. 53.

94 For Cosgrave's view on the effectiveness of the executions, see Garvin, *1922: The Birth of Irish Democracy,* p. 163. For the perspective of the Republicans, see Hopkinson, *Green Against Green,* pp. 228–9.

CHAPTER 8

'Without Further Hugger-Mugger': In Search of Peace and Clarity on the Boundary Question

> The President is very keenly aware of what all the Nationalists in the Six Counties have suffered and fully appreciates the patience and endurance with which they have awaited the time when they could join again with their fellow countrymen in working for a United Ireland.
>
> – Kevin O'Shiel[1]

As the Civil War was violently stumbling to a halt, the plight of the Northern minority was pushed back into the foreground once again. The need to find a solution to the boundary question had taken on a greater urgency for these nationalists as Northern Ireland's local elections approached in early 1923 but the renewed focus on the border also reflected Northern nationalists' overarching concerns about the Free State's apparently stalled Northern policy. Amidst increasing calls from Northern nationalists for a definitive policy statement from Dublin on the boundary, this chapter examines the trapped Northern minority's efforts to formulate their own positions as the economic impact of partition was made manifest through imposition of a customs border and the Irregular insurgency in the Free State finally came to a close.

Northern nationalists had a lot to lose by way of Northern Ireland's municipal elections, scheduled for 15 January. The Local Government Act had not only abandoned proportional representation in favour of a freshly gerrymandered ward system, it also forced an oath of allegiance on all individuals wanting to take their seats on local councils and many nationalists were not prepared to accept such a humiliating imposition. The local elections had been a significant area of concern for the deputation of border nationalists that had met with members of the Provisional Government several months earlier but, in disregarding President Cosgrave's advice and symptomatic of their 'dichotomous entrapment',[2] very little coordination or organisation had ensued. Devlinites, hoping to recover ground they had lost to Sinn Féin, had few qualms about participation and successfully ran eight candidates in Belfast's two Catholic wards advocating 'the essential principle of Unity'.[3] In the border regions, a more nuanced policy was employed. As a dossier prepared by the Free State government explained, anti-partitionists contested the elections and 'took the oath under protest where they had their proper share of the representation' but, '[w]here the only result of taking the oath would be to give the majority of the population a minority of seats', the elections were spurned and the oath refused.[4] Thus, the nationalists in areas like Enniskillen boycotted the election, as did those in Derry City – which did not elect another nationalist mayor until 1973[5] – while in contrast, anti-partitionists in Newry and Omagh successfully contested the election and took the oath under protest. There was logic in this approach but the border nationalists' apparent 'absence of definite aims'[6] led the *Irish News* to observe disapprovingly: 'The people of one urban centre elect Councillors: their neighbours take no part in public affairs. One section of the public officials decides on a certain course; their friends adopt another.'[7] If the incongruous policy employed by anti-partitionists on the border was not enough of an issue for the newspaper, the knowledge that Newry was 'now governed by a protesting Nationalist majority [while] the majority of Derry has no representatives on their city corporation' appeared almost too much to bear.[8]

This flexible, albeit patchy, approach to the local elections occurred at a time when anxieties were already heightened by the lack of progress on the boundary question and, in particular, by the 'Glenavy Intrigue'.[9] On his own initiative, Lord Glenavy, the Southern ex-Unionist and current Chairman of the Free State Senate, wrote a secret letter to Prime Minister James Craig in December 1922 advocating a form of Irish unity with safeguards for the partitioned counties.[10] Although the document was supposed to be kept confidential, the essence of its contents was divulged in January 1923 by the *Northern Whig*. Speculation about the secret document, hot on the heels of the local elections, only sharpened the *Irish News*' interest in the status of the stalled boundary issue and the nebulous position of the Northern minority. Claiming that Northern nationalists were 'just as ignorant of their position and their prospects as they were on the morning of December 7, 1921',[11] the *Irish News* urged either Glenavy or the *Northern Whig* to publish the mysterious document while strongly suggesting that the time was ripe for the Free State to release an authoritative statement regarding the status of the Boundary Commission. Such a statement was desired, the newspaper claimed, so that the 'puzzled and helpless' people of the North could 'shape a course in accordance with definite knowledge'.[12]

Since the Northern government was not inclined to endorse any measure that sought to make it subordinate to Dáil Éireann (as opposed to Westminster) – regardless of the terms – Lord Glenavy's proposal ultimately came to nothing. However, the incident seemed to awaken the Devlinite press to the increasing isolation of the trapped Northern minority within the context of relations between the North and South. Thus, claiming that Northern nationalists had been 'ignored with scrupulous care on all hands'[13] in the wake of the Glenavy affair, the *Irish News* demanded an end to the 'soul-destroying period of inactivity and doubt' that surrounded the Boundary Commission.[14] 'Let us know that the process of shelving has been decided upon,' wrote the newspaper on 17 February; 'if it is not to be shelved ... let the issue of the Commission be put to the test without further hugger-mugger'.[15]

Just as the *Irish News* was beginning to ratchet up its attack on the Free State's seemingly stalled Northern policy, Joe Devlin delivered a major speech on Ireland during an event celebrating his 'retirement from the Parliamentary Representation of West Belfast' held on 8 February. 'I feel, like yourselves, depressed by the present situation and grieved at all the miseries and misfortunes that have befallen the Nation in the last few years,' said Devlin as he declared his profound disappointment over the way constitutional methods had been 'paralyzed' by militarism. With an eye to the fratricidal Civil War still raging in the South of Ireland, he continued:

> I have never changed in my belief in Constitutional methods, and, if Ireland is to be saved, she must return to them. Bloodshed and destruction can bring nothing but hatred and desolation to the land, whether North or South … Surely it is better to battle against poverty and unemployment and slums and misery, which dog our footsteps … than to be waging a war of destruction with results such as are visible in Ireland and Europe to-day.[16]

Although Devlin's speech touched on various aspects of Irish affairs, North and South of the border, his remarks regarding the Boundary Commission and its connection to abstention from the Belfast parliament stood out. That some Devlinites were longing to recognise the Northern parliament and take their seats had been known since J.P. O'Kane's UIL speech in March 1922 but, significantly, the former Westminster MP was not yet ready to take that step.[17] 'For my part, until the Boundary question was settled, I felt it my duty to remain silent,' said Devlin as he explained:

> Many of our people whom I and others represent have chafed under the humiliating position which we occupy. That position has been taken up and maintained primarily and solely in order not to embarrass or make more difficult the task of those who are engaged in the difficult and delicate work of finding a solution to the Boundary question. We feel, and we have felt, that the delay in the settlement of this question has left us, and still leaves us, in a position which has brought many misfortunes upon our people and which is well-nigh intolerable. Therefore, we consider it vital to our existence, as well as our dignity and our citizenship, that this question should be settled without further or undue delay. (Hear, hear and applause). *When that question has been settled,* it will be for us to consider how far and in what way we can contribute our share to national unity and peace, for which the country, North and South, is passionately yearning. (Hear, hear).[18]

Although Devlin's comments about battling poverty and unemployment spoke to what he believed could *eventually* be done for the Northern minority via the Northern Ireland parliament, his contention that the boundary question would have to be settled before he entered the institution was intended to quell speculation that he would soon abandon abstention. The *Irish News* considered this somewhat subtle policy statement to have been unmistakably 'plain' but in order to further explicate his view on recognising the Belfast parliament, Devlin returned to the issue in a letter to the editor of the *Irish News* on 8 March. Insisting that his attitude had not changed since February, he reiterated the comments he had made at the retirement gala (cited above) adding: 'It will therefore be seen that until a decision has been come to with regard to the Boundary question – and the sooner a decision is arrived at the better for all the interests involved – there can be no question as to my attitude in relation to the Ulster parliament.'[19] While Devlin was undoubtedly less confident than were his border nationalist contemporaries about the prospect of a generous boundary settlement being able to end partition, he was not yet prepared to break ranks with them on the recognition issue and continued to resist mounting pressure to take his seat. 'I have good reasons for not going into the Northern Parliament,' he joked, adding, 'one is vanity – because I would have an audience there'.[20]

The *Irish News*' repeated requests for a statement on the status of the Boundary Commission and Joe Devlin's decision to break his self-imposed silence in February did not go unnoticed in Dublin. More importantly, there are clear indications that these Devlinite activities were making matters somewhat uncomfortable for the Free State government as it continued the fight against the anti-Treatyites. In a strictly internal and revealing memorandum accusing the Devlinites of working to subvert Dublin's Northern policy, NEBB Director Kevin O'Shiel warned members of the Free State cabinet that Devlin and 'his organ, the "Irish News"' were on 'the warpath' against the Southern government and were telling 'the Northern Catholics that they have been betrayed by the Free State and everybody'. Placing blame on the Glenavy letter for awakening the 'latent old uneasiness and old suspicions' and empowering Devlin, as the master-mind behind the *Irish News* assault, O'Shiel reported:

> His propaganda is already having an effect on our people: – not indeed to the extent of driving them into his Lodges, but to the extent of increasing and making articulate their suspicions of us. Whatever harm Devlin has done or will do in his new gallop to

> power the delectable moment was afforded by the Glenavy episode. Whilst he may not succeed in improving his own conditions very much at the moment, he may succeed in prejudicing our policy to some extent, thus adding to our troubles. Amongst our own particular supporters the suggested scrapping of the Boundary Commission has, of course, had its effect.[21]

As seen above, the *Irish News*' continued pursuit of a policy statement on the boundary question was apparently having an impact, yet no such statement was forthcoming from the Irish Free State. In the Dáil, Darrell Figgis had thrice asked President Cosgrave when and under what circumstance he planned to proceed with the appointment of the Boundary Commission but Cosgrave proved to be remarkably reticent on the matter[22] and, according to the London correspondent of the *Irish Independent,* had even joined James Craig in asking Britain to refrain from raising the issue.[23] Since the war was being fought, not surprisingly the Irish Free State's priorities appeared to lie outside the parameters of the boundary question. This was the period, Cosgrave would later recall, which had put the Free State in the greatest danger, since government was having difficulty financing a loan and a number of war-weary senators were showing a 'tendency to buckle' under the pressure.[24] However, the Free State was making progress in its war effort. Thousands of Republican prisoners were being held in captivity,[25] the National Army continued to expand – in part through recruitment in the North – and contemporary evidence suggests that the government's execution campaign was having a palpable affect on the morale of the Irregular forces during these early months of 1923.[26] New peace initiatives were also being bandied about by organisations such as the Neutral IRA, but for the moment, Irregular Chief-of-Staff Liam Lynch still stood in the way of peace, yet the pressure exerted on him from within his ranks was mounting.[27]

It was at this inopportune juncture that the Irish Free State announced that it intended to exercise its right under the Treaty settlement to install customs ports on its side of the Irish border.[28] Although the timing of the démarche was suspect, the notion of setting up revenue stations did not come entirely out of the blue. The subject had come up in November during the debate at Westminster over the Consequential Provisions Bill,[29] at which time the *Irish News* predicted that 'the Free State need not and will not, pay for a button in the coat of a Customs Officer along the "Boundary"'.[30]

Irrespective of the *Irish News*' view, shortly after Free State Economic Advisor Joseph Johnston issued a report on customs and excise, Dublin issued a 'preliminary notice' that it intended to have the customs barrier installed by 1 April.[31] Surprised by this move, the British government responded by announcing that it would install 'a similar line' if the Free State followed through with its plans. For his part, while urging Cosgrave to wait, Prime Minister Craig told a meeting of Belfast traders that if the Free State government imposed a 'barrier wall', it would only prove that the Free Staters were the real partitionists. Craig also instructed Northern Ireland exporters to redirect their trade to Scotland, England and the dominions where it would be welcomed.[32]

In keeping with the persistent internal divisions that plagued Northern Ireland's trapped nationalist minority over policy and methods, the imposition of a tariff frontier was one issue that caused concern in virtually all quarters, albeit for different reasons.[33] Since so much of Derry City's trade was dependant on its Donegal hinterland, the move to establish a customs frontier seemed to present serious economic hardships – especially given the Free State's rumoured desire to transform Buncrana, on Donegal's Inishowen Peninsula, into an international port. According to the *Fermanagh Herald*, the development of Buncrana would doom Derry City's fate as a commercial centre, while Newry and Enniskillen would also 'suffer commercially' by the imposition of a tariff barrier. Deeply concerned by the economic implications of the matter, the border newspaper was decidedly less concerned about political ramifications since it was still optimistic that the Boundary Commission would sit and deliver a generous reward to the Irish Free State. 'When this is accomplished,' wrote the *Fermanagh Herald*, 'the difficulties imposed by the new regulations will be overcome, as Derry City is the natural port for Donegal and the north west counties and Newry is the natural port for south Down and south Armagh.'[34]

The *Irish News* was equally concerned by the establishment of a customs frontier, for political as well as economic reasons.[35] Describing the move as 'a recognition of the validity and permanence' of partition by both the Free State and Great Britain,[36] the newspaper seized on the opportunity to continue its attack on Dublin's perceived indifference to the appointment of the Boundary Commission and the Free State's prolonged silence on the North. Arguing that the establishment of the customs ports implied that the Government of Northern Ireland 'need not trouble themselves further about the Boundary problem', the newspaper asked: 'Will anyone explain the delay in the issue of an authoritative statement from Dublin, or London – or both together?'[37]

In its vociferous clamouring for a policy statement from the Irish Free State, the *Irish News* drew a comparison between the seemingly detached approach employed by the Free State leadership and the transparency with which it attributed constitutional nationalism's ultimately unsuccessful attempt to avert partition in the 1910s. Thus, the newspaper contended, before the truce, Treaty and Civil War, nationalists made their case against partition in the British House of Commons 'with clearness and fullness that left nothing more to be said'. But now, more than a year after the Northern minority had accepted Dublin's assurances that the boundary question would be settled, the imposition of a tariff frontier said more about Free State policy than did the Cosgrave administration. Given the nature of the comparison being made, it was no mere coincidence that the *Irish News*' attack on the Free State's Northern policy appeared adjacent to a poetic tribute celebrating the fifth anniversary of John Redmond's death. The anonymous *aisling*, entitled 'To John E. Redmond', read:

You found her on the thorn-strewn way
 With torn and bleeding feet –
The sweet-faced lady with the patient smile.
 You gave her your strong arm to rest upon.
And helped her through the darkness towards the dawn.
 And watched until the hue of death had gone;
And then you toiled a while
 To bring the rich, red beauty to her cheeks,
A gleam of hopeful triumph to her eyes—
 The sweet-faced lady with the patient smile.
You pointed out the paths of greater power,
 And braved the trials of each gloomy hour,
And walked with her in sunshine and in shower
 Until each looming mile

Was conquered, and at last the golden gates
Of freedom's land ahead bade her rejoice –
The sweet-faced lady with the patient smile
And though you fell on that cold, straggling road
Where first you shared with her cold, weighty load
And ere you reached the long-yearned-for abode
Where peace might reconcile
The countless sorrows of dead centuries
And new-found liberty for all times bless
The sweet-faced lady with the patient smile—
Nor base Ingratitude besmirch thy name:
You smothered the once-so-rugged way – no blame
Thy life-work defile:
For all the griefs that fill her heart anew
As o'er your tomb she bends in love to-day –
The sweet-faced lady with the patient smile
And there in sad communion with her dead
The past is bridged to happier times ahead.[38]

Eulogies commemorating the life and work of John Redmond appeared in the *Irish News* every March near the anniversary of the IPP leader's death.[39] This particular piece paid homage to what the poem's author regarded as Redmond's selfless effort to bring hope to Ireland's long struggle for freedom – hope that, despite Southern Ireland's new-found liberty, seemed a distant memory in a partitioned and war-ravaged island that was so eager for happier times.

Not intending to rely solely on the *Irish News*' editorial page to further their agenda, Devlinite nationalists held a convention in Belfast on 9 April that was attended by Northern MPs, councillors and public board members.[40] The conventioneers unanimously adopted a resolution claiming that the only issue dividing Six-County nationalists was 'the Boundary Question', adding that as 'long as it remain[ed] in a nebulous state', united action was unlikely. The Devlinites called on the Free State to make 'an authoritative pronouncement' regarding the boundary and appointed a deputation to wait on President Cosgrave. A copy of this resolution and a letter signed by J.P. O'Kane and J. Gerald Kennedy was sent to Cosgrave on 11 April.

> We are an isolated community in a desperate situation. That situation can be retrieved by a simple act on your part and as fellow-countrymen we ask you to allow us to briefly indicate in an interview what we believe to be the solution of the difficulty … we believe that you keenly recognize that we are a minority surrounded on all sides by a rampant and intolerant ascendancy.[41]

Upon receiving the request for an audience with Cosgrave, O'Shiel advised the President that meeting with the Devlinites would 'cause very considerable heart-burning amongst our Sinn Fein supporters in the north' because it had been so long since he had received a deputation from that faction. Under these circumstances, Cosgrave followed O'Shiel's advice and arranged for the Devlinites to meet with Eoin MacNeill in order to 'prevent them from saying that they had been turned down'.[42] It was evident that the Devlinites had been snubbed but it was likewise clear that Northern Sinn Féiners were not getting any greater reassurances from the Free State government. The administration remained close-lipped about its boundary-related plans amidst unrelenting pressure from the *Irish News.*

As the Devlinite press continued its attack on the Irish Free State's Northern policy, significant events were occurring within the Republican movement South of the border. The Republican war effort was collapsing. Liam Lynch had refused repeated calls to bring together a meeting of the IRA Executive during the early months of 1923, partially out of fear that he would not be able to prevent the body from adopting a peace policy, but in March, the Republican Chief-of-Staff was finally forced to give in to the pressure.[43]

The IRA Executive, which had not assembled since October, held meetings over a period of four days during the last week of March. Although they provide a glimpse into the inner workings of the collapsing anti-Treaty movement, these meeting were, perhaps, less significant for what occurred during their proceedings than what happened after their adjournment. Having learned that the Republican leadership was preparing to meet in the Waterford–Tipperary area, the National Army flooded the region with troops intending to arrest the delegates. While the government's capture of several leading Republicans as the meetings disbanded represented a serious blow to the Irregular forces, the death of Liam Lynch, after a skirmish with Free State pursuers, had a far greater impact on the war. For months Lynch had prevented the Republicans' capitulation, yet now that he was dead, the prospect of peace became much more likely. On 20 April, Frank Aiken was chosen by the IRA Executive to succeed Lynch as the Republican Chief-of-Staff. Thereafter, with the support of the Executive and the Republican Government, Aiken ordered a suspension of military operations and de Valera began to seek a means to bring the protracted conflict to an end.[44] His first step in this regard was to issue a proclamation on 27 April, detailing the conditions on which peace could be achieved.

Describing de Valera's proclamation as one which 'no man in Ireland but the actual author could have fashioned',[45] the *Irish News* was left unmoved by the overture and with good reason. In an effort to salvage the credibility of the Republican movement, this initial bargaining position differed little from anything that had come before, since the announcement declared that de Valera and his Republican cohorts continued to eschew the Treaty's oath of allegiance.[46] Positing that the proclamation was 'not the way to liberty, unity, or peace', the *Irish News* was left wondering how the Free State would greet 'the white flag hoisted with so many gyrations of the pole that the color of the flag itself [was] almost indistinguishable'.[47] For its part, the *Derry Journal* was buoyed by definite signs of peace in the Dalkey region of Leinster, where Irregulars were voluntarily surrendering arms, but it too found de Valera's communiqué difficult to comprehend. 'After giving it 24 hours' study,' the newspaper maintained that 'its inner meaning ... is not fathomed, nor can it be said with certainty whether in whole or in part it will be acceptable to the Government as a basis for peace'.[48] The announcements made by de Valera and Aiken elicited no response from the government, which continued to execute prisoners.[49] These failed overtures did, however, mark the beginning of serious peace negotiations between the belligerents.

Watching with interest as de Valera attempted to seek some sort of *modus vivendi* with the Treatyite regime, the Devlinites continued to advocate unity and self-reliance within Northern nationalism in part through a series of mass rallies held across Northern Ireland.[50] In early May, delegates at AOH rallies in Armagh, Castlewellan and Magherafelt passed resolutions declaring their 'unchanging belief in the unity of Ireland' and demanding the immediate appointment of the Boundary

Commission and the release of Northern Ireland's political prisoners. Joe Devlin, who had been the National President of the AOH since 1905, was in excellent form at the Magherafelt rally. Arguing that Ireland was 'a Nation and ought to be an undivided nation', Devlin declared that no English or Irish statute could 'divide and sunder those whom God ha[d] united' adding that 'history, geography, material interest, commercial welfare' all recognised Ireland as one undivided nation. While Devlin's lengthy comments touched on the great sacrifices that had been made in the South for the Treaty and the punitive way Belfast used internment to stifle those who spoke out against the government, his remarks regarding the border question received some of the loudest cheers from the audience.

According to Devlin, it was a 'grave error' and a 'great mistake' that Dublin did not demand the convening of the Boundary Commission as soon as Northern Ireland availed of its right to contract out of the Free State. '[T]hat was the time,' he argued, 'at which the Boundary Commission should have declared what area in Ulster was to be governed and its destinies decided upon by the vote of those people. (Cheers).' As important as he thought it would be to end the uncertainty for his own followers who would not be repatriated, Devlin announced that his preferred approach would have been, and still was, 'to try and settle the Ulster question by peaceful negotiation, and by a statesmanlike approach to the question from the point of view of patriotism, North and South'. Apparently still unaware of the part Michael Collins had played in the border outrages of the previous year, Devlin argued that it was through this 'statesmanlike approach' that the slain Free State leader had 'passionately hoped to achieve' Irish unity. But, cautioning the audience of the need to 'recognize facts as they are', he proclaimed his determination to see the Boundary Commission assembled.

> [W]e, who for a quarter of a century have fought for the freedom of our country, demand here and now, in our own interests as well as in the general interests of the peace of the whole nation, that the Boundary Commission shall be set up, that our position shall be made clear, that we will know where we are and who are to control our destinies. When that is done we may proceed to discharge our duties and bear our responsibilities until the time comes when

> natural forces, economic interests and industrial demands shall make Ireland what Ireland will be yet if we have the courage and the wisdom to lay anarchy and bloodshed to one side amongst all sections and consecrate ourselves to the task of trying by peaceful and constitutional means to bring together North and South.[51]

As compelling as Devlin's oration may have been, it had come at a time when the Northern nationalists were as divided as they ever had been, and this helps to explain his emphatic pronouncements regarding the border. The persistent gulf separating the Devlinites from the border nationalists had actually widened in early May as a consequence of the *Irish News*' increasingly bellicose attacks on the Irish Free State's Northern policy and, in particular, an editorial it published on the Boundary Commission. In what was likely an attempt to drum up support for the AOH rallies, on 5 May, the newspaper dispensed with its demand for a definitive policy statement from Cosgrave and cast aside its usually cautious inferences about the futility of the Boundary Commission and stated bluntly: 'The main facts about the "Boundary Commission" are (1) that it will never materialise, and (2) that if it could possibly be established its operations would be fruitful of mischief and barren of good.' Claiming that 'the hand that sped the bullet that killed General Collins killed the Commission', the newspaper pleaded, '[i]n the name of Peace, Commonsense, and Ireland let the "Boundary Commission" vanish quietly from our minds'.[52]

Irrespective of the remarks he would make at the AOH rally later in the week, as the newly elected Chairman of the *Irish News* whose views were more pragmatic than many of his contemporaries, Joe Devlin would have agreed with the message of this editorial. For their part, border nationalists were clearly anxious about the delay in appointing the Boundary Commission and the *Derry Journal* had said as much in April when it argued that Northern nationalists had been 'unmistakably thrown back on their own resources' and needed to 'find some means of terminating the nebulous and "nightmare existence"'. The *Derry Journal*'s critique of the Free State's delay in activating Article 12 of the Treaty did not, however, imply any willingness to dispense with the Commission.[53] Thus, it is not surprising that the *Irish News* received harsh criticism after the newspaper called for the abandonment of the Commission in its 5 May editorial.

When queried about the *Irish News*' frank statement, NEBB Director Kevin O'Shiel assured a Dublin interviewer that '[t]he Boundary Commission Clause still stands, and there is no intention on the part of the (Free State) Government to waive it'.[54] O'Shiel's *Weekly Bulletin*, which pulled together news culled from the Dublin-friendly newspapers, was much more assertive in rejecting the call to abandon the Commission. Commenting on the punitive way that the Northern government had gerrymandered nationalist majorities out of existence, the *Bulletin* argued:

> The policy of disenfranchisement is the very axis on which the policy of the Belfast parliament swings. That policy has been pursued with particular zeal in the border areas to which the operations of the Boundary Commission are likely to apply. The powerlessness of the minorities in the Six-Counties to defeat the plans for their complete disenfranchisement, so far from being a reason for the abandonment of the Commission, supplies a strong extraneous reason for its employment at the moment in the circumstances which give it the maximum chance of efficacy.[55]

With respect to Northern Ireland's nationalist press, the newspapers of Michael Lynch's North West of Ireland Printing and Publishing Company were among the harshest critics of the *Irish News*' position. To take one example, the *Fermanagh Herald* lashed out at the Belfast newspaper and the Devlinites for using their discussions of the Boundary Commission as a 'guise' for the recognition of the Northern Ireland parliament. Such a ploy, argued the *Herald*, would 'condemn the people in the Six Counties who fought for the Treaty to years of servitude and separation from the life of the Free State, with which they have repeatedly demanded to be united'. Complementing the tack taken by O'Shiel's publication, the Enniskillen-based newspaper claimed that nationalist representation in the Belfast parliament would amount to nothing more than a 'milk and water opposition'. And, while it acknowledged that their distance from the border put the nationalists of Belfast and the interior in a wholly different position from the border nationalists and that it might be prudent for the Devlinites to form their own policy, the *Fermanagh Herald* also asserted:

'It would be nothing short of criminal, however, for the Nationalists of the minority areas, to try to drag along with them into the Belfast Parliament's mirage the Nationalists of Tyrone and Fermanagh, parts of Derry, South and East Down and South Armagh, which have clear majorities in favour of the Free State.' Contented that the Civil War – rather than Dublin's indifference or anything more nefarious – was the reason for the delay, the *Fermanagh Herald* concluded that the Free State's 'genuine supporters' in Northern Ireland had no doubt 'that no time would be lost' in appointing the Commission once the war ended.[56]

The *Fermanagh Herald's* condemnation of the *Irish News*' view on the Boundary Commission amounted to more than a simple editorial spat; rather it embodied the very essence of the distinction between border nationalists and the Belfast Devlinites. Nationalists on the periphery of the Northern state's territory could anticipate that a fair judgment from the Boundary Commission would facilitate their repatriation and thus anxiously awaited its appointment. In contrast, fearing retribution from a more compact and homogenously Orange Northern Ireland, nationalists living in areas that, as O'Higgins said, 'didn't have a dog's chance under the Boundary Commission'[57] would have preferred that it never met – even if it was dangerous to admit as much. But, as Devlin argued during the AOH rally, because of the hope that border nationalists continued to place in the Boundary Commission, these nationalists also knew that their uncertainty would only end once the Commission had delivered its reward and all the interested parties knew where they stood.

Fear that the nationalists of Belfast and the interior would become an even smaller and more isolated minority, a longing to end the ambiguity surrounding Article 12 and its own history of devotion to the cause of Irish self-government were effectively pulling the Devlinite *Irish News* in a number of different directions at once during this eventful period. While this helps to explain the newspaper's on again, off again demands that the Boundary Commission be assembled, a wider recognition that there were reasons behind the *Irish News*' inconsistent attitude towards Article 12 clearly did little to shield it from the wrath of the border press. The adverse reactions engendered by the newspaper's repudiation of the Boundary Commission in its 5 May editorial ultimately forced Joe Devlin to disavow the editorial publicly. He told a reporter from the *Manchester Guardian* that 'his opinions were exactly opposite to those given in the article and, in saying that, he spoke not only for himself but for all the other leading Nationalists'.[58] Realising that a line had been crossed in this instance, the *Irish News* ultimately went back to agitating for the appointment of the tribunal. But, all told, reactions to its 5 May editorial repudiating the Commission reveal just how divergent were the views of the *Irish News* from the border nationalist press and, in accordance with Rabinowitz's trapped minority model, this could not help but further diminish the nationalist credentials of the Devlinites in the eyes of both the Free State and their fellow Northern nationalists on the border.

And so it was at a time when the Northern minority was deeply divided on the question of how to defeat partition that Éamon de Valera and Frank Aiken brought an end to Republican military activity. Having been unable to come to terms with the government, the anti-Treatyite forces did not surrender but had simply laid down their arms. Nevertheless, by the third week in May the war was over and, so it seemed, preparations for the sitting of the Boundary Commission could finally begin in earnest.

During the eventful days of the Irish Civil War, both the border nationalists and the Devlinites were forced to accept the fact that the boundary question would not, and could not, be answered until hostilities ended. But, while impatiently enduring the delays, they could at least find solace in the expectation that the matter would be a priority for the Irish Free State once peace came. Thus, there was more than a kernel of wisdom to be gleaned from the words penned by Sinn Féiner Cahir Healy as he watched the terribly destructive course of the Civil War while languishing on board the prison ship *Argenta*. He wrote:

> There is no shadow in the sun,
> Nor any blackness in the snow,
> Neither is joy found in a gun
> Whose fruits taste bitter one by one.
> Fallen from boughs [of] woe.
>
> There are many tasks to do
> In the coming months and years

We can make old dreams come true,
    Build instead of burn that you
May dry away those tears.

There is no shadow in the sun,
    Neither is joy found in a gun.[59]

It is unknown exactly when during the period of his internment Cahir Healy committed these powerfully evocative words to paper; however, they appear to offer a clear indication of the expectations he had for the post-Civil War period. From the anti-partitionist perspective, there was indeed much work left to be done in order to achieve the lofty goals of Irish nationalism – work that could only be accomplished when the island was at peace. Inasmuch as this was the case, the title of Healy's poem – 'After' – seems entirely apt.

Notes

1 Proposed response to a Devlinite request to meet with President Cosgrave. It is unclear whether this letter was actually sent, but it reflects the Boundary Bureau's thinking on meeting Northern deputations. Kevin O'Shiel's draft reply to Messrs. J.P. O'Kane and Gerald Kennedy, 19 April 1923, Department of the Taoiseach, NAI/TSCH/S 2027, North East Boundary Secret Documents 1922–4, National Archives of Ireland, Dublin.

2 D. Rabinowitz, 'The Palestinian Citizens of Israel, the Concept of Trapped Minority and the Discourse of Transnationalism in Anthropology', *Ethnic and Racial Studies* 24, 1 (2001), p. 77.

3 *Irish News*, 13 January 1923. E. Phoenix, *Northern Nationalism: Nationalist Politics, Partition and the Catholic Minority in Northern Ireland, 1890–1940* (Belfast: Ulster Historical Foundation, 1994), pp. 268–9.

4 Emphasis in the original. 'Northern Minorities', n.d., E.M. Stephens Papers, 4239/1 Box VI File 1, Manuscript Department, Trinity College, Dublin.

5 In 1973, Raymond McClean of the Social Democratic and Labour Party became the first nationalist Mayor of Derry City since Hugh O'Doherty had left office. R. Gallagher, *Violence and Nationalist Politics in Derry City,1920–1923* (Dublin: Four Courts Press, 2003), p. 72.

6 *Irish News*, 25 January 1923.

7 Ibid., 23 January 1923.

8 Ibid., 25 January 1923.

9 Ibid., 26 January 1923.

10 This initiative did not have the backing of Boundary Bureau Director O'Shiel because Glenavy proposed scrapping Article 12 of the Treaty in exchange for

a scheme that would give Belfast what amounted to a veto in a quasi-federal arrangement. Even as a bargaining tactic, O'Shiel thought that the plan set the bar too low. Memorandum from Kevin O'Shiel, 'The Glenavy Affair', n.d., Department of the Taoiseach, NAI/TSCH/S 2027, North East Boundary Secret Documents 1922–4, National Archives of Ireland, Dublin.

11 *Irish News*, 23 January 1923.

12 Ibid.

13 Ibid., 31 January 1923.

14 Ibid.

15 Ibid., 17 February 1923.

16 Ibid., 9 February 1923.

17 Ibid., 13 March 1922.

18 Emphasis added. Ibid., 9 February 1923.

19 Devlin issued this re-statement of his position in response to allegations in the Unionist press in early March alleging that he was preparing to enter parliament. The exact nature of these allegations was not detailed in the *Irish News* or Devlin's letter but it appears that they related to a Devlinite convention held in Belfast on 5 March. The conventioneers did not release a statement to the press but 'the local Unionist papers' began to report that the Devlinites had decided to enter the Northern Ireland House of Commons. Devlin took great offense to these allegations as his letter to the editor of the *Irish News* indicated that, on his advice, the nationalist delegates had unanimously agreed not to abandon abstention. *Irish News*, 8 March 1923.

20 F. Whitford, 'Joseph Devlin: Ulsterman and Irishman' (MA thesis, London University, 1959), p. 161. Also see, E. Phoenix, *Northern Nationalism: Nationalist Politics, Partition and the Catholic Minority in Northern Ireland, 1890–1940* (Belfast: Ulster Historical Foundation, 1994), p. 279.

21 O'Shiel, 'The Glenavy Affair', n.d.

22 *Dáil Debates*, vol. 1 (15 November 1922), col. 2044; *Dáil Debates*, vol. 2 (17 January 1923), cols 843–4; *Dáil Debates*, vol. 2 (20 February 1923), col. 1476, https://www.oireachtas.ie/en/debates/find/ (accessed 23 July 2019).

23 *Irish News*, 17 February 1923.

24 K. Middlemas (ed.), *Thomas Jones Whitehall Diary, Volume III, Ireland, 1918–1925* (London: Oxford University Press, 1971), p. 220.

25 In April, O'Higgins told an interviewer that the enemy was 'fizzling by a policy of attrition', and that his government was taking in as many as 200 prisoners each day. *Irish News*, 9 April 1923. For details on the treatment of prisoners, see M. Hopkinson, *Green Against Green: The Irish Civil War* (Dublin: Gill & Macmillan, 2004) p. 228; J. Curran, *The Birth of the Irish Free State, 1921–1923* (n.p.: University of Alabama Press, 1980), p. 269.

26 For Cosgrave's view on the effectiveness of the executions, see Garvin, *1922: The Birth of Irish Democracy*, p. 163. For the perspective of the Republicans, see Hopkinson, *Green Against Green*, pp. 228–9.

27 Hopkinson, *Green Against Green*, p. 230; Curran, *The Birth of the Irish Free State*, pp. 270–1.

28 Phoenix, *Northern Nationalism*, p. 278; E. Staunton, *The Nationalists of Northern Ireland, 1918–1973* (Dublin: The Columba Press, 2001), p. 81.

29 This was a piece of legislation passed concurrently with the Irish Free State constitution that, among other things, provided for the establishment of a Privy Council and the appointment of a Governor. *Irish News*, 27 November 1922. For a discussion of the Bill, see K. Matthews, *Fatal Influence: The Impact of Ireland on British Politics, 1920–1925* (Dublin: University College of Dublin Press, 2004), p. 99.

30 *Irish News*, 29 November 1922.

31 Memorandum from Joseph Johnson, 'Suggested Modifications of Schedules of Customs and Excise Duties', n.d., Department of the Taoiseach, NAI/TSCH/S 2027, North East Boundary Secret Documents 1922–4, National Archives of Ireland, Dublin; *Irish News*, 28 February 1923. Also see Memorandum from Kevin O'Shiel, 'Customs on the Irish-British Land Frontier', 19 February 1923, Department of the Taoiseach, NAI/TSCH/S 2027, North East Boundary Secret Documents 1922–4, National Archives of Ireland, Dublin.

32 *The Times*, 3 March 1923. By the time that the Free State had readied the thirteen customs stations that were built on its side of the border, Britain had installed seven of its own on the Northern Ireland side. *The Times*, 2 April 1923.

33 In an exception to the rule, in an NEBB memorandum, O'Shiel made reference to an unidentified staffer in Derry who claimed that Unionist 'Derry traders' were put in a 'panic' by fear of the customs frontier and that this was working to the advantage of anti-partitionism. This view confirmed O'Shiel's own suspicions about the utility of the tactic. Memorandum from Kevin O'Shiel, 'Fiscal Independence and Customs Barrier', 2 March 1923, Department of the Taoiseach, NAI/TSCH/S 2027, North East Boundary Secret Documents 1922–4, National Archives of Ireland, Dublin.

34 *Fermanagh Herald*, 7 April 1922.

35 *Irish News*, 3 March 1923.

36 Ibid., 8 March 1923.

37 Ibid.

38 *Irish News*, 10 March 1923. Redmond died on 6 March 1918.

39 As another example of this form of eulogising, consider 'National's' tribute, entitled 'John E. Redmond: Died 6th March, 1918', which included these lines: 'How great and prosperous, and happy too/Would this island be,/If only all within its shores would seek/To emulate thee.' *Irish News*, 5 March 1921.

40 The information sent on behalf of these conventioneers does not include a list of the attendees but since there was no mention of him, it does not appear that Joe Devlin was in attendance.

41 Joseph P. O'Kane and J. Gerald Kennedy to President Cosgrave, 11 April 1923, Department of the Taoiseach, NAI/TSCH/S 2027, North East Boundary Secret Documents 1922–4, National Archives of Ireland, Dublin.

42 Kevin O'Shiel to President William T. Cosgrave, 17 April 1923, Department of the Taoiseach, NAI/TSCH/S 2027, North East Boundary Secret Documents 1922–4, National Archives of Ireland, Dublin. A draft reply to the deputation

was prepared by O'Shiel and it indicated that the President was 'very fully occupied'. The draft ended on a conciliatory tone that was far removed from the discourteous O'Shiel–Cosgrave communication on the matter: 'The President is very keenly aware of what all the Nationalists in the Six Counties have suffered and fully appreciates the patience and endurance with which they have awaited the time when they could join again with their fellow countrymen in working for a United Ireland.' It is unclear whether this letter was actually sent. Kevin O'Shiel's draft reply to Messrs. J.P. O'Kane and Gerald Kennedy, 19 April 1923, Department of the Taoiseach, NAI/TSCH/S 2027, North East Boundary Secret Documents 1922–4, National Archives of Ireland, Dublin.

43 Hopkinson, *Green Against Green*, pp. 228–9, 233–6.

44 Curran, *The Birth of the Irish Free State*, p. 274; Hopkinson, *Green Against Green*, pp. 237–8, 256.

45 *Irish News*, 28 April 1923.

46 A portion of the proclamation stipulated that a political oath, test or other 'device' should not preclude individuals or groups from taking 'their proper share and influence in determining national policy or from the councils and Parliament of the nation'. As the oath and what it stood for were the central reasons for the Sinn Féin split over the Treaty and the Civil War, it is not surprising why the *Irish News* was so perplexed by this peace proposal. M. Moynihan (ed.), *Speeches and Statements by Eamon De Valera, 1917–1973* (New York: St Martin's Press, 1980), p. 113.

47 *Irish News*, 30 April 1923.

48 *Derry Journal*, 30 April 1923.

49 Curran, *The Birth of the Irish Free State*, p. 274.

50 Phoenix, *Northern Nationalism*, p. 285.

51 *Irish News*, 11 May 1923.

52 Ibid., 5 May 1923.

53 *Derry Journal*, 11 April 1923.

54 *Irish News*, 10 May 1923.

55 *Weekly Bulletin*, n.d., J.H. Collins Papers, D 921/4/4/12, Public Record Office of Northern Ireland, Belfast.

56 *Fermanagh Herald*, 19 May 1923.

57 'Deputation to the Provisional Government', 11 October 1922, Department of the Taoiseach, NAI/TSCH/S 11209, National Archives of Ireland, Dublin, p. 19.

58 Cited by the *Weekly Bulletin*, n.d., J.H. Collins Papers, D 921/4/4/12, Public Record Office of Northern Ireland, Belfast.

59 C. Healy, 'After', n.d., Cahir Healy Papers, D 2991/C/28/60, Public Record Office of Northern Ireland, Belfast.

CHAPTER 9

'Not One Word!': Watchman, Kevin O'Shiel and Dublin's North Eastern Boundary Bureau

> It is difficult to know how far O'Shiel's views represented widespread thinking within Free State government circles but it is inconceivable that he could have remained head of an important department if his opinions were not shared.
>
> – John Dooher[1]

Of all the issues that confronted the Irish Free State in the aftermath of its Civil War, few were more crucial than, or as fraught with dangers as, the fight to secure Irish unity. In recognition of this, the *Irish News* had become increasingly critical of the Free State's Northern policy well before the Irregular military threat had diminished. But, while Devlinite disapproval did not go unseen, President Cosgrave and Cumann na nGaedhael, his newly formed political organisation, were decidedly more concerned by the uneasiness being expressed by Northern Sinn Féiners.[2] With both the Sinn Féiners and the Devlinites clamouring for the Boundary Commission to be put into operation for their own separate reasons, on 29 May, North Eastern Boundary Bureau Director Kevin O'Shiel sent a revealing memorandum to the Free State's Executive Council. In it, O'Shiel urged his government of the need to set its own agenda and pursue its Treaty rights 'in its own way and at its own time', even if this provoked the ire of Northern Ireland's nationalist minority.[3] Exactly when Dublin would be ready for its long-awaited boundary showdown and how Cosgrave intended to overcome Unionist obstructionism remained to be seen but there was little doubt that the Irish President's aloof attitude, lack of transparency and apparent waffling were trying the patience of even the most Dublin-friendly Northern nationalists. Amidst this growing Northern nationalist criticism, this chapter takes a glance inward at the steps that the Free State was taking clandestinely during the war to prepare itself for the Boundary Commission. While this approach will demonstrate that the Free State was far from inactive on the boundary front during these months, it also reveals the extent to which Dublin's proposed line of attack conflicted with perceptions held by the divided Northern minority.

Turning to Cumann na nGaedhael's Northern policy, it is instructive to note that as O'Shiel was privately advising Free State decision-makers of the need to proceed cautiously with the border dispute on 29 May, the *Irish News* became the forum for yet another barbed attack on President Cosgrave's seemingly stalled Northern policy. Occasioned in part by the release of the Free State's public service estimates, a correspondent known only as 'Watchman' lashed out at the administration for allotting £4,300 to the NEBB, which, the contributor claimed, had yet to do anything but produce a few 'nice little essays … [that] added nothing in the direction of information or argument'. However, Watchman's most pointed comments were firmly directed at Cosgrave and Local Government Minister Ernest Blythe. Days earlier Blythe had raised eyebrows by telling a Dún Laoghaire audience that a solution to the boundary question *could* be 'postponed for a generation',[4] yet the President did not even broach the topic when, on 27 May, he made his first public appearance since having been forced into seclusion by the war. As Watchman observed, Cosgrave 'had before his mind the strange statements made by his colleagues at Dun Laoghaire; he was well aware of the growing anxiety regarding [the] present and future position which [prevailed] amongst 450,000 Nationalists in all the Six Counties. Yet he said not a word about the Six Counties, or the Nationalists thereof, or the Commission. Not one word!'

Given all that was at stake for Watchman and the community that he/she claimed to represent, Cosgrave's silence on the boundary issue must have seemed deafening.[5] Indeed, the Irish President had said very little publicly about the thorny boundary issue during the war but the government that he led had been anything but idle. On his own initiative, Cavan TD Seán Milroy had begun compiling statistical and other evidence related to partition and the Six-County boundary while serving as the Treaty delegation's Northern advisor. The accumulated material was published in October 1922 as *The Case of Ulster: An Analysis of Four Partition Arguments* and even contained an essay written by fellow TD and Education Minister Eoin MacNeill. MacNeill and Milroy were well known in the North and appeared to take a greater interest in the region than did many of their colleagues but neither MacNeill's supposedly 'hurried' chapter nor the remainder of the book satisfied all readers.[6] Much of the tract had been serialised in *Young Ireland* between April and September of 1922 and the *Irish News* was particularly critical of MacNeill's 'disingenuous' account of the way intolerance paved the way for partition,[7] but the volume remains a notable piece of propaganda.

In addition to Milroy's contribution and despite Watchman's criticism of its 'nice little essays',[8] the Free State's propaganda agency was also very active during the final six months of the Civil War. But, while O'Shiel was devoting a great deal of time and effort to formulating a Northern policy,[9] it is clear that some of the Boundary Bureau's work also fell into the bracket of damage control. The Cosgrave government was well aware that its delay in bringing about the Boundary Commission was having an adverse affect on the Northern minority. O'Shiel's memoranda to the Executive Council frequently referenced Northern restlessness, suspicions that Dublin was 'ultimately going to shelve the whole issue' of the boundary[10] and the 'the greatest difficulties and the utmost delicacy' that the agency was taking to allay these fears. However, the NEBB actually attributed much of the disquiet amongst the border nationalists to Devlinite meddling. As O'Shiel informed his government during the Glenavy Affair in late January, 'Devlin and Coy. and the "Irish News" [are] on the warpath against us' and are telling 'the Northern Catholics that they have been betrayed by the Free State'.[11] Such a frank assessment speaks volumes about Sinn Féin/Cumann na nGaedhael fears of being outmaneuvered by the Devlinite nationalists and this, in and of itself, reveals a great deal about the diversity of opinion that existed at the time with respect to the finer points of Northern policy.

In this regard, the NEBB ultimately identified 'no less than four definite and distinct' nationalist perspectives on the boundary issue.[12]

The Southern nationalists were said to include both the supporters of the Cosgrave administration, who supposedly saw national unity as the Free State's 'next great milestone'; and their Republican enemies, who were hoping that a 'crash of the first magnitude' on the boundary issue would bring down the government. Not to be outdone, these Southern factions were matched in Ulster by the 'North-Eastern Irredentists' – the Sinn Féiners inhabiting the border regions – and the Devlinites. Although the administration continued to favour the former over the latter, NEBB Director O'Shiel did nothing to flatter the Northern Sinn Féiners when he intimated that they were a cluster of short-sighted malcontents who regarded 'themselves as the real advocates of National Unity' and individuals who were 'mainly concerned with the inclusion within the Free State of their own Parish'. These people, he claimed, were pressing for the immediate appointment of the Boundary Commission and had little regard for those who would be left in its wake.[13]

As for the Devlinites, O'Shiel was convinced that they were motivated by a latent desire to scrap the Boundary Commission altogether in favour of a 'compromise co-operation settlement with Craig', the Northern Prime Minister. Recognising that Belfast and other areas of Devlinite strength were not in the vicinity of the existing border, O'Shiel observed 'that no possible Boundary Commission could possibly get them out, and that therefore their best interests [were] served by having as big a hinterland of people of their own way of thinking as possible'. As reasonable an observation as this was, O'Shiel's assessment of the Devlinites (here and elsewhere) was also tinged by the lingering dislike that the Free Staters had of the Devlinites. Having lost so much of the influence they once had, O'Shiel firmly believed that the Devlinites' interest in the Boundary Commission had more to do with reviving their political fortunes within Northern Ireland than it did with an actual commitment to national unity.[14] In an earlier memorandum issued to the Executive Council, the NEBB Director dwelled at some length on this claim, suggesting that Devlin had made a career out of playing on the prejudices of Ulster politics. 'No man knows Nationalist Ulster, its conditions, and particularly its prejudices, better than Mr Devlin,' argued O'Shiel:

> It was by a subtle and insistent appeal to these prejudices that he was able to build up his, at one time, vast Hibernian Institution.

> It is by a similar appeal that he now hopes to rehabilitate it. Therefore, he has raised the Catholic standard once again, and whilst his organ, the 'Irish News,' tells the Northern Catholics that they have been betrayed by the Free State and everybody, he and his retainers have commenced a big reorganization campaign in the Six Counties. He hopes by this means to retrieve all that he has lost within the past six years; and then, having erected once again on a sound sectarian foundation his Order in almost its prestive [*sic*] glory, he hopes to bring off a special agreement, independent of us, with Sir James Craig in lieu of the Boundary Commission, and on the basis of Established Partition.[15]

Having resided in the North during the fateful days of 1916 when temporary exclusion was being bandied about, O'Shiel may have harboured more resentment against Devlin than did his Free State colleagues. Whatever explains his view, it is evident that the man at the helm of the NEBB neither trusted nor put much stock in cooperating with the Devlinite branch of Northern nationalism even when it came to the vital question of territorial reunification.

Given the variety of competing interests involved, elaborating a strategy to deal with the boundary question was a dangerous task for the Free State but, despite the *Irish News*' frequent claims to the contrary,[16] the foundations for such a policy were firmly in place before the end of the Civil War. Besides attempting to calm weary Northern nationalists and coordinating the collection of data within Northern Ireland, Kevin O'Shiel had also spent the first half of 1923 organising a London-centred publicity blitz[17] and overseeing the NEBB's investigation of analogous boundary issues, international law and the constitutional implications of the boundary question. The extent of the preparations being made by the Boundary Bureau may not have been appreciated – or, indeed fully known – by a nationalist minority that was too eagerly waiting for 'the thing [to be] brought to a head'[18] but this research ultimately formed the basis of the Free State's evolving Northern strategy and is, therefore, worth reconstructing.

Reflecting on the policy he had helped to create between January and May of 1923, O'Shiel described the Free State's Northern policy as one which enabled 'the Government to hold strongly to its pledges, yet [allowed] ample room for the operations of statesmanship'. This, he claimed, was 'as near to the policy of the late General Michael Collins as was humanly possible under the circumstances'. Characterising the strategy in such terms implied a reluctance to let the Boundary Commission actually run its course, while being unable to openly admit that, just like the Devlinites, the Free State was really 'angling'[19] for a round table conference. O'Shiel was convinced that the Free State would be able to 'hammer out a better and more lasting type of agreement than that provided by the very imperfect Boundary Commission' if it could make 'friendly contact with the North-East'.[20] As such, his confidential communications with the Executive Council frequently described the Boundary Commission as a 'weapon', like the customs frontier, to be wielded in the Free State's 'diplomatic war for National Union' but he was also firm in the opinion that Dublin should really be endeavouring to 'extract from it [the Boundary Commission] and its "by-products" every ounce of value, and only in the last resource, when all else fails and in the event of the North-East determining to continue obdurate to the bitter end, let it take its course to the ultimate'.[21] Inasmuch as they were both indisposed to view the Boundary Commission as a panacea for partition and notwithstanding the mutual mistrust they shared, the Devlinite and Free State perspectives on the boundary were not altogether dissimilar. By contrast, given the Northern Sinn Féiners' adverse reaction to Michael Collins' earlier attempt to set aside the Boundary Commission as a component of the first of two Craig–Collins pacts the previous spring,[22] knowing the details of the Cumann na nGaedhael plan of attack would surely have sent chills up the spine of every border nationalist.

Although it was not exactly forthright about its objectives, there is no doubt that the Free State was beginning to execute a Northern strategy during the final phase of its Civil War – one that was calculated to take advantage of the threat posed by the Boundary Commission – and the foundations upon which it sat owed as much to the work of Bolton C. Waller as it did to O'Shiel. As Waller was an acknowledged expert on international law and the League of Nations,[23] O'Shiel and NEBB Secretary E.M. Stephens had enlisted his services in order to investigate the procedures and precedents that governed boundary disputes stemming from the Treaty of Versailles. Waller's interpretation of these cases would greatly inform the Boundary Bureau's advice to the administration.

Bolton Waller's research for the NEBB identified two classes of Boundary Commissions established by the Paris Peace Conference. In the first class, the wishes of the inhabitants were not consulted and these Commissions had 'merely the humdrum task of measuring out an exact line'.[24] This class of Commission, Waller argued, applied to the Polish Boundary, as laid out in Article 87, and the Belgian Boundary, as indicated in Article 35. A second class of Boundary Commission stemming from the Versailles settlement was given 'totally different' powers. In the case of this second class, the Versailles Treaty:

> did not attempt to define the area to be ceded or to trace any boundary, but [left] the whole matter to be decided as the result of a plebiscite, fixing only the area in which the plebiscite was to take place and its method of procedure and setting up a Commission to supervise it and make a recommendation as to the frontier to be drawn as a result of the voting.[25]

This second class of Boundary Commission applied to Allenstein (Article 95) and Marienwerder (Article 97) in East Prussia, Upper Silesia (Article 88) and Schleswig (Article 109). According to Waller, 'there [was] a real attempt at self-determination' in areas where this alternate type of Boundary Commission was mandated. The people living in these areas were to 'express their wishes by popular vote' and the Commissions had 'the responsible task of fixing a boundary to carry out those wishes as nearly as possible'.[26]

From Waller's perspective, these European cases were significant in determining the intended function of the Irish Boundary Commission because the phraseology used to call it forth had 'been copied almost exactly' from articles in the Treaty of Versailles that pertained to East Prussia, Upper Silesia and Schleswig, and had 'no resemblance' to the language used in cases where self-determination was not the guiding principle.[27] He would subsequently advise the Irish government that it should 'take for granted that the clause in the Treaty means self-determination until that view [was] challenged'.[28]

Similarities aside, there was an important distinction to be made between the European Commissions and the proposed Irish

Boundary Commission, and this did not escape Waller's attention.[29] While he believed that the articles pertaining to both cases intended the wishes of the inhabitants to be considered as the primary criteria for determining borders, he acknowledged that the Irish article lacked the crucial qualifying clause 'as shown by the vote', which, in some way, formed a part of the articles that brought about the European commissions. But this oversight – if it was one – did not bother the Irish advocate nor did he think it imperilled the case for self-determination since, Waller argued, 'in Ireland ... the wishes of the inhabitants are already well known ... and where unnecessary the expense and possible danger of a plebiscite are best avoided'.[30]

While convenient for the Free State, such a view clearly contradicted a key assumption held by the Northern minority, and the border nationalists in particular, who were largely convinced that a plebiscite would be taken.[31] Yet, had they been apprised of Waller's research, his conclusions regarding the procedures used by the European Boundary Commissions would have appeared even more damaging to the nationalist minority. According to Waller, in the European cases, 'the principals in the dispute [were] the Governments which claim the territory, not the inhabitants of the disputed districts'.[32] The fact that the continental commissions had considered 'the peoples whose destinies were so vitally involved as of little importance' undoubtedly satisfied O'Shiel, who saw this as a wise precaution taken by Continental Commissioners who were 'well aware of the savage and easily roused passions that exist amongst "Irrendenta" border populations and of the simplicity with which the frontier regions are set ablaze by these passions'.[33]

For an administration that was already inclined to act as it saw fit,[34] Waller's contention provided a ready excuse to keep the Northern nationalists at arm's length. Accordingly, Kevin O'Shiel was to advise the Executive Council of the need to decide a course in light of Waller's investigations 'irrespective of the particular view-points of certain sections of the population'.[35] He recommended against giving the Northern nationalists the legal assistance they asked for and dismissed concerns they raised when the Free State proposed erecting a customs barrier, believing that it was 'good sound National policy in spite of all objection'.[36] In February 1923, at a time when the NEBB was expecting Northern deputations to become 'too frequent or importunate' in light of the Glenavy Intrigue and anticipating 'yet another outbreak of uneasiness', a memorandum from O'Shiel's office advised members of the Executive Council having to deal with the minority to remember that '[t]he future boundaries of Saorstat Eireann [were] not the special concern of the North-Eastern Nationalist populations' but had been entrusted, 'like the Land Question, the Unemployment Question, etc. etc. for settlement to the National Government'.[37] And, indicative of O'Shiel's influence on Northern policy, Cosgrave displayed the same haughty disregard for the Northerners as did the NEBB Director when, in April, he followed O'Shiel's advice and refused to meet with a Devlinite deputation that was seeking 'a clear statement as to the Boundary Commission and the policy of the Free State Government'.[38] The Irish President had, for some time, been avoiding Northern emissaries – be they Devlinites or Sinn Féiners[39] – and clearly viewed the arrival of this deputation as an attempt by the Northerners to 'stampede' Free State policy. He ultimately determined that 'adopting a policy and telling them we will carry it out whether the people in the North agree or not' was the best course to follow.[40] O'Shiel took matters a step further when he encouraged the President to 'ignore all Northern Ireland groups' and make any statements on Northern policy directly from the Dáil.[41]

As Clare O'Halloran's research aptly proves, the administration's penchant for jealously guarding its authority over the boundary question certainly predated Waller's counsel[42] but, if nothing else, his advice sanctioned the practice and helped to transform the inclination to go it alone into a hard and fast Free State policy. But, as revealing a development as this was, there was another aspect of Waller's work which, according to O'Shiel, was to 'entirely alter [the Free State's] whole pre-conceived notions of the practice and procedure of the Boundary Commission'.[43] This stemmed from the striking similarities that Waller saw between the wording of Article 12 of the Irish Treaty and the wording of the Articles used by the Treaty of Versailles to establish continental boundary commissions involving sovereign states. These similarities ultimately convinced Kevin O'Shiel that Dublin could, and indeed should, use its territorial claims in order to assert the dominion's newly acquired international status.

Bearing this objective in mind, on 9 January, the NEBB circulated a memorandum stressing how essential it was to have the Irish Boundary

Commission handled as an 'international Commission set up by a clause in an international Treaty', rather than appearing in any way similar to a 'Royal Commission set up by the King'. Summarising the constitutional implications of the boundary dispute for the Executive Council, O'Shiel argued:

> We won an international status by the Treaty, and Article 12 of this international document provides for a Boundary Commission, which we must insist is carried out in accordance with the rules governing international precedents. A Boundary Commission in the nature of a Royal Commission would endanger our status and create a bad initial precedent for the evolution of a position which must depend so much for its advancement on constitutional practice and procedure.[44]

The Boundary Bureau Director, who had served on the committee that drafted the Free State constitution,[45] assured the government that the international aspects of the Irish Boundary Commission were in no way compromised by the fact that Great Britain and the Irish Free State both belonged to the same Commonwealth or by the fact that Britain had 'an autonomous province called "Northern Ireland" within its sovereignty'.[46] And, determined as he was to have the Irish boundary treated 'as a great National problem, and not as a petty parochial problem',[47] O'Shiel advised the administration of the need to appear as England's equal – 'her peer in fact' – and strongly suggested using all of the 'formal courtesies'[48] nations normally used in their relations with one another, while he also encouraged the Executive Council to consider joining the League of Nations. Doing this, he argued, would mark 'very definitely before the world the immeasurable distance in status between Saorstat and Northern Ireland'.[49]

Having taken the time to digest the research that the NEBB was compiling, by early February 1923, O'Shiel was able to supply the Executive Council with a preliminary assessment of the Free State's prospects of successfully navigating the boundary dispute. The assessment characterised the government's case as being 'overwhelmingly strong' in light of the agency's 'recent researches on European Precedents', which led O'Shiel to conclude: 'Whether therefore as a weapon to force Craig to come to suitable terms with us, *or, in the last resource,* to push to the ultimate our advantage at the Boundary Commission our case, politically, economically, geographically, historically and according to the Treaty Article itself (as further emphasised by Versailles Precedents) would appear to be absolutely unanswerable.' He continued: 'Our case stated and the Commission itself provide us with extremely valuable diplomatic weapons which we can, and, in my opinion, should use for all we are worth in order to effect an enduring and lasting settlement on the basis *not in conflict with the ideal of National Union.*'[50]

As revealing as was the phrase 'not in conflict with the ideal of National Union', this important memorandum also brought to bear the appreciable differences that existed between the way that the NEBB was viewing the Boundary Commission and the way that the 'North-Eastern Irredentists' were disposed to see the tribunal. Anticipating a generous reward, border nationalists were anxious for the Commission to be convened and allowed to function, while O'Shiel's agency was more inclined to see its boundary-related Treaty rights as one of many 'diplomatic weapons' that could be used in order to pressure Belfast into a negotiated settlement and establish, even more firmly, independence from London. Motivated as the NEBB was by its leader's own conception of realpolitik, O'Shiel's approach clearly had more in common with the Devlinites than it did with the Northern Sinn Féiners. And, while it remained politically dangerous for either group publicly to admit as much given the stock that the border nationalists put into the tactic, the Southern leaders and the Devlinites were both now eager to end abstention from the Northern parliament.

The difference between the NEBB's nuanced approach to the boundary question and what the border nationalists had in mind was also made manifest by a timeline that was included in the 10 February memorandum. While not specifying a particular date for raising the boundary issue, O'Shiel advised, 'I am convinced that we should not at any rate go out of our way to seek' the Boundary Commission until:

1. The time is opportune
2. Our case is fully completed
3. We have made full use of all the privileges and advantages given us by our new position, particularly those of membership of

   a) the League of Nations
   b) the Imperial Conference
4. The unnatural folly of Partition has been demonstrated by the operations of a Customs chain along the present utterly untenable frontier and finally until
5. Every effort towards accomplishing an agreement with the North-Eastern Government along lines in conformity with the ideal of National Union has been fully and patiently exhausted.[51]

Given the fact that O'Shiel's fifth condition for convening the Boundary Commission could only be satisfied after the government had exhausted every effort towards reaching an agreement with Belfast – and had failed to do so – it is plain to see that there was a great deal of distance separating the NEBB's tentative and exploratory approach to the boundary question and the border nationalists' fervent demand that the Commission immediately set to work. Once again, O'Shiel's own position seemed much closer to the views that he had attributed to the Devlinites than it was to his natural (Sinn Féin) allies as he continued to search for a way to settle the boundary question by negotiation and without recourse to Article 12.

At the time when O'Shiel's list of conditions was put into the hands of the Executive Council, the Irish Free State was in no position to spearhead any sort of diplomatic démarche. Not only was the Civil War still raging but it had entered a particularly bitter phase, characterised by the kidnappings of Free State officials, a costly Irregular assault on the Irish railway system and the zealous use of execution as an adjunct to the usual methods of waging war.[52] Moreover, it was no secret that Bonar Law's 'strong Tory Government' in Britain sympathised with the 'Orange Cause'. But, while the time may not have been ripe for the 'ventilation of more "Irish Grievances"' during the early months of 1923,[53] by April and May the circumstances were much more favourable to the Irish administration.[54] With the Irregular revolt 'in the death agony'[55] and the prospect of peace finally looming large, the tenor of communication emanating from the NEBB became all the more upbeat and forceful.

Indicative of O'Shiel's conviction that the 'opportune moment for dealing with the issue' was imminent, on 21 April, the Boundary

Bureau laid out the 'four distinct stages' that it expected the Free State's showdown with Northern Ireland to take. These were:

> a) A Preliminary Stage, in which the opening announcement of policy which will set the ball rolling will be made, the British Government formally acquaintance [*sic*] of our purpose and the Boundary Commissioners all duly appointed.
> b) A Functioning Stage, in which the Boundary Commission will be engaged at its actual work as prescribed by Article 12.
> c) A Stage terminating with the promulgation of the Commission's findings, and
> d) A Final Stage (possibly) in which the findings of the Commission may be challenged, under certain circumstances, before a Higher Tribunal.[56]

Despite the expectation that James Craig intended to obstruct the preliminary stage by refusing to nominate his Commissioner, O'Shiel was convinced that, when pressed, the Northern Prime Minister would either 'swallow his brave "never, nevers" and appoint his man' or, what was more likely, Britain would break the stalemate by proposing a conference in lieu of the Commission.[57] This conviction was perched on the assumption that 'Britain [would] never let the matter get as far as a functioning Commission'[58] and this being the case, O'Shiel advised the government of the benefits to be gained if it could 'keep a stiff upper lip, and make a show of being very resolute and determined as to pressing forward our claims', adding '[a] little bit of the Ulster dourness and thick headedness at this stage will produce excellent results'.[59]

Thus, O'Shiel summed up the NEBB strategy for his colleagues with the motto 'Festina Lente' – a Latin expression meaning make haste slowly. While he thought that time was on the side of the Free State, he also believed that there was a definite diplomatic advantage to be had in appearing ready and willing to do battle with Belfast. This explains the NEBB Director's desire to have the administration nominate its Boundary Commissioner at this stage and his eagerness to offer recommendations as to the type of person that would be best suited to fill the post. According to O'Shiel, the Free State required 'a man of great weight and sagacity, and one of irreproachable name'.

Such a person would not need to have Northern roots or even be Irish but, O'Shiel continued:

> He should be a man without prejudice on the Northern Question, yet one who has a thorough mastery of the situation and with sufficient backbone to fight his corner hard and well ... Above all, he should be a person who is prepared to act on the Government's slightest suggestion – to go hard when the Government tells him to go hard, and to soften when the government tells him to soften.

From O'Shiel's perspective, James MacNeill, the brother of Education Minister Eoin MacNeill and the Free State's High Commissioner in London, was '[a]n ideal person', who possessed these prized characteristics.[60] It is also worth pointing out that, as these recommendations indicate, NEBB strategy was predicated on the assumption that Dublin's Boundary Commissioner would be in a position (and of a will) to take his cues from the administration while the body was deliberating. As O'Shiel would elsewhere suggest, irrespective of its supposedly non-partisan purpose, the boundary question was bound to become 'definitely, decidedly and undisguisedly a political game'.[61]

On 17 May, the NEBB submitted its proposed territorial claims for review by the Executive Council of the Irish Free State. The Bureau's so-called 'Maximum Line' represented 'the greatest possible amount of territory' available to the Free State and was based solely on 'one argument, viz., the wishes of the inhabitants'. The Maximum Line would leave a 148-mile border separating the Irish Free State from Northern Ireland and gave the Free State 'all Ireland save County Antrim, the extreme North-East corner of the County Derry, portion of North and Middle County Armagh ... and all of the County Down save the North and middle portions'. Accordingly, O'Shiel cautioned the government that this Maximum Line 'offends against every conceivable geographic and economic principle'.[62]

The NEBB's 'Minimum Line' presented to the Free State 'a considerable slice of County Derry, including Derry City', most of Tyrone, 'save a small quadrangle' in the vicinity of the Lough, in addition to Fermanagh and the southern sections of Armagh and Down, 'including the Borough of Newry'. This was regarded as 'the best possible line, taking into account the three considerations' – the wishes of the inhabitants in conjunction with economic and geographic factors. This line would reduce Northern Ireland's total area by as much as one-third, while shearing off approximately one-fifth of its population. And the NEBB also identified a third line known as the 'Middle Line' or 'Boundary Commission Line'. This line closely mirrored the Boundary Bureau's 'Minimum Line' but also laid claim to a few extra bulges of Northern Ireland's territory. The 'Boundary Commission Line' was intended to be used as an opening gambit if the Free State Commissioner felt that making a play for the embellished Maximum Line would fall flat.[63]

The precise location of these three potential borderlines was based on the NEBB's reading of the Anglo-Irish Treaty within the context of the Bureau's research on European precedents and analogous boundary disputes stemming from the Treaty of Versailles. While confidential, this work was of far greater consequence than the 'nice little essays' that the NEBB planted in the nationalist press and, had they known the particulars of these claims, nationalists living on the borders of Northern Ireland would likely have been pleased to know just how much Northern territory O'Shiel and the NEBB thought it would be possible to repatriate. By contrast, the more pragmatic anti-partitionists of Belfast and the interior – the Devlinite heartland – would surely have scoffed at the vast extent of the Boundary Bureau's claims. Knowing from the day that the Treaty had been signed that they did not have 'a dog's chance of getting out of the Boundary area'[64] had left those nationalists immune to such grand delusions. Despite the desire of successive British governments to be rid of the infernal Irish Question once and for all, to a certain extent, it did not really matter to James Craig how much territory the Free State was preparing to claim or even if some British politicians were inclined to yield to their demands. Rather, his was a strategy that had been bequeathed by generation after generation of Unionist standard-bearers, a strategy that was based on non-compliance: 'No Surrender' and 'Not an Inch.'[65]

Members of the Executive Council had O'Shiel's summary of the NEBB's territorial claims in their possession when, on 29 May, 'Watchman' used the pages of the *Irish News* to level his/her verbal assault on the Free State government.[66] Notwithstanding Cosgrave's failure to make any mention of the North during the speech that had so riled the mysterious correspondent, an investigation of the confidential memoranda emanating from O'Shiel's office between January and May of 1923 reveals just how much attention the Free State and the NEBB in particular, had been giving to the boundary issue during this heady period. Devlinite charges that the Irish administration lacked transparency certainly hold up under scrutiny but it is also clear that, for the Free State, the boundary issue did not exist in a vacuum. Those who were directing Northern policy knew all too well that the boundary could not be addressed in abstraction from the necessity of defeating the Republicans and the need to safeguard, if not expand upon, the measure of autonomy accorded the young dominion by the Anglo-Irish Treaty. These factors undoubtedly rendered the Free State's position on the North more complicated than Watchman and, indeed, most Six-County nationalists were inclined to acknowledge.

Notes

1 J. Dooher, 'Tyrone nationalism and the question of partition 1910–25' (MA, University of Ulster, 1986), p. 449.

2 In the Twenty-Six Counties, pro-Treaty Sinn Féiners reorganised themselves under the name *Cumann na nGaedhael* (Party of the Irish). The organisation was formally constituted on 8 April 1923.

3 Memorandum from Kevin O'Shiel, 'Alleged Delay in Holding the Boundary Commission. Should the Boundary Commission Be Held Now?' 7 February 1923, Department of the Taoiseach, NAI/TSCH/S 2027, North East Boundary Secret Documents 1922–4, National Archives of Ireland, Dublin.

4 According to Blythe: '[T]he next few years [will] determine whether this question [will] be settled within the next three or four years or postponed for a generation.' *Irish News*, 29 May 1923.

5 *Irish News*, 29 May 1923. In response to this anonymous piece, the NEBB's 'Weekly Bulletin' strongly intimated that the mysterious 'Watchman' was none other than *Irish News* editor Tim McCarthy, suggesting that the newspaper was 'fortunate in having a contributor who dovetails so neatly into the editorial scheme that the editor can inform his public of the very hour on which the contribution was penned'. *Weekly Bulletin*, 4 June 1923, J.H. Collins Papers, D 921/4/4/14, Public Record Office of Northern Ireland, Belfast. Aside from the timing issue noted by the *Weekly Bulletin*, there is a very strong similarity between the style, tone and phraseology used in this piece and the *Irish News*' editorial page.

6 This was the view of the *Irish News* as expressed in an editorial that was printed on 16 January 1923.

7 The *Irish News*' review of *The Case of Ulster* suggested that Milroy's compilation 'may yet prove useful' but the newspaper was unimpressed by the way MacNeill's chapter skirted over the impact that Sinn Féin abstentionism had had on the fight to avert partition. The review appeared during a particularly violent period of the war, leading the Devlinite organ to suggest that an end to the fighting would do more to end partition than any amount of stale statistics ever could. The review did not make note of the maps shown in Figure 21. *Irish News*, 16 January 1923.
8 Ibid., 29 May 1923.
9 With respect to the influence that O'Shiel had on the formation of the Free State's Northern policy, see Dooher, 'Tyrone nationalism and the question of partition 1910–25', p. 449.
10 Memorandum from Kevin O'Shiel, 'Alleged Delay in Holding the Boundary Commission. Should the Boundary Commission Be Held Now?', 7 February 1923.
11 Memorandum from Kevin O'Shiel, 'The Glenavy Affair', n.d., Department of the Taoiseach, NAI/TSCH/S 2027, North East Boundary Secret Documents 1922–4, National Archives, Dublin.
12 Memorandum from Kevin O'Shiel, 'The Boundary Issue', 29 May 1923; Memorandum from Kevin O'Shiel, 'Boundary Commission Memorandum', n.d., Department of the Taoiseach, NAI/TSCH/S 2027, North East Boundary Secret Documents 1922–4, National Archives of Ireland, Dublin.
13 Memorandum from Kevin O'Shiel, 'The Boundary Issue', 29 May 1923.
14 Ibid.
15 Emphasis in the original. Memorandum from Kevin O'Shiel, 'The Glenavy Affair', n.d.
16 The newspaper's increasingly harsh treatment of Free State policy began in earnest at the end of January 1923.
17 Memorandum from Kevin O'Shiel, 'Boundary Commission Propaganda', 27 January 1923, Department of the Taoiseach, NAI/TSCH/S 2027, North East Boundary Secret Documents 1922–4, National Archives of Ireland, Dublin. As O'Shiel reported on 10 February, the NEBB's London-centred publicity campaign was initially pursued but ultimately abandoned because of 'the many sensational and tragic news items which come from Ireland every day' that overshadowed his efforts. Memorandum from Kevin O'Shiel, 'The Boundary Commission – When? The Boundary Commission – Who?', 10 February 1923, Department of the Taoiseach, NAI/TSCH/S 2027, North East Boundary Secret Documents 1922–4, National Archives of Ireland, Dublin.
18 J.H. Collins to Kevin O'Shiel, 27 January 1923, J.H. Collins Papers, Public Record Office of Northern Ireland, Belfast.
19 Memorandum from O'Shiel, 'The Boundary Issue', 29 May 1923.
20 Memorandum from Kevin O'Shiel, 'The Boundary Issue and North-Eastern Policy', 21 April 1923, Department of the Taoiseach, NAI/TSCH/S 2027, North East Boundary Secret Documents 1922–4, National Archives of Ireland, Dublin.
21 Memorandum from Kevin O'Shiel, 'The Boundary Issue', 29 May 1923.

22 'Vigorous Protest from Newry, South Down, and South Armagh', n.d., J.H. Collins Papers, D 921/4/1/7, Public Record Office of Northern Ireland, Belfast.

23 A native of Cork, Waller would later serve as Secretary of the League of Nations Society of Ireland. He won the Filene Prize for an essay on the political situation in Europe in 1930 and he spoke widely on issues related to the League in the 1920s. He contested the Dublin University constituency as an Independent in 1927 and is the author of *Ireland and the League of Nations* (1925) and *Hibernia: Or, The Future of Ireland* (1928). *The Harvard Crimson*, 17 February 1930.

24 Memorandum from B.C. Waller, 'Memorandum on European Precedents for the North Eastern Boundary Bureau: Report A', n.d., Department of the Taoiseach, NAI/TSCH/S 2027, North East Boundary Secret Documents 1922–4, National Archives of Ireland, Dublin.

25 Memorandum from Waller, 'Memorandum on European Precedents for the North Eastern Boundary Bureau: Report A', n.d.

26 Ibid.

27 Ibid. For instance, after Article 88 of the Treaty of Versailles laid out the parameters on how a plebiscite was to be taken in Upper Silesia, the Article proceeded: 'On the conclusion of the voting, the number of votes cast in each commune will be communicated by the commission to the principal Allied and Associated Powers, with full report as to the taking of the vote and a recommendation as to the line which ought to be adopted as the frontier of Germany in Upper Silesia. In this recommendation *regard will be paid to the wishes of the inhabitants as shown by the vote, and to the geographical and economic conditions of the locality.*' Article 12 of the Anglo-Irish Treaty used a similar phraseology viz. 'a Commission consisting of three persons, one to be appointed by the Government of the Irish Free State, one to be appointed by the Government of Northern Ireland and one who shall be the Chairman to be appointed by the British Government *shall determine in accordance with the wishes of the inhabitants, so far as may be compatible with economic and geographic conditions, the boundaries between Northern Ireland and the rest of Ireland,* and for the purposes of the Government of Ireland Act, 1920, and of this instrument, the boundary of Northern Ireland shall be such as may be determined by such Commission.'

28 Memorandum from B.C. Waller, 'Procedure of Boundary Commission: Report C', n.d., Department of the Taoiseach, NAI/TSCH/S 2027, North East Boundary Secret Documents 1922–4, National Archives of Ireland, Dublin.

29 Of course, there were distinctions which he did not notice as well. As Geoffrey Hand has shown, the Upper Silesian commission did not employ representatives from Germany and Poland – the countries most involved in that dispute. G. Hand, 'MacNeill and the Boundary Commission', in F.X. Martin and F. J. Byrne (eds), *The Scholar Revolutionary: Eoin MacNeill, 1867–1945, and the Making of the New Ireland* (Shannon: Irish University Press, 1973), pp. 202–4.

30 Memorandum from Waller, 'Memorandum on European Precedents for the North Eastern Boundary Bureau: Report A', n.d.

31 Consider Cahir Healy's suggestion to George Murnaghan in 1924: 'We should insist on a plebiscite, and, if that is denied us, leave the Commission.' E. Phoenix,

Northern Nationalism: Nationalist Politics, Partition and the Catholic Minority in Northern Ireland 1890–1940 (Belfast: Ulster Historical Foundation, 1994), p. 310.

32 Memorandum from B.C. Waller, 'Notes on the Procedure of Boundary Commission, Report B', n.d., Department of the Taoiseach, NAI/TSCH/S 2027, North East Boundary Secret Documents 1922–4, National Archives of Ireland, Dublin.

33 Memorandum from Kevin O'Shiel, 'Procedure at the Boundary Commission', 9 January 1923, Department of the Taoiseach, NAI/TSCH/S 2027, North East Boundary Secret Documents 1922–4, National Archives of Ireland, Dublin.

34 This point was effectively emphasised in O'Halloran's study of Southern rhetoric. C. O'Halloran, *Partition and the Limits of Irish Nationalism: An Ideology Under Stress* (Dublin: Gill and Macmillan, 1987), pp. 31–56.

35 Memorandum from Kevin O'Shiel, 'Procedure at the Boundary Commission', 9 January 1923, Department of the Taoiseach, NAI/TSCH/S 2027, North East Boundary Secret Documents 1922–4, National Archives of Ireland, Dublin.

36 Memorandum from Kevin O'Shiel, 'Fiscal Independence and Customs Barrier', 2 March 1923, Department of the Taoiseach, NAI/TSCH/S 2027, North East Boundary Secret Documents 1922–4, National Archives of Ireland, Dublin.

37 Memorandum from Kevin O'Shiel, 'Alleged Delay in Holding of the Boundary Commission. Should the Boundary Commission be Held Now?' 7 February 1923.

38 This was the group led by J.P. O'Kane and J. Gerald Kennedy that was discussed in Chapter 3. The quotation above is taken from the resolution which their Belfast convention adopted. 'Nationalist Resolution', 9 April 1923, Department of the Taoiseach, NAI/TSCH/S 2027, North East Boundary Secret Documents 1922–4, National Archives of Ireland, Dublin.

39 Kevin O'Shiel to President William T. Cosgrave, 17 April 1923, Department of the Taoiseach, NAI/TSCH/S 2027, North East Boundary Secret Documents 1922–4, National Archives of Ireland, Dublin.

40 Memorandum from President William T. Cosgrave, 'Memo. by the President', 19 April 1923, Department of the Taoiseach, NAI/TSCH/S 2027, North East Boundary Secret Documents 1922–4, National Archives of Ireland, Dublin.

41 Memorandum from Kevin O'Shiel, 'The Boundary Issue and North-Eastern Policy', 21 April 1923.

42 O'Halloran, *Partition and the Limits of Irish Nationalism*, pp. 131–56.

43 Memorandum from Kevin O'Shiel, 'Procedure at the Boundary Commission', 9 January 1923.

44 Ibid.

45 A.J. Ward, *The Irish Constitutional Tradition: Responsible Government and Modern Ireland, 1782–1992* (Washington: The Catholic University of America Press, 1994), p. 168.

46 Memorandum from Kevin O'Shiel, 'The Boundary Commission – When? The Boundary Commission – Who?', 10 February 1923.

47 Emphasis in the original. Memorandum from Kevin O'Shiel, 'The Boundary Issue and North-Eastern Policy', 21 April 1923.

48 Memorandum from Kevin O'Shiel, 'Procedure at the Boundary Commission', 9 January 1923.

49 Memorandum from Kevin O'Shiel, 'The Boundary Commission – When? The Boundary Commission – Who?', 10 February 1923.

50 Emphasis added. Ibid.

51 Ibid.

52 For information on this stage of the war, see M. Hopkinson, *Green Against Green: The Irish Civil War* (Dublin: Gill & Macmillan, 2004), pp. 198–200, 228–9.

53 Memorandum from Kevin O'Shiel, 'The Boundary Commission – When? The Boundary Commission – Who?', 10 February 1923.

54 M. Hopkinson, *Green Against Green: The Irish Civil War* (Dublin: Gill & Macmillan, 2004), pp. 198–200, 228–9.

55 Memorandum from Kevin O'Shiel, 'The Boundary Issue and North-Eastern Policy', 21 April 1923.

56 Ibid.

57 Ibid.

58 Kevin O'Shiel said that he had it on 'fairly good authority' that Britain would not let the Commission function. While he never stated who his informant was or why this was the case, the claim was likely based on the belief that a Tory government would not want to risk party unity if a Boundary Commission were forced upon Northern Ireland. Memorandum from Kevin O'Shiel, 'The Boundary Issue and North-Eastern Policy', 21 April 1923.

59 Memorandum from Kevin O'Shiel, 'The Boundary Issue and North-Eastern Policy', 21 April 1923.

60 Ibid. For further information on James MacNeill's career and skill-set, see G. Hand, 'MacNeill and the Boundary Commission', pp. 210–11.

61 Emphasis in the original. Memorandum from Kevin O'Shiel, 'The Boundary Issue', 29 May 1923.

62 Memorandum from Kevin O'Shiel, 'Our Territorial Demand at the Boundary Commission', 17 May 1923, Department of the Taoiseach, NAI/TSCH/S 2027, North East Boundary Secret Documents 1922–4, National Archives of Ireland, Dublin.

63 Ibid.

64 'Minutes of the Northern Advisory Committee Meeting', 11 April 1922, Department of the Taoiseach, NAI/TSCH/S 1011, National Archives of Ireland, Dublin, p. 18.

65 St J. Ervine, *Craigavon: Ulsterman* (London: George Allen & Unwin Ltd, 1949), p. 491.

66 *Irish News*, 29 May 1923.

CHAPTER 10

'Too Full of Secrecy and Mystery to be Wholesome': Northern Nationalism, the Free State and Article 12 of the Treaty

> As far as the man in the street knows, practically nothing has yet been done to bring Clause 12 into effect. It is true we have the North-Eastern Boundary Bureau, but what has it done? Of course, Mr Kevin O'Shiel has assured us several times that he has been preparing his case, and once informed us that his case was nearing completion. But will Mr Kevin O'Shiel inform us what case he has been preparing? How could he prepare a case for the Boundary Commission without first finding out the wishes of the inhabitants? Has that been done? If it has, then it must have been when the inhabitants of the Six Counties were asleep.
>
> – P. Macken, Ballygawley, Co. Tyrone[1]

With its internal boundary-related preparations well underway, when peace finally came, Cumann na nGaedhael's attention veered sharply towards Dublin's constitutionally mandated commitment to hold a general election before the end of 1923.[2] Under these circumstances, the Cosgrave administration's inclination to ruthlessly guard its boundary-related intentions faded ever so slightly. In fact, it was the necessity of seeking a new mandate that explained Free State Minister Ernest Blythe's brazen remarks about the boundary in the Dún Laoghaire speech that had so unnerved Watchman in late May. With the vagaries of electoral politics in both

Ireland and the United Kingdom as its backdrop, this chapter examines Northern nationalists' perspectives on the apparent willingness of some Southern politicians to seek electoral advantage for themselves in the boundary question. Analysing how the trapped Northern nationalist minority reacted to Free State ministers' speeches and the Free State government's early efforts to set its Northern policy in motion is the chapter's primary purpose. It will show that, in the period between the end of the Civil War and the fall of the Andrew Bonar Law/Stanley Baldwin Tory government, Northern nationalists of all political stripes and hues were growing progressively impatient as they awaited news on how, practically, London and Dublin intended to overcome Ulster obstructionism and formally convene the Irish Boundary Commission.

Turning to the impact of the boundary on the Free State election, it is notable that, following the poor reception of his Dún Laoghaire statements, Blythe may have made matters even worse for himself and his government on account of the ambiguously curt comments that he delivered on the subject of the boundary three days later. On that occasion, the Local Government Minister told a Dublin audience that, if returned, Cumann na nGaedhael intended to use the 'boundary question' as a means of 'doing something to secure National Unity'.[3] Appearing more evasive than ever in light of his previous comments, the minister's remarks led the *Irish News* to the derisive conclusion that Article 12 had 'dropped out of current political vocabularies' and in the place of coherent policy statements on Irish unity, Blythe had 'been delegated by the Government to declare the official view on the "Boundary question" at intervals'. Further asserting that, '[a]nswers can come from the Free State Government only', the editorial exclaimed: 'In the Six Counties 450,000 faithful Nationalists are entitled to plain answers.'[4]

Although the Devlinite *Irish News* had built up a reputation for sparring with the Cosgrave administration over its Northern policy, the border press had, by and large, continued to support the Free State government. However, a letter penned by a correspondent known as 'Northern Nationalist' to the editor of the *Derry Journal* made it clear that suspicions of what Blythe's party might actually do to 'secure National Unity' were by no means reserved for the Devlinite press. This correspondent, who had identified himself as a resident of Derry City, offered readers of the *Journal* something akin to the 'plain answers' demanded by the *Irish News* when he suggested: 'It is generally accepted and believed that the Free State Government have no hope that any good will come out of the Boundary Commission, and that the portion of the Treaty dealing with it may be treated as scrapped.' He continued: 'No doubt a pretense will be made of forcing the appointment of arbitrators, but the number of people in the Six Counties who still believe that any practical good will come of it is very small, and every day getting less.'[5] For this correspondent, the situation facing the Northern Ireland's nationalist minority required a measure of self-reliance that could only come with political organisation. This, of course, was the same formula which the *Irish News* had advocated with regularity since the Treaty had been signed.

Northern Nationalist's letter to the *Derry Journal* elicited a similar response from another disillusioned reader of that newspaper that also bears mentioning. Tired of the marginal role that the trapped nationalist inhabitants of Northern Ireland had been unwittingly accorded by the Free State government, the *Derry Journal* correspondent, known as 'J.C.', strongly urged Six-County nationalists to 'cast aside their apathy [and] ... insist on their voice being heard to effect on this question which more than any other affects their very lives and destinies'. The Derryman reminded *Journal* readers that Hugh O'Doherty, former Mayor of Derry, had tried in vain to arrange a representative conference of Northern anti-partitionists during the autumn of 1922, only to be 'airily waved aside' by Seán Milroy and Eoin MacNeill, who had failed to produce any 'better plan'. And with respect to the NEBB research and preparations that Cumann na nGaedhael ministers had been alluding to with great frequency as they prepared to kick-start the Southern election campaign, J.C. retorted:

> The North-Eastern Boundary Bureau is simply a department of the Free State Government, which for all practical purposes is identical with the Second Dail, which sold us into bondage at the dictates of political expediency. Clearly, we can not entrust our interests to those over whose actions and policy we have no control ... The fact of the matter is that the atmosphere surrounding this boundary business is too full of secrecy and mystery to be wholesome.

J.C. concluded that if they could only devise an organisation competent enough to speak for the 'Nationalists of the new pale',[6] then they would be in a position to fight for 'the realization of the Boundary Clause of the Treaty and the relieving of all benevolent outsiders of the trouble of any longer managing our affairs for us'.[7]

Letters along the lines of those penned by Northern Nationalist and J.C. frequently appeared in the anti-partitionist press at this tense time and undoubtedly reflected the sense of powerlessness and anxiety that characterised the double marginality of being a trapped minority. As it was, these testimonials had come at a juncture when Derry nationalists were feeling especially stressed by internal matters. Owing to Belfast's Local Government Act (1922) – which reinstituted the ward system in the place of proportional representation – January's urban council elections had returned Derry City to the Unionist fold after it had been ruled (between 1920 and 1923) by its first Catholic mayor and corporation in more than 300 years.[8] The fact that the city's Catholic majority had been gerrymandered out of existence was bad enough but at the end of May, the *Derry Journal* revealed that the registration of anti-partitionist voters in Derry City had also been allowed to lapse. The registration agents who had been doing this important work were apparently terminated in January 1923 and it seemed that nothing had been done since then to combat the feverish work undertaken by unionist agents in the city. Upon learning from the border press of the 'Sad Position of [the] Nationalist Majority in the City', the *Irish News* advised its own readers of the dangers of inaction: 'If the Nationalists of the north sacrifice their own future for nothing, they will find themselves objects of pity hereafter – and pity is near akin to contempt.'[9]

Whether the Irish Free State had already progressed from pity to contempt remains to be seen but, since partition still stirred passions in the South, woolly pronouncements related to Irish unity continued to punctuate Cumann na nGaedhael's election speeches. For instance, on 10 June, Home Affairs Minister Kevin O'Higgins told an audience at Bray, Co. Wicklow, that 'the North-Eastern Boundary Commission' was one of the most significant issues that his government had to face, adding that the matter 'would have to be handled with great delicacy and skill' and by people blessed 'with a knowledge of all the under-currents'.[10] The Home Affairs Minister's speech left many anti-partitionists with the strong impression that Cumann na nGaedhael intended to appeal to the Irish electorate with the pitch that it alone had the 'comprehensive outlook' needed to deal with the boundary issue. Unconvinced and somewhat annoyed by O'Higgins' brash suggestion, the *Irish News* incredulously observed that ministerial murmurings 'about deep-laid schemes, and weird "under-currents," and marvellous knowledge confined to a few people in Dublin will deceive no one in this part of the country who does not want to be deluded'.[11]

Only days after O'Higgins' Bray speech, President Cosgrave and Eoin MacNeill caused a similar bout of displeasure in certain Northern quarters as a consequence of the election addresses they gave at a Limerick rally. Cosgrave's 'incidental remarks' on the issue of the North-Eastern boundary amounted to no more than one line: 'They (the Free State Government) intended to see that the Article of the Constitution (Treaty?) was carried into effect.'[12] For his part, MacNeill was content to leave his audience with the comfort of knowing that any differences between North and South 'would in due course pass away' if only they could 'quickly establish a good, fair, just, and successful Government in the rest of Ireland'. It is unclear how well these (and other) statements on national unity were received by the Southern audiences for whom they were intended but, as far as the Devlinite press was concerned, terse 'generalities' of this sort failed to inspire confidence in the government's ability – or its resolve – to deal with the vital issue.[13]

Unbeknownst to anyone in Ireland outside of Cosgrave's inner circle, the Irish President had already taken the first real step to make Article 12 of the Treaty operative more than a week before his Limerick speech. On 9 June, Cosgrave sent a preliminary letter to London warning Stanley Baldwin – who had, by then, replaced the ailing Bonar Law as British Prime Minister[14] – that the Irish Free State would soon be in a position to announce the name of its Boundary Commissioner.[15] This overture was intended as a courtesy along the lines of which O'Shiel and Bolton Waller had advised and news of the development was kept quiet on both sides of the Irish Sea pending a formal pronouncement from Cosgrave. Thereafter, deciding on the appropriate time for Cosgrave's announcement became a subject of debate within the government.[16]

Those who were hoping to push the boundary issue sooner rather than later ultimately won out. In what must have been an event orchestrated by the government, as the Dáil was preparing to adjourn on 20 July, Longford-Westmeath TD Peter Hughes asked President Cosgrave to clarify the government's position on the boundary question. 'There is a lot of unrest and dissatisfaction amongst a large section of the people in the north of Ireland as to why this Boundary Commission has been, as they call it, "shelved",' said Hughes, as he asked the government to state its policy on the North 'in order to allay the fears of a large section of people who are yearning to come in [to the Free State] and obtain their rights under the Treaty'.[17]

Peter Hughes was by no means the first TD to make such a request; Seán Milroy had also raised the issue in the Dáil and Darrell Figgis had made similar pleas for information on no fewer than three occasions without satisfaction;[18] however, this time was different. Indicating that his 'Government [was] of the opinion that the opportune moment [had] arrived to give effect to the remaining provisions of Article 12 of the Treaty', Cosgrave proceeded to announce that he had selected Dr Eoin MacNeill as the Free State's Boundary Commissioner. Having done this, Cosgrave took pains to 're-state' his government's position on the boundary question:

> On the 7th December last, as we know, the Northern Parliament exercised the undoubted right given it under the first part of this Article of the Treaty and voted itself out of the jurisdiction of Saorstát Eireann. This action of theirs has made inevitable and imperative the carrying out of the remaining provisions of that Article, viz., the establishment of the Boundary Commission. Until that Commission reaches a decision … it is plain to every man that it is impossible to say what the area and boundary of the future Northern Ireland, that sprung as it were from the first part of this Article, will be. It is, therefore, as I have said, essential; – essential for all parties, for ourselves, for Great Britain, and for Northern Ireland to have the new and actual proportions of the latter area definitely and justly established.[19]

Britain's Secretary of State for the Colonies, the Duke of Devonshire, had received formal notification of the Free State's decision to nominate MacNeill and pursue its rights under Article 12 of the Treaty on 19 July.[20]

While the NEBB had recommended Eoin MacNeill's brother James as the Free State's Boundary Commissioner, from Cosgrave's perspective, James MacNeill lacked an important qualification that his brother did not: he was not a minister in the Free State government. Indicative of O'Shiel's view that the work of the Commission had to be treated as a political exercise, Cosgrave thought that the post should be filled by a member of his Cabinet but the President also wanted his nominee to be a Northern Catholic. Only Eoin MacNeill met all three qualifications at the time of the appointment; he was the Education Minister and he was a Catholic from the Glens of Antrim.[21]

In advising Prime Minister Baldwin of Cosgrave's formal notification, the Colonial Secretary predicted that the Irish administration would push no further until the Free State election had passed.[22] For his part, Prime Minister James Craig responded to the appointment with rigidity that was typical of his government's determination to eschew any responsibility under Article 12 of the Treaty. Craig told one interviewer that he had 'no personal feeling against Prof. MacNeill' but the 'Boundary Commission was something Ulster [would] not recognize and [had] never agreed to'. According to the Northern Prime Minister, the very idea of the Commission was nothing more than 'a Lloyd George trick' and his government could not be blamed for the Welsh Wizard's failure to make Article 12 of the Treaty 'water-tight'.[23]

The press greeted the news of MacNeill's appointment with keen, albeit cautious, interest. The *Irish News* saw the nomination as an overwhelmingly positive development but its coverage of the event focused to a greater degree on what was left to be done rather than what had been accomplished by the move. Snidely contrasting its own efforts with those taken by the Free State, the newspaper observed:

> While the problem remains unsolved there must be dissatisfaction, uneasiness, and uncertainty. The longer it stood in the background the greater the danger of this unsettled feeling developing into a fever which might prove fatal to the chances of an amicable solution. This danger we have repeatedly impressed upon all concerned, and we are glad to find that at last the moment has

> been considered opportune to take the necessary steps to bring it to an end.[24]

Under the circumstances, the Devlinite organ pointed out that the 'necessary steps' taken by the Free State would be all for naught if James Craig did not appoint his own Commissioner. And, since it presumed that Stanley Baldwin's Tory government would ultimately be charged with handling any 'transactions' with Craig, the *Irish News* was not prepared to discount the Prime Minister's non-recognition strategy.[25]

The border nationalist press was less guarded in its response to Cosgrave's opening gambit than was the *Irish News*. For instance, the Enniskillen-based *Fermanagh Herald* touted MacNeill as a person whose Northern roots made him knowledgeable of, and sympathetic to, the beleaguered plight of Catholics and nationalists in the border counties and the newspaper was 'certain' that their interests were 'quite safe in his hands'. As such, the *Herald* used its columns in an attempt to contrast Northern Ireland's obstructionism with the Irish Free State's earnest effort to 'establish good relations' and seek an 'amicable understanding' with that supposedly loyal government of Northern Ireland. The *Fermanagh Herald* confidently observed that the 'responsibility for enforcement of the Treaty [rested] with the British Government, whose responsible Ministers have pledged themselves to observe the Treaty in the letter and in the spirit'.[26]

Bound to enforce the Treaty, Baldwin's Tory government may have been more sensitive to Northern Ireland's concerns than was the coalition government that had signed the document but, at this stage in the protracted dispute, he 'refused to meddle'.[27] Like most British parliamentarians, the Prime Minister wanted to be through with what Thomas Jones frequently described as the 'Irish bog', irrespective of Sir James Craig's refusal to cooperate with the Commission.[28] Thus, as the *Irish News* had pointed out, Baldwin's inability to enforce the Treaty was going to be the real crux of the problem.[29]

Devonshire's belief that Cosgrave would make no further moves to have the Boundary Commission assembled before the election proved to be correct. While the administration was keen to carry out the 'necessary originating steps', it was not eager to have the Commission actually sitting during the campaign, even if it were possible to do so.[30]

Thus, acting on knowledge imparted by Dublin, on 25 July, Devonshire presented his proposed course of action in a letter to Cosgrave, which was subsequently made public:

> His Majesty's Government note that, in accordance with Article 81 of the Irish Free State Constitution, a General Election must take place before December 6 next. So soon, therefore, as this election is concluded it is the intention of His Majesty's Government at once to enter into communication with your Government, and also the Government of Northern Ireland upon the further steps necessary to give effect to the provisions of Article 12 of the Treaty.[31]

If the publication of Devonshire's letter was intended to give Cosgrave some breathing space during the election, it proved to be woefully ineffective since criticisms of the government's Northern policy were unabated. For instance, perceived Free State dawdling on the boundary issue provided fodder for complaint during two large AOH rallies held in Dungannon, Co. Tyrone, and Kilrea, Co. Derry, on 15 August to mark the Assumption of the Blessed Virgin Mary.[32] Devlin, National President of the AOH, was not in attendance at either rally but he was well represented at the Dungannon rally by Armagh MP and AOH General Secretary John Nugent. Nugent found himself uncharacteristically praising the 'great sacrifices' the Free State had made to 'carry out their portion of the Treaty' but, in direct reference to the Colonial Secretary's 25 July letter, the ardent Devlinite still found himself asking: 'What on earth had an election to do with the appointment of the Commission? If the Treaty was genuine,' he mused, 'then an election would not alter it.' Hugh McAleer, chairman of the Tyrone meeting, was even less inclined to give the Free State government credit for its achievements than was Nugent. In his own rousing speech, McAleer cynically described the Boundary Commission as a mere 'political mirage ... which made excellent propaganda for the Free State elections' but was 'poor balm' for Catholics and nationalists who had to endure the persecution of James Craig's government.[33]

In keeping with the sentiment of these and other pronouncements, before disassembling, the Tyrone Hibernians passed a resolution reiterating their commitment to a united Ireland and urging swift action on the boundary front so that those nationalists that would be left behind could formulate their plans knowing all the facts. The resolution also called for the release of political prisoners, like Fermanagh–Tyrone MP Cahir Healy, who had been held by the Northern Ireland government without charges since May of 1922. Derry and Antrim Hibernians passed a similar resolution at their meeting but,[34] to no great surprise, the Hibernians' concerns failed to register with the Cosgrave administration as it proceeded on its way to the 27 August election, touting the MacNeill appointment as its grand stroke. Still, this was enough to secure the endorsement of Cardinal Logue, Archbishop of Armagh, who urged Free Staters to support the Cosgrave government.[35] Joe Devlin was asked by multiple Southern deputations to contest a Dublin City seat but turned down the suggestion out of hand,[36] later asserting: '[i]f I do that, the poor people of Belfast, who have stood by me loyally for the past thirty years and who are undergoing the tortures of the damned will, I fear, think I am taking this opportunity of slipping out of a difficult position'.[37]

Cosgrave's governing party won the highest seat total in the Free State's general election but lost its majority. Cumann na nGaedhael was able to elect sixty-three TDs, including Cosgrave's entire Cabinet but, despite de Valera's arrest under the Free State's Public Safety Act, he and forty-three other Republicans were also returned, along with fourteen Labourites, fifteen Farmers and seventeen Independents and non-aligned TDs. Notwithstanding the mixed results, the *Derry Journal* saw the elections as a 'complete success' for the administration and the 'intrepid and hard-working Head of the Dail Executive',[38] as it trumpeted the fact that Treatyites had outpaced the Republicans by a margin of four votes to one and in seats by two to one.[39]

Since the Republicans abstained and, as the *Derry Journal* observed, the great bulk of the remaining TDs backed the Treaty, Cosgrave was able to hold onto the Presidency and was, therefore, able to preside over the Irish Free State's formal admission to the League of Nations in early September.[40] There was a variety of reasons for joining the League and it was not without controversy in the South but it was also in keeping with the Northern strategy proffered by O'Shiel and Waller months earlier. It was not surprising, then, that an NEBB press release – proudly printed in the *Fermanagh Herald* – described the development in glowing terms.[41] In contrast, for the *Irish News*, League membership only meant international recognition of partition and the unwanted distinctions between North and South;[42] however, the Belfast newssheet had far greater concerns over what it was learning about the Free State's boundary-related preparations from the NEBB's *Handbook of the Ulster Question.*

Published in the autumn of 1923, the *Handbook of the Ulster Question* was the brainchild of Kevin O'Shiel and grew out of his effort to give the Free State's English advocates a better understanding of the Ulster question.[43] The book included chapters written by experts associated with the NEBB on such topics as ancient and modern Ulster history, the financial burdens of partition, the persecution of Northern Catholics and the history of recent European border disputes.[44] By and large, the *Irish News* had very little interest in this propaganda piece, seeing it as a needlessly convoluted rehash of its own arguments, but the *Handbook*'s presentation of the Free State's apparent territorial claims did draw the newspaper's attention. Using Poor Law Unions as the unit of transfer, one of the *Handbook*'s principal maps made the case that Dublin could reasonably lay claim to all of Cos Tyrone and Fermanagh, Derry City and a considerable chunk of Co. Derry, as well as southern Down and Armagh. This sizable block of territory even exceeded the 'Maximum Line' that the NEBB had privately presented to the Executive Council in May.

While the *Irish News* freely acknowledged that the Six-County border represented an 'awkward and unnatural series of curves, and twists, and turns' that in no way reflected the wishes of the inhabitants in the counties of contention, it had a much more conservative interpretation of Article 12 than did the NEBB or, indeed, the border nationalists. 'When – and if – a Boundary Commission is appointed,' the newspaper argued, 'its function will be the determination of a new Boundary', without taking the 'merits or demerits of Partition into account', adding:

> Someone should clarify the situation by providing a map in which a Boundary line deemed just to all concerned under the conditions laid down in the second part of Article 12 would be marked. Then the general public … would know with a degree of exactitude what is expected from the Commission. If such a map were published,

> the controversy would, almost certainly, become more vehement than ever, perhaps it would become more confusing – if possible – because an end would be made of vague generalities.[45]

As it rejected the possibility of land transfers large enough to end partition by contraction, the *Irish News*' reporting sought to lower expectations, which were, in its view, dangerously raised by propaganda like the *Handbook*. In truth, the NEBB likely saw the *Handbook*'s embellished territorial claim as part of its longstanding effort to use the Commission as a 'diplomatic weapon'[46] but the *Irish News* was more inclined to see this, and James Craig's obstructionism, as a matter of 'playing diplomatic games' with the fortunes of the trapped Northern minority.[47]

The publication of the NEBB's *Handbook* and territorial claims had brought even sharper focus to the unenviable position that the Devlinites had occupied since the prospect of a Boundary Commission emerged in 1921. They were unquestionably devoted to the pursuit of 'full national self-government' for all of Ireland[48] but they were, at the same time, cognisant of the dangers they would face as a more isolated nationalist enclave in Northern Ireland if the border nationalists were repatriated. The prospect of having to endure this undesirable situation helps to explain the *Irish News*' adverse reaction to the *Handbook* and the way it had oscillated between clamouring for the Commission to sit and fearing that it eventually would.

Whether it amounted to deceitful game-playing or not, there was a diplomatic endeavour in the works during September and October and this venture, once revealed, caught many Irish nationalists by surprise. On 22 September, the British government invited the Irish Free State and Northern Ireland to attend a round table conference aimed at finding a solution to the boundary issue that was 'satisfactory to all parties'.[49] The proposed conference was not immediately disclosed to the press and the summit itself was delayed by the October meeting of the dominion leaders in London but this was just the sort of opportunity that the Free State, not to mention the Devlinites, had been banking on.

For Stanley Baldwin, the possibility of securing a negotiated settlement of the boundary question had as much to do with British politics as it did with Anglo-Irish relations. The Ulster Question was sure to embitter the diehard wing of his party, which was 'still grumbling against the Treaty of 1921'. Baldwin also had reason to fear the reconstitution of the coalition and political rebirth of Lloyd George; but, since he could delay it no longer, addressing the boundary issue via the conference route surely seemed the lesser of the evils.[50] The participants were to hold a preliminary conference on 15 December and, for the time being, the status of the talks remained cloaked in secrecy.[51]

The invitation and the resultant delay in acting on the démarche no doubt informed the Boundary Bureau's decision to send Hugh McCartan on a tour of Belfast and Derry City in mid-October. Filing his report before the month had elapsed, McCartan painted a grim picture of a 'disorganized' Northern minority that had yet to recover from the sectarian fighting of 1920–2 and was left cowed and beaten by the imposition of an unfriendly government in Belfast.[52] The abolition of proportional representation in local elections and the burdensome oath of allegiance to the Northern government were particularly galling for Six-County nationalists but, as McCartan learned, these concerns were further heightened as a consequence of Lord Londonderry's Education Act (1923).

Despised in virtually all quarters, Northern Ireland's Education Act withdrew the bulk of funding from denominational schools unless they agreed to a measure of secular control and this was something Northern Catholics would not do.[53] As McCartan discovered, the Act had caused 'much discontent' among Northern Catholics, who saw the corresponding curriculum changes as an effort to teach Catholic children to look at England as 'their mother country' while encouraging them 'at frequent intervals to salute the Union Jack'. Moreover, McCartan's discussions with a Father O'Neill on the subject seemed to reveal the religious underpinning of the supposedly non-denominational Act. According to O'Neill, when an MP objected to the oath that was being forced upon Catholic teachers during the debate stage of the Bill, a government member retorted: '[W]e who pay the piper will call the tune and that tune will be God Save the King,' to which a second MP interjected 'or Dolly's Brae'.[54] There was a deep sectarian resonance to the mere mention of this aggressively Orange song, and the nineteenth-century battle it chronicled, that required no further elaboration from Father O'Neill.

On 12 October, before McCartan's arrival in Ulster, the Northern bishops published a stern condemnation not only of the Education Act but of the general state of affairs that Northern Catholics were living under. Significantly, the statement included a plea for Northern nationalists 'to organize openly on constitutional lines, and resolve to lie down no longer under this degrading thralldom'. It is unclear whether the Bishops intended this as a general call for nationalist MPs to enter the Belfast parliament[55] but the idea of political organisation definitely did have traction amongst the nationalists that Hugh McCartan conversed with a couple of weeks later. For instance, George Martin, the NEBB's representative in Belfast,[56] advised McCartan of the advantages that could be mustered if the Free State were to spearhead 'a new Union of Ireland movement'[57] in Northern Ireland. Tellingly, Martin was convinced that Northern Sinn Féiners would be 'willing to cooperate with the old Nationalists' and were even prepared 'to accept Mr Devlin's leadership' in such a movement. *Irish News* editor Tim McCarthy had made political organisation a motto of his newspaper since the Treaty debates and, if his interpretation of 'Craig's future policy' was correct, a strong and united nationalist machine would become all the more important in the months ahead.

McCarthy, who also met with Hugh McCartan during the tour, was certain that James Craig intended to obstruct the Free State's Northern policy by presenting an intentionally unworkable unity scheme based on autonomy for historic (nine-county) Ulster. According to McCartan, *Irish News* reporters had proof that the idea had been 'canvassed', while McCarthy saw the seeds for such a plan in a speech Lord Londonderry gave in which he said that Unionists from Donegal, Monaghan and Cavan would 'play a part in the re-enactment of the Act of Union'. McCarthy warned the NEBB agent of the need to proceed cautiously should this trap be laid. While any unity plan putting current Free State counties under Belfast's jurisdiction was sure to be rejected by Dublin, the political fallout of rebuffing such an offer would serve Craig's purpose by marking the Free State as an unreasonable negotiator. As it was, McCarthy held out little hope for the future under the unsavoury circumstances that prevailed.

McCarthy's views largely confirmed McCartan's pessimistic conclusions regarding wider Northern conditions. Although the NEBB man observed general dissatisfaction with the Craig administration and the customs frontier, he did not think that Unionist unhappiness with the Craig regime 'cut very deep' or amounted to 'a definite revolt' in favour of Irish reunion. Rather, since the most ardent Unionist critics of the government were forced to 'stress their "loyalties" so as to avoid the charge of being disguised Sinn Feiners', McCartan was left with the strong impression that 'there [was] no evidence of any real desire for political union among the Unionists'. This certainly did not bode well for the tripartite talks that had been put temporarily on hold but it did speak to the 'disorganized and apathetic condition of the Catholic minority', which gave McCartan pause. He informed the Boundary Bureau: 'Again and again I heard the opinion expressed that the Free State took no interest in their [Northern nationalists'] position. They have lost faith in the Boundary Commission and many of them think it would do more harm than good.' He continued: 'When the Treaty was signed the Belfast Catholics were almost wholly in favour of it, but I met many Republicans who had become so on account of the Free State's apparent lack of interest in their position and the humiliations heaped on them.' Given what he had been told by Martin, McCarthy and others, Hugh McCartan speculated that a new nationalist movement 'based on current needs' could counteract the minority's sullen apathy and re-connect *nouveau* Republicans with the Treatyite position. It was, nonetheless, certain that damage had already been done to the relationship between Northern nationalists and their Southern counterparts.[58]

It was at this juncture that rumours about the still-unannounced border summit began to appear. The first hints that such a diplomatic endeavour was in the works actually came from a vague, albeit carefully worded, speech delivered by Kevin O'Higgins on 29 October. O'Higgins advised his Dún Laoghaire audience:

> We have at all times been willing to meet and confer with the representatives of our fellow-countrymen in the North-East. Any other attitude on our part would be inconsistent with the fact that the unity of the country is our dearest wish. If, as the result of such a Conference, we were to arrive at an arrangement even more conducive to the welfare of the country as a whole than the operation of the Treaty provisions – that is a contingency in which we would deem it our duty to consult the Parliament to which we

> are responsible. In default of such a desirable development the Treaty stands, as a policy of the Government.[59]

O'Higgins made no mention of a definite invitation to confer with his fellow-countrymen but, notwithstanding the painful subtlety of the minister's remarks, together with the fact that James Craig had made a casual reference to the possibility of a conference in late October, it seemed obvious that something was stirring.[60]

Despite its general approval of the conference route, the absence of definite facts in Kevin O'Higgins' speech sent the *Irish News* reeling. Convinced that the Home Affairs Minister was not just casting blindly, the newspaper complained that 'Northern Nationalists know nothing about these proposals until they read about them in the public Press.' The editorial continued:

> there has been no indication of the slightest regard for the opinions of the Nationalists of the Six Counties from those in authority either in Dublin or Belfast. Even now, when Mr O'Higgins announces that he and his colleagues are willing 'to meet and confer with the representatives of our fellow-countrymen in the North-East,' he means with the members of Sir James Craig's Government: if the idea that representatives of those 'fellow-countrymen in the North-East' who are Nationalist possess a right and title to have their views taken into account was entertained by the Minister, he forgot to mention it at Dun Laoghaire.

Confirmation that the Free State and Northern Ireland had accepted invitations to a boundary conference finally broke on 1 November. On the basis of the rumours that were leaking out, the *Irish News* responded positively to the development. So long as it was 'reasonable and just', the newspaper mused, a boundary settlement by way of a conference would be 'cordially welcomed – for all the many reasons stated in these columns time after time while futile belligerency was the prevailing mood'.[61] In contrast to these hopeful comments, the idea of going into conference with Britain and Northern Ireland sparked immediate concerns from other quarters. For instance, Tyrone Sinn Féiners were aware of the conference plan when they assembled in Omagh on 2 November. Ostensibly brought together to protest the manifold concerns raised by the 12 October bishop's statement, Revd Philip O'Doherty, one of the many clerics at the meeting, advised the crowd that the 'only remedy' for the inhospitable conditions Northern Catholics were toiling under was 'the fulfillment of the Treaty *in all its terms*'. Significantly, he added that 'Ulstermen should be fully consulted before and during the Conference.' This sentiment was shared by Father Donnelly of Carrickmore, who adamantly declared, '[c]onference or no conference we must insist on our rights now, for now is the time and not later'.[62]

While the NEBB fully expected the 'East-Ulster Irredentists' to be suspicious of anything that seemed to threaten the Boundary Commission, these initial concerns were intensified as a result of a report written by the Belfast correspondent of the Press Association as the story was breaking. That report claimed that James Craig had agreed to the conference 'on the basis of the Craig–Collins Agreement entered into in January, 1922'.[63] In this, the first of two pacts between the Irish leaders that spring, James Craig and Michael Collins had agreed to dispense with Article 12 of the Treaty in favour of a border settlement by mutual consent. It should also be remembered that border nationalists had come out harshly against the pact, which ultimately fell apart within weeks of its appearance.

The Press Association's report was eventually refuted by all three governments but not before President Cosgrave was forced to address the concerns under less than favourable conditions. Questioned in the Dáil by Cavan TDs Seán Milroy and Patrick Baxter, Cosgrave assured the Deputies that any rumours they had heard were not based on any information 'furnished directly or indirectly by the Irish Government', to which he added, 'there has been no question of a conference on the basis of the agreement of January, 1922, and there will be none'.[64]

As might be expected given its predilection for the negotiation route, the *Irish News* accepted Cosgrave's assurances at face value as it chastised those seeking to complicate the talks by clinging to the 'relics of futile negotiations'. Unless the failures of 1922 were laid to rest, the newspaper noted, 'we may find ourselves discussing the Act of Union, the Treaty of Limerick, and the paper signed by Hugh O'Neill at Mellifont in the quest for a formula applicable to the present-day problem'.[65]

Border nationalists were not easily convinced by the President's assurances. Indicative of the lingering mistrust, Ernest Blythe, then Minister of Finance, received an angry letter from Father Eugene Coyle on the matter, with the Fermanagh Sinn Féiner informing the minister that Free State supporters on the border were 'tremendously suspicious' that Dublin was preparing to jettison Article 12. As the priest warned Blythe, '[o]ne thing is for certain, your government will live or die by it [Article 12]'. In a similar vain, Archdeacon Tierney, the 'leading Sinn Fein priest', purportedly saw the tripartite conference revelation as the sign of 'a broken Treaty'.[66] And, Cahir Healy, writing from the prison ship *Argenta*, advised Kevin O'Shiel that, although he understood that Free State had to 'take the long view' rather than 'look at the matter from an area standpoint', a boundary conference would be worthless unless it led to Irish unity. Healy forcefully explained that, for border nationalists like himself, unity was the only 'satisfactory' solution to the boundary dispute.[67]

In not an entirely new development, the plight of the *Argenta* men like Healy and other internees became a *cause célèbre* for all anti-partitionist groups as they waited anxiously for more details on the proposed boundary conference. The press had made frequent references to the condition of these men throughout the summer and autumn of 1923,[68] as had the Northern bishops in October.[69] Border nationalists passed resolutions calling for the release of these men when they met in Omagh and Armagh[70] and on 15 November, Joe Devlin, Bishop MacRory, Hugh O'Doherty, Thomas Harbison and a number of other nationalist leaders made a spirited plea for the release of the prisoners in a public letter they addressed to Stanley Baldwin.[71] However, by mid-November, Ireland was the last thing the British Prime Minister had on his mind. On 12 November, nearly three weeks after harnessing his party to tariff reform at the Conservative Party Conference in Plymouth, Stanley Baldwin announced that the UK would go to the polls on 6 December.

Since he had inherited a healthy Tory majority from Bonar Law, there has been much debate over Baldwin's reason for calling an election barely a year into the mandate.[72] Whatever his underlying motivation may have been, in Great Britain, protectionism was the issue that decided the contest. In a telling contrast, in Northern Ireland the election was fought over partition just as the 1922 election had been. Where Unionist candidates, like T.E. McConnell, were telling their supporters that a Liberal or Labour victory meant that 'Ulster would be coerced, the Boundary would be changed, and all they would have left would be a strip of land along the Belfast Lough', anti-partitionists played up the propaganda value of winning Fermanagh–Tyrone for a second time in twelve months.[73] In 1923, as it was in 1922, these were the only two seats that anti-partitionists had a fair chance of winning and the incumbents, Cahir Healy and Thomas Harbison, were again selected to contest the joint constituency (despite T.P. O'Connor's attempt to engineer Joe Devlin's nomination).[74] Since the West Belfast constituency that Devlin had held for so long had been enlarged and gerrymandered, the consummate parliamentarian was again left without a Westminster riding to contest.[75] Yet, as the election occurred at a time when Devlin was described by Dick McGhee as looking 'ghastly' and being too ill to witness the internment of their mutual friend, Devlin may not have been fit for an electoral fight.[76]

When all of the votes were tallied, the Conservatives remained the largest party in parliament but their seat total dropped from 345 to 258 – a staggering loss of eighty-seven – which put the party in minority status against 159 Liberal and 191 Labourite free traders. Protectionism had clearly found little favour amongst the British electorate and, since this was the issue upon which the election was fought, there was no way for Baldwin to continue as Prime Minister.[77] As the *Irish News* told its readers, under these circumstances, 'it is quite unlikely that a Tory Government will rule England for many years to come'.[78]

Baldwin's fate and the composition of the next government were not immediately clear and the situation was left unsettled during the six-week Christmas holiday during which time he remained Prime Minister.[79] In Northern Ireland, the election results were unequivocal. Unionist candidates secured eleven out of the thirteen seats available in Northern Ireland, although Healy and Harbison were returned in Fermanagh–Tyrone. Their victory was interpreted, in nationalist quarters, as a definite sign that all of the gerrymandering and dirty tactics applied by the Northern government could not disguise the wishes of the inhabitants in those counties.[80] By way of a letter sent to his election agent, Cahir Healy thanked all those who had come out to vote, not for himself or Thomas Harbison, 'but (1) as a protest against partition and (2) as an expression of their desire to be included in the Free State', adding 'I sincerely trust there will not be an hour's unnecessary delay in putting Clause 12 of the Treaty into operation.'[81]

The 'jubilant' atmosphere on the Six-County border after the election produced at least one deputation of nationalist representatives demanding the immediate assembly of the Boundary Commission.[82] Whether the boundary issue was to be settled by way of Article 12 or 'by agreement involving the abolition of the Boundary' as it openly preferred, the *Irish News* found profound meaning in the advice that Cahir Healy imparted from the vantage point of his prison cell onboard the *Argenta.* Said the MP, 'A not unimportant factor in National affairs is the distrust with which the North looks at the West and South.' He continued:

> Between both there is a swift river flowing, and so far only the foundations of a bridge that is to connect them are visible. It must be a bridge of civic honesty, civic courage and toleration ... The courage to do the right thing by the community in all circumstances is the keystone alike of National union, and National ardency.

While Healy was a Sinn Féiner, the Devlinite *Irish News* declared without reservation that any man able to write in such moderate terms after being detained without charges under such harsh conditions was entitled to 'more than a "hearing" from the people on both sides of the "swift river"'.[83] Healy's fate was to become a much discussed topic when the British parliament resumed.

Notes

1 Originally appearing in a Dublin newspaper, Mr Macken's letter was reprinted in the *Irish News* on 11 August 1923.

2 K. Matthews, *Fatal Influence: The Impact of Ireland on British Politics, 1920–1925* (Dublin: University College of Dublin Press, 2004), p. 120.

3 *Irish News*, 28 May 1923.

4 Ibid.

5 The *Irish News* reprinted 'Northern Nationalist's' letter to the *Derry Journal* in conjunction with a second letter written on the same topic which had also appeared in the border press. The author of the second letter identified himself as 'J.C.' from Derry City. *Irish News*, 31 May 1923.

6 The English enclave centred around Dublin, which housed the administration, was known as the Pale or the English Pale. The designation was in use as early as 1495. M.A. Lyons, 'Pale, or English Pale', in B. Lalor (ed.), *The Encyclopedia of Ireland* (New Haven: Yale University Press, 2003), pp. 852–83.

7 *Irish News*, 31 May 1923. The *Irish News* had similar disdain for the much touted – yet largely unknown – research being conducted by the NEBB. For instance, on 6 June, an editorial entitled 'Futile Special Pleading' argued: 'The "North-Eastern Boundary Bureau" has not a word of information, or a promise of performance, or even the ghost of a suggestion that action leading to the setting-up of a Boundary Commission is intended.' The Devlinite newssheet wondered how anyone in the North of Ireland could be expected to design a plan to end partition without knowing the facts. *Irish News*, 6 June 1923.

8 R. Gallagher, *Violence and Nationalist Politics in Derry City, 1920–1923* (Dublin: Four Courts Press, 2003), p. 17.

9 It seems that news of the neglected state of the Derry City register was first revealed by the *Derry Journal*. The particulars on the situation given here have been provided by the *Irish News*' coverage of the issue. *Irish News*, 5 June 1923.

10 Ibid., 11 June 1923.

11 Ibid.

12 The parenthetical information appeared in the original source. *Irish News*, 18 June 1923.

13 Ibid.

14 Andrew Bonar Law was forced into retirement upon being diagnosed with terminal throat cancer. He resigned from the Premiership on 20 May 1923 after having served in that post for 210 days. Matthews, *Fatal Influence*, pp. 109–10.

15 Cosgrave advised Baldwin: 'I assume that any interests adverse to ours have similarly got to work since the presentation of the addresses that made the Commission inevitable [i.e., Northern Ireland's decision to contract out of the Free State as was its right under the first section of Article 12]; but my Colleagues and I think it fair to you that I should let you know a little in advance that a formal request that the Commission proceed will shortly be made on our part.' Baldwin, it seems, appreciated the informal advanced notice. K. Middlemas (ed.), *Thomas Jones Whitehall Diary, Volume III, Ireland, 1918–1925* (London: Oxford University Press, 1971), p. 221. Cosgrave had dispatched a similar letter to Bonar Law on 16 May but, under the circumstances, O'Shiel advised that Cosgrave take no further action. As the NEBB director put it: 'The success of the Boundary Commission depends so much on there being good men in power in England – men, not necessarily favorable to us, but prepared to deal straightly and honorably with us.' Memorandum from Kevin O'Shiel, 'Changes in British Government and Boundary Commission', 22 May 1923, Department of the Taoiseach, NAI/TSCH/S 2027, North East Boundary Secret Documents 1922–4, National Archives of Ireland, Dublin.

16 For information on the internal debate that went on among members of the Executive Council as well as the Governor General and some business interests,

see Memorandum from Kevin O'Shiel, 'Changes in British Government and Boundary Commission', 22 May 1923.

17 *Dáil Debates*, vol. 4 (20 July 1923), col. 1223, https://www.oireachtas.ie/en/debates/find/ (accessed 23 July 2019).

18 Figgis had raised the question on 17 January, 20 February, and 13 April and on each occasion his request for information was curtly brushed aside by the government.

19 *Dáil Debates*, vol. 4 (20 July 1923), cols 1223–5, https://www.oireachtas.ie/en/debates/find/ (accessed 23 July 2019).

20 The Governor General of the Irish Free State to the Secretary of State for the Colonies, 19 July 1923, in *Correspondence between His Majesty's Government and the Governments of the Irish Free State and Northern Ireland relating to Article 12 of the Article of Agreement for a Treaty between Great Britain and Ireland* (London: His Majesty's Stationary Office, 1924), p. 5.

21 G. Hand, 'MacNeill and the Boundary Commission', in F.X. Martin and F.J. Byrne (eds), *The Scholar Revolutionary: Eoin MacNeill, 1867–1945, and the Making of the New Ireland* (Shannon: Irish University Press, 1973), pp. 210, 216.

22 Devonshire to the Prime Minister, 20 July 1923, *Thomas Jones Whitehall Diary, Volume III, Ireland*, pp. 221–2.

23 *Fermanagh Herald*, 28 July 1923.

24 *Irish News*, 23 July 1923.

25 Ibid.

26 *Fermanagh Herald*, 28 July 1923.

27 K. Middlemas and J. Barnes, *Baldwin: A Biography* (London: The Macmillan Company, 1969), p. 207.

28 *Thomas Jones Whitehall Diary, Volume III*, p. 227.

29 *Irish News*, 23 July 1923.

30 Memorandum from Kevin O'Shiel, 'The Boundary Issue', 29 May 1923, Department of the Taoiseach, NAI/TSCH/S 2027, North East Boundary Secret Documents 1922–4, National Archives of Ireland, Dublin; Memorandum from Kevin O'Shiel, 'Boundary Commission Memorandum', n.d., Department of the Taoiseach, NAI/TSCH/S 2027, North East Boundary Secret Documents 1922–4, National Archives of Ireland, Dublin.

31 The Secretary of State for the Colonies to the Governor General of the Irish Free State, 25 July 1923, in *Correspondence*, pp. 5–6.

32 The Kilrea meeting was said to be '[o]ne of the largest Nationalist demonstrations witnessed in County Derry for the past number of years'. Thousands were in attendance and, according to the *Irish News*' estimate, the processions at the two meetings reached over two miles in length. *Irish News*, 16 August 1922.

33 *Irish News*, 16 August 1923.

34 Ibid. Co. Derry AOH President Luke Devlin chaired the Kilrea meeting and was every bit as antagonistic as McAleer had been. He argued that the Six-County nationalists had been 'basely deserted by the so-called leaders of the Twenty-six Counties and robbed' of their democratic freedoms by the Northern government.

35 Ibid., 11 August 1923.

36 Ibid., 16 August 1923.

37 A.C. Hepburn, *Catholic Belfast and Nationalist Ireland in the Era of Joe Devlin, 1871–1934* (Oxford: Oxford University Press, 2008), p. 249.

38 *Derry Journal*, 29 August 1923.

39 Ibid., 31 August 1923.

40 According to B.C. Waller, the Free State's entry into the League of Nations 'meant an express and clear recognition by the world at large of our distinct nationhood and of our newly re-established freedom and autonomy'. B.C. Waller, *Ireland and the League of Nations* (Dublin: Talbot Press Ltd, 1925), p. 3.

41 *Fermanagh Herald*, 22 September 1923.

42 It was also miffed at the suggestion in the press that Ireland – as opposed to the Irish Free State – had joined the League. Said the newspaper: 'Ireland is not a member of the League of Nations. Ireland is a country of 32 Counties ...The Free State comprises 26 Counties. It is not Ireland.' *Irish News*, 11 September 1923.

43 Memorandum from Kevin O'Shiel, 'The Boundary Issue', 29 May 1923. The *Handbook* made use of some of the statistical information compiled by Seán Milroy but it was very different in scope and content from Milroy's 1922 book. Whereas Milroy's *The Case of Ulster* took the form of a rebuttal of many of the arguments Unionist advocates had given for maintaining partition, the *Handbook of the Ulster Question* approached the topic by delving more deeply into the political history of Ireland dating back to the Norman Conquest, while also examining the economic repercussions of partition and the connections that could be drawn between the Irish Boundary Commission and the boundary disputes that sprang from the Treaty of Versailles. More importantly, the *Handbook* had the sanction of the Free State government and was prepared on its behalf. Milroy's book may (or may not) have been welcomed by the Southern government but was not an official publication.

44 Eoin MacNeill, J.W. Good, E.M Stephens, G.A. Ruth, Joseph Johnston, Bolton Waller and an unspecified Mr Murphy were identified as the primary contributors. Memorandum from Kevin O'Shiel, 'The Boundary Issue', 29 May 1923.

45 *Irish News*, 1 October 1923.

46 Memorandum from Kevin O'Shiel, 'The Boundary Commission – When? The Boundary Commission – Who?', 10 February 1923, Department of the Taoiseach, NAI/TSCH/S 2027, North East Boundary Secret Documents 1922–4, National Archives of Ireland, Dublin.

47 *Irish News*, 20 October 1923.

48 According to a 1912 report prepared for the National Directory of the UIL by Joe Devlin, the 'full national self-government of Ireland' was the organisation's first and most important objective. *The Times*, 8 February 1912.

49 The Secretary of State for the Colonies to the Governor General of the Irish Free State, 22 September 1923, in *Correspondence*, pp. 6–7.

50 Middlemas and Barnes, *Baldwin: A Biography*, 207; Matthews, *Fatal Influence*, pp. 129, 133–4.

51 'Proposed Conference RE Boundary. Copy of Notes By President', n.d., Department of the Taoiseach, NAI/TSCH/S 2027, North East Boundary Secret Documents 1922–4, National Archives of Ireland, Dublin.

52 H. McCartan, 'North Eastern Boundary Bureau. Report on Visit to Belfast and Derry', n.d., Department of the Taoiseach, NAI/TSCH/S 2027, North East Boundary Secret Documents 1922–4, National Archives of Ireland, Dublin.

53 S. Farren, 'Catholic–Nationalist Attitudes to Education in Northern Ireland, 1921–1947', *Irish Educational Studies* 8, 1, (1989), pp. 60–3.

54 Emphasis in the original. McCartan, 'North Eastern Boundary Bureau. Report on Visit to Belfast and Derry', n.d.

55 Michael Farrell used this statement to suggest that 'if the bishops had to choose between accepting the northern state and losing their schools then they were going to keep their schools'. See M. Farrell, *Northern Ireland: Orange State* (London: Pluto, 1976), p. 101. Phoenix suggested that the Bishops' statement 'stopped short' of encouraging recognition. E. Phoenix, *Northern Nationalism: Nationalist Politics, Partition and the Catholic Minority in Northern Ireland, 1890–1940* (Belfast: Ulster Historical Foundation, 1994), p. 293. M. Harris, *The Catholic Church and the Foundation of the Northern Irish State* (Cork: Cork University Press, 1993), pp. 154–5.

56 Phoenix, *Northern Nationalism*, p. 296.

57 McCartan, 'North Eastern Boundary Bureau. Report on Visit to Belfast and Derry', n.d.

58 Ibid.

59 *Irish News*, 30 October 1923.

60 Ibid.

61 Ibid., 2 November 1923.

62 Emphasis added. Ibid., 5 November 1923.

63 Ibid.

64 *Dáil Debates*, vol. 5 (2 November 1923), cols 693–702, https://www.oireachtas.ie/en/debates/find/ (accessed 23 July 2019).

65 *Irish News*, 3 November 1923.

66 Phoenix, *Northern Nationalism*, p. 294.

67 Emphasis in the original. Letter from the Assistant Legal Advisor's Office to each member of the Executive Council, 17 November 1923, Ernest Blythe Papers, P 24/204, University College Dublin Archives (UCDA).

68 For instance, see the *Irish News*, 6 June 1923; 17 July 1923.

69 Phoenix, *Northern Nationalism*, pp. 293–4.

70 *Irish News*, 3 November 1923.

71 Ibid., 15 November 1923.

72 Bonar Law had pledged not to abandon free trade without putting the question to the country and the former Prime Minister's pledge likely informed Baldwin's decision to call an election once he decided that high unemployment required abandoning economic orthodoxy. In 1925, Baldwin changed his story, claiming

that the early election was a calculated attempt to re-unify the party in the face of lingering divisions between coalitionists and non-coalitionists. Historian Nick Smart supports this view but his contention is disputed by Robert Self. A decade later Baldwin changed his story and he began to suggest that the move came as a way to outmanoeuvre Lloyd George, whom he felt was on the verge of taking up protectionism. A recent article by political scientist Andrew Taylor posits that Baldwin had called the 'disastrous' election because he, as a 'party politician', was trying to 'maximize his party's vote by moving towards the median voter on the economic class dimension'. Given the discrepancies and the historical debate that has been generated, the exact reason for this important election remains somewhat unclear. N. Smart, 'Baldwin's Blunder? The General Election of 1923', *Twentieth Century British History* 7, 1 (1996), pp. 110–39; R. Self, 'Baldwin's Blunder: A Rejoinder to Smart on 1923', *Twentieth Century British History* 7, 1 (1996), pp. 140–50; A. Taylor, 'Stanley Baldwin, Heresthetics and the Realignment of British Politics', *British Journal of Political Science* 35, (2005), p. 430; R. Jenkins, *Baldwin* (London: William Collins Sons & Co. Ltd, 1987), pp. 71–8.

73 For instance, at a Tyrone rally on 2 December Harbison informed the crowd that '[i]f they registered their votes unanimously the Boundary Commission must be set up, and it must find that Tyrone and Fermanagh belong to Ireland (cheers)', while Alex Donnelly told the same audience that 'the result of the election would be the death of Partition and the creation of a free and undivided Ireland'. *Irish News*, 3 December 1923.

74 In this instance, it seems that Harbison was willing to stand down but the move was blocked by prominent border nationalists, who, consequently, disproved George Martin's supposition that the Sinn Féiners were ready to accept the Old Party and Devlin's leadership. Phoenix, *Northern Nationalism*, p. 297; Hepburn, *Catholic Belfast and Nationalist Ireland in the Era of Joe Devlin*, pp. 244, 248–9; McCartan, 'North Eastern Boundary Bureau. Report on Visit to Belfast and Derry', n.d.

75 According to the *Irish News*, after changes were made to the electoral boundaries in the city, the formerly safe nationalist seat in West Belfast had nearly 20,000 voters added to it from North and South Belfast, making West Belfast 'the biggest constituency returning one Parliamentary representative in the Six Counties and Great Britain'. In raw numbers, West Belfast had 67,162 voters on the register as compared with only 44,289 in the East; 46,844 in the North; and 44,054 in the South. *Irish News*, 1 December 1923.

76 Hepburn, *Catholic Belfast and Nationalist Ireland in the Era of Joe Devlin*, p. 253.

77 Middlemas and Barnes, *Baldwin: A Biography*, pp. 248–53; Jenkins, *Baldwin*, pp. 77–9.

78 *Irish News*, 8 December 1923.

79 Jenkins, *Baldwin*, pp. 78–9.

80 In this connection, the *Irish News* compared the tactics of the Northern government to the eighteenth century's 'rotten boroughs'. *Irish News*, 11 December 1923.

81 Ibid., 12 December 1923.

82 *Weekly Digest*, 17 December 1923, Ernest Blythe Papers, P 24/204, University College Dublin Archives (UCDA); *Irish News*, 10 December 1923.

83 Healy's comments were originally published in the *Irish Statesman* but were re-published in the *Irish News* in an editorial advocating fair dealing in any settlement that was to be reached between the Irish governments. *Irish News*, 11 December 1923.

CHAPTER 11

'Do it Without Them': Convening the Irish Boundary Commission

> The 'Boundaries question' is simply and plainly insoluble – for no man, or Commission, can ever devise a scheme that will satisfy all concerned, or that will not add, perhaps immeasurably, to the discontent and bitterness presently prevailing.
>
> – *Irish News*, 3 February 1922[1]

After much uncertainty, the political situation precipitated by Britain's December election was finally sorted out when, on 22 January 1924, James Ramsay MacDonald was appointed as the first Labour Prime Minister of the United Kingdom. MacDonald's minority government was the fourth British administration to hold the reins of power in the three years since the Anglo-Irish Treaty had been signed and, not unexpectedly, it, too, would be short-lived. While emphasising Northern nationalist views of Free State's stewardship during this most vital and volatile time, this chapter continues to examine the drawn-out fight to convene the Irish Boundary Commission.

Although the impact that the Labour government was to have on Ireland and Article 12 was not initially clear, some of the uncertainty was alleviated when J.H. Thomas, the new Colonial Secretary, extended a fresh offer to meet with the two Irish governments.[2] Both governments ultimately agreed to meet 'on the same terms' as Stanley Baldwin had offered; however, Northern rumblings seemed to indicate that there would be little chance of success.[3] On 31 January, Sir James Craig appeared before a meeting of the UUC where he repeated his oft-cited determination to 'stand firm'. Decidedly less circumspect, the Northern Finance Minister, Hugh Pollock, openly boasted that 'any arrogant claim to Ulster territory would be resisted to the death'. And, reminiscent of the dangerous days of 1914, these Unionist heavyweights clearly still had the backing of Lord Carson, who confidently assured the UUC, via telegram, that Ulster 'would always be ready' to face 'whatever difficulties may confront [it] in the future'.[4] The fact that Unionism was apparently prepared to go into the tripartite talks with 'absolutely unruffled composure' left the *Derry Journal* without much hope about their outcome.[5]

The *Irish News* shared its sister newssheet's pessimism about the long-anticipated talks but it also took this opportunity to vent on the vexing question of minority representation. 'As it was at the beginning of November, 1923,' said the newspaper, 'so it is at the close of January, 1924. Nearly half a million Nationalists in the Six Counties will have no spokesmen or representative at the forthcoming conference.' Presuming that Dublin was, by now, fully aware of the nationalist minority's desire to have the boundary question 'settled – and settled without delay', the newspaper was nonetheless peeved that 'the voicelessness of the Nationalist people of the Six Counties' did not matter in the least to Belfast, London or even Dublin.[6]

Gloomy predictions about the round table talks proved to be well founded. Representatives from the Free State, Northern Ireland and Great Britain met for four hours on 1 February and less than three hours on 2 February without coming to any sort of conclusion but they did agree to meet again within twenty-eight days. Keeping what the *Irish News* called a 'solemn Treaty of silence', the conference participants agreed not to divulge any details of their discussions to the press[7] but it is now known that the Colonial Secretary's plan for sidestepping Article 12 amounted to the resurrection of the Council of Ireland. Cosgrave had raised the possibility that a suggestion of this sort might arise in a memorandum that he circulated to his ministers in mid-January and the President did not altogether reject the idea then,[8] but '[t]he snag', as Thomas Jones put it, was on Craig's demand for equal representation in the Council.[9] J.H. Thomas' proposal also provided for Northern Ireland's continued representation at Westminster and neither of these eventualities sat right with the Free State. President Cosgrave framed his major concern with the question: 'Is there not a great danger of such a plan tending in time to pull the whole of Ireland, through the north, more and more towards London?'[10]

Irrespective of the policy of secrecy, the adjournment of the conference spawned the usual spate of recriminations, accusations and rabble-rousing. Former editor of the *Northern Whig* and noted barrister Joseph R. Fisher wrote to *The Times* arguing that the Articles of Agreement did not alter a single word of the Better Government of Ireland Act of 1920, while insisting that Article 12 of the Treaty could do nothing but render a minimal 'rectification of [the] boundary'.[11] The ultra-Unionist *Morning Post* likened the Anglo-Irish conference table to a 'powder barrel containing enough explosives to lift the whole of the British Isles six feet into the air',[12] while the disillusioned *Irish News* instructed its readers to remember the Ninth Beatitude in the Christian tradition: 'Blessed are they that expect nothing, for they shall not be disappointed.'[13] One of the most interesting reactions to the official account of the conference came from a disgruntled correspondent of the *Derry Journal*, who cynically observed:

> The Belfast Government had, according to the Treaty, a month in which to make up its mind as to whether it would 'contract out' or 'go in' the Free State. Catholics in the Enclave know the result. Now Belfast is to have yet another month … Perhaps inside that month they may be able to squeeze a million out of the Labour Government to pay for the 'Specials.' Has President Cosgrave any guarantee that the Labour Government will even be in office for a month? While at all times in favour of peaceful solution to the Boundary problem, I think the time has come for settling the matter one way or another … The Treaty provides the remedy for the Six-county minority.[14]

Complementing the frustrated sentiments of this unidentified reader, on 11 February, the *Derry Journal* gave this stern warning for the Free State: '[T]he policy of leaving the problem to the "shifting winds of chance," in the hope that some fine day an acceptable solution might be borne on the breeze, cannot be pursued interminably.'[15]

Irrespective of appearances, in the aftermath of the February conference, Dublin was no longer inclined to simply wait for such a solution to be 'borne on the breeze'. The official correspondence between T.M. Healy, Irish Governor General, and J.H. Thomas suggests that the Cosgrave administration was intent on re-convening the talks as soon as was possible as a way of testing the waters one last time before taking a new approach.[16] The sticking point here was Craig's apparent ill health, which prevented an early re-convening of the talks but, while the timetable was being worked out, it must have been becoming clear in Dublin that the NEBB's carefully laid plans were not having their desired affect. The negotiation route had thus far been unsuccessful, as Craig had not budged beyond his initial 'Not an Inch' policy despite considerable pressure from Britain.[17] Notwithstanding the fact that communication between Belfast and London was carried out through the Home Ministry rather than the Colonial Office, what O'Shiel had once called the 'immeasurable distance in status between Saorstat and Northern Ireland'[18] was clearly not preventing the subordinate parliament of Northern Ireland from controlling this exercise in high politics, just as the Craig government had got its way with its Local Government Bill of 1922.[19]

To those outside government circles, the reasons for delaying the resumption of the conference were not known and this, naturally enough, caused much ill will in the nationalist North. As the no longer patient *Derry Journal* asked on St Patrick's Day, with February 'fled' and half of March 'vanished' without movement, 'How much longer have expectant people to wait for "results"?'[20] Taking up the *Irish News*' frequent tag, Derry Devlinite George Leeke found himself wondering why no steps had been taken 'to consult the interests of those most concerned – namely those of the minority in the Six Counties'. After all, Leeke proclaimed, it was the Northern minority whose 'whole future [was] staked on the results'.[21]

Leeke and his colleagues powerlessly waited for others to decide their fate; however, the Six-County minority did have one victory to celebrate. After months of protesting and considerable discussion at Westminster, in mid-February 1924, the Northern government finally released Cahir Healy from detention.[22] Encouraged by Dublin and his constituents to take his place at Westminster,[23] the Fermanagh nationalist did so on 14 March after trying to make it clear to both the press and any detractors[24] that he 'was taking [his] seat for a definite object [and] for a limited period'. The MP, who now eschewed the Sinn Féin label for all its anti-Treatyite connotations, declared 'as soon as [the] Treaty has been carried out, or even if G[rea]t Britain refuses to [carry] it out, I am through with Westminster'.[25]

According to Healy, one of the chief reasons that he agreed to enter the British House of Commons was because certain colleagues had pointed out that he could 'do some good with [the] English press'[26] on account of his journalistic background. In mid-February Cosgrave and Eoin MacNeill had advised him to take his seat with this purpose in mind[27] but no one knew then that a stunning turn of events in Dublin would leave the Free State government clamouring for as much friendly press as it could get.

In mid-March, the Treatyite regime came under attack from within. Attempting to prevent any further demobilisation of the Free State army, elements within its structure having ties to the IRB presented the government with an ultimatum, demanding that it suspend its demobilisation efforts and find a way to work towards a republic. Initially the problem appeared to be swept away rather painlessly by the promise of an inquiry but on 18 March, a number of the officers who had signed the ultimatum were arrested in rather dramatic fashion under the suspicion that they were fomenting a mutiny. The confusing debacle that followed split the Executive Council, leading to the resignations of Defence Minister Richard Mulcahy and Joseph McGrath, Minister of Industry and Commerce, along with much of the GHQ and eight TDs, including Cavan's Seán Milroy. Cosgrave's government was both shaken by the threat that the Army Mutiny posed and left in disarray on account of the political fallout.[28]

Although its origins bore no real connection to the boundary dispute, Healy was prepared to use the mutiny for all it was worth as a means of pushing the Free State's case in London. In a piece provocatively titled 'Will the Free State Fall?: Another Civil War Threatened', he argued that the 'Free State's only chance of survival [was] the full delivery of the Treaty'. This was the case, Healy maintained, because Dublin's inability to proceed with the Boundary Commission had produced 'a perilous situation' characterised by discontent that could no longer be suppressed. 'The British public must know the truth,' wrote the Northern MP, since 'they alone can prevent further chaos. The Treaty must be fully honoured.'[29]

It may indeed be tempting to view this plea for movement on the boundary issue as overly dramatic (as did the *Irish News*)[30] or even opportunistic but it is also certain that the mutiny and its aftermath genuinely concerned Healy and other Northern nationalists. After hearing the Republican Sean T. O'Kelly tell a Six-County audience that the Irish Free State was on 'the point of collapse', Healy wrote to Minister for Finance Ernest Blythe expressing trepidation over the 'heart-breaking situation' caused by Free State 'bickering'. Until these sorry conditions were reversed, warned Healy, '[a]ll visions of either a settlement or a B/C fade out'.[31]

To keep the prospect of reengaging the tripartite conference from completely fading out, on Lionel Curtis' urging, Britain's Colonial Secretary decided to send a reluctant Thomas Jones back to Dublin at the end of March.[32] In a reversal of what had been the case, Jones now found it exceedingly difficult to lure Cosgrave back to the conference table and he was probably correct to place some of the blame for this on the 'psychological effect' of the Army Mutiny.[33] Whatever the cause of Dublin's new reluctance to talk, in order to get the Free State back to the table, it took a definite assurance that the Labour government would 'exercise all the powers vested in them by Article 12 of the Treaty to constitute the Boundary Commission' if the Free State became convinced that the conference had failed. With this promise made, the long-overdue conference resumed on 24 April.[34]

The discussions during this second round of talks focused on the idea of a 'voluntary Commission', consisting of local experts working on the basis of mutual consent. Although Cosgrave would later tell Jones and Curtis that there had been 'utmost good feeling between [himself] and Craig' during the meeting, the voluntary Commission, not to mention the conference itself, faltered when Craig demanded that the Free State renounce its right to invoke Article 12 should the voluntary body fail. As Jones freely admitted upon learning of this ploy, had Cosgrave accepted these terms, 'it would be open for the North, unobtrusively but effectively, to block any agreement by voluntary Commission' thereafter.[35] The official statement issued at the termination of the conference said only that, '[a]fter prolonged discussion [,] it was not found possible to reach an agreement'.[36]

Despite its ignorance of the actual deliberations, the *Irish News* was not far from the truth when it claimed, after the conference broke down, that 'it was silly to say that the result was not anticipated' since 'Sir James Craig's attitude precluded the possibility of agreement.' For his part, Cosgrave had 'no information whatsoever to give' in the Dáil or otherwise[37] but in the wake of the disappointing conference, Six-

County nationalists marshalled whatever forces they could to appeal to London's sense of principle, honour and respectability in an attempt to keep the Labour government engaged. As the *Derry Journal* pointed out on 28 April, 'British honour is pledged to carry out the Treaty.'[38] Writing in the *Westminster Gazette* in early May, Cahir Healy argued that the Free State had 'scrupulously carried out their part of the contract', adding 'it becomes a simple matter of honour with Great Britain now to carry out hers'.[39] And, in a pamphlet appropriately entitled 'Some Facts about the Ulster Boundary', a group of leading Six-County nationalists proffered the claim that the Free State had already 'made good' on its Treaty obligations as they pressured England to do as much.[40] This subtle arm-twisting represented the sum total of Northern nationalism's influence on a situation that so dearly affected them. Moreover, with local elections scheduled for Northern Ireland's county and rural district councils on 1 June, time was now of the essence for the nationalist minority since gerrymandering had all but guaranteed Unionist victories in key border contests.[41]

Having failed to produce any alternative to the Boundary Commission via the conference route and recognising that, as Cosgrave told Jones, 'speed was the important thing',[42] when the talks faltered, the Free State finally asked Britain, on 26 April, to proceed with the establishment of the Boundary Commission. Three days later, Home Secretary Arthur Henderson formally asked Northern Ireland to appoint its Commissioner.[43] Faced with this official request, Craig did not 'swallow his brave "never, nevers"' as Kevin O'Shiel had once predicted.[44] Rather it took Belfast until 10 May to word a refusal that was sufficiently polite to send to the Home Secretary and thereafter the matter was transformed from a dangerous political issue into a convoluted constitutional dilemma requiring the intervention of the Judicial Committee of the Privy Council (JCPC).[45] Responding to the possibility that Northern Ireland would refuse to nominate its Boundary Commissioner during the debate at Westminster on the Irish Free State (Agreement) Bill in 1922, Joe Devlin had offered this simple one-sentence suggestion: 'Do it without them.'[46] As that eventuality had now come to pass, the British government was keen to determine if Northern Ireland's Governor, the Duke of Abercorn, could appoint the Six-Counties' Commissioner or, barring this, whether the Boundary Commission could function with only two Commissioners. On 21 May, the cabinet agreed to refer the matter to the JCPC[47] and news of the impending referral was made public on 4 June.[48]

Predicting that this new course of action would be 'indistinguishable from a cul de sac', the downtrodden *Irish News* no longer saw even the semblance of honour in the politics of treaty-making. In what it now regarded as the appropriate epitaph for Article 12 of the Anglo-Irish Treaty, the newspaper recalled these lines of verse: 'Fame's but a hollow echo; Gold pure clay;/Honour, the darling of but one short day.' The Devlinite newssheet offered its own postscript to this poetic rendering: 'Treaties and Pacts, undertakings and promises, are frequently dishonoured within the space of one short day.'[49] These cynical lines of verse, attributed to the English, poet and coloniser Sir Walter Raleigh, were all the more evocative in light of what Archdeacon Tierney called the 'plantation of Orangemen in Fermanagh and Tyrone'. While the tripartite negotiations were sliding into nothingness, border nationalists chose to boycott the 1 June municipal elections, rather than allowing them to be lost via a rigged vote, and Unionist councils were returned across the board.[50]

It would be well into July before any word from the JCPC arrived but in the meantime, J.H. Thomas did offer those anxious for an end to the dispute one consolation; on 5 June, Britain announced Richard Feetham, South African Judge (on the Transvaal provincial division), as its choice to Chair the Boundary Commission. Evidently, Feetham was an acceptable choice to the Free State. Boundary Bureau Secretary E.M. Stephens is known to have considered him 'a good appointment'[51] and the *Irish News* cast Feetham as a 'conscientious adjudicator' even as it admitted that 'few people, if any, in the North or South of Ireland had ever heard of him'.[52] As a long-time confidant of Lionel Curtis (who had suggested his appointment),[53] a member of Lord Milner's Kindergarten and contributor to the *Round Table*, the English-born jurist certainly had his champions within the Colonial Office even if his name was not more widely known. Following the appointment, Curtis wrote reassuringly to Churchill: 'Feetham is just the Chairman you wanted, of conservative temperament, and a man who could be relied upon to reject the preposterous and extravagant claims being advanced by the Free State.'[54]

As he, too, was now left waiting on the decision of the JCPC, Feetham made use of his time by meeting with the two Irish leaders, touring the border regions and giving careful consideration to the meaning of the Treaty's boundary clauses.[55] As far as the *Manchester Guardian* was concerned, however, there should have been no real mystery attached to the interpretation of the infamous Article 12. 'Everybody knows what Article 12 means,' argued the *Guardian*. 'What the Judicial Committee is to decide upon is what are the means legally and constitutionally to carry that Article out.' Pointing to the real crux of the problem, the newspaper continued: 'That need has come because the north of Ireland has refused to obey not a "midnight Treaty" but a daylight statute passed by a House of Commons in which the Unionist Party had a majority and by a House of Lords which knew perfectly well what it was doing.'[56] Irish nationalists had spent many months making this same argument. While loyal Ulster might be able to justify its refusal to abide by a 'midnight Treaty' that it had not signed, this *right* could not possibly extend to the Irish Free State (Agreement) Bill: the British statute that gave the Treaty force of law. This was indeed a compelling argument and one rendered stronger still in light of the fact that Northern Ireland had knowingly and unabashedly made use of the first part of Article 12 on 7 December 1922 when it voted itself out of the Irish Free State. Nationalist-oriented newspapers were brimming with articles and editorials concerning both of these lines of argument throughout the summer of 1924.

Still able to draw a big crowd, on 19 June, Joe Devlin appeared before a large demonstration of Antrim Hibernians in Carnlough. In this, one of the few known political engagements that he had made since the summer of 1923, Devlin delivered a major speech calling for consultation between the two Irish governments, an end to the 'inactivity' and a voice for Northern Catholics on the intractable boundary issue. 'For three years we, the Nationalists of North-East Ulster, have been practically inarticulate,' said Devlin:

> We have waited with phenomenal patience that might justifiably be regarded as exhausted ... You and I have been waiting for three years; and what did that waiting mean? It meant intolerable humiliation; it meant that our citizens' rights were flinched from us, that we were reduced to the degrading position of helots in this area; that we had neither power nor authority to direct our destinies or to defend our interests. We are one-third of the

> citizens of Ulster, and yet we have not been permitted to exercise our rights and we have been left without a single spokesman [in the Northern parliament] ... We are waiting to know where we are.[57]

As the great bulk of Northern nationalists had little knowledge of, not to mention influence on, the way that the boundary question was being handled, Devlin saw every justification for demanding that their voices be heard. But, even had this call been heeded, no one could have said with any degree of certainty exactly where the situation stood until the JCPC rendered its decision.

The JCPC was given the formal order of reference on 25 June and heard testimony from the crown and Northern Ireland during the third week in July. But, because the Free State viewed this dispute as a 'domestic' matter between the British government and a subordinate legislature and was determined to guard its own international status at any cost, Dublin chose not to be represented when 'The Trial of Article Twelve' began.[58] The verdict eventually came down on 31 July and, as Thomas Jones recorded in his diary, the 'decision was "beastly awkward"'.[59] The Law Lords had decided that a Boundary Commission could not function in the absence of a representative from Northern Ireland and that neither Abercorn nor the Imperial parliament could appoint a Commissioner for Belfast. Equally important, in light of later events, the JCPC also decided that, if the Boundary Commission was ever assembled, majority rule (as opposed to unanimity) would be sufficient to produce a report and deliver a territorial reward.

Beastly awkward or not, unless the Northern Prime Minister could be convinced to change his mind, there was but one way out of the impasse. The Labour government would have to pass corrective legislation allowing Britain to appoint a representative for Northern Ireland. So, when last-ditch discussions failed to avert this unpleasant alternative, Labour introduced its Irish Free State (Confirmation of Agreement) Bill on 5 August, just before the parliamentary session came to a close. The corresponding Irish legislation was put before the Dáil a week later.[60]

The period between the introduction of the British Bill in August and the resumption of parliament on 30 September was filled with intrigue and speculation. It was by then clear that the minority Labour government was on shaky ground for reasons entirely unrelated to Ireland.[61] Cognisant that an election would soon be called, the opposition parties may well have been tempted to use the Irish legislation for political advantage but neither the Liberals nor the Tories had any great desire to be enveloped by what Herbert Gladstone had once called 'the grim vapors of the past'.[62] This was why Baldwin tried, in early August, to dissuade Craig from carrying on the troublesome course he had set in motion.[63] However, Baldwin's reassurances were all for naught. Craig seems to have taken to heart Edward Carson's warning – issued in December 1923 – that Ulster unionists 'could not really trust ... English politicians'[64] and the Northern Prime Minister refused to budge.

Eager to confirm his newly found place within the Tory ranks, it was at this juncture that former Liberal coalitionist Winston Churchill came up with an idea that he, together with Lords Balfour and Birkenhead, hoped would give Craig all the political collateral he would need in order to appoint his own Commissioner.[65] On 19 August, Churchill sent Craig a copy of a letter that Birkenhead had written to Balfour in March of 1922, explaining the meaning that the then Lord Chancellor and Treaty signatory had attributed to Article 12.[66] In the letter, made public on 8 September,[67] Birkenhead claimed that the Commission was never meant to do anything more than rectify glaring problems with the poorly drawn border. Attributing Michael Collins' well-known assumption that the Boundary Commission would give the Free State control of Fermanagh and Tyrone to the Irish leaders' hotheadedness and 'overheated imagination',[68] Birkenhead observed: 'I have no doubt that the Tribunal, not being presided over by a lunatic, will take a rational view of the limits of its own jurisdiction, and will reach a rational conclusion.'[69]

Although Lloyd George supported Birkenhead's narrow interpretation of Article 12 in an important policy speech he gave at Penmaenmawr,[70] the Churchill–Birkenhead–Balfour masterstroke did nothing but muddy the waters. Irish nationalists saw the letter as a blatant attempt to re-write history and the *Irish News* wasted no time in printing contrary statements delivered by Birkenhead in the immediate aftermath of the Treaty negotiations.[71] Thomas Harbison, at a Derry City protest meeting, went so far as to suggest that the

Birkenhead letter was just as likely to have been 'written in March last or during the present month' as it was in 1922.[72] And, freed from detention in the South, Éamon de Valera also got into the game of re-interpretation by publishing dispatches on the Northern issue sent in October 1921 between himself and Arthur Griffith. The sum of the newsprint taken up with the issue of interpretation during the first weeks of September amounted to this: in spite of guarantees given to him by Baldwin, Birkenhead and others, James Craig had cornered the market on 'Ulster dourness and thick headedness',[73] as he still refused to appoint his own Commissioner. Fears brought on by the British signatories' efforts to narrowly cast the meaning of Article 12 led the Free State and border nationalists to redouble their efforts to secure a plebiscite. And, despite their eagerness to bring down the Labour government, neither the Liberals nor Tories wanted Ireland to be the cause. As a result, both parties supported the Labour government's Irish Bill in the end.[74]

Although the Labour administration was taking its last shallow breaths when parliament resumed on 30 September, the Irish Free State (Confirmation of Agreement) Act was carried before the government fell. Empowered by the legislation to appoint a Boundary Commissioner for Northern Ireland, Thomas immediately approached the Unionist Joseph Robert Fisher, former editor of the *Northern Whig* (1891–1913), with the intent of securing his services as the tribunal's third representative.[75] This would be one of the last actions Thomas would take as Colonial Secretary. Before any appointment could be made or the Commission assembled, domestic issues brought down the Labour government on 8 October. The UK was going to the polls for the third time since the demise of the coalition.

Writing in June 1924, the *Irish News* had mused that Northern nationalists did not really care 'whether a Tory Die-hard Government, or a Liberal gang of Die-easys, or a Labour host of Talk-hards command[ed] the majority at Westminster'.[76] While this jibe at the instability of British politics undoubtedly still held true during the autumn election, it did not reflect any desire to relinquish control of the two nationalist seats in the Fermanagh–Tyrone constituency. Since this was the one riding that was able to return anti-partitionist MPs, Northern nationalists were understandably on edge when Éamon de Valera broached the idea of running a slate of Republican and abstentionist candidates in this and a number of other Northern constituencies.[77]

Worried that the introduction of Republican candidates would split the nationalist vote in the crucial border contest, reaction from both wings of Northern nationalism was extremely hostile. Alex Donnelly, former Chairman of the Tyrone County Council, speculated that nationalist voters in the Six Counties would sooner 'refrain altogether from exercising the franchise' than vote for Republicans. Such a prospect left the Sinn Féiner convinced that 'de Valera [could] do no good by nominating candidates' since anti-Treatyites could not possibly win any of the contests. Archdeacon Tierney was even more adamant in his rejection of the Republicans than was Donnelly.[78] 'No necessity [e]xists for compromise or haggling of any kind,' argued the Fermanagh cleric. 'The issue is clear; we know our strength; we know our supporters; we know our business, and we shall put forward the candidates of our own choice, or none at all.'[79] Shielded to some extent by the fact that this was a border issue, the *Irish News* observed that de Valera's proposal left the nationalists of Tyrone and Fermanagh in a state of 'confusion and uncertainty', especially since no one was sure whether the 'once-beloved leader' was 'bluffing' or was really intending to 'stab the opponents of Partition in the back'.[80]

This mystery was soon solved when the anti-Treatyites officially nominated candidates in Fermanagh–Tyrone, in addition to West Belfast, North Belfast, Antrim, Armagh and Derry.[81] De Valera appears to have had this course in mind even before the Labour government fell. Lamenting the fact that the 'full anti-partition strength [could not] be registered', in September, the Republican leader had written to his old nemesis Joe Devlin suggesting that the time might be ripe for them to sit down 'for a short talk'. There is no indication that Devlin answered the request[82] but once it was certain that de Valera was prepared to follow through with his election ploy, border nationalists began plotting a loud response of their own.

Knowing that Republican candidates would siphon votes away from any Treatyite standard-bearers and that splitting the vote would give the two Unionist candidates an electoral and propaganda victory, Healy and Harbison – the incumbents – decided not to contest the election.[83] Refusing to participate in electoral contests that pro-Treaty nationalists were bound to lose – because of gerrymandering or, as in this case, the fear of a split vote – was a tactic frequently employed by the border nationalists. The *Irish News* had frowned upon this tactic when it had been used in the past and, in truth, its actual value as anti-partitionist propaganda is difficult to gauge. Despite their considerable anger at the thought of losing the vital Fermanagh–Tyrone seats to what one Devlinite called the forces of 'retrogression', the Devlinites ultimately agreed not to nominate candidates either and the joint constituency was left open to de Valera's Republicans.[84] When asked what the likely electoral result would be, Cahir Healy scornfully responded: 'Partitionists will be returned instead of Mr Harbison and myself. The new members will not ask Mr de Valera's permission to go to Westminster.' For Harbison, a man from the IPP tradition, the Republican intervention amounted to 'one of the greatest political crimes in the annals of the two Counties'.[85]

While many Six-County nationalists saw consolation in the fact that anti-partitionists had taken the border seats in the previous two elections, the anxiety level was high. East-Ulster nationalists were 'sick to death with Dublin intermeddlers', Healy declared, because '[n]one of them cared a d____ what happened to the Six County Nationalists. They simply play them off as a pawn in the Southern game.'[86] The frustrated outgoing MP continued: 'All that the people of Fermanagh and Tyrone ask is that Mr de Valera and other outsiders should leave us alone. They cannot help us; let them not try to make trouble for us.' And in a retort that seemed to say as much about his dissatisfaction with the Treatyite regime's guardianship as it did about de Valera's Republicans, Healy told his interviewer:

> If the people of the Free State could settle their own internal bickerings and jealousies they might have some claim to advise the Nationalists of the Six Counties, *who have hitherto presented a united defense* to the Orange Party … I have long been convinced that Northern Nationalists must work out their own political salvation in their own way. We have rights under the Treaty which we will press to the last inch.[87]

Despite the dubious claim of anti-partitionist unity, Healy's call for Six-County nationalists to find 'their own political salvation' meshed nicely with the long-time agenda of the *Irish News*. Just as it had been saying all along, the Belfast newspaper continued to argue that the only avenue open to the Northern minority compelled them to 'shake off the apathy which placed them at the mercy of a few juntas and coteries, and organise themselves into a phalanx, united and disciplined'. Unlike border newssheets, however, the Devlinite organ was decidedly less sure that 'running away from the Ascendancy Party because Mr de Valera appear[ed] on the scene' was the best of tactics.[88]

As was fully expected, de Valera's candidates were handily defeated by the Unionists in Fermanagh–Tyrone but not before the Republican chief was himself arrested in Derry for violating a prohibition order.[89] On the whole, the election debacle had the effect of souring relations between de Valera and the Six-County nationalists but, more importantly, it also left the Northern minority without any parliamentary representation at Westminster. In Britain, the 1924 general election was just as bitter an affair. On 25 October, four days before the election was to take place, the Conservative *Daily Mail* released a letter, purported to have been written by Grigori Zinoviev of the Comintern, urging British communists to step up their agitation when relations normalised between Britain and the USSR. The Zinoviev letter was a fake but the British Conservatives were able to use the spectre of communist infiltration in Britain to their advantage and, under these circumstances, Stanley Baldwin was returned to power with a large Tory majority.[90]

Thus, in 1924, Stanley Baldwin once again inherited an Irish policy that had been formulated by a previous government. Not only had the key piece of legislation been passed allowing for the appointment of Northern Ireland's Boundary Commissioner but days before the election, Labour had formally announced that J.R. Fisher had agreed to accept that appointment. Fisher was an Ulster native and, like Justice Feetham, he had also been a barrister of some repute.[91] Although he had 'dropped out of Ulster politics' when he left Belfast, J.R. Fisher remained a strong defender of the union and had kept in close touch with English Unionists. As Northern Ireland was being born in 1922, he had also written to Craig, urging the Northern Prime Minister to make a play for Donegal if the opportunity arose for, in his view, 'Donegal belong[ed] to Derry, and Derry to Donegal.'[92] Craig was purportedly 'delighted' by Fisher's appointment, even if he refrained from saying so publicly.[93] Seeing Fisher as no friend to Ireland, the *Irish News* had a slightly different view of the appointment:

> no citizen of the Six Counties, from Stormont to Derry and thence to Southernmost Fermanagh, can question Mr J.R. Fisher's credentials as a representative of Ascendancy. His partisanship is open and above board, its 'true fixed and lasting quality' should satisfy Sir James Craig himself. The fact that Mr Fisher has accepted this appointment as a man born in the North-East closely identified with its Ascendancy politics for many years, still active as an advocate of Ascendancy's demands, and continuously associated with its recognized leaders, is an important circumstance. Who in the local Parliament will dare to rail against the Government's selection?[94]

Although pleased that the work of the Boundary Commission could finally get under way, the *Irish News* then raised another issue that bears noting. Casting doubts upon Eoin MacNeill's suitability for the task at hand, the newspaper wrote:

> Mr MacNeill was engaged as a Civil Servant in the Dublin Law Courts at an early stage of his career: but he has not had a legal training and his duties as a Professor of Early (including Medieval) Irish History in the Dublin College of the National University have probably made him more familiar with the austerities of the Brehon Code than with the meticulous intricacies of modern Constitutional problems.[95]

As the *Irish News* pointed out, a lack of legal training could not help but leave MacNeill at a disadvantage with respect to his fellow Commissioners but MacNeill was limited by other factors as well. Whereas Feetham and Fisher could be full-time Boundary Commissioners, MacNeill remained Minister of Education throughout his time on the tribunal. Moreover, it is also evident that the Free State missed out on an important opportunity to have Kevin O'Shiel, E. M. Stephens or some other Free Stater join F.B. Bourdillon (Commission Secretary) and C. Beerstecher (Justice Feetham's private secretary) on the Boundary Commission staff.[96] Had it been more widely known that Bourdillon, an acknowledged authority on European boundary commissions, had authored a policy paper critical of the NEBB's *Handbook Of the Ulster Question*, perhaps greater care would have been taken to balance out his influence on the Commission with a Free State appointee.[97]

In any event, the three members making up the Irish Boundary Commission met for the first time in their official capacity on 6 November in London and it was at this early stage that the Commissioners agreed on a policy of secrecy.[98] This was a development which the Boundary Bureau had not anticipated when the bulk of its preparations were being carried out in 1923. The vow of secrecy essentially meant that none of the representatives would be in a position to act on their Government's 'slightest suggestion', as Kevin O'Shiel had hoped, without violating pledges made to their fellow Commissioners. Under these conditions, whether or not MacNeill had the 'backbone' and ability to 'fight his corner hard and well' became an even greater factor than it otherwise would have been.[99]

In early December, the Commission Secretary, F.B. Bourdillon, sent a dispatch to the press indicating that the Commissioners would be receiving written evidence until the end of December and planned to hold formal sittings in Ireland thereafter.[100] A subsequent announcement set out the Commission's plan to take a 'preliminary tour' of the border 'for the purpose of seeing portions of the country, acquainting itself with economic and geographic conditions and ascertaining what sources of information [were] likely to be available for the purpose of its work'. While the press release made it clear that the Commissioners would not be conducting formal interviews during their initial visit, it noted that they were looking 'forward to coming into contact with some of those persons who may be prepared to assist' the Commission.[101]

The *Derry Journal*'s response to news of the Boundary Commission's impending arrival was representative of Northern nationalist opinion as a whole.

> While the desire of the Commission to get a thorough grasp of the situation by actual contact with it is welcomed, we would again stress the point that the main thing – in our opinion the first thing – is to ascertain the wishes of the inhabitants. This must be done

> by the vote, and the measures essential for a plebiscite should be expedited.[102]

Putting the matter to a vote in the border regions was widely regarded as a necessity by those hoping to be transferred to the Free State. Expecting to be 'diddled' otherwise, Cahir Healy thought that the Free State should 'leave the Commission' unless the terms of reference were fixed and the right to hold a plebiscite was secured.[103] The possibility of taking a vote seems to have entered Justice Feetham's mind very early on but when he inquired about it in July 1924, he was told by the Labour government's law officers that the Boundary Commission would have no such authority without enabling legislation.[104] Since Bolton Waller had reached a similar conclusion in early 1923, the Free State should have anticipated this eventuality[105] but it seems that the administration was still working on the assumption that a vote could be taken and nothing regarding Feetham's inquiry was ever passed on to Dublin. What is more, while the many rival interpretations of Article 12 were swirling about in September, Feetham broached the idea of having provisions for a plebiscite appended to the Irish legislation but, unbeknownst to any of the interested Irish parties, this effort was blocked by the Colonial Office.[106]

Given the weight that Irish nationalists had placed on holding a vote, it is no surprise that this issue was front and centre when, on 4 and 5 December, Free State Attorney General John O'Byrne accepted an invitation to meet with the tribunal in advance of their border tour. By this point, Feetham knew that the Commission did not have the power to conduct a plebiscite, yet he entertained a myriad of suggestions (and asked as many questions) regarding who in Northern Ireland would be permitted to cast a ballot when a vote was taken.[107] Despite the Chairman's goading, his observation that 'most elaborate' provisions had been made in the Treaty of Versailles for holding plebiscites and 'no provision at all' was found in the Irish Treaty must have alerted the Irish delegation to the legal defeat that was coming.[108] Shortly before the second meeting ended, Feetham at last admitted that the Commission lacked the 'the necessary powers to enable [it] to take a vote'.[109] This was not the only bad news for O'Byrne. Feetham's assertion that a reconfigured Northern Ireland had to be 'capable of maintaining a Parliament and Government'[110] seemed to exclude any large-scale transfers of territory, while his observation that 'mixed populations' existed on either side of the Irish border implied that land transfers were likely to go in either direction.[111]

Given the way that O'Byrne had been baited throughout the meetings by Justice Feetham, it does not seem possible for the Irish Attorney General to have left his two interviews with the Boundary Commissioners in a hopeful mood. Although O'Byrne 'declined to say a word as to the proceedings before the Commission' in an interview he gave to the *Manchester Guardian*, the Attorney General was definitely on the defensive and it was evident that the prospect of losing – rather than adding – territory was now Dublin's biggest concern.[112] But when asked what he thought would be the 'proper methods' of ascertaining the wishes of the inhabitants, O'Byrne replied wilily: 'I will say no more than that there are precedents in the Treaty of Versailles dealing with the determination of boundaries in Upper Silesia and East Prussia in which provision was made for taking a plebiscite', adding: 'There is no reason why a similar proceeding should not be followed in Northern Ireland.'[113] Nothing that O'Byrne said about the Treaty of Versailles was untruthful and, as all is politics in Ireland, it is likely that his comments were intended to ruffle Orange feathers. Still, invoking the Upper Silesian example in this manner while knowing that the requisite provisions for a vote did not exist in Ireland only served to mislead and deceive anti-partitionists in the North. The interview was reported with misguided enthusiasm in Northern Ireland's nationalist newssheets.

Notes

1 This passage was part of an *Irish News* editorial that appeared in response to the unravelling of the first Craig–Collins pact.

2 Secretary of State for the Colonies to the Governor General of the Irish Free State, 24 January 1924, in *Correspondence between His Majesty's Government and the Governments of the Irish Free State and Northern Ireland relating to Article 12 of the Articles of Agreement for a Treaty between Great Britain and Ireland* (London: His Majesty's Stationary Office, 1924), pp. 10–11.

3 *Irish News*, 30 January 1924.

4 *Derry Journal*, 1 February 1924.

5 Ibid.

6 *Irish News*, 30 January 1924.

7 Ibid., 4, 5 February 1924.

8 Cosgrave's acceptance of such a scheme depended upon Dublin being seen as the dominant partner. He told his cabinet that a plan of this sort would only work if '[w]e preside'. K. Matthews, *Fatal Influence: The Impact of Ireland on British Politics, 1920–1925* (Dublin: University College of Dublin Press, 2004), p. 138; E. Phoenix, *Northern Nationalism: Nationalist Politics, Partition and the Catholic Minority in Northern Ireland, 1890–1940* (Belfast: Ulster Historical Foundation, 1994), p. 297.

9 K. Middlemas (ed.), *Thomas Jones Whitehall Diary, Volume III, Ireland, 1918–1925* (London: Oxford University Press, 1971), p. 226.

10 Matthews, *Fatal Influence*, p. 139.

11 *The Times*, 4 February 1924.

12 *Irish News*, 5 February 1924.

13 The Beatitudes are words of blessing from the Christian tradition and are mostly found in the Gospel of Matthew; however, there is some discrepancy regarding how many Beatitudes there actually were and not all theologians number Beatitudes in the same way. *Irish News* editor Tim McCarthy evidently regarded the words cited in the text above as 'the Ninth Beatitude' and I do the same in this book. *Irish News*, 8 February 1924.

14 *Derry Journal*, 4 February 1924.

15 Ibid., 11 February 1924.

16 In particular, see the official correspondence between Governor General Healy and Colonial Secretary Thomas dated: 16 February and 4, 11, 15 March 1924, in *Correspondence*, pp. 13–17.

17 St J. Ervine, *Craigavon: Ulsterman* (London: George Allen & Unwin Ltd, 1949), p. 491.

18 Memorandum from Kevin O'Shiel, 'The Boundary Commission – When? The Boundary Commission – Who?', 10 February 1923, Department of the Taoiseach, NAI/TSCH/S 2027, North East Boundary Secret Documents 1922–4, National Archives of Ireland, Dublin.

19 For two months the British government refused to give assent to this Bill that aimed to abolish PR in local elections and only submitted after Craig and his administration threatened to resign. 'After that,' argued Paul Arthur, 'there was little resistance from London to Belfast's actions.' P. Arthur, *Special Relationships: Britain, Ireland and the Northern Ireland Problem* (Belfast: The Blackstaff Press, 2000), p. 23.

20 *Derry Journal*, 17 March 1924.

21 *Irish News*, 19 March 1924.

22 At Westminster, Healy's internment had brought condemnation from a number of MPs, including fellow Northerner Thomas Harbison but Asquithian Liberal William Pringle was among the most ardent critics of the Craig government on this issue. Using his intimate knowledge of parliamentary procedure, Pringle sought to secure the Sinn Féiner's release by making it a matter of parliamentary privilege – 'privilege of freedom from arrest'. As a consequence of Pringle's efforts, Ramsay MacDonald appointed a committee to examine whether Cahir Healy should have been protected from incarceration because he was an elected

MP. Due to the pressure which the committee and Prime Minister MacDonald exerted on Craig, Northern Ireland released Healy but some 400 other internees remained in custody until 1925–6. *Parliamentary Debates*, Commons, 5th ser., vol. 169 (15 January 1924), cols 56–76; D. Kleinrichert, *Republican Internment and the Prison Ship Argenta, 1922* (Dublin: Irish Academic Press, 2001), pp. 232–4. For the details on the initial restrictions that the Northern government put on Healy's movement within Northern Ireland, see Phoenix, *Northern Nationalism*, pp. 300–1.

23 In April, Healy told a meeting of Fermanagh nationalists that he had 'no intention of going to Westminster' but he had received many letters urging him to do so and only two letters 'conveying a contrary opinion'. Given this outpouring from his constituents, the MP felt it necessary to override his own wishes and take his seat. *Fermanagh Herald*, 19 April 1924.

24 Seamus McManus, the Donegal-born author and friend of Healy's, delivered if not the harshest, then certainly the most personal, critique that the MP was to receive. McManus' letter read in part: 'For 20 years they strove in vain to either break or sweep away the master plank of the Sinn Fein platform. And after they had given up their efforts as a vain task, unable to break, bribe, or intrigue even the weakest advocate of the policy, a Donegal man, and a man of thought culture [and] ability voluntarily gives them their victory! That a Donegal man should be the betrayer is the poignant part of the shame to me. Too bad!' There was no indication that Healy ever answered this assault on his character. Seamus McManus to Cahir Healy, 15 April 1924, Cahir Healy Papers, D2991/D/6/11, Public Record Office of Northern Ireland, Belfast.

25 This quotation is drawn from a series of rough, hand-written and untitled notes found in the Healy Papers which shall be identified as 'Recollections of Westminster' hereafter. It is unclear when the notes were written or if they were eventually published in some form, as was his apparent intent, but they do offer an interesting glimpse at his recollections of this heady period. In the original, Healy used a backslash to signify the word 'the' and a plus sign to signify the word 'and' but in the above excerpt these shortened forms have been replaced – using square brackets to demarcate changes – for the benefit of the reader. C. Healy, 'Recollections of Westminster', n.d., Cahir Healy Papers, D2991/B/140/13, Public Record Office of Northern Ireland, Belfast.

26 Healy, 'Recollections of Westminster', n.d.

27 For the advice Cosgrave and MacNeill imparted in this regard, see Phoenix, *Northern Nationalism*, pp. 300–1.

28 For a critical review of the Army Mutiny and its aftermath, see J.R. Regan, *The Irish Counter-Revolution 1921–1936: Treatyite Politics and Settlement in Independent Ireland* (Dublin: Gill and Macmillan, 1999), pp. 163–97.

29 C. Healy, 'Will the Free State Fall?: Another Civil War Threatened', *The People*, 23 March 1924, Cahir Healy Papers, D2991/E/26/1, Public Record Office of Northern Ireland, Belfast.

30 *Irish News*, 24 March 1924.

31 Cahir Healy to Ernest Blythe, 29 March 1924, Ernest Blythe Papers, P 24/204, University College Dublin Archives (UCDA).

32 D. Lavin, *From Empire to International Commonwealth: A Biography of Lionel Curtis* (Oxford: Clarendon Press, 1995), p. 220.

33 *Thomas Jones Whitehall Diary, Volume III, Ireland*, pp. 227–8.

34 The Secretary of State for the Colonies to the Governor General of the Irish Free State, 10 April 1924, in *Correspondence*, p. 20. The demand for assurances came via the Governor General's dispatch of 7 April 1924.

35 *Thomas Jones Whitehall Diary, Volume III*, pp. 229–30. For a fuller account of this meeting from the British perspective, see Matthews, *Fatal Influence*, pp. 143–4.

36 Conference Statement, issued 24 April 1924, in *Correspondence*, p. 23.

37 *Irish News*, 25 April 1924.

38 *Derry Journal*, 28 April 1924.

39 C. Healy, 'Ulster M.P. and Sir James Craig', *Westminster Gazette*, 7 May 1924 Cahir Healy Papers, D2992/D/6/11, Public Record Office of Northern Ireland, Belfast.

40 A.E. Donnelly, John McHugh, Thomas Harbison and Cahir Healy, 'Some Facts about the Ulster Boundary', 1924, Ernest Blythe Papers, P 24/204, University College Dublin Archives (UCDA).

41 Phoenix, *Northern Nationalism*, p. 302.

42 *Thomas Whitehall Diary, Volume III*, p. 229.

43 The Governor General of the Irish Free State to the Secretary of State for the Colonies, 26 April 1924; The Secretary of State for the Home Department to the Governor of Northern Ireland, 29 April 1924, in *Correspondence*, pp. 23–5.

44 Memorandum from Kevin O'Shiel, 'The Boundary Issue and North-Eastern Policy', 21 April 1923, Department of the Taoiseach, NAI/TSCH/S 2027, North East Boundary Secret Documents 1922–4, National Archives of Ireland, Dublin.

45 A draft reply having 'derogatory descriptions of the Treaty' was deemed to be 'not suitable for the King's representative' to impart. G. Hand, 'MacNeill and the Boundary Commission', in F.X. Martin and F.J. Byrne (eds), *The Scholar Revolutionary: Eoin MacNeill, 1867–1945, and the Making of the New Ireland* (Shannon: Irish University Press, 1973), p. 217.

46 *Parliamentary Debates*, Commons, 5th ser., vol. 152 (16 February 1922), col. 1347.

47 For the complete text of the JCPC reference questions, see The Secretary of State for the Colonies to the Governor General of the Irish Free State, 23 May 1924, in *Correspondence*, pp. 26–7.

48 Hand, 'MacNeill and the Boundary Commission', p. 222.

49 *Irish News*, 6 June 1924.

50 The Fermanagh and Tyrone County Councils and eight Rural District Councils became Unionist. Phoenix, *Northern Nationalism*, pp. 300, 302.

51 Ibid., p. 303.

52 *Irish News*, 5 February 1924.

53 Lavin, *From Empire to International Commonwealth*, p. 222.

54 P. Murray, *The Irish Boundary Commission and its Origins, 1886–1925* (Dublin: University College Dublin Press, 2011), p. 199.

55 Hand, 'MacNeill and the Boundary Commission', pp. 217–23.
56 *Manchester Guardian*, 11 June 1924.
57 *Irish News*, 20 June 1924.
58 Ibid., 23 July 1924; Hand, 'MacNeill and the Boundary Commission', p. 222.
59 *Thomas Jones Whitehall Diary, Volume III*, p. 233.
60 Hand, 'MacNeill and the Boundary Commission', pp. 224, 226–7.
61 D. Marquand, *Ramsay MacDonald* (London: Jonathan Cape, 1977), pp. 364–77; A. Morgan, *J. Ramsay MacDonald* (Manchester: Manchester University Press, 1987), pp. 113–21.
62 Matthews, *Fatal Influence*, p. 173.
63 Hand, 'MacNeill and the Boundary Commission', p. 228.
64 The *Irish News* recoded this revealing, if rambling, warning that Carson gave to a contingent of Belfast Unionists as follows: the one 'thing they had always to remember was – he was not talking of any particular individual but of the present system – that they could not really trust – and he was sorry to say it – English politicians'. *Irish News*, 7 December 1923.
65 Churchill's correspondence during August and September reveals that Stanley Baldwin, Lloyd George and Edward Carson were each in on, if not parties to, this démarche. Stanley Baldwin to Winston Churchill, 22 August 1924; Winston Churchill to Lord Balfour, 1 September 1924; Winston Churchill to Lord Balfour and Lord Carson, 1 September 1924, in M. Gilbert (ed.), *Winston S. Churchill: Volume V Companion Part I Documents: The Exchequer Years, 1922–1929* (London: William Heinemann Ltd, 1979), pp. 181, 189–93.
66 For a good synopsis of the issues surrounding the Birkenhead letter, see Matthews, *Fatal Influence*, pp. 169–77.
67 *The Times*, 8 September 1924; *Irish News*, 8, 9 September 1924.
68 The original letter Birkenhead wrote employed the qualifier 'honest if hot-headed'. Matthews, *Fatal Influence*, p. 170.
69 *The Times*, 8 September 1924.
70 Lloyd George told his audience: 'I stand by Lord Birkenhead's letter and all that it contains', as he suggested that Birkenhead's was the 'only reasonable interpretation of that important clause'. *The Times*, 11 September 1924.
71 At issue here were the comments Birkenhead made in Birmingham just hours after he had signed the Treaty. He told the audience that the Boundary Commission 'shall examine into the boundary lines with a view to rendering impossible such an unhappy incident as that of a few days ago, in which the popularly elected bodies of one or two of these districts [Fermanagh and Tyrone] were excluded from their habitations by representatives of the Northern Parliament for discharging their duties properly. I am not making criticism; but such a system cannot be consistent with the maintenance of order.' Nationalist newspapers like the *Irish News* saw an admission that self-determination was intended when Birkenhead made reference here to the suppression of public bodies for refusing to submit to Belfast's authority but they seem to gloss over the fact that he also said that they did 'not propose to interfere with the arrangement of a year ago [partition] in relation to Counties' and his frequent

use of the word 'rectification' to describe the Commission's intentions. *Irish News*, 8 September 1924.

72 *Irish News*, 12 September 1924.

73 A phrase once used by O'Shiel to describe the Northern mentality. Memorandum from Kevin O'Shiel, 'The Boundary Issue and North-Eastern Policy', 21 April 1923.

74 Matthews, *Fatal Influence*, pp. 165–8, 174–80.

75 Thomas wrote to Fisher on 10 October regarding the position. Hand, 'MacNeill and the Boundary Commission', p. 230.

76 *Irish News*, 13 June 1924.

77 J. Bowman, *De Valera and the Ulster Question 1917–1973* (Oxford: Clarendon Press, 1982), pp. 83–5.

78 *Irish News*, 16 October 1924.

79 *Fermanagh Herald*, 18 October 1924.

80 *Irish News*, 16 October 1924.

81 Ibid., 20 October 1924.

82 Bowman, *De Valera and the Ulster Question*, p. 84.

83 Meeting in Omagh on 16 October, a convention of more than one hundred primarily Sinn Féin border nationalists passed a resolution indicating that, since the Irish Free State (Confirmation of Agreement) Act had been ratified, 'there was nothing to be gained from having representatives at Westminster'. A corresponding manifesto advised 'all supporters of the Treaty and Boundary Commission to abstain from going to the poll' while making a firm demand that a plebiscite be carried out in the border counties. *Derry Journal*, 17 October 1924.

84 *Irish News*, 20 October 1924.

85 'Tyrone Nationalists' Seats Presented to Orangemen', n.d., Cahir Healy Papers, D2991/D/10/92, Public Record Office of Northern Ireland.

86 'Tyrone Nationalists' Seats Presented to Orangemen', n.d. The *Irish News* gave less detailed coverage of these interviews than did the source cited here but it is interesting to note how it chose to insert the word 'straw' in the place of the 'd___' which appeared in the above citation. *Irish News*, 20 October, 1924.

87 Emphasis added. 'Tyrone Nationalists' Seats Presented to Orangemen', n.d.

88 *Irish News*, 17 October 1924.

89 According to John Bowman, de Valera was jailed for a month 'under conditions worse than he had experienced in either Free State or British custody'. This being the case, Mary MacSwiney's advice to the electors of Armagh seems completely wrong-headed. While campaigning for the Republican candidate Dr McKee, she said that 'the "Specials" were no worse than the Black-and-Tans. A bully was only dangerous whilst one knuckled under. "Stir up square to him ... Say to him, if he does attempt to interfere with you, what right have you to interfere with me?"' For reference to de Valera's arrest, see J. Bowman, *De Valera and the Ulster Question, 1917–1973* (Oxford: Clarendon Press, 1982), p.84. For Mary MacSwiney's advice, see 'Tyrone Nationalists' Seats Presented to Orangemen', n.d.

90 Marquand, *Ramsay MacDonald*, pp. 381–2, 387; K. Middlemas and J. Barnes, *Baldwin: A Biography* (London: Weidenfeld & Nicolson, 1969), pp. 275–6.

91 Among other things, he had published a book on the *Law of the Press*. See Hand, 'MacNeill and the Boundary Commission', p. 230.

92 Ervine, *Craigavon*, pp. 481–2.

93 On 31 October 1924, Lady Craig recorded in her diary that Fisher 'is a most excellent choice, as he will have our interests absolutely at heart, and be as firm as a rock ... James is really delighted with the appointment'. B. Follis, *A State Under Siege: The Establishment of Northern Ireland, 1920–1925* (Oxford: Clarendon Press, 1995), p. 164.

94 *Irish News*, 24 October 1924.

95 Ibid.

96 Hand, 'MacNeill and the Boundary Commission', pp. 236, 248. Bourdillon had worked for the Commission set up in Upper Silesia and had sharply (and publicly) criticised the NEBB's *Handbook of the Ulster Question*. This should have raised eyebrows in Dublin. Matthews, *Fatal Influence*, p. 206.

97 Based on his prior experience with European precedents, Bourdillon's paper had found fault with the NEBB assumption that the Irish Boundary Commission would be a one-way tribunal that could only extract territory from Northern Ireland. He also challenged nationalist assumptions that the border would be determined by a vote and that Article 12 empowered the Commission to take a plebiscite. Bourdillon had shared his paper with Lionel Curtis in December of 1923. Murray, *The Irish Boundary Commission and its Origins*, pp. 204–7.

98 Hand, 'MacNeill and the Boundary Commission', p. 232.

99 Memorandum from Kevin O'Shiel, 'The Boundary Issue and North-Eastern Policy', 21 April 1923.

100 *Irish News*, 5 December 1924.

101 Ibid., 8 December 1924.

102 *Derry Journal*, 8 December 1924.

103 Phoenix, *Northern Nationalism*, p. 310.

104 Hand, 'MacNeill and the Boundary Commission', p. 224.

105 Memorandum from Bolton C. Waller, 'Memorandum on European Precedents for the North Eastern Boundary Bureau', Report A, n.d., Department of the Taoiseach, NAI/TSCH/S 2027, North East Boundary Secret Documents 1922–4, National Archives, Dublin.

106 Hand, 'MacNeill and the Boundary Commission', pp. 224, 228–9.

107 G. Hand (ed.), *Report of the Irish Boundary Commission 1925* (Shannon: Irish University Press, 1969), pp. Appendix I, 22–7, 38. References are made to a verbatim report of the two meetings which Hand published with the Commissioners' final *Report*.

108 Ibid., p. 24.

109 Ibid., p. 40.

110 Ibid., p. 9.

111 Ibid., p. 7.

112 In this interview, O'Byrne argued that the Treaty represented an agreement between the whole of Ireland and Great Britain, advising the reporter: 'In the settlement of the Irish Boundary issue the onus is not on us to prove how much of Northern Ireland should be in the Free State, but on Northern Ireland to show how much of it should remain out of the Free State.' He continued: 'It follows therefore that when Article 12 speaks of the Boundary Commission consulting the wishes of the inhabitants it means the wishes of the inhabitants of Northern Ireland, and the Commission has no right to go on the other side of the Boundary of the Six Counties. The Boundary Commission have [*sic*] to deal with a problem within the Six Counties. They have to ascertain what populations within Northern Ireland do not desire to be within the jurisdiction of the Free State, and Northern Ireland must justify every claim it makes to keep any area out of the Free State.' *Irish News*, 9 December 1924.

113 *Irish News*, 9 December 1924.

CHAPTER 12

'Bartered and Sold': The Wishes of the Inhabitants Denied

Once the ball has commenced to roll in this game we shall be to a greater or lesser extent victims of circumstances.

– Kevin O'Shiel[1]

By the time that Attorney General John O'Byrne's interview appeared in the press, the Boundary Commissioners were already engaged in their border tour, accompanied by their escorts from Northern Ireland's Special Constabulary.[2] As it was the only nationalist daily in Northern Ireland, the *Irish News* provided Northern anti-partitionists with the most up-to-date information on the activities of the Boundary Commissioners as they began their investigation of the border. Focusing on the functioning of the long-awaited Irish Boundary Commission, this chapter analyses how Northern Ireland's trapped nationalist minority reacted to the Commissioners' arrival, anti-partitionists' participation in the so-called Boundary election and the sequence of events that ultimately caused the Commission to collapse without rendering its decision.

Having decided to make their first base of operations in Armagh, Justice Feetham, Eoin MacNeill and J.R. Fisher arrived 'almost unnoticed' in the primatial city on 9 December. F.B. Bourdillon, 'a most curious gentleman', was given the task of keeping reporters at bay and the *Irish News* charged that 'little information [could] be got from him by Pressmen as to what exactly the Commissioners intend[ed] doing'. True to their word, Feetham, Fisher and MacNeill did not meet with reporters or announce their movements during the two weeks they spent surveying the border but a dogged band of pressmen 'shadowed the Commissioners like sleuths of the law' every step of the way.[3]

The Commissioners spent their time in Ireland both visiting places of interest along the border and meeting informally with the individuals and groups who awaited them. From their base in Armagh, the trio initially concentrated their travel in Newry; the area around Carlingford Lough; and the Armagh–Louth and Armagh–Monaghan borders. As was expected, the Commissioners also paid considerable attention to the new Silent Valley Reservoir (near Kilkeel) that the Craig government had begun building in order to supply Belfast with water.[4] Although the reservoir represented the second stage of a water procurement scheme that had begun in the 1890s,[5] many anti-partitionists viewed Craig's decision to advance the project as a calculated attempt to create additional economic and geographic justification for maintaining the existing border.[6] The fact that Edward Carson had taken part in the launch ceremony for stage two of the project seemed to confirm anti-partitionist suspicions.

The Northern government still refused to recognise the Boundary Commission, believing that to do so would weaken the resolve of English Unionists[7] but to the great concern of the *Irish News*, initially only deputations of 'prominent Unionists' sought to present their views before the body.[8] A contemporaneous report generated by E.M. Stephens observed that the 'people were nervous of any boundary' in Armagh and that there was 'very considerable apathy prevailing and great skepticism about the Boundary Commission doing anything effective' in Newry. Although Republicans in the region were supposedly 'standing aloof' from the work of the Commission, Stephens attributed the indifference he noticed there to Frank Aiken's lingering presence and Republican propaganda.[9]

To be sure, not all nationalists in southern Armagh and Down were as languid as were those whom Stephens encountered. One of the very few Catholic members of the Northern civil service, Patrick Shea, later recalled in his autobiography that the 'nationally-minded' people of the area 'confidently expected' Newry to be repatriated and that the crowds abounded when the Commissioners appeared in the city. What was perhaps most telling of the mood, according to Shea, was that the residents of Newry were so convinced that the city would be transferred that a Newry Unionist had actually agreed to swap houses with a nearby Republican so that 'each would be a secure citizen of his preferred state'.[10]

To the great relief of the *Irish News*, nationalist deputations – and crowds of spectators – made their presence known as early as the second day of the tour when the Armagh and Keady Urban Councils interviewed the Commissioners. On 11 December, Bishop Mulhern of Dromore was known to have 'placed certain views before the Commissioners' and it was believed that a deputation of Warrenpoint nationalists 'urged the unwisdom of the policy of splitting ... Carlingford Lough for the purpose of making a boundary that was not wanted'. Before they were detected, a band of reporters was able to eavesdrop on the proceedings when Richard O'Hagan, speaking for the Newry Urban Council, told the Commissioners that Newry was 'overwhelmingly nationalist' and that 'the question of the Boundary was one which affected their existence very much, and they wanted to have it settled'. O'Hagan claimed that Newry nationalists 'had nothing to hide. They had a straightforward claim and a straight story to tell, and they would give it in all honesty.'[11] On 13 December, the Council, of which O'Hagan was a member, sent the Commission a copy of a resolution demanding to 'be relieved from the authority of the Belfast parliament'. They also struck a committee to prepare a statement.[12]

Having moved their headquarters to Enniskillen on 13 December, the Commissioners spent considerable time on the Fermanagh–Monaghan border around Roslea and the predominantly Protestant Clones area of Monaghan. The Boundary Commissioners also investigated Fermanagh's borders with Cavan and Leitrim. In keeping with the divisions over policy that had dogged the trapped Northern minority in recent years, Fermanagh nationalists chose not to meet with the trio during their three days in Enniskillen.[13] In advance of the Commission's arrival, a nationalist convention was held in which Father Eugene Coyle and Cahir Healy put forward a resolution urging the Free State, as 'custodians of [their] rights, under Article 12' of the Treaty, to use all its influence to have a plebiscite taken. The resolution maintained that 'any ascertainment of the views of individuals meantime, or of public boards elected for gerrymandered constituency areas, [could] only be regarded as unduly delaying the fulfillment of the Treaty and misrepresenting the views of the people'.[14] Still unaware that the Boundary Commission did not have the authority to hold a vote, the resolution passed unanimously and Fermanagh nationalists refused to meet with the Commissioners.

The investigation of Donegal's border with Fermanagh and Tyrone required the Commissioners to move their headquarters to Newtownstewart, where they spent three days before moving on to Derry City on 19 December. During a day visit to Omagh on 17 December, the Commissioners met with Tyrone nationalists, including Father Philip O'Doherty, Thomas Harbison, Alex Donnelly and Michael Lynch. Reporting on the occurrences, the Omagh correspondent of the *Irish News* observed that the nationalist deputation 'gave one the impression of not being a bit too pleased with the result of their interview'. One of the nationalists shouted that the proceedings were 'all bosh', while another claimed that the group came out of the interview 'just about as wise as they went in'. The reporter later determined that the deputation had 'laid stress on the fact that in their opinion the Border to which the Commissioners ought to be devoting their attention lay ninety miles north of the line they had been on, by which, of course, they meant the Derry, Tyrone, Donegal border'. Naturally upset by fears that the Commission was taking a narrow view of its duty, it did not help matters that a Unionist group left their meeting with the Commissioners in good spirits taunting, 'it is all right: we have fixed it all up'. As the reporter noted, the nationalists of Tyrone were 'relying on the plebiscite provided for in Article 12, and believe that this [would] have to be finally resorted to as a means of ascertaining the wishes of the inhabitants'.[15]

That the Commission was holding rather close to the existing Six-County border was a major concern for anti-partitionists but the most shocking moment in the border tour came in Derry on 20 December. In an informal conversation with the city's nationalist representatives, Chairman Feetham 'intimated that they [the Commissioners] were not at present empowered to hold a plebiscite, to take a vote of the inhabitants, but that all records, including census returns, and the results of contested elections would be taken into consideration'.[16]

Indicative of the differences that had estranged the Devlinites of the interior from border nationalists, the *Irish News* devoted surprisingly little attention to the plebiscite issue after the story surfaced. Rather its 22 December editorial actually toasted 'the Dauntless Three' for fording rivers and navigating rugged roads and mountains in the Irish mist, fog and rain.[17] For border newssheets like the *Derry Journal*, the fact that the Commission could not hold a plebiscite amounted to a 'startling confession' and the newspaper did not understand why the truth had been hidden for so long. 'In calling for a plebiscite, therefore, we are told that the people are merely beating the air,' wrote the *Journal* as it noted that there was 'not the slightest chance of having their demand acceded to for the necessary legislation could not be obtained in the British Parliament'. While pointing out the similarities that NEBB propaganda had consistently identified between the Irish Treaty and the Treaty of Versailles, the *Derry Journal* scornfully observed:

> The Anglo-Irish Treaty ... contains no provision in regard to a plebiscite, and, as stated, so far as this means of getting the wishes of the inhabitants is concerned, the Commission is powerless at present. We cannot help thinking that the fact was realised long ago in certain quarters, and that propaganda based on the assumption that a vote would be taken was quite insincere.[18]

Given what had transpired between the Free State Attorney General and the Commission before the border tour, it is difficult to question this conclusion.

Since so much weight had been placed on allowing the wishes of the inhabitants to speak for themselves, when that avenue was unequivocally closed in December 1924 much of the enthusiasm that the nationalists felt about the Commission dissipated. Yet, despite this discouraging development, nationalist-controlled public bodies continued to busy themselves with boundary-related preparations. Before 1924 had elapsed, the Urban Councils of Armagh, Newry and Strabane, had each passed resolutions enabling them to draft statements and send deputations to be heard by the Commission. The Omagh Urban Council even raised the idea of holding its own county-wide plebiscite during its contentious 31 December meeting. Nothing came of this idea but, by a vote of nine to eight, nationalists on the Council were able to pass a motion allowing it to take steps in line with those taken by nationalists elsewhere to present its case.[19]

Clerics took a leading role in the gathering of evidence and the organising of meetings during the early months of 1925 and this caused the advocates of partition considerable displeasure. While he argued forcefully that '[n]o influence was brought to bear on [parishioners] from the Altar', Bishop Mulhern of Dromore unapologetically admitted to the Commission later that spring that clergy had 'an opportunity of summoning meetings that nobody else [had]'.[20] Although the new Primate of All Ireland, Patrick Cardinal O'Donnell, would eventually have a part to play in papering over the divisive politics of Northern nationalism,[21] for the moment he tried to remain above the fray. Elaborating in some detail on the need to bury the differences that separated all Irish men and women, the Cardinal told an Armagh gathering on 1 February that 'Governments [had] a special obligation to protect minorities' and he applied this proviso to both 'the sparse [Protestant] minority in the Twenty-six Counties' and 'the large [Catholic] minority in the Six Counties'. Comparing the Cardinal's plea for toleration with the ecumenical nationalism of Young Irelander Thomas Davis, the *Irish News* hoped to convince those with particularist interests of the value in these oft-cited lines of Davis' verse:

> What matter if at different shrines we
> pray unto one God?
> What matter if at different times our
> fathers won the sod?
> In nation and in name we're bound by
> stronger links than steel,
> And neither can be safe nor sound
> but in the other's weal.

That the 'Catholic Primate sprang from the race of O'Donnell' – the chief allies of the Ulster O'Neills during the Tudor period – and Davis was a 'Protestant Anglo-Welshmen', with Cromwellian blood running through his veins, did not matter to the *Irish News*. In its view, Davis and Cardinal O'Donnell 'preached the self-same doctrine of rational unity and common devotion to the welfare of all' that Ireland dearly needed if it was ever to remove the blight of partition.[22] The fact that the Cardinal cited Davis' 'A Nation Once Again' in his 1925 Lenten Pastoral suggests that he would not have minded the comparison.[23]

Having pushed back its deadline, the Boundary Commission received 103 pieces of written communication by the end of January.[24]

These ranged from calls for the re-creation of historic Ulster within a federally united Ireland[25] to an attempt by the Unionist Fermanagh County Council to trade participation in the proceedings for assurances that the Commission would confine its duties to 'the mere rectification of anomalies on both sides of the existing border'.[26] In the case of the latter communication, it was necessary for Secretary Bourdillon to post a public letter in the press indicating that the Commissioners were unable to make assurances of any kind. This was not the only such instance that required clarification by the Commission.[27]

At the end of January, the Boundary Commissioners made the decision to begin their formal hearing of evidence in March. Because some unionist public bodies, such as the Fermanagh County Council,[28] eventually declared an interest in presenting evidence of their own, nationalists had a glimmer of hope that the Commission's findings would be accepted, however reluctantly. Unionist backpedalling of this sort also suggested increased anxiety on the part of the partitionists. Symptomatic of unionist anxiety, in a January editorial, the *Derry Standard* even advocated electoral reform as a way of reaching out to Northern Ireland's Catholic minority.[29]

Having returned to Ireland on 2 March, the Boundary Commission issued a communiqué indicating that press representatives would not be accorded access to the proceedings, as the Commissioners believed that 'witnesses would give freer expression to their views at private sittings'.[30] On the following day, the Commission heard evidence in Armagh and the proceedings held in that county town, as well as in Rostrevor and Newcastle, concerned with claims relating to the southern portions of Counties Armagh and Down. A committee representing the nationalist inhabitants of Middletown, situated on the Armagh–Monaghan border, was first to give evidence on 3 March and the Keady Urban District Council presented the case for both Keady and nearby Granemore two days later.[31] Seeking to challenge conventional wisdom during this early stage in the proceedings, advocates of partition frequently claimed that their Catholic neighbours were not unhappy with the existing boundary.[32] According to Mary Harris' tabulations, on the first day of the hearings alone, no fewer than thirteen people stated that Six-County Catholics were 'indifferent' to the border issue and only said otherwise on account of clerical intimidation. This was the background that informed Bishop Mulhern's previously noted defence of the clergy's involvement in organising meetings. Mulhern was one of only two Bishops whose diocese was untouched by the border – being entirely within Northern Ireland – but he was the only Bishop to present evidence.[33]

The bulk of nationalist testimony given while the Commissioners were in Armagh concerned the primatial city itself. However, when the hearings shifted to Co. Down, Newry and the area around Carlingford Lough became the primary nationalist focus. It was during these hearings that there emerged further indications that anti-partitionists had a need to worry. In the course of an interview with the Warrenpoint Urban District Council, Chairman Feetham divulged his view that 'Carlingford Lough might be regarded as a good natural boundary.'[34] This, of course, fell well short of nationalist expectations, as it would leave all of South Down in Northern Ireland and could only be justified on conditions other than the wishes of the inhabitants. Witnesses were also perturbed to discover that, as Chairman Feetham informed the East Down contingent, the Boundary Commission would not be entertaining evidence based on any 'statements made by the signatories of the Treaty'.[35] The Commission's hearings were temporarily stalled at this juncture on account of James Craig's decision, on 10 March, to ask for a dissolution of parliament on the very day that its new session was to begin.[36] Craig's request was duly granted and 3 April was set as the date of the election.

The 1925 Northern Ireland election has been seen as a 'cheap maneuver' that aimed to pull Craig's Unionist critics into his 'electoral net' on false pretences.[37] In this respect, it was, according to J.H. Collins, 'the most dishonest election ever held'.[38] Despite nationalist haranguing of this sort, however, because his government had declined to give evidence before the Boundary Commission, Craig had little choice but to call an election as a way of marshalling his forces.[39] Initially, the divided nationalist minority responded to the election in the same way they had since the Treaty; the Devlinites, Sinn Féiners and the Republican supporters of Éamon de Valera each attempted to marshal forces in support of their own particularist interests. Pro-Treaty Sinn Féiners met or planned meetings at various points in the border regions and the *Irish News* reported with considerable displeasure that there was 'evidence of activity on the part of the Republicans'.[40] And for their part, on St Patrick's Day, the AOH held a large rally in Ballinderry that was alleged to have brought together 20,000 Hibernians from Derry, Antrim and Tyrone. As the long-time Hibernian Thomas Harbison saw it, the massive turnout represented but 'a further revelation that the spirit of Owen Roe, of Hugh, of Sarsfield, Emmett, and Grattan was still burning hot and bright in the hearts of Derry, Tyrone, and Antrim'.[41]

While his name was on the lips of many of the Hibernian speakers at Ballinderry,[42] AOH National President Joe Devlin was not in attendance. But in a remarkable reversal of fortunes, Devlin soon found himself being courted by both Republicans and members of the Cumann na nGaedhael/pro-Treaty Sinn Féin group. Contemplating 'another experiment',[43] a Republican Advisory Committee voted nine to seven in favour of seeking an electoral agreement with Devlin.[44] In light of the speeches the long-time MP had given in early March extolling the memory of his friend John Redmond and chastising the 'rattle of musketry and terror of civil war',[45] it is difficult to imagine how de Valera could have expected anything but the 'polite and reasoned refusal' Devlin ultimately tendered.[46] However, the prospect of united pro-Treaty action was entirely another matter. Devlin expressed a 'willingness to co-operate' with any joint efforts; however, the Belfast leader denied press reports suggesting that he had been approached by Free State representatives urging him to assemble a nationalist conference.[47]

As it turns out, the press reports were correct. Devlin had, in fact, been asked by Free State representatives to serve as the Joint Chair of a nationalist conference with Sinn Féiner Alex Donnelly. Cardinal O'Donnell and his bishops had been instrumental in putting together this long overdue démarche. Devlin was apparently pleased 'at the confidence shown in him' by the Cosgrave regime (which later agreed to foot the election expenses) but, conscious that some Northern Sinn Féiners had still not forgiven him for Black Friday, Devlin thought that greater success might be had if someone 'less controversial' took the lead. The conference ultimately emerged with Harbison and Donnelly as Joint Chairs.[48]

The meeting took place in Belfast on 21 March and, significantly, two-thirds of the twenty-seven conventioneers were from the Devlinite tradition – a fact which Phoenix claims highlighted the declining stock of the Northern Sinn Féin.[49] As the bishops, the Free State government and both factions of Northern nationalism all shared a common desire to register as large a vote for anti-partitionism as was possible in light of the Boundary Commission, the delegates agreed to revive the 1921 election pact, which, this time, allowed for eleven candidates to be fielded: six Devlinites (including Devlin for West Belfast) and five coming from the pro-Treaty Sinn Féin. Indicative of the changed mood and desire for unity, Northern Sinn Féiners finally dropped the Sinn Féin name and they all ran as 'Nationalists'.[50]

Whether or not those elected would be permitted to take their seats was not a clear-cut issue, but the delegates ultimately agreed that those elected in regions that had a chance of being transferred to the Free State would not take their seats before the Boundary Commission delivered its award. However, it was quite clear that considerable pressure was being brought to bear on Devlin to take his West Belfast seat, should he be elected, and he did not mask his intention to do so.[51]

Devlin set out his views regarding abstention in a letter to the editor of the *Irish News* announcing his nomination.[52] Firmly asserting that the rationale for abstentionism was swept away by the Treaty and establishment of the Boundary Commission and convinced that the Commission's report would not be long in coming, Devlin told the newspaper's readers:

> I have decided that as soon as its deliberations are concluded and its decision arrived at, it shall be my duty, if elected, to enter the Northern Parliament, and to apply myself to the task of fighting for those National and Democratic interests to which I have given a life-long devotion, and to resume the work on which I had been engaged in another Parliament, and which has been suspended for the last four years. Permanent abstention means permanent disenfranchisement; and to any such a policy, leading as it inevitably would, to helplessness, confusion, and failure, I could not give the slightest continuance.

Carefully explaining that he still 'believ[ed] in the largest possible measure of Self-Government for Ireland' and was prepared to 'do everything possible to promote, by conciliation and good-will, the union of all sections of Irishmen, north and south, in the service of their common country', Devlin concluded his letter noting that he was prepared to 'accept the judgment of the electors'.[53] The letter was dated on the day of the Belfast convention but was held from publication until nomination day, on 24 March.

All told, the Belfast convention was a rousing success with historic implications. Every segment of anti-partitionist opinion, save the Republicans, backed the efforts of the united Nationalist candidates. As an indication of the new co-operative mood that existed between Devlin's supporters and nationalists of the Sinn Féin tradition, the *Derry Journal*, reporting on the proceedings of an election rally for George Leeke and Basil McGuckin, candidates for Derry City and the county, touted the new 'buoyant spirit' that allowed both Devlinites and Sinn Féiners to appear on the same stage. When Revd Father Laurence Hegarty took the Chair of that 'historic' event, he proudly noted that all Catholic and nationalist interests were now being represented by men who 'agreed to sink minor differences and to meet on the common platform of anti-partition'.[54] In a letter endorsing Devlin for West Belfast, Archdeacon Convery expressed his wish to see 'the Catholic voters united like a bar of steel all over the Six Counties'[55] and in a hitherto unthinkable event, J.H. Collins and diehard Hibernian John Nugent even campaigned together in Armagh. Collins freely admitted that he and Nugent 'were as opposed as the Poles in many of their political convictions' but he also said that they were prepared to bury their differences 'in the face of the grave menace to their common interests'.[56]

For Collins and Nugent, it was the Republican Eamon Donnelly who presented the biggest challenge but Collins maintained throughout the campaign that the election amounted to a 'question of the boundary pure and simple' and had nothing to do with the Republicans' enfeebled cause.[57] Equally candid, Cahir Healy told a meeting in Roslea that it was no longer 'a question of Free State versus Republic' because 'unfortunately they had neither'.[58] As 'insatiable' as was the Republicans' 'unnatural appetite for dissention', the *Irish News* only hoped that nationalist voters would stand firm against the Republicans' persistent attempts to thwart pro-Treaty candidates.[59]

In the end, only two Republicans were returned. Eamon Donnelly edged out Devlinite John Nugent for the final seat in Armagh and de Valera was among the eight candidates in Down who were returned unopposed.[60] As Nugent was the only Treatyite to go down to defeat, the Nationalists were able to win ten seats and they out-polled the Republican candidates by more than 70,000 votes across Northern Ireland.[61] Four Independent Unionists and three members of the Northern Ireland Labour Party were also elected, reducing James Craig's Ulster Unionist Party majority to twelve seats. But the biggest triumph was that of Devlin in West Belfast, where he received 17,558 first preference votes.[62] One admirer's relief at Devlin's election was rendered poetic in 'Victory For Devlin', which appeared in the *Irish News* on 6 April:

Victory has crowned the efforts of the
    people of the West:
In rallying around their candidate the voters
    did their best;
Contented now they all should be, and
    proud they all should feel –
They know their rights, they now will get
    the right man at the wheel.
On platform or in Parliament, he always
    speaks his mind,
Regardless of what people say – his equal
    you can't find.
Years now have passed since last he sat,
    and now that he is back
Few of the other members can follow in
    his track.
O'er hill and dale in clarion notes the name
    of Devlin sounds,
Re-echoed loud in West Belfast the clarion
    note rebounds.
Dreaded by his opponents, beloved by all
    his friends,
Each word he speaks is to the point, he
    always gains his ends.
Victory follows in the train wherever
    Devlin leads,
Loved well by all where'er he goes for
    many gallant deeds,

In years to come, when he is gone, his
troubles at an end,
No man can ever fill his place, you'll get
no stauncher friend.[63]

Symbolic of the devotion that Devlin still managed to court, this elaborate poem is an example of an *acrostic* as the first letter of each protruding line on the left-hand margin spells out the message 'Victory for Devlin.'

Pressure from publicans, his working-class constituents, and unknown admirers of the sort noted above meant that Devlin would not long be able to stand outside the Northern parliament; nor was that his desire. As such, on 28 April, Devlin and Antrim MP T. MacAllister became the first two anti-partitionists to sit in the partition parliament.[64] Anticipating this eventuality, about a week before the election, Cahir Healy expressed the view that he personally 'did not believe any good cause could be served by going into the Belfast Parliament, but Mr Devlin and his friends had a right to look after themselves'.[65]

The 1925 Northern Ireland election campaign and the stunning volte-face that allowed Sinn Féiners and IPP members to close ranks seemed to breathe new life into Joe Devlin, whom T.P. O'Connor thought 'looked at least ten years younger'. And as John Dillon noted in a letter to O'Connor that April, Cosgrave was now 'extremely anxious to cultivate friendly relations with Joe and the Northern Nationalists'.[66] This meant that Devlin was once again welcomed in Dublin's halls of power. Significantly, Devlin had also made a new friend and ally in Cahir Healy.[67]

With the so-called Boundary election settled, attentions once again returned to the work of the Commission itself, which was reengaged on 22 April when the tribunal assembled at Enniskillen, before its sittings moved to Derry and finally Omagh.[68] Appearing before the Commission, Fermanagh nationalists devoted some of their attention to the way that the border interfered with the regulation of water flow in Lough Erne and the prospect that the customs port would force the closure of certain railway lines.[69] Inconveniences of this sort had also informed the testimony of Tyrone nationalist Michael Lynch, the Managing Director of the North West of Ireland Publishing Company.

As his company printed a number of newspapers that were sold on either side of the border, Lynch complained of the time wasted and expense incurred by his deliverymen as they were forced to pass through the customs frontier at multiple points while distributing his products. However, for Lynch, there was more at stake than business interests. 'The people of these districts have been accustomed to look to Dublin as the seat of Government and as the center of the political and social life of the country,' observed the Tyrone nationalist while making his case against partition.[70]

As NEBB representatives had cautioned against laying too much stress on economic and geographic conditions, the bulk of the evidence presented in these hearings focused on showing the will of the people and cataloguing democratic grievances of Catholics and nationalists. Father Eugene Coyle, for example, complained of 'terrorism at the hands of the Specials',[71] while Cahir Healy devoted considerable time to the issue of gerrymandering and the 'octopus shaped' constituencies that had been contrived in order to suffocate anti-partitionist representation. That problem, Healy said, was only compounded by the irregularities in the voter register that allowed members of the USC on border patrol to vote in Fermanagh, regardless of the location of their primary abode.[72]

Emphasising the 1911 census statistics as a way to show that the inhabitants in the county wanted to be included in the Free State, Healy advised the Commissioners that '[i]n Fermanagh one can, with rare exceptions, take a Catholic as a nationalist and a Protestant as a Unionist'. The census figures, while outdated, had become the primary means of determining the wishes of the inhabitants when holding a plebiscite was ruled out but the Fermanagh Nationalist Committee also submitted election returns showing the small but clear margin of victory that Healy and Harbison had achieved over their Unionist opponents in 1922 and 1923. Justifying the nationalist claim for inclusion in the Free State on the idea of 'Ireland a Nation' while laying bare the grievances that prevented nationalists from accepting Belfast's jurisdiction, the Fermanagh nationalists worked to separate their own reasoned arguments from the mean-hearted arguments they associated with their Unionist opponents. It was Healy's contention that the Unionists based their claim to the county 'on the possession of bullocks and grass [more] than the goodwill of human beings'.[73]

As was the case during the earlier round of hearings, MacNeill and Fisher appeared largely 'passive' during the sessions but Chairman Feetham was not and his questions led some of the witnesses to think that the Chairman had ruled out conceding any large land transfers. At one point Feetham asked Basil McGuckin, the MP for Derry City, whether he thought that 'the transference of Derry to the Free State would be a serious surgical operation', which naturally unnerved the MP, while certain other comments Feetham made suggested that much of Donegal's Inishowen peninsula was bound to be put under Belfast's jurisdiction.[74]

Observations of this sort surely caused anxieties for the witnesses, but anti-partitionist worries certainly would have been compounded had they known that J.R. Fisher had not kept his pledge of secrecy. Rather, the Northern Ireland Commissioner had been forwarding status reports to some of his Unionist colleagues as the hearings occurred. In a report sent as the Commission sat in Omagh, Fisher informed Mrs Reid (the wife of David Reid, Unionist MP and Chairman of the Ulster Unionist Parliamentary Party, 1923–1939) that the tribunal had rejected the nationalists' 'extreme claim' and the Commissioners were, at that point, confining their attention to 'a matter of border townlands for the most part'.[75] Despite pressures from E.M. Stephens and Kevin O'Higgins, MacNeill had not been so forthcoming in providing information to his government.[76]

With the conclusion of the Omagh hearing in July, the Boundary Commission set to work formalising and finalising the basis of their award and this took them into October. The Commission records indicate that a total of 575 witnesses were heard, representing fifty-eight groups or public bodies, while an additional ten individuals presented evidence on their own behalf. Of these, forty were classed as 'Negative Claims', which meant that their advocates wanted no changes to the border without the mutual consent of both the Free State and Northern Ireland. Most of the claims related to small, specific areas on or near the existing border but there were also a number of claims 'of a comprehensive character involving several counties'. These included claims seeking to move the border in accordance with the NEBB's recommended line; the recreation of a nine-county Ulster; and an unusual proposal calling for Northern Ireland to be divided into two provinces after further Free State territory was added.[77]

In anticipation of the tribunal's conclusions, the British and Free State governments spent the summer months determining the provisions under which the Commissioners' report would be implemented. It is clear from Geoffrey Hand's thorough investigation of the intricate deliberations that neither government had any knowledge of the Commission's findings as the autumn approached.[78] It is also clear that the nationalists of Northern Ireland, and border nationalists in particular, were growing increasingly apprehensive about their prospects for transfer. Cahir Healy's 6 November letter to Kevin O'Higgins offers insight into the Northern mind during these stressful moments. Healy requested an interview with the Executive Council in order to discuss the following questions:

1. Will the Saorstat representative on the Boundary Commission submit to the E.C. [Executive Council], for their consideration the proposed border line?
2. Will the E.C. approve of any boundary that does not involve the acquisition by the Soarstat of substantial areas out of the six counties?
3. Will the representatives of the areas claiming to be part of the Free State be consulted before any decision is arrived at?
4. Cannot the minutes and reports of the London Conference of 1921 with reference to the Ulster proposals be published?

The word 'No' was scribbled in the margins of the letter beside questions (1) and (3).[79] It would have been interesting to see exactly how O'Higgins would have replied to the concerns of the man whom Kevin O'Shiel once called 'one of the sanest and most far-seeing leaders' of the Northern minority.[80] No reply was forthcoming as developments much further afield had queered the pitch literally overnight.

On 7 November, the Conservative London daily, the *Morning Post*, published a forecast of the impending award of the Boundary Commission and a map indicating where the changes were likely to occur. This 'inspired document'[81] suggested that only small patches of Tyrone, Fermanagh and Armagh were to be transferred to the Free State while intimating that fertile portions of Donegal's Inishowen peninsula – and with it, control of the Foyle and the Swilly – would be transferred in the other direction. Equally disturbing from the anti-partitionist perspective, according to the forecast, Derry City, Newry and Enniskillen were to remain in Northern Ireland.[82] On the whole, the map and forecast represented a fairly accurate reflection of the draft award that all three Commissioners had approved two days earlier. Given what is now known about his breach of secrecy, there is absolutely no doubt that the information upon which this material was based can be traced back to Fisher.

The *Morning Post* forecast was certainly not the first to emerge and Bourdillon wasted no time informing the press that the story was 'purely speculation' but it quickly gained traction on both sides of the Irish Sea. Not yet ready to put any credence in the Tory newssheet's prediction, the *Irish News* attempted to downplay the rumours and speculation already swirling. 'Neither the Commission as a body nor an individual Commissioner has made a public statement that could indicate the character of the Report' wrote the newspaper, adding: 'More than 100 "forecasts" of the Report – or Reports – have been published. The total may have been 500, as 100 is a modest estimate. All versions have differed from one another ... no doubt, it will be found that the authors of some "forecasts" were not far away from the truth.'[83] The newspaper made other attempts to calm weary nerves throughout the week but to no avail.

Border hysteria was now beginning to take over in the North. On 12 November, the attendees of a Derry City meeting passed a resolution expressing 'all the vehemence at [their] command' at the allegation that the Commission intended to 'ignore ... the wishes of the inhabitants' of their City as they simultaneously decried any attempt to 'dissect the Nationalist Peninsula of Inishowen' from Donegal.[84] Initially unsure what to make of the forecast, the *Fermanagh Herald* urged the Free State to 'withdraw their representative from the Commission' if it was convinced Feetham had adopted a 'partisan role'.[85] Cahir Healy, writing in the *Irish Independent*, called for the resignation of Eoin MacNeill and,[86] while it also thought that it was MacNeill's duty to 'retire forthwith' as a first step, Manchester's *Catholic Herald* went further in suggesting that the Free State would have 'to consider the question of boldly repudiating the Treaty, refusing to recognize the Governor General, and summoning de Valera and his colleagues to their councils'.[87] Beginning as an outbreak of jitters on account of unsubstantiated rumours of a bad report, the story had quickly deteriorated into a full-blown crisis in which Cosgrave and MacNeill were left stalling for time as pressure and criticism mounted in the Dáil.[88]

As events were carrying MacNeill and Northern Ireland's border nationalists ever closer to the edge, Six-County deputations began appearing in Dublin. A Strabane group led by three priests informed the Free State government on 17 November that they 'would prefer to leave the border lie as it [was] rather than have the line suggested by the *Morning Post* forecast'.[89] According to a letter President Cosgrave sent to MacNeill two days later, the Strabane deputation's view was confirmed by a subsequent Tyrone group led by Alex Donnelly. When asked their thoughts 'on the question of no report and a bad report', according to Cosgrave, Donnelly's deputation said 'they favoured unequivocally no report'.

Significantly, Cosgrave concluded this letter to his Minister of Education with the suggestion that he should 'retire [from the Commission] and leave nothing undone to bring about no report'. Before Cosgrave's letter had found its way to MacNeill, the beleaguered Free State Commissioner had already reached the same conclusion. Eoin MacNeill resigned from the Commission on 20 November and ultimately from the Executive Council amidst bitter and often personal recriminations in the Dáil.[90]

MacNeill's resignation only served to confirm Six-County nationalists' fears that they had been done over but the fact that the two remaining Commissioners were determined to press forward with their findings only muddied matters further.[91] With the suppression of the Commission's report as his first priority, Cosgrave entered into discussions with a less-than-pleased British administration on 25 November.[92] A marathon of negotiations soon followed involving Britain and both Irish governments, during the course of which Cosgrave was inundated by representations from Northern nationalists determined not to let their fate be decided without their prior consent. A telegram of this variety, sent by Richard O'Hagan, Patrick O'Neill and J.H. Collins on 2 December, warned:

> The overwhelming majority of the inhabitants of Newry, South Down, East Down, and South Armagh protest against any deal

> settling their destiny behind closed doors. They are not sheep or cattle to be given from one Government to another against their wishes. They insist on self-determination. They urge that you demand documents and evidence given by them before the Commission and see their expressed rights. Irish nationality is not to be bartered or sold. It is not for the market place.[93]

The 5 December edition of the *Fermanagh Herald* – a weekly newspaper – put the issue in these terms:

> The Free State Government should not make any settlement without first consulting the representatives of the Nationalists of the border counties and placing before them the full terms of the proposals, and before coming to a definite decision on any point or question at issue, they should take every possible care to safeguard the interests of the people whose trustee they are.[94]

The *Fermanagh Herald*'s advice was, of course, out of date before it was even in print. After a teary-eyed Cosgrave and his negotiating team had fought through days of intense negotiation, on 3 December, Britain, Northern Ireland and the Irish Free State reached an agreement. As Jones would record, the British Foreign Secretary Austen Chamberlain and Winston Churchill, then Chancellor of the Exchequer, had been instrumental in bringing about the compromise. Yet, despite his refusal to give ground on boundary revision, Jones also maintains that Sir James Craig was 'very helpful to the Free State' with regard to the discussion of monetary matters.[95] The settlement that was ultimately reached put to death the long defunct Council of Ireland and cancelled financial burdens owed to the Imperial exchequer by the Free State in relation to Article 5 of the Treaty.[96] In exchange, Dublin agreed to accept financial liability for damages done during the Anglo-Irish War and Civil War to the property of Southern Unionists, while rescinding any territorial claims under Article 12.

The status of the Northern minority under the Craig regime was a topic of heated discussions during these negotiations. Indicative of the British desire to dispense with the boundary issue once and for all, Lord Salisbury even urged Craig to appoint Joe Devlin to liaise between his government and the Northern Catholic community at the tidy sum of £10,000 per year[97] but nothing came of this suggestion. Kevin O'Higgins' push for the return of proportional representation for local elections in Northern Ireland and the release of the remaining political prisoners held by the Northern government offered a more realistic, albeit no more successful, approach to dealing with the plight of the Six-County nationalists.[98] In the end, however, the agreement did not contain any safeguards for the protection of the Northern nationalist minority.

'Money decided the great "Boundary Question" at last,' observed the *Irish News*, which once again found 'consolation in the terms of the ninth Beatitude: "Blessed are they that expect nothing, for they shall not be disappointed."'[99] For the *Derry Journal*, the agreement amounted to 'the betrayal and abandonment of the Catholics of Ulster'.[100] The *Journal*'s headlines reflected the tone of its reportage as the agreement was making its way through the British and Irish legislatures: 'No Relief for Six County Catholics', 'Ourselves Alone' and 'Sacrifice of Six Counties'.[101] For his part, Cahir Healy argued:

> The nationalists of Fermanagh are overwhelmed with amazement that any men representing the country could sign such a document. It is a betrayal of the Nationalists of the North and a denial of every statement put forward by the Free State in their alleged support of our case since 1921. They are doing exactly as Judge Feetham proposed to do; they are ignoring the wishes of the people ... For what have the Nationalists been sold? Is it the cancellation of Article 5?

Content to let history determine 'if the betrayal [would] not bring its own retribution', Healy concluded with this ominous observation: 'John Redmond was driven out of public life for even suggesting partition for a period of five years. The new leaders agreed to partition forever.'[102]

In the end, twenty copies of the Boundary Commission's Report were printed before its suppression was ultimately decided upon. One of these, signed by Chairman Feetham and J.R. Fisher, eventually made its way to the Cabinet Office. Feetham, Fisher and Bourdillon supposedly kept souvenir copies for themselves as well but the remaining copies were destroyed along with their printing plates.[103]

Given the beleaguered position in which Northern nationalists were ultimately left in December of 1925, it is worth reflecting upon the closing days of the Civil War, when anti-partitionists of all stripes were madly clamouring for the provisions of Article 12 to be put in force. At that time, Kevin O'Shiel prepared a memorandum for the Executive Council that offered instructions on how to deal with the impertinent demands of the overly anxious Northern minority. The then Boundary Bureau Director observed:

> all the Government asks is to be judged by the ultimate results of its policy, and not by what it is, or is not doing, or what other people may suspect it may be doing in connection with the matter ... For 750 years they have waited in a condition of uncertainty as to their future. They can certainly hold on in patience for a little longer.[104]

Northern nationalists, and border nationalists in particular, were unmistakably clear in their emphatic rejection of the Free State's 'ultimate results' but, callous as O'Shiel's words now seem,[105] they pointed to the only silver lining that could be found in the tripartite settlement. As the *Irish News* said in relation to the agreement: 'We have gained one advantage – and it is neither small nor mean: we have passed out of a period of uncertainty, deceit, false pretense and humbug, and we find ourselves face to face at last with the stern realities of the situation so many amongst us declined to consider during the past three or four years.'[106] It certainly was not a settlement that any Irish nationalist had hoped to achieve but, after four years of waiting, it was at least a settlement.

Notes

1 Memorandum from Kevin O'Shiel, 'The Boundary Issue', 29 May 1923, Department of the Taoiseach, NAI/TSCH/S 2027, North East Boundary Secret Documents 1922–4, National Archives of Ireland, Dublin.

2 P. Murray, *The Irish Boundary Commission and its Origins, 1886–1925* (Dublin: University College Dublin Press, 2011), p. 157.

3 *Irish News*, 10, 11 December 1924.

4 Ibid., 11, 12 December 1924.

5 Alarmed at the rate of population increase in Belfast, in the early 1890s, the Belfast City and District Water Commission asked civil engineer Luke

Livingstone Macassey to develop a long-range plan for supplying water to the city. For Macassey, the natural geography of the Mourne Mountains and their relative proximity to Belfast made the region the ideal place to locate the hydro-project that was required. Between 1893 and 1899, the Water Commission purchased land in the region and in 1901, tunnels, conduits and pipelines were installed. In 1904, a 9,000-acre drainage basin was created by the building of the Mourne Wall and, put together, these building projects represented stage one of the project. The Water Commission began to prepare for stage two – the Silent Valley Reservoir – in 1910 and the designs for the facility were nearing completion at the start of the First World War. Nothing more was done until the Craig government requested tenders in 1922. The project actually got underway on 10 October 1923 when Lord Carson symbolically broke the ground and it took ten years to complete the facility. J. Thompson, 'A Century of Water from the Mournes: A Concise History', BBC Northern Ireland: Your Place and Mine, https://www.bbc.co.uk/northernireland/yourplaceandmine/down/A1068518.shtml (accessed 23 July 2019); J. Thompson, 'A Century of Water from the Mournes – Part 2', BBC Northern Ireland: Your Place and Mine, https://www.bbc.co.uk/northernireland/yourplaceandmine/down/A1068527.shtml (accessed 23 July 2019).

6 G. Hand, 'MacNeill and the Boundary Commission', in F.X. Martin and F.J. Byrne (eds), *The Scholar Revolutionary: Eoin MacNeill, 1867–1945, and the Making of the New Ireland* (Shannon: Irish University Press, 1973), p. 201.

7 St J. Ervine, *Craigavon: Ulsterman* (London: George Allen & Unwin Ltd, 1949), p. 492.

8 *Irish News*, 10 December 1924. Craig had earlier given his approval to these private initiatives.

9 Of the latter, Isadore B. Mooney's 'Ulster Betrayed: The Startling Admissions of Eoin MacNeill' was having an appreciable affect. Described by Stephens as 'an irregular leaflet circulating in Newry', Mooney claimed that he had been told by Eoin MacNeill in April 1922 that the 'Free State Government had come to the decision of freely handing Fermanagh, Tyrone, South Armagh, and South Down to Sir James Craig's Government without waiting for any Boundary Commission'. According to Stephens, it was concern about this alleged 'betrayal of the North' that had left the nationalists of the vital region both discouraged and in want of greater assistance from the Free State. E.M. Stephens, 'Report of Visit to Armagh and Newry, December 18 & 19', 22 December 1924, Ernest Blythe Papers, P24/204, University College Dublin Archives (UCDA).

10 P. Shea, *Voices and the Sound of Drums: An Irish Autobiography* (Belfast: Blackstaff Press, 1981), pp. 95–6.

11 *Irish News*, 12 December 1924.

12 Ibid., 13 December 1924.

13 Ibid., 15, 17 December 1924.

14 Ibid., 12 December 1924.

15 Ibid., 18 December 1924.

16 *Derry Journal*, 22 December 1924.

17 *Irish News*, 22 December 1924.

18 *Derry Journal*, 22 December 1924.

19 *Irish News*, 1 January 1925.

20 M. Harris, *The Catholic Church and the Foundation of the Northern Irish Church* (Cork: Cork University Press, 1993), p. 166.

21 Ibid., pp. 168–9; E. Phoenix, *Northern Nationalism: Nationalist Politics, Partition and the Catholic Minority in Northern Ireland, 1890–1940* (Belfast: Ulster Historical Foundation, 1994), p. 317.

22 *Irish News*, 6 February 1925.

23 Ibid., 23 February 1925.

24 G. Hand (ed.), *Report of the Irish Boundary Commission 1925* (Shannon: Irish University Press, 1969), p. 10.

25 'Evidence of H. Melley', 16 December 1924, Irish Boundary Commission Papers, P. 6521, National Library of Ireland, Dublin.

26 *Irish News*, 18 February 1925.

27 Ibid. For the letter sent to the Armagh County Council, see the *Irish News*, 4 February 1925.

28 According to that Council's Basil Brook, 'There [was] no use ignoring the Commission, as it was a fact and because its findings would be upheld, no matter how [the Unionists] might dislike it.' See the *Irish News*, 18 February 1925. For the change of mood among Northern nationalists, see Phoenix, *Northern Nationalism*, p. 314.

29 The unionist organ said it would be 'the duty of the Government to so redistribute electoral areas that the Roman Catholic population may be given a representation in keeping with their numbers, influence, and standing' if Belfast really wanted their co-operation. *Irish News*, 27 January 1925. The newspaper was in a decidedly less conciliatory mood on 2 March when it reported: '[W]hile the Commission may not have the authority to do what it [was] set up to do, still that is no reason why it should be made use of as a medium through which the enemies of the Northern Government should be allowed to publish unchallenged and uncontradicted statements wholly at variance with the real facts.' *Irish News*, 3 March 1925.

30 Ibid., 3, 4 March 1925.

31 Ibid., 4, 5 March 1925.

32 Murray, *The Irish Boundary Commission, 1886–1925*, p. 179.

33 Harris, *The Catholic Church and the Foundation of the Northern Irish State*, pp. 165–6.

34 Hand, 'MacNeill and the Boundary Commission', p. 237.

35 'Evidence of the East Down Committee of Nationalist Inhabitants', 18 March 1925, Irish Boundary Commission Papers, P. 6521, National Library of Ireland, Dublin.

36 *The Times*, 11 March 1925.

37 *Irish News*, 11, 18 March 1925. If there was anything to Hugh McCartan's claim that critics of the Craig government were forced to 'stress their "loyalties" so as to avoid the charge of being disguised Sinn Féiners' then there could be something to the *Irish News* charge, as McCartan plainly implies that one's disposition towards the union trumped all other issues in Northern Ireland

regardless of party affiliation. H. McCartan, 'North Eastern Boundary Bureau. Report on Visit to Belfast and Derry', n.d., Department of the Taoiseach, NAI/TSCH/S 2027, North East Boundary Secret Documents 1922–4, National Archives of Ireland, Dublin.

38 'What Collins Stands For', 31 March 1925, J.H. Collins Papers, D921/4/5/1, Public Record Office of Northern Ireland, Belfast.

39 As the final words of Craig's election manifesto plead for his followers to '[s]ave Derry, Tyrone, and Fermanagh, and the Border', there was little doubt as to why the election had been called. *The Times*, 16 March 1925; Ervine, *Craigavon*, p. 495.

40 *Irish News*, 16 March 1925.

41 Ibid., 18 March 1925.

42 For instance, in an attempt to contrast the 'sane' Devlin/Redmond tradition of constitutional nationalism with 'the heartburnings' that Ireland had suffered in more recent years, Derry Devlinite George Leeke told the crowd that 'it was something for their Order to feel that they at no time swerved from the path marked out by their great leader, Joseph Devlin, who, he was sorry, was unable to be [there] with them'. *Irish News*, 20 March 1925.

43 Ibid.

44 E. Staunton, *The Nationalists of Northern Ireland, 1918–1973* (Dublin: The Columba Press, 2001), p. 94.

45 On 8 March, supporters and friends of John Redmond gathered in Wexford to remember the late IPP leader on the seventh anniversary of his passing. While commemorations (and pilgrimages to Wexford) were more subdued the previous year, in 1925, the Wexford event attracted thousands of people and many from Northern Ireland. Devlin was an honoured guest at the proceedings where he spoke glowingly about Redmond in a way that could only have been interpreted as a rejection of all that followed from 1918. The lines cited above are from that speech which later appeared in an *Irish News* editorial regarding the election. *Irish News*, 9, 16 March 1925.

46 Staunton, *The Nationalists of Northern Ireland*, p. 94.

47 *Irish News*, 18 March 1925.

48 Staunton, *The Nationalists of Northern Ireland*, p. 93; Phoenix, *Northern Nationalism*, p. 317.

49 Phoenix, *Northern Nationalism*, p. 318.

50 Although they incorrectly cite the date as 1922 rather than 1925, Rumpf and Hepburn have suggested that the pro-Treaty Sinn Féiners effectively 'came over to the Nationalists'. E. Rumpf and A.C. Hepburn, *Nationalism and Socialism in Twentieth-Century Ireland* (New York: Barnes & Noble Books, 1977), p. 184.

51 Phoenix, *Northern Nationalism*, pp. 317–20. For greater emphasis on the clerical role, see Harris, *The Catholic Church and the Foundation of the Northern Irish State*, pp. 167–70.

52 Although the official announcement that Devlin planned to seek a nomination for West Belfast came on 21 May this was not much of a secret. On the previous evening, he presided over an event slated to raise funds for the Belfast Celtic

Football and Athletic Club and on that occasion the dignitary who thanked Devlin for his support assured him 'that his re-entry into the political life of Belfast and Ireland would be received with joy everywhere'. Not to miss a chance to campaign, the parliamentarian told his audience: 'I am not now looking for votes but I say this – that I have always been on the side of democracy, and I have tried during my life to make [the people's] lives brighter and happier – and therefore I should like to see them being made comfortable at football matches and everywhere else.' *Irish News*, 21 May 1925.

53 Ibid., 24 March 1925.

54 *Derry Journal*, 30 March 1925.

55 Indicative of the clerical influence that the *Irish News* was attempting to make use of in its support of Devlin, this letter by Belfast's Archdeacon originally ran on 25 March as part of a large spread but this section of the letter continued to appear thereafter in a small, well-placed text box. *Irish News*, 25 March and 2 April 1925.

56 'What Collins Stands For', 31 March 1925.

57 Ibid.

58 *Fermanagh Herald*, 4 April 1925.

59 *Irish News*, 23 March 1925.

60 The pro-Treaty anti-partitionists did not want a contest in Down for fear that it might reveal the extent of Unionist strength in the county as a whole, so de Valera was not challenged. Devlinite Patrick O'Neill and the six Unionists also won their seats by acclimation. Phoenix, *Northern Nationalism*, p. 320.

61 Nationalist candidates received 91,452 first preference votes while Republican candidates received only 20,615 first preference votes. Thus, Nationalists received 81.6% of the first preference votes given to anti-partitionist candidates. S. Elliott (ed.), *Northern Ireland Parliamentary Elections Results 1921–1972* (Chichester: Political Reference Publications, 1973), p. 89.

62 After the redistricting of 1921 anti-partitionists, candidates were no longer able to win the single Westminster seat returned from West Belfast on the basis of the first past the post system but Northern Ireland elections returned four MPs from West Belfast using proportional representation. Joe Devlin was able to win one of these four Northern Ireland seats in both 1921 and topped the poll in 1925. In terms of first preference votes, the closest candidate to Devlin in 1925 was the Independent Unionist P.J. Woods, who received 9,599. Elliott, *Northern Ireland Parliamentary Elections Results*, p. 9.

63 The poem was submitted to the *Irish News* by 'F.P.H.' *Irish News*, 6 April 1925.

64 Phoenix, *Northern Nationalism*, p. 321.

65 *Fermanagh Herald*, 4 April 1925.

66 Hepburn, *Catholic Belfast and Nationalist Ireland in the Era of Joe Devlin*, p. 258; Staunton, *The Nationalists of Northern Ireland*, p. 94.

67 They had not met before the Belfast convention. Staunton, *The Nationalists of Northern Ireland*, p. 93.

68 Hand, *Report of the Irish Boundary Commission*, p. 12.

69 'Evidence of the Fermanagh Nationalist Committee', 2 July 1925, Irish Boundary Commission Papers, P. 6516, National Library of Ireland, Dublin; 'Evidence of

the Fermanagh Nationalist Committee – Healy Interview', 24 April 1925, Irish Boundary Commission Papers, P. 6517, National Library of Ireland, Dublin. Copies of all testimony given by Healy also appear in the Cahir Healy Papers, D2991/B/1 file at Public Record Office of Northern Ireland, Belfast.

70 'Written Evidence of M. Lynch', 29 December 1924, Irish Boundary Commission Papers, P. 6521, National Library of Ireland, Dublin.

71 Harris, *The Catholic Church and the Foundation of the Northern Irish State*, p. 166.

72 'Evidence of the Fermanagh Nationalist Committee', 2 July 1925; C. Healy to F.B. Bourdillon, 4 May 1925, Irish Boundary Commission Papers, P. 6516, National Library of Ireland, Dublin.

73 Ibid.; 'Evidence of the Fermanagh Nationalist Committee – Healy Interview', 24 April 1925.

74 Hand, 'MacNeill and the Boundary Commission', p. 338.

75 Ibid., pp. 338–9. For more on Fisher's indiscretions, see K. Matthews, *Fatal Influence: The Impact of Ireland on British Politics, 1920–1925* (Dublin: University College of Dublin Press, 2004), p. 217.

76 Murray, *The Irish Boundary Commission, 1886–1925*, p. 197.

77 Hand, *Report of the Irish Boundary Commission*, pp. 12–18.

78 Hand, 'MacNeill and the Boundary Commission', p. 246; Murray, *The Irish Boundary Commission, 1886–1925*, pp. 197, 211.

79 C. Healy to Kevin O'Higgins, 6 November 1925, Department of the Taoiseach, NAI/TSCH/S 1801/O, National Archives of Ireland, Dublin.

80 Letter from the Assistant Legal Advisor's Office to each member of the Executive Council, 17 November 1923, Ernest Blythe Papers, P 24/204, University College Dublin Archives (UCDA).

81 *Irish News*, 14 November 1925.

82 *Morning Post*, 7 November 1925.

83 *Irish News*, 9 November 1925.

84 'Resolution Unanimously Adopted at a Meeting of Derry Nationalists', 12 November 1925, Eoin MacNeill Papers, LA 1/M/19, University College Dublin Archives (UCDA).

85 *Fermanagh Herald*, 14 November 1925.

86 There are references to this, and Healy's recantation, in the Eoin MacNeill Papers, LA 1/F/302, University College Dublin Archives (UCDA).

87 *Fermanagh Herald*, 14 November 1925.

88 Hand, 'MacNeill and the Boundary Commission', pp. 252–4.

89 Harris, *The Catholic Church and the Foundation of the Northern Irish State*, p. 171.

90 Hand, 'MacNeill and the Boundary Commission', p. 256.

91 Owing to the JCPC's decision that the Boundary Commission would function on the basis of majority rule, as opposed to unanimity, this was a definite possibility and one which Feetham and Fisher pursued. Hand, 'MacNeill and the Boundary Commission', p. 160.

92 Matthews, *Fatal Influence*, pp. 223–4.

93 *Irish News*, 5 December 1925.

94 *Fermanagh Herald*, 5 December 1925.

95 K. Middlemas (ed.), *Thomas Jones Whitehall Diary, Volume III, Ireland, 1918*–1925 (London: Oxford University Press, 1971), pp. 239–45.

96 Article 5 stated: 'The Irish Free State shall assume liability for the service of the public debt of the United Kingdom as existing at the date hereof and towards the payment of war pensions as existing at that date in such proportion as may be fair and equitable, having regard to any just claims on the part of Ireland by way of set off or counter-claim.' 'The Anglo-Irish Treaty, 6 December 1921', in A.C. Hepburn (ed.), *Ireland, 1905–1925: Volume 2 Documents and Analysis* (Newtownards: Colourpoint Books, 1998), p. 203.

97 *Jones Whitehall Diary, Volume III*, p. 243. The suggestion was made on 1 December in the presence of Churchill, Craig, John Anderson and Jones.

98 'Irish Boundary Commission: Notes of a Conference, 1 December 1925', in M. Gilbert (ed.), *Winston S. Churchill: Volume V Companion Part I Documents: The Exchequer Years* (Boston: Houghton Mifflin, 1981), p. 606; *Jones Whitehall Diary, Volume III*, p. 244.

99 *Irish News*, 4 December 1925. Also see footnote 15 in this chapter for an earlier reference to the Ninth Beatitude, as understood by *Irish News* editor Tim McCarthy.

100 *Derry Journal*, 11 December 1925.

101 Ibid., 4, 18 December 1925.

102 Ibid., 7 December 1925.

103 *Thomas Jones Whitehall Diary, Volume III*, p. 246; Hand, 'MacNeill and the Boundary Commission', p. 262.

104 Memorandum from Kevin O'Shiel, 'Alleged Delay in Holding of the Boundary Commission. Should the Boundary Commission Be Held Now?', 7 February 1923, Department of the Taoiseach, NAI/TSCH/S 2027, North East Boundary Secret Documents 1922–4, National Archives of Ireland, Dublin.

105 To his credit, O'Shiel's biographer reports that the former NEBB Director was forever haunted by 'loss of his homeland' and 'the sense that he had been complicit in the betrayal of his fellow countrymen'. See E. Sagarra, *Kevin O'Shiel: Tyrone Nationalist and Irish State-Builder* (Dublin: Irish Academic Press, 2013), p. 222.

106 *Irish News*, 4 December 1925.

EPILOGUE AND CONCLUSION

'Blessed are they that Expect Nothing …'

> It will interest you to know that some folks, lay and clerical, who used not to understand you, are completely changed. Unanimously they agree that if a Party were formed you should be the pivot.
>
> – Cahir Healy to Joe Devlin[1]

In a January 1924 *Irish Times* interview, the Belfast-born author, journalist and nationalist Robert Lynd observed: 'Partition is not a mortal wound. It counts for as little in the history of a nation as does the incision made by a clumsy surgeon in the body of a healthy patient who ought not to have been operated on at all.'[2] It is doubtful that Lynd would have found many to support this view amongst the nationalists of Northern Ireland once the Boundary Commission fiasco was brought to its inauspicious end. 'The Free State leaders told us that our anchor was Article 12,' wrote an angry Cahir Healy in December 1925, yet 'when the time of trial came they cut our cable and launched us, rudderless, into the hurricane, without guarantee or security even for our ordinary civic rights'.[3] Contrasting the blemishes on his own record with those of the Treatyite regime, Joe Devlin averred:

> If I made an error it was a venial sin compared with that of the more extreme patriots who signed the Treaty of 1921 and the Pact of 1925. I would never have agreed to the setting up of a Parliament in Belfast and the permanent partition which it foreshadowed. They signed away the rights of Northern nationalists for all time, putting them under the heel of an intolerant anti-Catholic junta.[4]

The feeling of being let down by those whom many had regarded as the custodians of minority rights remained an open wound for Northern anti-partitionists as nationalist Ireland, north and south of the reconfirmed Six-County border, underwent a period of change.

In the Irish Free State, Cosgrave and his able Minister of External Affairs, Kevin O'Higgins, set out to transform the Free State from a semi-independent dominion born of the Treaty into a fully autonomous political entity by using the Commonwealth apparatus. While certainly not alone in this endeavour, the Irish Free State played a leading role in the process of re-defining dominionhood, and the Statute of Westminster (1931), codifying the dominions' co-equal status with Great Britain, was the ultimate result of the dominions' handiwork.[5]

Other changes were occasioned by Éamon de Valera's political rebirth as the leader of a new organisation known as Fianna Fáil – *Soldiers of Destiny*. Considered a 'slightly constitutional' party by one of de Valera's lieutenants, Fianna Fáil was initially abstentionist but when abstentionism became illegal after O'Higgins was assassinated in 1927, de Valera took the much-maligned oath, signed the book and led his followers into Dáil Éireann. That the anti-Treatyite TDs had refused to enter the Dáil in time to block the 1925 Tripartite Agreement provided yet another sore spot for some Northern nationalists[6] but since most of them had come to believe that Cumann na nGaedhael had forfeited its trusteeship of the Six-County minority when Cosgrave accepted the 'damn good bargain' of 1925,[7] it was to de Valera that they looked for salvation.

Even before Fianna Fáil emerged as a viable vehicle for achieving the unrequited aims of anti-partitionism, significant changes were already afoot among the nationalists of Northern Ireland. Despite Cahir Healy's claim in December 1925 that 'Border Nationalists [were] so sore as a result of [the border] betrayal that they' did not want to 'have anything further to do with political action',[8] George Leeke, Basil McGuckin and Patrick O'Neill joined Joe Devlin and Thomas McAllister in the Northern Ireland House of Commons by the spring of 1926 and by 1928, most of the remaining nationalist holdouts had also taken their seats. Informed by Cahir Healy that he 'was never so necessary to the people of Ulster as today',[9] Devlin and Healy worked to sustain the measure of co-operation entered into during the 1925

Northern Ireland election by organising their nebulous grouping of MPs into the National League of the North – the name under which the non-abstentionist Northern nationalists campaigned until the movement faded after Devlin's death in 1934.[10]

As an indication of all that had changed during these years, in 1929, an ailing Joe Devlin was able to secure one of the two nominations and was returned unopposed in the Westminster constituency of Fermanagh–Tyrone – a traditionally Sinn Féin-held constituency that had been hitherto off limits to him.[11] Given the divisions that had separated them for so long, Northern nationalist unity was itself a virtue but in terms of practical politics, the National Leaguers were not able to have much of an impact on the legislative agenda of their Unionist adversaries.[12] As a result, their attendance at the regional parliament in Belfast was at first erratic and then non-existent.[13] Devlin never set foot in the Northern parliament once it had removed to Stormont Hill in 1932.

In 1928 and again in 1933, Devlin and Healy floated the idea of merging their group with Fianna Fáil but de Valera had little interest in the suggestion lest the North interfere with his reemergence from the political wilderness and on both occasions, the Northerners were spurned, much as they had rebuffed de Valera in 1924–5.[14] Irrespective of this rejection, many Six-County nationalists became loyal champions of de Valera in the late 1920s. For instance, J.J. McCarroll, the managing editor, director and company secretary of the *Derry Journal* switched the newspaper's allegiance from Cumann na nGaedhael to Fianna Fáil as early as 1927,[15] after which it became a ready carrier of anti-Cosgrave propaganda, such as the 1932 election poem 'Vote For Fianna Fail'.

> Now, gents and ladies, one and all, attention
> to me pay,
> 'Till I tell you of the work we've done near
> deep Sheephaven Bay.
> We have canvassed well and truly, and now
> you can bail
> We'll shift 'our Willie' and his pals, and
> elect Fianna Fail.

The 'damned good bargain' makers must
join the unemployed,
Or else cross o'er to England, their sorrow
there to hide;
These hypocrites at freedom's cause did long
and loudly rave,
But now, thank God, our day has come –
We'll vote Fianna Fail.[16]

De Valera was able to form a minority administration in 1932 and when he gambled on exchanging this for the prospect of a clear Fianna Fáil victory the following year, Healy and J.H. Collins campaigned for him in the border counties.[17]

Fianna Fáil's landslide victory over the pro-Treatyites in 1933 solidified its hold on power and, while Cosgrave's party wilted, de Valera set to work shedding Southern Ireland of the remaining constitutional restrictions that he and the moderate anti-Treatyites of Fianna Fáil had so strenuously objected to in the Treaty.[18] The decade witnessed a deterioration of Anglo-Irish relations, an economic war between the two countries and the implementation of a new constitution for the Free State, which was re-styled as 'Éire, or in the English language, Ireland'. In addition to casting aside the last vestiges of Imperial rule and making Éire into a near republic, Article 2 of the 1937 constitution also laid (symbolic) claim to all of the island's thirty-two counties. However, as a clear indication that de Valera's stated claim to the North was merely anti-partitionist sabre-rattling, he refused to allow parliamentary representatives elected in the North to sit in Dáil Éireann.[19]

Writing in 1936, a year before the birth of Éire and the constitution's claim to Northern territory, Cahir Healy mused:

> I doubt if Ireland yet feels for the 'Lost Province' as France felt for her Alsace and Lorraine. In time, when lesser issues, like Republic versus Commonwealth, which now divides the people of the Free State, shall have receded into their proper place in the National scheme, will this nation begin to put first things first. Then will the question of Partition overshadow every other, and a solution will have been brought a lot nearer than it is to-day.[20]

Such a day appeared imminent when de Valera entered into negotiations with Britain in 1938 with the intent of ending the economic war and securing a general Anglo-Irish settlement.

During the course of the conference, de Valera found himself confronted by a deputation of Northern nationalists. Hoping that the nationalists of Northern Ireland might be seen, for propaganda purposes, but not heard, lest they have an impact on his attempts to completely re-cast the relationship between Éire and Britain, this was a group that de Valera had not intended to consult during the meetings, did not invite and was none too pleased to see.[21] Prior to their arrival in London, the nationalists had passed a motion at a Belfast meeting expressing their 'determination to regard with the utmost disapproval any settlement with England that [ignored] the plight of the Six County Nationalists and [did] nothing to undo the crime of Partition'. The deputation brought with them a letter written by the Bishop of Down and Connor informing de Valera that Northern Ireland's nationalist minority was 'fearful' that the conference would bring about a settlement of Éire–British differences that 'would fail to right the grave injustices of Partition, and would leave unchanged the intolerable position of almost half a million of [his] people in the North-East [who were] deprived of their national rights as Irishmen'. Cahir Healy was no less candid than the bishop. 'However strong we have been behind Mr de Valera in the North,' said the long-time nationalist agitator, 'we would regard it as a betrayal of all our interests if he ignored the problem of Partition by getting trade and defence agreements only, although, of course, we think he has no intention of doing such a thing.'[22]

Whether Healy meant this as a warning or a plea is uncertain but it was clear that the Northern nationalists whom this group represented were trying desperately to avoid being marginalised as they had been in 1925. The Anglo-Irish Agreements of 1938 did not brush away the blight of partition as they had hoped and, according to a statement issued by all the leading Northern nationalists, this news was greeted with 'profound disappointment'. Exasperated by the development, Senator John McHugh declared himself 'more satisfied than ever that Mr de Valera [had] no policy about the North' and was only 'using [the Six-County nationalists] for his own purposes'.[23] Such an unhappy turn of events seemed once again to bear out the sagacity of the Ninth Beatitude.[24]

De Valera's inability to unify Ireland in 1938 only compounded the sense of abandonment, betrayal and exploitation that anti-partitionists had felt since the collapse of the Boundary Commission. Although Ulster Unionists had more weapons at their disposal and proved more adept at defending their interests, circumstances surrounding both instances make it difficult to deny that they, and the nationalists of Northern Ireland, each found themselves being used as pawns in the Dublin–London game throughout the 1920s and 1930s.

Reflecting on the eventful period that led up to the debacle of 1925, it seems clear that the first five years of the 1920s represented a distinct chapter in the history of Irish nationalism – a chapter in which the ultimate failure of Home Rule to solve the Irish Question was made manifest by Sinn Féin's eclipse of the Redmond/Devlin brand of constitutional nationalism and the republicans' subsequent inability to prevent partition. This was the juncture at which the clumsy surgeon of Robert Lynd's metaphor amputated six of Ireland's thirty-two counties in order to establish a safely unionist Northern Ireland. Yet, because the cut was not as clean as it could have been, nearly half a million Irish nationalists were left to brood on the wrong side of the incision.

Convinced that the nationalists whom partition stranded within Northern Ireland still considered themselves to be a vital part of the Irish nation, a primary objective of this book has been to re-connect them to the wider Irish nationalist movement by emphasising Northern nationalists' relations with their Southern peers, as well as examining their responses to the events that dominated Free State politics after partition. While my concentration on the relationship between Northern and Southern nationalism sets this work apart from the existing historiography, with its incorporation of hitherto unexamined nationalist poetry and songs and an extensive, detailed and systematic use of the Devlinite *Irish News*, this study also breaks new ground by presenting the nationalists of Northern Ireland as an example of a trapped minority.

Believing that scholarship related to the transnational Palestinian minority of Israel had been stunted by an 'analytical straightjacket' that prioritised understanding the nature of the Israeli state rather than the Palestinians themselves, Dan Rabinowitz devised the trapped minority framework in order to redirect scholarly focus onto that minority group and others like it.[25] Rabinowitz identified a number of characteristics that he considered common to trapped minorities but, when distilled to its essence, it is clear that the quality that differentiates a trapped minority from a distinct national group that is wholly contained within a single state is the fact that the former is a part of an external mother nation that it considers materially different from the dominant population of the host state in which it has been entrapped. Thus, because it puts priority on a trapped minority's relationship with its mother nation and how the nature of that relationship is perceived by its host state, the framework is a very useful tool for examining the nationalist minority of Northern Ireland. As my research has shown, the Northern nationalists were not just a distinct community that happened to live in, and interact with, the unionists who dominated the Northern state; rather, they were a nationalist community that lived in Northern Ireland but continued to see themselves as part of a larger transnational ethnic, religious and political group that was figuratively and, at times, literally in conflict with Northern Ireland. In this regard, I have presented Great Britain's partition of Ireland as the prerequisite 'sudden external interference'[26] that led to the confinement of the Northern nationalists as a trapped minority, while demonstrating that they fit the other criteria that Rabinowitz identified as common to trapped minorities.

According to Rabinowitz, a lack of unity on policy and tactics is one of the chief characteristics of a trapped minority and, during the period under study, the nationalists of Northern Ireland were very much divided between the constitutionally minded followers of Joe Devlin and the Northern branch of Sinn Féin. Although these divisions pre-dated partition and were partly related to the Devlinites' ideological aversion to using physical force, it is demonstrably clear that the divisions became more acute after partition when the prospect of repatriation via a Boundary Commission emerged. This was the case because it was widely held in nationalist Ireland that a fairly constituted Boundary Commission would rescue the primarily Sinn Féin-oriented border nationalists but would not be able to repatriate nationalists who resided in the inland areas where the Devlinites were predominant. As Kevin O'Higgins once observed, this was the basic division between those who did, and those who did not, have a 'dog's chance' of getting out of the partitioned area[27] and it manifested itself in a key division over policy. While the border nationalists were eager to have the Commission convened and remained staunch advocates of abstentionism as they waited, the Devlinites of Belfast and the interior would have preferred abandoning the Boundary Commission in favour of a negotiated settlement and entry into the Northern parliament as a more practical, albeit long-term, path to Irish reunification.

Notwithstanding the important differences that Sinn Féiners and Devlinites had over policy and tactics, pressure from the border nationalists and the Free State government kept the Devlinites from abandoning abstention until 1925 which, despite the naivety of the tactic, conforms to what Rabinowitz has said about the tendency of trapped minorities to be non-assimilating. Yet, for the nationalists of Northern Ireland, non-assimilation was not just a matter of refusing to recognise the Northern Ireland government; it was also a symptom of what Omagh nationalist Michael Lynch called the tendency of the minority to 'look to Dublin as the seat of Government and as *the center of the political and social life of the country*'.[28]

The Northern nationalists' orientation towards Dublin also had an influence on the nature of their interactions with the Northern government – another consistency with the trapped minority model. Regarding them with suspicion, and sometimes fear, the Unionist government in Belfast was – at best – insensitive to the concerns of the minority, as seen by its disproportionate use of internment against Catholics and nationalists, as well as its determination to remove the one aspect of the Better Government of Ireland Act that provided practical safeguards to the Northern nationalists – proportional representation. As a result of the measures adopted by the Unionist government of Northern Ireland and their own refusal to participate in partition politics, Northern nationalists ultimately found themselves marginalised within what had become a Unionist state.

Northern nationalists might have expected to be marginalised by a government led by their political enemies in Belfast but what neither nationalist group had expected was how little their views would matter to the Southern nationalists of the Free State after partition. Michael Collins' willingness to enter into negotiations with the Prime Minister of Northern Ireland without the involvement of any Northern emissaries – Devlinites or Sinn Féiners – as well as the Cosgrave administration's preference for 'ignor[ing] all Northern Ireland groups' as it worked out its own boundary policy,[29] both speak to the way in which the Northern minority saw its nationalist credentials devalued by the Free State government. Thus, in a way that conforms to yet another salient feature of the trapped minority framework, the nationalists of Northern Ireland became marginal twice over: once within their host nation and once within their mother nation.

Divided amongst themselves, confined to the segregated regions of Belfast and the borders, marginalised within Irish politics as a whole and left waiting on the wrong side of the Irish border as others determined their fate – in many ways there could be no better example of a trapped minority than the nationalists of Northern Ireland. Yet there was one significant way in which the Northern nationalists varied from the Rabinowitz model. Living under the jurisdiction of Belfast's regional parliament, Six-County nationalists endured hardships and faced challenges that were different from those encountered by Southern nationalists but, unlike the archetypal trapped minority, this did not cause the Northern nationalists to lose a sense of their history and culture. Rather, this study proves that these differing conditions served to reinforce, rather than diminish, their sense of Irishness and their connections to Irish history and culture. The frequent use of the language of 'The Cause'[30] in the speeches minority leaders gave, the columns of the anti-partitionist press and the poetry and songs Northern nationalists wrote are all sure signs that they not only embraced, but also found comfort in, their history and culture.

Indicative of the enduring connectedness that Northern nationalists felt towards the Irish mother nation and the history they shared with Southern nationalists, their grievances towards Britain and James Craig's government in Belfast were very often described in terms of plantation and Ascendancy politics. The anti-partitionist press made frequent references to Ireland's 750 years of struggle dating back to Henry II and fears that the Anglo-Irish Treaty of 1921 would be broken as was the Treaty of Limerick. Moreover, no effort was spared to relate the conditions in which the Northern minority lived to the depravity that Cromwell and Carew and the Act of Union had inflicted on Ireland. And where heroes were concerned, it was not just to the Ulster O'Neills and the Belfast branch of the United Irishmen that the Six-County nationalists looked; rather, Emmet,

O'Connell, Butt, Parnell, the Young Irelanders and especially Thomas Davis were never far from mind.

Autograph books kept by the *Argenta* men, the speeches delivered by political and religious leaders and the editorial pages of the *Irish News* often made references to Davis, which is itself indicative of just how well-versed Northern anti-partitionists were in the literary nationalism of the Young Irelander. But in keeping with traditions that dated at least as far back as the penal era, Northern nationalists not only found meaning in the songs and poetry of the United Irishmen and Young Irelanders but also wrote their own verse describing the joy felt when the Treaty had been signed, anguish that Ireland was falling prey to an internecine struggle and the fear of being abandoned by a Southern government that was too caught up in its own particularist affairs.

Telling and re-telling history, singing patriotic songs and writing poetry were all a vital part of constructing a sense of Irishness and this process of identity construction and reinforcement was an extremely important aspect of Irish nationalism during the eighteenth, nineteenth and early twentieth centuries. While Rabinowitz's archetypal trapped minority sought to suppress its history, I demonstrate that Northern nationalists' continued efforts to tap into this evocative material and make their own contributions to it only bound them closer to the Irish mother nation as they expressed their feelings of elation, angst and exploitation *as a consequence of their entrapment.* This process, I contend, does not provide cause to disqualify the nationalists of Northern Ireland as a trapped minority but rather, encourages us to re-think the criteria and refurbish the model.

Seen from this perspective, it is abundantly clear that the enduring cultural connectedness that Six-County nationalists sought to the Irish mother nation represented an attempt to avoid being excluded from what Rabinowitz would describe as the 'thrust of national revival'[31] in the Irish mother nation and, in hindsight, this makes the Boundary Commission fiasco appear all the more tragic. With the confirmation of the Six-County border in 1925, it seems that the mere hours which were allowed to elapse between the activation of the Free State constitution on 6 December 1922 and the following day when Northern Ireland formally contracted out of its jurisdiction, represented the last time that the island was to be politically united. For the nationalists of Northern Ireland, the 1921–5 period was filled with moments of both anxiety and excitement but, in the end, these years only served to re-enforce the wisdom of the Ninth Beatitude: Blessed are they who expect nothing, for they will not be disappointed.

Notes

1 Cahir Healy to Joe Devlin, 12 January 1928, Cahir Healy Papers, D2991/A/1/60, Public Record Office of Northern Ireland, Belfast.

2 As cited by the *Derry Journal*, 1 February 1924.

3 *The Irish Statesman*, 18 December 1925.

4 C. Healy, 'Late Joseph Devlin, MP: An Intimate Sketch by a Colleague', 1934, Cahir Healy Papers, D2991/B/140/19, Public Record Office of Northern Ireland, Belfast.

5 For an argument emphasising the Irish Free State's role in the re-definition of dominionhood see D. Harkness' *The Restless Dominion: The Irish Free State and the British Commonwealth of Nations, 1921–31* (Dublin: Gill and Macmillan, 1969). A contrary view which stresses actions taken by Canada and the other dominions has been presented by G. Martin in his 'The Irish Free State and the Evolution of the Commonwealth, 1921–49' which appeared in R. Hyam and G. Martin (eds), *Reappraisals in British Imperial History* (London: The Macmillan Press Ltd, 1975).

6 C. Healy, 'De Valera and the March of a Nation', 1956, Cahir Healy Papers, D2991/C/15/1, Public Record Office of Northern Ireland, Belfast.

7 A 'damn good bargain' is an unfortunate tag which Cosgrave used to describe the Tripartite Agreement. J. Curran, 'The Anglo-Irish Agreement of 1925: Hardly a "Damn Good Bargain"', *Historian* 40 no.1 (1977), p. 50.

8 *The Irish Statesman*, 18 December 1925.

9 A.C. Hepburn, *Catholic Belfast and Nationalist Ireland in the Era of Joe Devlin, 1871–1934* (Oxford: Oxford University Press, 2008), p. 261.

10 The National League of the North was not affiliated with William Redmond's National League, established in 1926, but both names were attempting to conjure up an association with Parnell.

11 His running mate was Thomas Harbison in 1929. Harbison died a year later and Devlin and Cahir Healy contested and won the joint constituency in 1931.

12 According to Phoenix, the Wild Birds Protection Act of 1931 was 'the party's sole legislative achievement'. E. Phoenix, *Northern Nationalism: Nationalist Politics, Partition and the Catholic Minority in Northern Ireland 1890–1940* (Belfast: Ulster Historical Foundation, 1994), p. 368.

13 E. Staunton, *The Nationalists of Northern Ireland, 1918–1973* (Dublin: The Columba Press, 2001), pp. 101–5, 107.

14 J. Bowman, *De Valera and the Ulster Question 1917–1973* (Oxford: Clarendon Press, 1982), pp. 133–5.

15 The *Journal*'s 225th Anniversary Supplement recalled that the 1927 switch in the newspaper's editorial policy was not without repercussions. A shareholder named Johnny Shan McLaughlin made an unsuccessful attempt to unseat McCarroll and, when that failed, he founded the *People's Press*. Ironically, the *Derry Journal* acquired that splinter newspaper in 1995. *Derry Journal*, 6 June 1997.

16 *Derry Journal*, 15 February 1932.

17 Staunton, *The Nationalists of Northern Ireland*, p. 110.

18 A. Ward, *The Irish Constitutional Tradition: Responsible Government and Modern Ireland, 1782–1992* (Washington: The Catholic University of America Press, 1994), pp. 212–38.

19 Bowman, *De Valera and the Ulster Question*, pp. 133–5.

20 C. Healy, 'An Englishwoman with a Notebook', 6 May 1936, Cahir Healy Papers, D2991/C/15/1, Public Record Office of Northern Ireland, Belfast.

21 Bowman, *De Valera and the Ulster Question*, p. 175.

22 'Voice of the People', 1938, Cahir Healy Papers, D2991/D/9/12, Public Record Office of Northern Ireland, Belfast.

23 'The Omission of Partition', 1938, Cahir Healy Papers, D2991/E/5/1, Public Record Office of Northern Ireland, Belfast.

24 In keeping with Alexander Pope usage, *Irish News* editor Tim McCarthy declared the following to be a Ninth Beatitude: 'Blessed are they that expect nothing, for they shall not be disappointed' and he cited it a number of times during the boundary debacle of 1924–5.

25 D. Rabinowitz, 'The Palestinian Citizens of Israel, the Concept of Trapped Minority and the Discourse of Transnationalism in Anthropology', *Ethnic and Racial Studies* 24, 1 (2001), pp. 65, 69.

26 Ibid. p. 73.

27 'Deputation to the Provisional Government', 11 October 1922, Department of the Taoiseach, NAI/TSCH/S 11209, National Archives of Ireland, Dublin, 18.

28 Emphasis added. 'Written Evidence of M. Lynch', 29 December 1924, Irish Boundary Commission Papers, P. 6521, National Library of Ireland, Dublin.

29 Memorandum from Kevin O'Shiel, 'The Boundary Issue and North-Eastern Policy', 21 April 1923, Department of the Taoiseach, NAI/TSCH/S 2027, North East Boundary Secret Documents 1922–4, National Archives of Ireland, Dublin.

30 M. Wheatley, *Nationalism and the Irish Party: Provincial Ireland, 1910–1916* (Oxford: Oxford University Press, 2005), p. 80.

31 Rabinowitz, 'Trapped Minority', p. 75.

Select Bibliography

I. Archival Sources

Linen Hall Library, Belfast
Northern Ireland Political Collection, in particular:
Pre-1966 Anti-Unionist Material (1922–) Boxes 1 and 2

National Archives of Ireland, Dublin
Department of the Taoiseach files, in particular:
NAI/TSCH/S1011 North-East Ulster Advisory Committee
NAI/TSCH/S1801 Boundary Commission
NAI/TSCH/S2027 Northern Ireland Boundary, Secret Documents

National Library of Ireland, Dublin
Irish Boundary Commission Papers P. 6509–32
National Photographic Archive

Public Record Office of Northern Ireland, Belfast
J.H. Collins Papers
Joseph Devlin Papers
Cahir Healy Papers
George Leeke Papers
Seamus MacCall Papers
J.J. McCarroll Papers
Patrick O'Neill Papers

University College, Dublin
Ernest Blythe Papers, P24
Hugh Kennedy Papers, P4
Eoin MacNeill Papers, LA1
Richard Mulcahy Papers, P7

Trinity College, Dublin
John Dillon Papers
E.M. Stephens Papers

II. Parliamentary Papers

Northern Ireland
The Stormont Papers, http://stormontpapers.ahds.ac.uk/search.html (accessed 23 July 2019)

The Irish Free State/Eire/Republic of Ireland
Dáil Debates, https://www.oireachtas.ie/en/debates/find/ (accessed 23 July 2019)

The United Kingdom
Parliamentary Debates: Official Report, House of Commons, 1921–1972
Parliamentary Debates: Official Report, House of Lords, 1921–1972

III. Newspapers

Derry Journal
Fermanagh Herald
Freeman's Journal
Irish News
The Manchester Guardian
The Times
Weekly Bulletin
Weekly Digest

IV. Printed Documents and Contemporary Sources

Buckland, P. (ed.), *Irish Unionism, 1885–1923: A Documentary History* (Belfast: Her Majesty's Stationary Office, 1973).

Churchill, R., *Winston S. Churchill: Companion Volume II Part 2, 1907–1911* (Boston: Houghton Mifflin Company, 1969).

Correspondence between His Majesty's Government and the Governments of the Irish Free State and Northern Ireland relating to Article 12 of the Articles of Agreement for a Treaty between Great Britain and Ireland (London: His Majesty's Stationary Office, 1924).

Gilbert, M. (ed.), *Winston S. Churchill: Volume IV Companion Part 3 Documents April 1921–November 1922* (London: William Heinemann Ltd, 1977).

Gilbert, M. (ed.), *Winston S. Churchill: Volume V Companion Part I Documents: The Exchequer Years, 1922–1929* (London: William Heinemann Ltd, 1979).

Handbook of the Ulster Question (Dublin: State Paper Office, 1923).

Hand, G. (ed.), *Report of the Irish Boundary Commission, 1925* (Shannon: Irish University Press, 1969).

Hepburn, A.C. (ed.), *Ireland, 1905–1925 Volume 2: Documents and Analysis* (Newtownards: Colourpoint Books, 1998).

Middlemas, K., (ed.), *Thomas Jones Whitehall Diary, Volume III, Ireland, 1918–25* (London: Oxford University Press, 1971).

Milroy, S. (ed.), *The Case of Ulster: An Analysis of Four Partition Arguments* (Dublin: The Talbot Press Limited, 1922).

Treatment of the Minority in the Six Counties Under the Government of Northern Ireland (Belfast: The Internees Dependants Committee, 1924).

V. Secondary Material: Books

Anderson, B., *Imagined Communities: Reflections on the Origin and Spread of Nationalism* (3rd ed., London: Verso, 2006).

Arthur, P., *Special Relationships: Britain, Ireland and the Northern Ireland Problem* (Belfast: The Blackstaff Press, 2000).

Bardon, J., *A History of Ulster* (Belfast: Blackstaff Press, 2001).

Bowman, J., *De Valera and the Ulster Question, 1917–1973* (Oxford: Clarendon Press, 1982).

Boyce, D.G., *Nationalism in Ireland* (London: Routledge, 1995).

Boyce, D.G., *Nineteenth-Century Ireland: The Search for Stability* (Dublin: Gill and Macmillan Ltd, 1990).

Buckland, P., *A History of Northern Ireland* (Dublin: Gill and Macmillan, 1981).

Buckland, P., *James Craig: Lord Craigavon* (Dublin: Gill and Macmillan Ltd, 1980).

Buckland, P., *The Factory of Grievances: Devolved Government in Northern Ireland, 1921–39* (Dublin: Gill and Macmillan, 1979).

Buckley, P., *Faith and Fatherland: The Irish News, the Catholic Hierarchy, and the Management of Dissidents* (Belfast: Belfast Historical and Educational Society, 1991).

Canning, P., *British Policy Towards Ireland, 1921–1941* (Oxford: Clarendon Press, 1985).

Clayton, P., *Enemies and Passing Friends: Settler Ideologies in Twentieth Century Ulster* (London: Pluto Press, 1996).

Clyde, T., *Irish Literary Magazines: An Outline History and Descriptive Bibliography* (Dublin: Irish Academic Press, 2003).

Coogan, T.P., *Ireland in the Twentieth Century* (London: Hutchinson, 2003).

Curran, J., *The Birth of the Irish Free State, 1921–1923* (n. p.: University of Alabama Press, 1980).

de Nie, M., *The Eternal Paddy: Irish Identity and the British Press, 1798–1882* (Madison: The University of Wisconsin Press, 2004).

Doherty, G. and Keogh, D. (eds), *Michael Collins and the Making of the Irish State* (Boulder: Mercier Press, 1998).

Elliott, M., *The Catholics of Ulster: A History* (London: Penguin Books, 2000).

Ellison, G. and Smyth, J., *The Crowned Harp: Policing Northern Ireland* (London: Pluto Press, 2000).

Ervine, St J., *Craigavon: Ulsterman* (London: George Allen & Unwin Ltd, 1949).

Farrell, M., *Arming the Protestants: The Formation of the Ulster Special Constabulary and the Royal Ulster Constabulary, 1920–27* (London: Pluto Press, 1983).

Farrell, M., *Northern Ireland: The Orange State* (London: Pluto, 1976).

Follis, B., *A State Under Siege: The Establishment of Northern Ireland, 1920–1925* (Oxford: Clarendon Press, 1995).

Gallagher, R., *Violence and Nationalist Politics in Derry City, 1920–1923* (Dublin: Four Courts Press, 2003).

Garvin, T., *1922: The Birth of Irish Democracy* (New York: St Martin's Press, 1996).

Garvin, T., *Mythical Thinking in Political Life: Reflections on Nationalism and Social Science* (Dublin: Maunsel & Company, 2001).

Gilbert, M., *Churchill: A Life* (London: William Heinemann Ltd, 1991).

Hachey, T. and McCaffrey, L. (eds), *Perspectives on Irish Nationalism* (Lexington: The University Press of Kentucky, 1989).

Hampton, M., *Visions of the Press in Britain, 1850–1950* (Chicago: University of Illinois Press, 2004).

Harkness, D., *The Restless Dominion: The Irish Free State and the British Commonwealth of Nations, 1921–31* (Dublin: Gill & Macmillan, 1969).

Harris, M., *The Catholic Church and the Foundation of the Northern Irish State* (Cork: Cork University Press, 1993).

Hart, P., *Mick: The Real Michael Collins* (New York: Viking Penguin, 2006).

Hart, P., *The IRA & its Enemies: Violence and Community in Cork, 1916–1923* (Oxford: Oxford University Press, 1999).

Hepburn, A.C., *A Past Apart: Studies in the History of Catholic Belfast, 1850–1950* (Belfast: Ulster Historical Foundation, 1996).

Hepburn, A.C., *Catholic Belfast and Nationalist Ireland in the Era of Joe Devlin, 1871–1934* (Oxford: Oxford University Press, 2008).

Heslinga, M.W., *The Irish Border as a Cultural Divide: A Contribution to the Study of Regionalism in the British Isles* (The Netherlands: Assen, 1971).

Hill, J.H., (ed.), *A New History of Ireland VII: Ireland, 1921–84* (Oxford: Oxford University Press, 2003).

Hopkinson, M., *Green Against Green: The Irish Civil War* (Dublin: Gill & Macmillan, 2004).

Hughes, M., *Ireland Divided: The Roots of the Modern Irish Problem* (Cardiff: University of Wales Press, 1994).

Jackson, A., *Ireland, 1798–1998: Politics and War* (Oxford: Blackwell Publishers, 1999).

Jackson, A., *The Ulster Party* (New York: Oxford University Press, 1989).

Jalland, P., *The Liberals and Ireland: The Ulster Question in British Politics to 1914* (Sussex: The Harvester Press, 1980).

Johnson, P., *Ireland: A Concise History from the Twelfth Century to the Present Day* (Chicago: Academy Chicago Publishers, 1996).

Kee, R., *The Green Flag: A History of Irish Nationalism* (Toronto: Penguin Books Canada Ltd, 2000).

Kendle, J., *Walter Long, Ireland, and the Union, 1905–1920* (Montreal & Kingston: McGill-Queen's University Press, 1992).

Kennedy, D., *The Widening Gulf: Northern Attitudes to the Independent Irish State, 1919–49* (Belfast: Blackstaff Press, 1988).

Kleinrichert, D., *Republican Internment and the Prison Ship Argenta, 1922* (Dublin: Irish Academic Press, 2001).

Knirck, J., *Imagining Ireland's Independence: The Debates Over the Anglo-Irish Treaty of 1921* (New York: Rowman & Littlefield Publishers, Inc., 2006).

Laffan, M., *The Partition of Ireland, 1911–1925* (Dundalk: Dublin Historical Association, 1983).

Legg, M.L., *Newspapers and Nationalism: The Irish Provincial Press, 1850–1892* (Dublin: Four Courts Press, 1999).

Lynch, R., *The Northern IRA and the Early Years of Partition, 1920–1922* (Dublin: Irish Academic Press, 2006).

Lyons, F.S.L., *Ireland Since the Famine* (London: Weidenfeld and Nicolson, 1971).

Martin, F.X. and Byrne, F.J. (eds), *The Scholar Revolutionary: Eoin MacNeill, 1867–1945, and the Making of the New Ireland* (Shannon: Irish University Press, 1973).

Matthews, K., *Fatal Influence: The Impact of Ireland on British Politics, 1920–1925* (Dublin: University College of Dublin Press, 2004).

McCaffrey, L., *The Irish Question: Two Centuries of Conflict* (Lexington: The University Press of Kentucky, 1995).

McDermott, J., *Northern Divisions: The Old IRA and the Belfast Pogroms, 1920–22* (Belfast: Beyond the Pale, 2001).

McMahon, S., *Wee Joe: The Life of Joseph Devlin* (Belfast: Brehon Press Ltd, 2011).

Moody, T.W. and W.E. Vaughan, W.E. (eds), *A New History of Ireland: IV Eighteenth-Century Ireland, 1691–1800* (Oxford: Clarendon Press, 1986).

Moody, T.W. and Martin, F.X. (eds), *The Course of Irish History* (Cork: Mercier Press, 2001).

Morgan, K., *Consensus and Disunity: The Lloyd George Coalition Government, 1918–1922* (Oxford: Clarendon Press, 1979).

Murray, P., *The Irish Boundary Commission and its Origins, 1886–1925* (Dublin: University College Dublin Press, 2011).

O'Halloran, C., *Partition and the Limits of Irish Nationalism: An Ideology Under Stress* (Dublin: Gill and Macmillan Ltd, 1987).

Oram, H., *The Newspaper Book: A History of Newspapers in Ireland, 1649–1983* (Dublin: MO Books, 1983).

Parkinson, A., *Belfast's Unholy War: The Troubles of the 1920s* (Dublin: Four Courts Press Ltd, 2004).

Phoenix, E., *Northern Nationalism: Nationalist Politics, Partition and the Catholic Minority in Northern Ireland, 1890–1940* (Belfast: Ulster Historical Foundation, 1994).

Phoenix, E. (ed.), *A Century of Northern Life: The Irish News and 100 Years of Ulster History, 1890s–1990s* (Belfast: Ulster Historical Foundation, 1995).

Rafferty, O., *Catholicism in Ulster, 1603–1983: An Interpretative History* (London: Hurst & Company, 1994).

Regan, J. M., *The Irish Counter-Revolution, 1921–1936: Treatyite Politics and Settlement in Independent Ireland* (Dublin: Gill & Macmillan Ltd, 1999).

Ryder, C., *The Fateful Split: Catholics and the Royal Irish Constabulary* (London: Methuen Publishing Limited, 2004).

Sagarra, E., *Kevin O'Shiel: Tyrone Nationalist and Irish State-Builder* (Dublin: Irish Academic Press, 2013).

Staunton, E., *The Nationalists of Northern Ireland, 1918–1973* (Dublin: The Columba Press, 2001).

Thuente, M.H., *The Harp Re-Strung: The United Irishmen and the Rise of Literary Nationalism* (Syracuse: Syracuse University Press, 1994).

Townshend, C., *Ireland: The Twentieth Century* (New York: Oxford University Press, 2001).

Urquhart, D., *Women in Ulster Politics, 1890–1940: A History Not Yet Told* (Dublin: Irish Academic Press, 2000).

Vance, N., *Irish Literature Since 1800* (London: Pearson Education Limited, 2002).

Ward, A., *The Irish Constitutional Tradition: Responsible Government and Modern Ireland, 1782–1992* (Washington: The Catholic University of America Press, 1994).

Wheatley, M., *Nationalism and the Irish Party: Provincial Ireland, 1910–1916* (Oxford: Oxford University Press, 2005).

Whyte, J., *Interpreting Northern Ireland* (Oxford: Clarendon Press, 1990).

VI. Secondary Material: Articles

Curran, J., 'The Anglo-Irish Agreement of 1925: Hardly a "Damn Good Bargain"', *Historian* 40, 1 (1977), pp. 36–52.

Farren, S., 'Catholic–Nationalist Attitudes to Education in Northern Ireland, 1921–1947', *Irish Educational Studies* 8, 1 (1989), pp. 56–73.

Gallagher, M., 'The Pact General Election of 1922', *Irish Historical Studies* 21, 84 (1979), pp. 404–21.

Hart, P., 'Michael Collins and the Assassination of Sir Henry Wilson', *Irish Historical Studies* 28, 110 (1992), pp. 150–70.

Hopkinson, M., 'The Craig–Collins Pacts of 1922: Two Attempted Reforms of the Northern Ireland Government', *Irish Historical Studies* 27, 106 (1990), pp. 145–58.

Howard, K., 'Diasporas and Ambiguous Homelands: A Perspective on the Irish Border', *Institute for British–Irish Studies, Working Paper no. 62* (2006), pp. 1–22.

Johnson, D.S., 'The Belfast Boycott, 1920–1922', in J.M. Goldstrom and L.A. Clarkson (eds), *Irish Population, Economy, and Society: Essays in Honour of the late K.H. Connell* (Oxford: Clarendon Press, 1981), pp. 287–307.

Keane, R., 'The Governor-General and the Boundary Commission Crisis of 1924–5', in T. Garvin, M. Manning and R. Sinnott (eds), *Dissecting Irish Politics: Essays in Honour of Brian Farrell* (Dublin: University College of Dublin Press, 2004), pp. 19–30.

Kiberd, D., 'Irish Literature and Irish History', in R.F. Foster (ed.), *The Oxford Illustrated History of Ireland* (Oxford: Oxford University Press, 1989), pp. 275–337.

Kinsella, A., 'The Pettigo–Belleek Triangle Incident', *Irish Sword* 20, 82 (1997), pp. 346–66.

Phelan, M., 'The Critical "Gap of the North": Nationalism, National Theatre, and the North', *Modern Drama* 47, no. 4 (2004), pp. 594–606.

Rabinowitz, D., 'The Palestinian Citizens of Israel, the Concept of Trapped Minority and the Discourse of Transnationalism in Anthropology', *Ethnic and Racial Studies* 24, 1 (2001), pp. 64–85.

Rankin, K.J., 'The Role of the Irish Boundary Commission in the Entrenchment of the Irish Border: From Tactical Panacea to Political Liability', *Journal of Historical Geography*, 34 (2008), pp. 422–47.

VII. Unpublished Theses

Day, C., 'Political violence in the Newry/Armagh area, 1912–1925' (Ph.D. diss., Queen's University, Belfast, 1999).

Dooher, J., 'Tyrone nationalism and the question of partition, 1910–25' (M.Phil. thesis, University of Ulster, 1986).

Whitford, F., 'Joseph Devlin: Ulsterman and Irishman' (MA thesis, London University, 1959).

Index